Elizabethan Poetry

A Study in Conventions, Meaning,
and Expression

HALLETT SMITH

HARVARD UNIVERSITY PRESS
CAMBRIDGE · MASSACHUSETTS

1964

Mr. Smith is Professor of English
and Chairman of the Division of the
Humanities at the California Institute of Technology. He is a co-
editor of the anthologies *The
Golden Hind* and *The Critical
Reader*.

PREFACE

THIS book is neither a systematic chronological survey of Elizabethan nondramatic poetry nor a purely critical and evaluative judgment of it. I have included some historical narrative and a good deal of critical comment, but my principal purpose is to study the nature of the creative process in the last quarter of the sixteenth century in England.

To understand the creative process you must of course have before your eye the things created. The beginning is obviously the fairly large body of Elizabethan verse, which I wish it were possible to represent more fully in my illustrative quotations. But the poetry by itself cries out for connections, for context; the reader whose acquaintance with the period is incomplete will anachronistically provide a context from his own time and thus distort the poetry. The relevant context for Elizabethan poetry is rather different from the one we are accustomed to. We normally think, in the nineteenth and twentieth centuries, of the context of poetry as the private experience and biography of the poet—his particular feelings and "personality" which give him his own identifiable voice.

In the sixteenth century, it seems to me, the appropriate context for poetry is a series of ideals, values, commonplaces, or conventions. The modern reader can observe these commonplaces readily enough in the poetry, but he has difficulty in responding to them because they seem to him dead conventions, without significance beyond their own time. My effort has been to reanimate some of these conventions and to show how the poetry they fathered gets from its source a characteristic vitality and versatility. I am trying to explain, in part, the "Elizabethan-ness" of Elizabethan poetry. The mystery of this quality, or of the reasons for it, has often been felt. Somehow, it seems, an obscure force worked on everybody in the latter part of the sixteenth century to contribute to a dazzling display of poetry, the work of soldiers, courtiers, sea dogs, parsons, tavern-brawlers, scholars, merchants, lawyers, and apprentices. As Jusserand put it, in his *Literary History of the English People:* "One other phenomenon surprises the spectator more than all the rest: the richness, the variety, the incredible literary fecundity of this country, erstwhile so far behind, and whose principal poets, representing half a century of efforts, had barely supplied Tottel with enough to fill his slender volume. Indefatigable, the poets now sing verses worthy of remembrance, on every subject, amorous, religious, epic, satirical, pastoral, didactic, moving from the world of insects to the world of heroes. Songs rise naturally to their lips, no one knows why, they do not know why."

I begin with pastoral, felt by the Elizabethans to be the humblest kind of poetry and the most appropriate for a beginner (they remembered Virgil). For them pastoral constituted a positive ideal and was not merely an artificial game or an escape from life. In the second chapter I proceed to the amatory-mythological poetry which the Elizabethans derived from Ovid, tracing the changes in the English attitude toward those myths which combined imaginative invention and sophisticated sensuality. My treatment of the sonnet cycles shows how the Elizabethans coped with the problem of securing vitality in their exploitation of the tremendously popular Petrarchan mode; I suggest rather sharper distinctions among the principal sonneteers, Sidney, Spenser, Daniel, Drayton, and Shakespeare, than have before been made. In the chapter on satire, I take the opportunity to explore the relationship between Elizabethan poetic expression and the social and economic changes which so profoundly affected the sixteenth century. In showing the interplay among motives economic, moral, and psychological which agitated the men of the age, I also deal with the problem of the valid ground for the satirist as the Elizabethans saw it.

The most difficult, and in some ways the most interesting, relationship of Elizabethan poetry is that with music. I have offered no more than a minimum of detail in my chapter on poetry for music, because I did not wish to burden the reader with technicalities. But I have, I trust, indicated how the association with music influenced the tone and character of the Elizabethan lyric, and how the vexed problem of quantitative rhythm in English was finally solved by applying the principles of music to verse.

To complete a rough analogy between the organization of this book and the career of some hypothetical archetype of the Elizabethan poet, I end with heroic poetry, as I began with pastoral. Here the limitations of space are most evident and I am compelled to give only small fragments of the poetry I am discussing. But I bring to bear upon Elizabethan epic verse another commonplace, or symbol, or myth, which, though it had great power in the sixteenth century, is almost forgotten now; and I consider the Elizabethan approach to Homer and to Ariosto as the appropriate introduction to Spenser's *Faerie Queene*.

Long as this book is, I am conscious of several omissions, and I regret them. A chapter on religion as a source of poetic feeling and expression would probably have been longer than any chapters now in the book. I have neglected philosophical poems, like Davies' *Nosce Teipsum* and Daniel's *Musophilus* and much of Chapman. I have left aside the long historical and geographical poems which are so characteristically and inevitably Elizabethan. These omissions, and others unmentioned, merely mean that I am not writing a history but a critical and historical study, intended for anyone who is interested in poetry, where it comes from and what it does.

My obligations to others are very great; this is not the kind of book one writes by himself. Louis B. Wright, then of the Huntington Library, provided me the chief impetus and encouragement to write the book. I was given the time to do it by the generous and sympathetic attitude of the President and Trustees of Williams College and of my colleagues in the English Department there. I was supported first by the Class of 1900 Fund of Williams College and later by a fellowship of the John Simon Guggenheim Memorial Foundation. Without any one part of this assistance I could not have finished the work.

In 1947–48 at the Huntington Library I did the actual writing. William Haller stimulated, encouraged, and guided me. Margaret Gay Davies saved me from making a good many mistakes in Elizabethan economic history. And the incomparable staff of the Henry E. Huntington Library again and again saved my time and my temper. I have benefited from criticism of the manuscript by James Wortham, Ellsworth Mason, Harold Wilson, and George R. MacMinn. Successive drafts were typed, with patience and accuracy, by Jane Thomason and Mary McNamee. Mary Stockly helped with the final preparation of the manuscript, and Elizabeth Treeman of the Harvard University Press greatly improved the book with her editorial skill and acumen. I am profoundly grateful to all of them.

HALLETT SMITH

California Institute of Technology
Pasadena
April 1952

CONTENTS

ELIZABETHAN POETRY

NOTE

Elizabethan books may be identified, and copies located, by *A Short-Title Catalogue of Books Printed in England, Scotland and Ireland . . . 1475–1640*, compiled by A. W. Pollard and G. R. Redgrave (London: The Bibliographical Society, 1926), supplemented by *A Checklist of American Copies of "Short-Title Catalogue" Books*, compiled by William Warner Bishop (Ann Arbor: University of Michigan Press, 1944).

Abbreviations frequently used in the footnotes are:

AJP	*American Journal of Philology*
EETS	Early English Text Society
ELH	[Journal of English Literary History]
HLB	*Huntington Library Bulletin*
HLQ	*Huntington Library Quarterly*
JEGP	*Journal of English and Germanic Philology*
MLN	*Modern Language Notes*
MLQ	*Modern Language Quarterly*
MLR	*Modern Language Review*
MP	*Modern Philology*
OED	*Oxford English Dictionary on Historical Principles*
PMLA	[Publications of the Modern Language Association of America]
PQ	*Philological Quarterly*
RES	*Review of English Studies*
SAB	*Shakespeare Association Bulletin*
SP	*Studies in Philology*
STC	*A Short-Title Catalogue*
TLS	*Times Literary Supplement,* London

PASTORAL POETRY

The Vitality and Versatility
of a Convention

THE Elizabethan poet usually began, as Virgil had done, by writing pastoral poetry. And, since many poets begin and not all of them continue, the proportion of pastoral to the whole literary production of the Elizabethan period is fairly high. There have been many attempts to account for this prominence of the shepherd in the literature of an age of sea dogs and explorers, of courtiers and usurers, of magnificent Leicester, dashing Essex, and staid Burleigh.

One critic maintains that pastoral is always a vehicle for something else: "The pastoral, whatever its form, always needed and assumed some external circumstance to give point to its actual content. The interest seldom arises directly from the narrative itself." [1] Another commentator shakes his head over the whole pastoral tradition and seems to think that in the Elizabethan period it is merely a literary fad which got out of hand. "The exquisitely artificial convention of the pastoral poetry of the late sixteenth century and its stylized vocabulary, at times so dazzling and yet so often monotonous, gave little scope for original expression." [2] A more sensitive critic finds the reason for the popularity of pastoral in artistic

[1] W. W. Greg, *Pastoral Poetry and Drama* (London, 1906), p. 67.
[2] Anonymous review of *England's Helicon*, ed. Hyder E. Rollins, 2 vols. (Cambridge: Harvard University Press), in *TLS*, April 11, 1935, p. 240.

considerations: "It was the peculiarly combined satisfaction of freedom and formalism which attracted so many Elizabethans to pastoral." [3] Probably the most commonly held view is that pastoral is merely escape literature, especially attractive at a time when populations are shifting, life is becoming more complex, and the townsman dreams nostalgically of life in the country.

It is certainly true that pastoral was a convention. Shepherds thronged in the entertainments for royalty, in the pageants and devices like those presented at Kenilworth in 1575 and in the royal entertainments of 1578. These shows are in part literature, and they had their influence on works which were more purely literature.[4] But to establish the occasion, and even the fashion, of a work of art is not to explain its significance. The more conventional it is, the more likely it is to have some central core of meaning from which individual treatments may originate. "Originality" cannot be estimated until we know what the convention meant to the writers working in it.

Whatever may be said of other times and places, Elizabethan England saw a meaning in pastoral. This meaning was, or constituted, a positive ideal. It was an ideal of the good life, of the state of content and mental self-sufficiency which had been known in classical antiquity as *otium*. The revival of this ideal is a characteristic Renaissance achievement; it would have been impossible in the Middle Ages, when time spent in neither work nor communion with God was felt to be sinful. By projecting this ideal, poets of the age of Shakespeare were able to criticize life as it is and portray it as it might be. Their shepherds are citizens of the same Arcadia as that inhabited by the shepherds of Milton and Matthew Arnold.

The Elizabethan mind took over its conception of pastoral

[3] Kathleen Tillotson in *The Works of Michael Drayton*, ed J. W. Hebel, 5 vols. (Oxford, 1931–1941), V, 4.

[4] See, for example, Thomas Blenerhasset's *Revelation of the True Minerva*, ed. J. W. Bennett (New York, 1941), and I. L. Schulze, "Blenerhasset's *A Revelation*, Spenser's *Shepheardes Calender*, and the Kenilworth Pageants," ELH, XI (1944), 85–91.

from many sources. The most general and the most obvious of these sources was the Bible. In Genesis, the first great event after the fall of man is one which involves a shepherd; it is the story of Cain and Abel. What it meant to the Elizabethans is explained by Bacon:

> We see (as the Scriptures have infinite mysteries, not violating at all the truth of the story or letter), an image of the two estates, the contemplative state and the active state, figured in the two persons of Abel and Cain, and in the two simplest and most primitive trades of life; that of the shepherd, (who, by reason of his leisure, rest in a place, and living in view of heaven, is a lively image of a contemplative life,) and that of the husbandman: where we see again the favour and election of God went to the shepherd, and not to the tiller of the ground.[5]

Moreover, David, perhaps the most romantic figure in the Old Testament, was a shepherd, as well as being the principal poet and singer of songs among the ancient Hebrews. Of his psalms, the twenty-third was of course a special favorite. It reflected not only the atmosphere of green pastures but also the doctrine of content as the greatest of God's blessings. "The Lord is my shepherd; I shall not want" was explained by the preachers as a pastoral metaphor expressing the truth of Christian content.[6]

In the New Testament there is the central pastoral imagery of Christ the Good Shepherd, and of course the episode of the shepherds hearing from heaven the good tidings of Christ's birth. As Michael Drayton wrote, "In the Angels Song to Shepheards at our Saviours Nativitie Pastorall Poesie seemes consecrated." [7]

Characteristically, the Renaissance mixed examples of the shepherd from Greek and Roman tradition and history with those from the Bible. In Mantuan's seventh eclogue, Moses and Apollo are mentioned in pastoral roles.[8] Paris, the son of

---

[5] *Sir Francis Bacon, Works,* ed. James Spedding, R. L. Ellis, and D. D. Heath, 15 vols. (Boston, 1860–1864), VI, 138.

[6] See, for example, *Davids Pastorall Poeme: or Sheepeheards Song. Seven Sermons, on the 23. Psalme of Dauid,* by Thomas Jackson (1603).

[7] "To the Reader of his Pastorals" in *Works,* ed. Hebel, II, 517.

[8] *The Eclogues of Baptista Mantuanus,* ed. W. P. Mustard (Baltimore, 1911), p. 97. Translations or adaptations of this passage are in Alexander

Priam, King of Troy, was the most famous of all classical shepherds because from his actions sprang the whole epic narrative of the siege of Troy. Besides Paris, James Sandford's translation of Cornelius Agrippa (1569) cites Romulus and
Remus, Anchises, and the emperor Diocletian as shepherds.
Thomas Fortescue's translation from Pedro Mexía, *The
Foreste* (1586) adds Galerius and Tamburlaine. A shepherd in Drayton's "Dowsabell" is described as resembling
Tamburlaine in looks and Abel in temper.[9]

The Elizabethan attitude toward Paris reveals much of the
meaning and significance of pastoral in the poetry of the age.
The story of Paris is of course one of the great stories: how a
king's son, living as a shepherd, is in love with the nymph
Oenone; how he is chosen to be umpire among the three goddesses, Juno, Venus, and Pallas Athena, to decide which of
them deserves the golden apple inscribed "For the fairest";
how he decides in favor of Venus and is given as a reward the
love of the most beautiful of women, Helen; how he deserts
Oenone, brings Helen to Troy, and precipitates the Trojan
War with all of its consequences—this plot is surely one of
the great achievements of the Western imagination.

Dramatic treatments of the story of Paris are mentioned by
Saint Augustine;[10] the subject is inherently dramatic, both
for the power of the rival claims of the goddesses and for the
world-shaking consequences of Paris' choice. The death of
Hector and Achilles, the destruction of Troy, the wanderings
of Ulysses and of Aeneas, the founding of Rome (and of
Britain, too, as the Elizabethans thought), all resulted from
this one simple decision by a shepherd on the hills of Ida.

Purely as plot, then, the story of the shepherd's choice had
color and vitality. But it was also symbolic, and an understanding of what was represented to the Elizabethan mind by
the offers of Juno, Pallas, and Venus while Paris was trying

Barclay's fifth eclogue (about 1514), lines 469–492; in Turbervile's translation (1567), sig. K2ᵛ; in Spenser's July eclogue in *The Shepheardes Calender*
(1579), lines 131–160; and in Francis Sabie's *Pan's Pipe* (1595), sigs. D2ᵛ–D3ʳ.
[9] *Works*, ed. Hebel, I, 89.
[10] *De civitate Dei*, XVIII, 10.

to make up his mind is essential to an appreciation of poetic treatments of the myth. From classical times on down, the principal myths had been interpreted morally, if not allegorically, and the Judgment of Paris was one which lent itself to such treatment in a very natural way. Athenaeus says, in the *Deipnosophistae,* "And I for one affirm also that the Judgment of Paris, as told in poetry by the writers of an older time, is really a trial of pleasure against virtue. Aphrodite, for example—and she represents pleasure—was given the preference, and so everything was thrown into turmoil." [11]

Fulgentius, Bishop of Carthage, also moralized the myth of the Judgment of Paris. The three goddesses, he says, represent the three ways of life: the active, the contemplative, and the voluptuous. Jove himself, continues Fulgentius, could not make judgment among the three contending goddesses or the ways of life they represent; it is essentially a human dilemma. A shepherd, in Fulgentius' opinion, is the most suitable of all men to be the judge, though of course, according to the bishop, Paris made a foolish choice. Spenser agrees, and in the July eclogue of *The Shepheardes Calender* goes out of his way to condemn Paris:

> For he was proude, that ill was payd,
> (no such mought shepheards bee)
> And with lewde lust was ouerlayd:
> tway things doen ill agree.[12]

To the Renaissance, Paris' mistake was intended as a powerful warning. Italian treatises on nobility considered the Judgment of Paris story to represent the choice which must actually be made by the young man deciding upon a course of life.[13]

[11] *The Deipnosophists,* XII, 510 c, trans. C. B. Gulick, Loeb Classical Library, 7 vols. (1922–1949) , V, 295.

[12] The same point had been emphasized by Horace in *Epistles,* II, 10. The idea was also familiar to Renaissance Platonists and was elaborated by Ficino, for example, in his commentary on Plato's *Philebus.* See P. O. Kristeller, *The Philosophy of Marsilio Ficino* (New York, 1943) , pp. 358–359.

[13] The passage in G. B. Nenna's treatise is so typical, and the reputation of his book in England is so amply attested to by Edmund Spenser, Samuel Daniel, George Chapman, and Angel Day, that it must be quoted: "Now let

In the most popular of the pastoral romances, the Judgment of Paris is a subject for debate; in Montemayor's *Diana,* for example, Delia and Andronius spend the greater part of a night in arguing the question whether Paris gave the apple to the right goddess or not and whether the inscription on it referred to physical or mental beauty.[14] The shepherds and shepherdesses in Elizabethan pastoral poetry often allude to the Paris story or compare themselves with figures in it. An example is from "Phillidaes Loue-Call to her Coridon, and his replying," by "Ignoto" in *England's Helicon;*[15] another is Willye's compliment to Cuddie, the umpire of the singing match in Spenser's August eclogue:

> Neuer dempt more right of beautye I weene,
> The shepheard of Ida, that iudged beauties Queene.[16]

Drayton's Rowland, on the other hand, compares himself to the deserted Oenone.[17]

Whatever the faults of Paris' decision, the son of Priam remained, for the Elizabethan, the archetype of the shepherd. Spenser's Sir Calidore, when he takes off his armor and puts

---

vs consider what fruit may be gathered by the shadowe of fables, especially of this which I euen now recited. For indeed vnder those vailes we may receiue no lesse pleasant then profitable instruction . . . After that a man is once framed, and that he hath attained to that age, that hee beginneth nowe to discourse within himselfe, what kinde of life hee were best to followe as the most noble in account amongst men: whether that which is grounded vppon knowledge, which the Philosophers were wont to cal a contemplatiue kind of life: or otherwise, yt which guideth a man that addicteth himself only to worldly matters, which they terme actiue: or else that which consisteth wholy in pleasure, which they name delightfull. Then straightwaie discord entreth: of which three sortes of liues, Soueraigne Iupiter will not giue sentence which is the best, least that in approuing the one, he should condemne the other two; and so the life of man should rather be constrained then free, but hee leaueth them to the judgement of man, to the end that he may as pleaseth him, tie himselfe to that kind of life that shall best like him; it may be, shewing vs thereby, the free choice which is granted to vs by him. Of the which notwithstanding he that is caried away to follow the delightfull kind of life, doth bring vnto him selfe vnspeakeable detriment" (*Nennio, or a Treatise of Nobility,* trans. William Jones, 1595, sig. H3ʳ).

[14] Trans. Bartholomew Yong (1598), p. 53.
[15] Rollins ed., I, 70.
[16] Lines 137–138.
[17] *Idea The Shepheards Garland* (1593), Eclogue IX, lines 55–60.

on shepherd's weeds in order to woo Pastorella, suggests the obvious model, "Phrygian Paris by Plexippus brooke." [18]

The Judgment of Paris had of course been treated in medieval love allegories such as Froissart's *L'Espinette Amoureuse,* Machaut's *Le Dit de la Fontaine Amoureuse,* and Lydgate's *Reson and Sensuallyte;* there had been continental dramas on the subject in the fifteenth and early sixteenth centuries; and most important of all for the English pastoral, the Paris story was a common subject of the pageants—for Queen Margaret at Edinburgh in 1503, for the coronation of Anne Boleyn in 1533, and at a marriage masque in 1566.[19] It also appeared in the emblem-books. In Whitney's *Choice of Emblemes* the account of the Judgment is much abbreviated, but full justice is done to the interpretation.[20]

It is obvious, then, that the major Elizabethan treatment of the Paris story, George Peele's play *The Arraignment of Paris* (1584), is in a well-established tradition. It is in dramatic form, but it is so important as an indication of the significance of pastoral in the Elizabethan mind that it must be discussed briefly here.

In the temptation scene, when the three goddesses in turn offer their rewards to Paris, they are more abstract than personal. Juno offers the shepherd "great monarchies, Empires, and kingdomes, heapes of massye golde, scepters and diadems," symbolized theatrically by the appearance of a golden tree, the fruit of which is diadems. Pallas offers fame, wisdom, honor of chivalry and victory, "but yf thou haue a minde to fly aboue." The reward is symbolized by nine knights in armor treading a warlike Almain. Venus offers Paris the services of Cupid, kisses from herself, and finally (here the reward and the symbol become the same thing) Helen.[21] Paris is

---

[18] *Faerie Queene,* VI, IX, xxxvi.

[19] See C. R. Baskervill, "Early Romantic Plays in England," *MP,* XIV (1916–17), 483; T. S. Graves, "*The Arraignment of Paris* and Sixteenth Century Flattery," *MLN,* XXVIII (1913), 48–49; A. H. Gilbert, 'The Source of Peele's *Arraignment of Paris,*" *MLN,* XLI (1926), 36; and Douglas Bush, *Mythology and the Renaissance Tradition in English Poetry* (Minneapolis, 1932), pp. 51–52.

[20] Ed. of 1586, p. 83.

[21] Sig. C^r.

constantly a symbolic figure; he is suggestive. I do not mean that the artist had nothing to do with this suggestiveness and that the audience could be counted upon to do it all. A sixteenth-century Italian treatise on painting makes clear the artist's obligation in the matter and uses Paris as an example:

> Hence then the painter may learne how to expresse not onely the proper and naturall motions, but also the accidentall; wherein consisteth no small part of the difficulty of the Arte, namelie in representing diversities of affections and passions in one bodie: A thing much practized, by the ancient Painters (though with greate difficulty) who ever indevored to leaue no iotte of the *life* vnexpressed.
>
> It is recorded that *Euphranor* gaue such a touch to the counterfeit of *Paris,* that therein the beholder might at once collect, that hee was *Vmpire* of the three *Goddesses,* the *Courter of Helena,* and the slaier of *Achilles.*[22]

But Paris, with the alternatives clearly before him, chooses Venus. When he defends himself before the court of the gods, in Peele's play, he speaks first as a man, blaming his fault, if any, on the judgment of his eye. Then he adds a *reason:* that it was only for beauty he gave the ball, and if other virtues had been concerned he would have chosen Pallas or Juno. Furthermore, he says, he was tempted more than man ever was, and as a shepherd he was relatively immune to offers other than that of Venus.[23] The simplicity of the shepherd's conditions makes for an invulnerability to appeals in the name of wealth or of chivalry. It is only beauty, of the three ideals represented by the goddesses, which has any significant power in a pastoral life.

Paris is the judge precisely because the conditions of the pastoral life provide the greatest independence, the greatest security. The shepherd is not motivated by ambition or by greed. Free from these two common human passions, he enjoys "content," or the good life. Elizabethan pastoral poetry is essentially a celebration of this ideal of content, of *otium.* The contemplative state enjoyed a freedom, not only from

[22] G. P. Lomazzo, *A Tracte Containing the Artes of Curious Paintinge,* trans. Richard Haydocke (1598), sig. Bb6r.

[23] Sig. D4r.

ambition or greed, but from the vicissitudes of fortune. The popular tradition of the fall of princes, represented in Elizabethan literature by the *Mirror for Magistrates* and the poems added to it, had stressed ominously the dangers in the turn of Fortune's wheel. Kings and princes, the high and mighty, were exhibited in tragic circumstances, the victims of their own high position, their ambition, or their greed. The poetic tragedies of the *Mirror* therefore supported, negatively, the same ideal celebrated by pastoral. Occasionally the warning in a *Mirror* tragedy concludes with a direct endorsement of the quiet life of content. In one of the tragedies in Blenerhasset's *Mirror,* for example, the herdsman who kills Sigebert and is hanged for it concludes with the lesson:

> And happy he, who voyde of hope can leade.
> A quiet lyfe, all voyde of Fortunes dread.

This makes the following Induction deal with the question of why it is that formerly the wisest men were content to be shepherds, but now "in these our dayes, none bee Heardmen but fooles, and euery man though his witte be but meane, yet he cannot liue with a contented mind, except he hath the degree of a Lorde." [24]

In order to respond adequately to the appeal of the Elizabethan ideal of the mean estate, content, and *otium,* it is necessary to feel the force of its opposite, a form of ambition which the sixteenth century called most commonly the aspiring mind. Marlowe's Tamburlaine is of course the great representative of the aspiring mind, as he is its philosopher:

> Nature that fram'd vs of foure Elements,
> Warring within our breasts for regiment,
> Doth teach vs all to haue aspyring minds.[25]

But there are many other examples of the concept in Elizabethan England. Mr. Secretary Walsingham, summing up the

---

[24] *Parts Added to the Mirror for Magistrates,* ed. L. B. Campbell (Cambridge, England, 1946), pp. 462–463.

[25] Lines 869–871. For evidence that Tamburlaine was a symbol of this Renaissance spirit before he appeared in Marlowe's play, see my "Tamburlaine and the Renaissance," *Elizabethan Studies in Honor of George F. Reynolds* (Boulder, Colo., 1945), pp. 128–129.

personal charges against Mary Queen of Scots, said that she had an aspiring mind; [26] and Queen Elizabeth herself, writing a poem about Mary, included the line

But clowds of tois vntried, do cloake aspiring mindes.[27]

Blue, as the color of the sky, was symbolic of the aspiring mind, according to Lomazzo:

Persius sat. 1. speaking of Blew garments, sheweth that they belong only to such persons, as aspire vnto high matters: and Cicero vsed sometimes to weare this color, giuing men thereby to vnderstand, that he bare an aspiring minde.[28]

There were many other Roman examples of the aspiring mind; a typical one is Pompey.[29] That the aspiring mind was a dangerous and possibly sinful state is made clear by Du Bartas, who contrasts it to the attitude of the angels.[30] The first example of the aspiring mind, according to Du Bartas, was in the hunter, Nimrod, "that was the first Tyrant of the world, after the time of Noah, the first Admiral of the worlde: his aspiring minde & practises in seeking the peoples fauour, his proud and subtle attempt in building the Tower of Babel, & Gods iust punishment thereof in confounding the language of the builders." [31]

The central meaning of pastoral is the rejection of the aspiring mind. The shepherd demonstrates that true content is to be found in this renunciation. Sidney expresses the preference in terms of a contrast between pastoral and court life:

Greater was that shepheards treasure,
Then this false, fine, Courtly pleasure.[32]

---

[26] Conyers Read, *Mr. Secretary Walsingham and the Policy of Queen Elizabeth,* 3 vols. (Oxford, 1925) , I, 69.

[27] George Puttenham, *The Arte of English Poesie,* ed. Gladys D. Willcock and Alice Walker (Cambridge, England, 1936) , p. 248.

[28] *The Artes of Curious Paintinge,* trans. Haydocke, p. 122.

[29] *Fennes Frutes* (1590) , sig. E3ᵛ.

[30] *The First Day of the Worldes Creation,* trans. Joshua Sylvester (1595) , sig. E1ᵛ.

[31] *Babilon,* trans. William L'Isle (1595) , sig. A3ᵛ.

[32] "Disprayse of a Courtly life," first published in *A Poetical Rhapsody* (1602) , ed. Hyder E. Rollins, 2 vols. (Cambridge: Harvard University Press, 1931, 1932) , I, 9–12.

In the pastoral episode in Book VI of *The Faerie Queene,*
Sir Calidore envies the apparent happiness of the shepherds;
he comments that their life seems free from the "warres, and
wreckes, and wicked enmitie" which afflict the rest of the
world.[33] In reply to this, the sage old Meliboee then answers
with an analysis of the pastoral existence which is in effect a
definition of "the good life." It consists of four elements:
(1) being content with what you have, however small it is
—this is the way taught by nature (contrast Tamburlaine's
statement that nature teaches us to have aspiring minds);
(2) enjoying freedom from envy of others and from excessive
care for your own possessions (the flocks multiply without
your doing much about it); (3) avoiding the dangers of pride
and ambition and also the insomnia that plagues those who
hold positions of responsibility (see the testimony of Shakespeare's kings in *2 Henry IV*, III, i, 1–31, and IV, v, 20–27;
Henry V, IV, i, 266–290); (4) doing what you like. Old
Meliboee does not speak from provincial ignorance, either.
He once spent ten years at court, but returned to the pastoral
life from choice.

The question of the moral validity of pastoral life when
compared with life at court is not difficult to answer: the long
tradition of dispraise of the court is always, by implication or
by direct statement, an endorsement of the pastoral life. But
there is a more difficult question when the alternatives are
the quiet, retired life of the shepherd on the one hand or a
mission of chivalric and honorable achievement on the other.
The pastoral romance, both in Sidney and in his sources like
Montemayor's *Diana,* mingles pastoral and heroic elements.
The question of the relative value of the two kinds of life is
naturally raised. The pastoral sojourn of Erminia in the
seventh book of Tasso's *Jerusalem Delivered* is used as a
contrast to the heroic actions of the main part of the poem.
It is also obvious that pastoral and heroic put a different light
upon the feelings of love; these might or might not be a detriment to the heroic life, but they are sanctioned in the world
of pastoral.

[33] VI, ix, xix.

The commentators on the sixth book of Spenser's *Faerie Queene* have been at odds over the meaning of the pastoral interlude there, the Pastorella episode. T. P. Harrison says, "Spenser obviously censures Sir Calidore's pastoral aberration; yet he, like Sidney, is inclined to paint the rural picture sympathetically." [34] The opposite view is expressed by C. S. Lewis:

> The greatest mistake that can be made about this book is to suppose that Calidore's long delay among the shepherds is a pastoral truancy from Spenser's moral intention . . . Courtesy, for the poet, has very little connection with court. It grows "on a lowly stalke"; . . . according to Spenser, courtesy, in its perfect form, comes by nature; moral effort may produce a decent substitute for everyday use, which deserves praise, but it will never rival the real courtesy of those who
>
> > so goodly gracious are by kind
>
> That every action doth them much commend.[35]

Lewis is certainly right about Spenser's endorsement of the pastoral life, or his justification of Sir Calidore, for the opening stanzas of Canto x make it clear.[36] Spenser's own words do not, however, support conclusively the suggestion that courtesy is wholly natural. When in the beginning of Canto xii the poet makes a kind of apology for the wandering structure of the narrative, he is careful to defend the idea behind it.[37] The pastoral environment is a further test and demonstration of Sir Calidore's courtesy, but it is not its source. Calidore treats his shepherd rival, Coridon, with great generosity and magnanimity.[38] The pastoral ideal, then, is reconcilable somehow with the code of chivalry and honor, even though its emphasis is different. As the climax and goal of a life of heroic effort there is a state of heavenly contemplation not too different from the state of mind of the pastoral ideal. But this state may be reached only after the knightly quest is achieved, as we see in the tenth canto of Spenser's Book I.

[34] "The Relations of Spenser and Sidney," *PMLA*, XLV (1930), 720.
[35] *The Allegory of Love* (Oxford, 1936), pp. 350–353.
[36] VI, x, iii.
[37] VI, xii, ii.
[38] VI, ix, xlv.

Closer to pastoral is the Horatian praise of the country gentleman's life, of which there are many examples in Elizabethan poetry. Wyatt's first satire, a translation of Alamanni, and Thomas Lodge's "In Praise of the Countrey Life," a translation of Desportes, are typical. This type of poetry, like pastoral, proclaims the moral and emotional advantages of the country over the court. Lodge, for example, sings:

> Amidst the pallace braue puft vp with wanton showes
> Ambicions dwell, and there false fauors finde disguise,
> There lodge consuming cares that hatch our common woes:
> Amidst our painted feelds the pleasant Fayrie lies,
>   And all those powers diuine that with vntrussed tresses,
>   Contentment, happie loue, and perfect sport professes.[39]

This kind of thing moves in the direction of satire, and it will be considered again later in connection with the other elements of satire in the pastoral.

The theme of the Golden Age is one of the great commonplaces of Elizabethan literature.[40] The creation of an Arcadia which is primitive and pastoral, which may be identified with the early period before the birth of Jupiter, and which finally is a country located not so much in central Greece as in some Utopian space, is a result of the work of Polybius, Ovid, and Virgil.[41] There are many sources in antiquity for the theme; it was especially popular among the Stoics, and it was congenial to Stoic thought because it explained the Law of Nature as a survival from the Golden Age.[42] Accordingly, the best example of it may be chosen from Seneca;

> 'Twas in such wise, methinks, they lived whom the primal age produced, in friendly intercourse with gods. They had no blind love of gold;

[39] "Sonnets" appended to *Scillaes Metamorphosis* (1589), sig. D4ʳ.

[40] For the general background, see A. O. Lovejoy and George Boas, *Primitivism and Related Ideas in Antiquity* (Baltimore, 1935); Paul Meissner, "Das goldene Zeitalter in der Englischen Renaissance," *Anglia*, LIX (1935), 351–367; E. Lipsker, *Der Mythos vom goldenen Zeitalter in den Schäferdichtungen Italiens, Spaniens und Frankreichs zur Zeit der Renaissance* (Berlin, 1933).

[41] Erwin Panofsky, "Et in Arcadia Ego," *Philosophy and History*, ed. Raymond Klibansky and H. J. Paton (Oxford, 1936), pp. 225–227.

[42] See L. I. Bredvold, "The Naturalism of Donne in Relation to Some Renaissance Traditions," *JEGP*, XXII (1923), 471–502.

no sacred boundary-stone, judging betwixt peoples, separated fields on the spreading plain; not yet did rash vessels plough the sea; each man knew only his native waters.[43]

Spenser in the Proem to Book V of *The Faerie Queene* follows the convention of idealizing the Golden Age,[44] even though his friend Harvey was of the newer school of Jean Bodin, which thought that the earliest periods of history were the worst and that something like progress had taken place.

The first information given the audience about the pastoral atmosphere in Shakespeare's *As You Like It* compares pastoral life to the Golden Age; the wrestler Charles, informing Oliver, and at the same time the audience, of the circumstances of the banished Duke, says:

They say he is already in the Forest of Arden, and a many merry men with him; and there they live like the old Robin Hood of England; they say many young gentlemen flock to him every day, and fleet the time carelessly, as they did in the golden world.[45]

The identification of the pastoral life with the conditions of the Golden Age was natural enough. One was a criticism of life by means of adopting the point of view of its simplest and purest elements; the other was a criticism of the present way of life by describing an ideal past.

It is also true that pastoral was considered the earliest form of poetry and would therefore be the natural expression of the earliest blissful age.[46] Not all English opinion agreed with this conventional account, however. George Puttenham, bearing in mind the humanistic use of eclogues for satire, considers that the form cannot be primitive.[47] He insists that the eclogue is a sophisticated form, but he concedes that the pastoral lyric does come down from "the first idle wooings," "the

[43] *Hippolytus*, in *Seneca's Tragedies*, trans. F. J. Miller, Loeb Classical Library, 2 vols. (1916–17), I, 525–539.

[44] V, Proem, ix.

[45] I, i, 109–114.

[46] For a Renaissance account of this historical side of pastoral, see F. M. Padelford, *Selected Translations from Scaliger's Poetics* (New York, 1905), pp. 21–32.

[47] *The Arte of English Poesie*, ed. Willcock and Walker, pp. 37–39.

first amorous musicks." The Golden Age, associated with pastoral as we have seen, was supposed to have been an age of free love.[48] It is so celebrated in a song from Tasso's *Aminta* which Samuel Daniel translated under the title "A Pastorall." [49] And since the shepherd is insensitive to the claims of power and wealth, as Paris was, it is sometimes emphasized in pastoral that his susceptibility to love is a cruel bondage. As Montemayor puts it:

> The shepherd busied not his thoughts in the consideration of the prosperous and preposterous successe of fortune, nor in the mutabilitie and course of times, neither did the painfull diligence and aspiring minde of the ambitious Courtier trouble his quiet rest: nor the presumption and coye disdaine of the proude and nice Ladie (celebrated onely by the appassionate vowes and opinions of her amorous sutours) once occur to his imaginations. And as little did the swelling pride, and small care of the hawtie priuate man offend his quiet minde. In the field was he borne, bred and brought vp: in the field he fed his flockes, and so out of the limits of the field his thoughts did neuer range, vntill cruell loue tooke possession of his libertie, which to those he is commonly woont to doe, who thinke themselues freest from his tyrannie.[50]

Love in a pastoral environment is first exploited in the second-century Greek romance *Daphnis and Chloe,* written by someone whose name was perhaps Longus. It is the only one of the Greek romances which is pastoral in character, and it is the great forerunner of the Renaissance pastoral romances —those of Sannazarro, Montemayor, and their many imitators. It plays with the adventures in love of two perfectly simple and naïve pastoral people; their innocence of sex along with their captivation by it is presented with amused sophistication by the author for an equally sophisticated reader. S. L. Wolff well describes the peculiar salacious quality of the ro-

---

[48] The differing attitudes possible on this and other points are noticed by Lois Whitney, "Concerning Nature in *The Countesse of Pembrokes Arcadia,*" *SP*, XXIV (1927), 207–222.

[49] This is the final poem in Daniel's *Works* (1601); it did not, as Grosart asserts, appear in the *Delia* of 1592 (*Complete Works of Samuel Daniel,* ed. A. B. Grosart, 5 vols. [London, Spenser Society, 1885–1896], I, 260).

[50] *Diana,* trans. Yong, sig. A1ᵛ.

mance: "Longus with all his art did not—or rather did not try!—to take his emphasis off the teasing succession of Daphnis and Chloe's attempts, and place it wholly or even preponderantly upon their idyllic simplicity, their idyllic environment. *They* are simple enough, but *we* are not; and Longus knows it."[51]

There was an Elizabethan translation of *Daphnis and Chloe,* by Angel Day from the French of Jacques Amyot, in 1587. Day's version does not include the more salacious parts of the Greek romance, substituting instead pastoral lyrics and inserting a pastoral praise of Queen Elizabeth under the title "The Shepheardes Holidaye." Day's language is often colloquial and vivid, especially in descriptive scenes, but his tone is softened and sobered; the conscious absurdity and the conscious aphrodisiac quality of the original are quite lacking.[52] The great translation of *Daphnis and Chloe* into English is not Day's but that of George Thornley in the mid-seventeenth century.

The innocent and naïve, but pagan, lover immediately calls to mind such figures as Shakespeare's Adonis and Marlowe's Hero and Leander. Marlowe especially may have been influenced by Longus, but the significant point here is that pastoral is touching the boundary of still another literary genre, that of Ovidian-mythological poetry. In the Ovidian tradition sexuality was of course an important element, and the shepherds of pastoral, if made creatures of myth (and Paris could be treated as mythology or pastoral) became suitable subjects for the Ovidian love poem.

The general tendency of English pastoral literature was to subdue the sexual element and make the love scenes romantic and innocent. The innocence of rustic lovers is not exploited for the superior feeling of more worldly readers; what humor there is develops from gentle satire of rude and boorish characters. A conventional comic device is the detailed description

---

[51] *The Greek Romances in Elizabethan Fiction* (New York, 1912), p. 131.
[52] It is impossible to agree with Wolff that "Angel Day's version is pervaded by this indulgent ridicule of rustic wits, manners, speech and dress" (*ibid.,* p. 122, n. 6). Day presents it all quite seriously.

of a costume which is inappropriate or absurd.[53] The love is generally idyllic, lending itself to lyrical treatment, fitting in with the idealized setting, timeless and remote.

The element of love in pastoral romance works in two directions—toward lyric simplicity, as I have said, and toward plot complication. The events of pastoral plot usually come from outside and are not the result of the lovers' characters. Brigands, unscrupulous rivals, uncoöperative parents all provide motion and direction for the plot. The oracle, the exposed child, the changeling motif supply a frame for the beginning and conclusion of the story. Essentially, however, there is nothing complex about the course of love itself in the pastoral plot. Fortune and villains provide the difficulties; they do not lie in the nature of love itself. Love expressed as emotion (rather than as plot) is simple and lyric; love used as plot entanglement (not as feeling) is involved and complicated.

Pastoral emphasizes the irrationality of love. That is, it agrees with the general Elizabethan view. Lovers are subject to the whims of fortune (although Fortune is kinder in Arcadia than elsewhere), but there is no blame imputed to anyone for falling in love. It is irrational but unavoidable. The lyric, then, accepts the fate of love but complains at its sorrows just as it rejoices at its pleasures. "Since that in love there is no sound/ Of any reason to be found" is a basic assumption.[54]

Love is simple in essence, but the variety and complexity of its consequences make for a total paradox. Though there is no jot of reason in love, the lover invariably reasons about it. Pastoral provides amply for this paradox. It utilizes for the purpose various devices which taken out of their context seem absurd. The most common perhaps is the "cross-eyed Cupid" situation, in which A loves B, B loves C, C loves D, and D loves A. It is used in Montemayor,[55] and of course it is a device

[53] I have pointed out an example of this in Lodge's *Rosalynde*. See *The Golden Hind*, ed. Roy Lamson and Hallett Smith (New York, 1942), p. 665. There is another in Montemayor's *Diana*, trans. Yong, sig. E6^v.

[54] Montemayor, *Diana*, trans. Yong, sig. D5^r.

[55] *Diana*, trans. Yong, sig. B6^r.

in Lodge's *Rosalynde* and Shakespeare's *As You Like It*, as well as in the woodland part of *A Midsummer Night's Dream*. The paradox is that love itself is so simple; the lyric and plot elements of pastoral romance work together to enforce the contrast between simplicity and complexity.

Another aspect of pastoral love is the contrast between the direct, personal, subjective expression of the feeling and the same feeling seen in some other way, reflected, as in a mirror. In Book XI of the *Diana* Syrenus hears three nymphs singing his own farewell song to Diana—a song which one of them got from a shepherd who heard it long ago and memorized it. A similar effect is produced by having a pastoral lover hang his poems on trees, to be read or recited by others, sometimes in his hearing. There is an absence of self-consciousness in both these devices which makes the paradoxical effect possible. The naïveté of the whole pastoral convention is being utilized.

The ancestry of much pastoral poetry has something to do with its quality. The primitive song-and-dance games of the countryside, which often kept the color of their native surroundings, were in large part wooing ceremonies or complaints of the rejected lover who wore willow at the wedding and was expected to display his sorrows to heighten the merriment of the occasion. There were also celebrations of the beauty of the shepherdess who was crowned queen of the May. These popular customs were beginning to die out in Elizabethan times, or rather to be relegated to the use of children. But the courtly vogue, picking them up, made of them something both sophisticated and naïve. There is an awareness on the part of the Elizabethan poet of pastoral that he is exploiting a quality which works in two ways.[56]

This combination of "distance" and familiarity, of formalism and freedom, gives the Elizabethan love lyric and the song of good life their characteristic tone. Their "Elizabethanness," that quality which makes them popular in the antholo-

[56] A good account of the popular dance-song background of Elizabethan pastoral is given in C. R. Baskervill, *The Elizabethan Jig* (Chicago, 1929), chap. I.

gies, which permits enjoyment of them without any concern for the authorship, derives from this suspension.

If we turn to the greatest storehouse of Elizabethan pastoral lyric, the anthology published in 1600 called *England's Helicon*,[57] we may examine the concrete results of the fashion. The compiler of this anthology had under survey the whole body of Elizabethan literature, from *Tottel's Miscellany* on down to the end of the century. He selected poems from translated pastoral romances (Montemayor's *Diana* translated by Bartholomew Yong), from original romances in English (Sidney's *Arcadia,* Greene's *Menaphon,* and Lodge's *Rosalynde*), from the songbooks of Byrd and Morley and Dowland, from plays, from other anthologies (*The Passionate Pilgrim,* 1599), and from manuscripts. His volume has remained popular from 1600 to the present time, and his modern editor says it would be hard for anyone to compile a better anthology of the period without lavish use of Shakespeare and Jonson.[58]

I shall consider the poems in the volume under several headings, without suggesting that these headings constitute rigid "types" or kinds. For purposes of clarity it is easier to talk about pastoral lyrics as complaints, invitations, palinodes, love dialogues, blazons, and dance songs than to group them all together.

More of the poems in *England's Helicon* are complaints than any other kind. Most commonly the shepherd himself is the speaker, although sometimes the complaint is "framed" within the poem as something overheard by the speaker. This latter is an old medieval device, familiar in such poems as Chaucer's *Book of the Duchesse.* The cause of the shepherd's complaint is of course always unrequited love, or a mistress who has proved fickle, and his sorrow is almost always reflected in the change made not only upon himself but also upon his flocks, his dog, upon nature itself. No. 35 (which had already appeared in Weelkes' *Madrigals,* 1597, and *The Passionate Pilgrim,* 1599) begins:

[57] Edited by H. E. Rollins in two volumes (Cambridge: Harvard University Press, 1935).   [58] Rollins, II, 3-4.

My Flocks feede not, my Ewes breede not,
My Rammes speede not, all is amisse:
Loue is denying, Faith is defying,
Harts renying, causer of this.[59]

This kind of complaint serves, of course, as a description of the values in pastoral life by bewailing their loss. The emphasis is not so much sentimental, in that sympathy is asked for the lovelorn shepherd, as it is pictorial, in which the "merry jigs," the clear-wells, and the happy herds are thrown into strong relief by having their basic attributes reversed.

Quite frequently some object of comparison is found, so that the rhetorical expression of the shepherd's grief can be saved for a climax. This principle of economy is apparent in a fine lyric by Thomas Lodge:

A Turtle sate vpon a leauelesse tree,
    Mourning her absent pheare,
    With sad and sorrie cheare.[60]

The contrast of bitter and sweet is the complaining shepherd's constant theme; sometimes it is expressed more lavishly, as by Lodge in a poem which he himself described as Italianate in manner.[61]

Sometimes the shepherd's complaint takes the form of a narrative and is elaborated in such a way as to make the effect of a pageant or little drama. In this case the pastoral element is likely to be mere stage setting for the central situation, which derives from medieval allegory or Anacreontic cupid-lore. A good example is No. 126 in *England's Helicon*, by Michael Drayton.[62]

[59] Rollins ed., I, 56.
[60] Rollins ed., I, 58.
[61] Rollins, I, 85, and II, 134.
[62] Rollins, I, 167. This poem was used by Drayton to take the place of a more direct song of complaint which he had published in his second eclogue in *Idea The Shepheards Garland* (1593). The version as given in *England's Helicon* was printed in the 1606 edition of Drayton's eclogues and revised further for publication in 1619 (see *Works*, ed. Hebel, I, 53, and II, 525). Mrs. Tillotson remarks that "the song [as given in *E. H.*] gives a much more detached and playful impression of Rowland's love than the song of *Shepheards Garland*" (*ibid.*, V, 184).

Fifteen of the poems in this pastoral anthology are by Sidney; all are taken from the 1598 folio volume containing the *Arcadia, Astrophel and Stella,* and miscellaneous poems. Actually, fewer than half of the Sidney poems in the *Helicon* are pastoral when taken out of context, but Sidney's name gave prestige to the volume and he was thought of as a writer who had lent seriousness and dignity to the pastoral mode. Thomas Wilson, for example, confessed to a certain embarrassment about his translation of Montemayor's *Diana:* "Soe it may bee said of mee that I shewe my vanitie enough in this litle, that after 15 yeares painfully spent in Vniversitie studies, I shold bestow soe ·many ydle howres, in transplanting vaine amorous conceipts out of an Exotique language." But his justification was that however vain and frivolous the *Diana* might seem, Sir Philip Sidney "did very much affect and imitate the excellent Author there of." [63]

The best known of Sidney's poems in the volume is "Ring out your belles, let mourning shewes be spread," a more elaborate and subtle poem than Drayton's "Antheme" and of the same type; but there is nothing specifically pastoral about the poem. Sidney's characteristic touch and his skill in conveying a mood by indirection are best exemplified in No. 5, called "Astrophell the Sheep-heard, his complaint to his flocke." It begins in the usual mood of the forlorn shepherd, telling his merry flocks to go elsewhere to feed so they may have some defense from the storms in his breast and the showers from his eyes. The poet leaves us uncertain how to interpret this extravagant feeling until the shepherd states to the sheep the extent of his love, in terms the sheep could understand:

Stella, hath refused me,
    Stella, who more loue hath proued
In this caitiffe hart to be,
    Then can in good eawes be moued
    Towards Lambkins best beloued.[64]

[63] Preface, reproduced in *Revue Hispanique*, L (1920), 372.
[64] I have substituted the correct reading "eawes" of the 1598 folio for the meaningless "by us" of *England's Helicon*.

Sidney is pushing homely pathos to the point at which it is felt as humor also, and the comic tone is underlined two stanzas later:

> Is that loue? Forsooth I trow,
>   if I saw my good dogge greeued:
> And a helpe for him did know,
>   my loue should not be beleeued:
>   but he were by me releeued.

Finally, at the conclusion, the identification of the shepherd's emotions with his pastoral environment, a stock feature of the mode, is used for comic purposes. The complaints of the shepherd-lover are whimsically identified with the bleatings of his sheep.

Parody is not the most difficult art. The "distance" between pastoral and reality (which Panofsky says is intimately connected with that other Renaissance invention, perspective) can easily be foreshortened or flattened out so as to make a fantastic effect. But it is not so easy to make the pathetic and absurd felt at once, as partners in the result. This Sidney was able to do. As Theodore Spencer accurately expresses it, "The pastoral setting, the traditional tone of lament, the rigorous form of the verse have been revitalized not merely by Sidney's superb technique, but by the fact that he has put into them something more than the purely conventional emotion." [65]

The other kind of pastoral complaint besides that of the rejected shepherd is of course that of the betrayed or abandoned shepherdess. She is the Oenone of the Judgment of Paris story. In *England's Helicon* Oenone's complaint from Peele's *Arraignment* is No. 149, the next to the last poem in the book. There are half a dozen other nymph's complaints in the volume, of which the most interesting are Selvagia's song from the *Diana*, as translated by Bartholomew Yong

---

[65] "The Poetry of Sir Philip Sidney," *ELH*, XII (1945), 267. Spencer is speaking of a poem not included in *England's Helicon*, the double sestina "You goat-herd gods." It is certainly true that a better selection from Sidney's poetry in the 1598 folio could be made than that of the editor of *England's Helicon*.

(No. 103), with its graceful return at the end to the chorus of the beginning,

> It is not to liue so long,
>   as it is too short to weepe,

and No. 118, "Lycoris the Nimph, her sad Song," from Thomas Morley's *Madrigals to Four Voices* (1594).[66] The varied line length of the second poem and the feminine rhymes suggest the fragility of the nymph and the insecurity she feels. And the poem progresses very prettily from idyllic description to rhetorical exclamation to the final taunt and pout, conveyed by the strikingly simple and direct language of the last two lines. Its sudden transitions of mood are characteristic of the poem-for-music.

Some half dozen of the poems in *England's Helicon* are invitations, a few of them the most attractive and famous poems in the volume. At its best, the invitation poem is simple in language and in versification, preferring short lines and a direct rhetoric. The strategy of the shepherd is to call attention to the beauty and innocence of the pastoral setting and to use these qualities as arguments naturally reinforcing his simple desires:

> Faire Loue rest thee heere,
> Neuer yet was morne so cleere,
> Sweete be not vnkinde,
> Let me thy fauour finde,
>   Or else for loue I die.

[66] Rollins' note (*England's Helicon*, II, 173), is possibly misleading when it says that the poem was taken from Morley's book "with very lavish changes." Rollins depends upon E. H. Fellowes' *English Madrigal Verse, 1588–1632* (Oxford, 1913), p. 126, for what he calls "the original." But Dr. Fellowes' text is a reconstruction from the various part-books of Morley, and in his reconstruction Dr. Fellowes is markedly classical. Every variant from Fellowes' text in *England's Helicon* can be found in some one of the part-books. The editor of the *Helicon* simply made a different reconstruction, pruning away the "Aye me's" and the like less rigorously. I grant that he arranged the first line incorrectly for the rhyme. The whole point is of some importance in that it raises the question of what *are* the words that make up a poem when they occur as words to a madrigal. For Fellowes' method of reconstruction, and his triumph in reconstructing a poem by Ben Jonson, see *English Madrigal Verse*, pp. xv–xvii; most Elizabethans, I am convinced, were not as firmly sealed of the tribe of Ben as Dr. Fellowes. Certainly the editor of *England's Helicon* was not.

This (No. 74) is Drayton, who well understands the Elizabethan art of securing a beauty and simplicity which seems
almost impersonal. Passion and thought are carefully strained
out; the poem must be self-contained and must cast no
oblique lights. The humorous and the sentimental attributes
of the complaint are entirely lacking. The *aubade* and the
May-morning song are cousins to it, but the clearest and
simplest form for this state of mind is the pastoral lyric of
invitation.

> Come away, come sweet Loue,
> The golden morning breakes:
> All the earth, all the ayre,
> Of loue and pleasure speaks.

This is an anonymous poem, taken from Dowland's *First
Booke of Songes or Ayres* (1597). I have cited these two
poems of invitation to show that the most famous of them,
Marlowe's "The passionate Sheepheard to his loue" (No.
137), is not alone in its class, even though it is superior to
all of its kind.[67] The greatness of Marlowe's poem consists
in the completeness of his pastoral picture and its total identification with the state of mind which the pastoral lyric of
invitation is intended to induce. It includes gowns, shoes,
beds of roses, cap, kirtle, slippers, and belt, all rural and
simple, but rich and fine; more significantly, it includes the
entertainments fit for the contented mind: to see the shepherds feed their flocks, to listen to the music of the shallow
rivers, and best of all to watch the shepherd swains dancing
and singing. These are delights to move *the mind* (as the
last stanza in the *Helicon* version specifies), and there is of
course no ground for refusal to this invitation—except the
one given in the answer ascribed to Ralegh, that the pastoral
picture assumes a youthful, single-hearted, timeless world;
deny this premise and you destroy the force of the whole

---

[67] R. S. Forsythe, in *"The Passionate Shepherd* and English Poetry," *PMLA*,
XL (1925), 692–742, provides an elaborate treatment of the imitations of
Marlowe's poetry in English and some account of earlier uses of the invita-
tion motif.

thing. Just so, in Spenser's garden of Adonis, there is no disturbing element but Time:

> But were it not, that Time their troubler is,
> All that in this delightfull gardin growes
> Should happy bee, and have immortall blis:
> For here all plenty and all pleasure flowes,
> And sweete Love gentle fitts emongst them throwes,
> Without fell rancor or fond gealosy:
> Franckly each paramor his leman knowes,
> Each bird his mate, ne any does envy
> Their goodly meriment and gay felicity.[68]

The extreme popularity of Marlowe's poem caused many parodies and imitations of it, one of which is given in the *Helicon* as No. 139; to some extent these parodies show that the original poem ceased to be felt as a pastoral invitation. Modern criticism can more readily approach the famous poem from the point of view of its contemporaries if it takes into account the whole pastoral mode and the special nature of the lyric of invitation.

The palinode, a song in rejection of love, is represented in *England's Helicon* by a few examples. One of them, No. 54, is a definition of love put in such terms as to warn the inexperienced away from it. The poem is an example of those which were not originally pastoral but were doctored by the editor of *England's Helicon* to make them fit the pastoral character of his anthology. Lifting it from *The Phoenix Nest* (1593), the editor added speech tags for two shepherds, Melibeus and Faustus, and substituted phrases like "Sheepheard, what's" for "Now what" and "good Sheepheard" for "I praie thee." A better example of the rejection of love is the well-known ballet of William Byrd, "Though Amarillis daunce in greene" (No. 110). It has a pastoral and rustic atmosphere, since the chorus to each stanza is the humorously resigned exclamation, "Hey hoe, chill loue no more," and the second stanza begins "My Sheepe are lost for want of foode." It is interesting that there is so little of the rejec-

---

[68] *Faerie Queene*, III, VI, xli.

tion of love in the anthology. Perhaps a reason is that in the pastoral romances no shepherd ever cures himself of love by philosophy; it can be done only by magic or a drug. Therefore there is no tradition within this mode of a rejection of love, as there is in others. The Ovidian *remedia amoris* or the Platonic "Leave me, O love, which reachest but to dust" has no place in pastoral.[69]

The "blazon," or catalogue of the lady's beauties, is in style if not in origin a pastoral adaptation of one of the main conventions of the Petrarchan sonnet. As such it is subject to the same limitations as those felt by the sonneteers, but perhaps pastoral praise exhausts itself sooner because the comparisons must be those which are possible for a shepherd. Further, the naïve quality of the shepherd does not fit with his being an accomplished fine courtier (unless there is allegory, of course; I am here dealing only with the lyric); wit and ingenuity are out of place among sheep-flocks, as Shakespeare points out in *As You Like It*. Accordingly, we get blazons which are effective because of their subdued tone and restraint; they are likely to be plaintive, as for example the one by J. Wotton in *England's Helicon*, No. 41.

The finest and most elaborate blazon in all English pastoral poetry is of course Spenser's praise of Queen Elizabeth in the April eclogue of *The Shepheardes Calender,* which is printed in *England's Helicon* as No. 6. The comment on this poem has mostly concerned itself with the flattery of royalty and with the versification. Considered purely as a blazon, however, its structure and proportion are very impressive. The style itself is first established, as a "siluer song," and the Muses are invoked for aid. Then comes the justification for the heightened praise: that the lady is "of heauenly race" and therefore without mortal blemish. Within this frame-

[69] The poem printed by Albert Feuillerat (ed., *The Complete Works of Sir Philip Sidney*, 4 vols. [Cambridge University Press, 1922–1926], II, 344–346) from Harleian MS. 6057, entitled by him "A Remedie for Love" and said in the manuscript to be "An old dittie of Sr Phillipp Sidneyes omitted in the Printed Arcadia," may seem to be a contradiction of this statement. Actually, the poem is a version of the "mock-blazon" on Mopsa which I discuss below, p. 53.

work, she is first presented as a picture; [70] the following stanza forms a bridge from her physical beauty to her "heauenly hauiour, her Princely Grace," and this makes possible the association with her of the sun and the moon in the two succeeding stanzas. The summary of this part is the line "Shee is my Goddesse plaine," and we are brought back to the lowly pastoral atmosphere by the shepherd's promise to offer her a milk-white lamb when the lambing season comes. The musical glorification of Eliza then follows, with the Muses trooping to her and playing their instruments, while the Graces (she herself making the fourth) dance and sing. The Ladies of the Lake then come to crown her with olive branches symbolizing peace, and this leads to the lovely flower stanza in which the Queen is again associated with the beauties of earth. As such she is to be attended by the "Sheepheards daughters that dwell on the greene," and we have the pastoral atmosphere reaffirmed. Finally, the attendant maidens are dismissed, with the quaint promise by the shepherd of some plums if they will return when he gathers them.

The most remarkable quality of the poem considered as a pastoral blazon is the firm and sure control the poet exercises over his transitions and the harmonious blending of many motifs. Classic myth, abstract divine qualities, the reality of earth, music, and color—all are here. The poem has an organic motion, wavelike, easy, and natural. Its stability comes from its pastoral inspiration and method.

The gayest pastoral lyrics are the roundelays, jigs, and dance songs, of which *England's Helicon* exhibits a half dozen examples. Spenser is again represented as the most expert maker of this type of poem, thanks to the fact that the editor did not pick up the "Cupid's Curse" roundelay when he was going through Peele's *Arraignment of Paris*. The roundelay from the August eclogue of *The Shepheardes Calender* is No. 11 in *England's Helicon*. It seems probable that Spenser's poem was written to an already existing tune,

[70] The editor of *England's Helicon* apparently liked a more regular line than he found in Spenser. He changes line 6 from "With Damaske roses and Daffadillies set" to "With Daffadils and Damaske Roses set."

"Heigh ho Holiday." [71] Either because of the popularity of the old tune or the success of Spenser's poem, there are several imitations, two of them in the *Helicon:* No. 81 from Lodge's *Rosalynde,* "A Blithe and bonny Country-Lasse," and No. 125 by H. C., "Fie on the sleights that men deuise." [72] These poems were to be sung by two singers, alternating; the editor of *England's Helicon* has removed the speech-tags and has left the indication of how the songs were sung only in the heading to No. 125: "two Nimphes, each aunswering other line for line."

Two shepherds' jigs, "Damaetas Iigge" by John Wotton (No. 28) and "The Sheepheard Dorons Iigge" from Greene's *Menaphon* (1589; No. 32), have the same carefree spirit. The characteristic feeling is that of Wotton's first stanza:

Iolly Sheepheard, Sheepheard on a hill
   on a hill so merrily,
   on a hill so cherily,
  Feare not Sheepheard there to pipe thy fill,
Fill euery Dale, fill euery Plaine:
   both sing and say; Loue feeles no paine.

This atmosphere of merriment and naïveté distinguishes some of the *Helicon* poems which are otherwise hard to classify, such as the pleasant narrative poem of Nicholas Breton's, "Phillida and Coridon" (No. 12), which merely relates, in short lines appropriate to the fresh and simple feeling of the poem, a pastoral betrothal.[73] Although this

[71] See Bruce Pattison, "The Roundelay in the August Eclogue of *The Shepheardes Calender,*" *RES,* IX (1933), 54–55, and his *Music and Poetry in the English Renaissance* (London, 1948), pp. 173–174.

[72] This poem, although Rollins (*England's Helicon,* II, 178) says it is known only in the *Helicon,* appears in Thomas Deloney's *Garland of Good Will,* 1631 (*Works,* ed. F. O. Mann [Oxford, 1912], pp. 344–346); whether it was in the *Garland* as entered in 1593 and published in 1596, hence before its publication in the *Helicon,* is not known.

[73] Perhaps the closest parallel to Breton's poem is the "Dowsabell" song in Drayton's eighth eclogue of *Idea The Shepheards Garland,* 1593 (see *Works,* ed. Hebel, I, 88–91). But Drayton's poem is much more "naturalized," with English place names and very specific details about the materials of the shepherds' clothing and equipment. It moves the pastoral environment out of Arcadia to the English countryside. This realism no doubt had a comic effect for the Elizabethans, and Drayton uses a comic meter, that of Chaucer's *Sir Thopas.*

poem reads like a mere pretty narrative, it, too, was originally set to music and as a song in three parts was sung to
Queen Elizabeth by three musicians "disguised in auncient
Countrey attire" as she opened the casement of her gallery
window about nine o'clock on a September morning. According to the account published in 1591, the song pleased Her
Highness so much, both in words and music, that she com-
manded a repeat performance and graced it highly "with her
chearefull acceptance and commendation." [74]

The royal progress was, incidentally, one of the important
sources of pastoral poetry and pageant. In the next year, 1592,
the Queen was again entertained with a shepherd's speech at
Sudeley, and she would have seen a pastoral play except that
the Cotswold weather prevented its production. [75] In 1599
when Elizabeth visited Wilton, she was entertained by a song
in praise of Astrea, sung by two shepherds, Thenot and Piers,
the words written by her hostess, the Countess of Pembroke. [76]
Whether the progress was primarily responsible or not, much
of the glorification of Her Majesty took a pastoral form. In
fact, William Empson thinks that "it was this Renaissance
half-worship of Elizabeth and the success of England under
her rule that gave conviction to the whole set of ideas." [77]

Sometimes the shepherd's complaint was transformed into
a song, and, when the naïveté was emphasized and the chorus
lines made prominent, something like a comic tone tempered
the declaration of love. An example is *Helicon* No. 68, by
H. C.

---

[74] *The Honorable Entertainement gieuen to the Queenes Maiestie in Progresse, at Eluetham in Hampshire, by the right Honorable the Earle of Hertford* (1591), sig. D2ᵛ.

[75] *Speeches Delivered to Her Maiestie this Last Progresse, at the Right
Honorable the Lady Rvssels, at Bissam, the Right Honorable the Lorde
Chandos at Sudley, at the Right Honorable the Lord Norris, at Ricorte* (Ox-
ford, 1592), sigs. B–Cʳ.

[76] Printed as No. 4 in Davison's *A Poetical Rhapsody* (1602), ed. Rollins,
I, 15.

[77] *English Pastoral Poetry* (New York, 1938; American edition of *Some
Versions of Pastoral*), p. 34. For a discussion of Elizabeth in this role and a
survey of the many relevant works, see E. C. Wilson, *England's Eliza* (Cambridge: Harvard University Press, 1939), chap. IV, "Fayre Elisa, Queene of
Shepheardes All."

England's Helicon contains several examples of the song of good life to which we have already referred. The editor was no doubt aware that some of his readers would tire of love songs, and he may have been as willing to please them as is the clown Feste in *Twelfth Night,* when he asks the two tippling knights, who have demanded a song, "Would you have a love-song, or a song of good life?" Feste, as a professional entertainer, knows the conventional types of song well enough, though the commentators have not done much to illuminate the passage.

Examples of the good-life song in *Helicon* are No. 10 by Lodge, a piece preferring the shepherd's life to that of kings and worldlings, and No. 104, taken from a songbook of Byrd's. The second poem in *England's Helicon,* mainly a blazon of the shepherd's mistress, begins with two stanzas on the good life, in which it is claimed that

> Good Kings haue not disdained it,
> > but Sheepheards haue beene named:
> A sheepe-hooke is a Scepter fit,
> > for people well reclaimed.
> The Sheepheards life so honour'd is and praised:
> That Kings lesse happy seeme, though higher raised.[78]

The pastoral lyric concerns itself largely, as we have seen, with love and the good life. It is less psychologically and rhetorically complex than the Petrarchan sonnet, less troubled by the sexual paradox than the poetry of the Ovidian-mythological tradition. A few more comments on its treatment of love may be useful. In general, love in the pastoral world is thought of as innocent, chaste, childlike. The final lines of No. 147 in *England's Helicon* (by "Shepherd Tonie") are representative:

> Take hands then Nimphes & Sheepheards all,
> And to this Riuers musiques fall
> Sing true loue, and chast loue
> > begins our Festiuall.

---

[78] I have found about forty-five additional Elizabethan poems which would be called "poems of good life."

So general is this atmosphere that one wonders if the editor of the great pastoral anthology realized that one of the poems he took from Yonge's *Musica Transalpina* (Nos. 131 and 132) exploits a *double entendre* on the word "die." It is curious indeed to encounter here a poem not very far in intention from Dryden's song, "Whil'st Alexis lay prest," in *Marriage à-la-Mode*.

There is little in common between Elizabethan pastoralism and the transparent pretense of Restoration shepherds and shepherdesses. The Elizabethan view of pastoral is at once more serious and more gay. It emphasizes the value of *otium* and the mean estate, and, possibly because a realization of that value produces a legitimate feeling of freedom, Elizabethan pastoral gaiety is natural, untainted, and harmonious:

> Harke iollie Sheepheards,
>   harke yond lustic ringing:
> How cheerefully the bells daunce,
>   the whilst the Lads are springing?
>
> Goe we then, why sit we here delaying:
> And all yond mery wanton lasses playing?
>   How gailie Flora leades it,
>   and sweetly treads it!
>   The woods and groaues they ring,
>   louely resounding:
>   With Ecchoes sweet rebounding.

This is the note on which the reader of *England's Helicon* in 1600 closed the book.

II

The pastoral lyric distills emotion from an ideal of content and the good life. It is the purest of the pastoral forms and the one in which Elizabethan style and manner are most clearly evident. But the pastoral eclogue is more typical and more conventional; it is more important historically, because Spenser used the form to usher in a great new age of English poetry. A critical appreciation of the Elizabethan eclogue is not easy for a modern reader, because he does not discriminate as the Elizabethans did and because the commonplaces upon which pastoral is built have now lost some of their vitality.

The models for pastoral eclogue available to the Elizabethans were both classical and modern, Latin and vernacular, great and mediocre. The tradition is one which has often been traced from Theocritus to Virgil to the humanists of the Renaissance to Marot and Spenser. It now seems clear that Spenser's sources, or perhaps inspirations would be a better word, were largely Renaissance rather than ancient.[79] Of special interest among the neo-Latin eclogues are 'those of Baptista Spagnuoli, called Mantuan. They were used in Elizabethan school textbooks and became a part of the knowledge of anyone who learned Latin in the period. Mantuan was a Carmelite monk, and his eclogues contain satire on the Roman church which naturally pleased the taste of Protestant Englishmen. Moreover, his Latin was of about the right degree of difficulty for schoolboys, the content was one which schoolmasters would believe healthy for their charges, and there is the illusion of pleasantness about the eclogues which is always a consideration in a textbook.[80]

Alexander Barclay's eclogues of about 1514 contain imitations of Mantuan and of Aeneas Sylvius; Barnabe Googe's *Eglogs Epitaphs and Sonnets* in 1563 includes translations from eclogues in Montemayor; and George Turbervile translated into English verse the whole of Mantuan's eclogues in 1567. This is the extent of the pastoral eclogue in English before the appearance of Spenser's *The Shepheardes Calender* in 1579.

Spenser's sources have been elaborately worked out; his covert allusions to contemporary persons and events have been so laboriously and painfully investigated that it is with some difficulty that a modern reader threads his way through all the apparatus that has been provided for the poetry to

[79] M. Y. Hughes, *Virgil and Spenser* (Berkeley, Calif., 1929), Part I.

[80] See the edition by W. P. Mustard for text, comment, and notes on Mantuan's literary influence.

the poetry itself. Yet the very commentators who have erected such a mountain of lumber around *The Shepheardes Calender* justify themselves by pointing, quite rightly, to the quality and significance of the twelve eclogues contained in it. It was the publication of these poems, everybody agrees, which ushered in the New Poetry of the Elizabethan age. Spenser's metrical experiments were bold and, for the most part, effective. His language, although serious critics like Sidney might be doubtful about it, utilized archaic and provincial words in such a way as to provide a diction suitable to the characters who are speaking. Most of all, he demonstrated with amazing confidence and flair that English verse was capable of the most varied and complex effects, all within a traditional mode which had a general European acceptance.

The Shepheardes Calender appeared anonymously, with a dedication to Sir Philip Sidney; its authorship could hardly have been a secret long, but whether the success of the poem made the poet or only the poem famous is not a matter of much concern to us. The volume did appear, however, with the annotations of one E. K., whose identity has fascinated many antiquarians but has never been perfectly established. E. K., whoever he was, was a mixed blessing. His confusions and his errors have been straightened out by modern scholarship, but one of his contributions, a classification of the eclogues, seems to have been very little utilized.[81]

These xij. Aeclogues euery where answering to the seasons of the twelue monthes may be well deuided into three formes or ranckes. For eyther they be Plaintiue, as the first, the sixt, the eleuenth, and the twelfth, or recreatiue, such as al those be, which conceiue matter of loue, or commendation of special personages, or Moral: which for the most part be mixed with some Satyrical bitternesse, namely the second of reuerence dewe to old age, the fift of coloured deceipt, the seuenth and ninth of dissolute shepheards and pastours, the tenth of contempt

[81] There is no comment on the classification in the Spenser Variorum (9 vols.; Baltimore, 1932–1949). O. Reissert, in "Bemerkungen über Spensers *Shepheards Calender* und die frühere Bukolik," *Anglia*, IX (1886), 205–224, takes up the eclogues according to E. K.'s classification but only for purposes of source study.

of Poetrie and pleasaunt wits. And to this diuision may euery thing herein be reasonably applyed: a few onely except, whose speciall purpose and meaning I am not priuie to.[82]

This classification would read as follows:

Plaintive: 1st (January), 6th (June), 11th (November), 12th (December)

Moral: 2nd (February), 5th (May), 7th (July), 9th (September), 10th (October)

Recreative: 3rd (March), 4th (April), 8th (August)

A glance at this list will show that the three kinds, if the distinction between them is valid, are quite skillfully scattered through the pattern of the whole. There are five moral eclogues, four plaintive, and three recreative. The division into kinds, even though it is of course not absolute, serves as a means to achieve variety, and it bears some relationship to the adherence of some of the eclogues to the atmosphere of the season concerned. The variety of verse forms is another means by which the *Calender* distinguishes itself. But with all this care to achieve variety, there is also a principle of continuity stronger than the mere sequence of the months. In each of the three "forms or ranks," as E. K. calls them, two of the examples occur consecutively: the third and fourth eclogues are recreative, the ninth and tenth are moral, and the eleventh and twelfth are plaintive. The over-all structure of the *Calender,* then, is one which combines similarity and contrasts, variety and continuity. The complex relationships of theme, of style, and of "rank or form" give *The Shepheardes Calender* a vitality and interest which no other collection of pastoral eclogues in English can boast.

The *Calender* begins and ends with plaintive eclogues. This is appropriate to the winter season of January and December, and it also sets the over-all tone for the series. The total effect must not be harsh and satirical, as the moral eclogues tend to make it, not gay and carefree, as the recreative eclogues would suggest. The poet is our sage and serious

---

[82] "The Generall argument of the whole booke," Variorum *Minor Poems,* ed. C. G. Osgood and H. G. Lotspeich, 2 vols. (Baltimore, 1943, 1947), I, 12.

Spenser, but his seriousness must be conveyed in tone and mood; doctrine and belief must be expressed primarily as poetry, and for this purpose the tone of the complaint will best serve.

"January" is simple in style. The plaintive eclogues increase in complexity up through "November" (a piece which E. K. says he prefers to all the rest), and then the style is somewhat simpler again for the final "December." "January" mainly equates the lovelorn shepherd's state of mind with nature around him. The poem might be called an extended simile:

> Thou barrein ground, whome winters wrath hath wasted,
> Art made a myrrhour, to behold my plight.

Rather than a simile, it is a mirror situation; the comparison between object and image extends both ways, and each has its validity. For example, stanza 5 describes the shepherd's heart, blood, and pain in terms of winter weather. The sixth stanza does the reverse: it turns the woodland into an abandoned and disconsolate lover of birds and flowers. What does this leave for the spectator as a point of view? It is impossible to keep the position of the shepherd, for he is sometimes only a reflection of nature; it is impossible to keep the point of view of nature, for it is often only a reflection of the moods and feelings of the shepherd. The result is a kind of "distance" or objectivity, which gives us both shepherd and nature in perspective, in the round. We are not sure which is object and which is reflection because they reverse roles. Sometimes this is made explicit by means of rhetorical figures, which commentators who belong to the tribe of E. K. have noticed:

> With mourning pyne I, you with pyning mourne.

This, addressed to the sheep, seems stilted and frigid under the comment of those who merely give the name for the rhetorical figure; seen as a detail which reinforces the whole mirror device of the eclogue, it acquires some artistic significance.

The device of lovers in series, or the fragmentary cross-eyed Cupid situation, is also used here. As Hobbinol is to Colin ("His clownish gifts and curtsies I disdaine," line 57), so Colin is to Rosalind ("And of my rurall musick holdeth scorne," line 64). This device also provides scale and "distance." Finally, it leads up to the resolution, in which Colin breaks his pipe (the symbolic significance of poetry as such is very great in the *Calender,* and this is an unobtrusive and yet powerful way of opening the theme) and concludes his outburst. The final stanza shows how delicately the point of view of the spectator has been adjusted:

> By that, the welked Phoebus gan availe
> His weary waine, and now the frosty Night
> Her mantle black through heauen gan ouerhaile,
> Which seene the pensife boy halfe in despight
> > Arose, and homeward droue his sonned sheepe,
> > Whose hanging heads did seeme his carefull case to weepe.

The effect here should be compared with that achieved by Milton in *Lycidas,* when he shifts from a tone of austere rejoicing at the picture of Lycidas being entertained by all the Saints above

> In solemn troops and sweet societies
> That sing, and singing in their glory move
> And wipe the tears for ever from his eyes

to a return to the pastoral environment and level of feeling:

> Thus sang the uncouth swain to oaks and rills,
> While the still morn went out with sandals grey:
>
> .   .   .   .   .
>
> At last he rose, and twitched his mantle blue:
> Tomorrow to fresh woods, and pastures new.

There is something more here than the mere formal close to a pastoral elegy; there is the sudden involvement of the reader himself in the attitude and position of the shepherd. The same kind of shift occurs at the end of Gray's *Elegy* when the meditations on the reluctance of the dying culminate in "Ev'n in our Ashes live their wonted Fires" and give

way to the placing of the melancholy youth among his subjects, and the reader of the poem is directed by "some hoary-
headed Swain" to the youth's epitaph. In comparison with
these two famous examples, Spenser's art seems more delicate
and particular. He involves the reader in the fortunes and
feelings of Colin less sentimentally, with more reserve.[83]

"June," the second of the plaintive eclogues, is a dialogue
in form; the complaint here derives its strength from the
conflict of two situations and points of view and finally proceeds to paradox. The contrast is between Hobbinol and
Colin. Hobbinol represents the standard, happy pastoral existence. He has found, according to Colin, that Paradise
which Adam lost. This is one way of making the equation
between mind and nature, content and Arcadia. But Colin
is not so fortunate; he has grown older, sadder, and wiser.
His youth was marked by love and poetry, "But ryper age
such pleasures doth reproue"; sad experience has turned him
away from vain love and "those weary wanton toyes" of
poetry.

The paradox develops when Hobbinol praises his poetry:
Colin was able to teach the birds themselves how to sing,
and when the Muses heard him, even they had to confess
themselves outdone in their art. Colin replies by denying
all the ambitious implications of this praise and asserts that
his aims are very modest:

> But pyping lowe in shade of lowly groue,
> I play to please my selfe, all be it ill.

> Nought weigh I, who my song doth prayse or blame,
> Ne striue to winne renowne, or passe the rest:
> With shepheard sittes not, followe flying fame:
> But feede his flocke in fields, where falls hem best.

[83] Whether this emotional treatment of the shepherd and the "distance"
achieved by Spenser owe anything to pictorial art is an interesting question.
The investigators of Spenser's relationship to the fine arts have so far considered mostly color and illustrative details. See Rosemond Tuve, "Spenser
and Some Pictorial Conventions," *SP*, XXXVII (1940), 149–176; Frederick
Hard, "Clothes of Arras and of Toure," *SP*, XXVII (1930), 162–185; J. B.
Fletcher, "The Painter of the Poets," *SP*, XIV (1917), 153–166.

This is, of course, the shepherd's denial of ambition, the literary form of the central pastoral philosophy of life. And Spenser uses this poetic equivalent of "the quiet mind" as a background for Colin's proudest boast:

The God of shepheards Tityrus is dead,
Who taught me homely, as I can, to make.
He, whilst he liued, was the soueraigne head
Of shepheards all, that bene with loue ytake.

Colin, although he protests his verses are rough and rude, is still the true heir of Chaucer. Here is the paradox: he is both uncouth and unambitious, yet he is the pupil of great artists and proud to be in their tradition. There is a contrast of mood, too. Chaucer, as Tityrus, was able to dampen the flames that love bred in him and to entertain the shepherds with merry tales to keep them awake, but Colin cannot achieve this gaiety. Therefore, in the act of bewailing his sad state, he says he is not able to continue, and instructs the other shepherds (inferior to him in ability at complaints) to tell Rosalind what she has done.

The involutions of the complaint are quite elaborately exploited in this eclogue, and the contrasts and paradoxes might absorb all of our attention. It is worth noticing, however, that Spenser has really shifted the grounds for the pastoral complaint. There is a good deal more about poetry here than about love. The unhappy love situation is felt to be important chiefly because it is said to affect Colin's poetry. The shift has been subtly managed, and no doubt those gullible readers who follow E. K.'s challenge and speculate on the identity of Rosalind miss it; but they are hardly reading the poem anyway; they are playing with biographical puzzles. E. K. in the argument to the eclogue says nothing about poetry, but of course poetry is the main theme of "June"; there is a link here with the next plaintive eclogue, "November," and with "October," its predecessor, also.

"November," like "December," follows the model set by Marot in pastoral. The November poem is a dialogue between Thenot and Colin, leading up to the elaborate pastoral elegy which Colin composed to celebrate the death of Dido, the great shepherd's daughter. The most interesting thing about "November" is not the identity of Dido, whatever the commentators say; it is the elaborateness of the elegy, at the most formal and most elevated level of the complaint. E. K. did not know the identity of Dido, but he declared this eclogue his favorite, "farre passing his [Marot's] reache, and in myne opinion all other the Eglogues of this booke." Plaintive poetry starts with the complaining lover, then has to refine him out of it for the sake of the form and objectivity of the work of art; finally, it discovers in the formal pastoral elegy a vehicle which permits elaborate verse technique together with heightened rhetorical style and a subject which is large enough to permit the expression of deeply felt personal sorrow within the limits of decorum. It is the emancipation of the lover's complaint.

Formally, "November" contains the invocation to the Muse (line 53), the calling on others to wail (lines 63ff.), the description of the effects of her death on Nature (lines 83ff. and 123ff.), the parade of the nymphs (lines 143ff.), and the change from grief to joy (lines 163ff.), which characterize the conventional pastoral elegy.[84] From these conventional features of the elegy the poet has his opportunity in varying and increasing the emotion. The combination of grief and joy makes a "doleful pleasaunce," as Thenot calls it; he hesitates whether to rejoice or weep. This fine balance is what the pastoral elegy tries to achieve.

Spenser's metrical form in this poem is very remarkable. He varies line length, adds a fifth line to his modified quatrain, and finishes the stanza with a lyrical chorus section which links the stanzas together and provides a continuity of emotion. The flexibility and fluidity of the versification do much to keep the formal elements from seeming stiff and rigid.

[84] See George Norlin, "The Conventions of the Pastoral Elegy," *AJP*, XXXII (1911), 294–312, and T. P. Harrison, Jr., "Spenser and the Earlier Pastoral Elegy," *Texas Studies in English*, XIII (1933), 36–53. The relationship between Spenser's "November" and Marot's *Loyse de Savoye* can be studied conveniently in *The Pastoral Elegy*, ed. T. P. Harrison, Jr., and H. J. Leon (Austin, Texas, 1939).

"November" is connected rather more definitely with the season than some of the other eclogues.[85] The mood of the elegy is prepared for by the explanation of Colin that other types of poetry are unsuitable for this time of year. This contrast calls to mind another, that between the elaborate elegy for Dido in "November" and the elaborate praise of Eliza in "April." The two are in a sense complementary, and their importance is clearly marked for us by the wealth of metrical invention Spenser lavished upon them.

"December," the final eclogue, returns to monologue and rounds out the tonal pattern "even as the first beganne," as E. K. says. This poem, too, is dependent on Marot, but a more important influence is that of the calendars, with their symbolic representations of the four seasons as representing the stages of a man's life.[86] The career of Colin, which I take to be somewhat more fictional than the commentators do, is here summed up. In spring he experienced exuberance and freedom, felt pride in his songs. In summer he learned his craft, but was smitten with love. In harvest he reaped only a weedy crop of care. And now winter comes:

> Winter is come, that blowes the balefull breath,
> And after Winter commeth timely death.

The paradox here depends upon the idea of a calendar: it runs out as time runs out; and yet the calendar of months is still good, it records something which is permanent. Just so the poet, saying adieu to his delights, to his love, to his sheep and his woods, to his friend, as Colin does in the last stanza, is by the very form in which he says it achieving something that stops time, that contradicts and denies the Death which is the subject. The detachment or the "distance" between the content or argument and the poetry itself produces a paradoxical relationship between them. That Spenser's use of the calendar device was useful for "scale" was first pointed out, I

[85] See Mary Parmenter, "Spenser's *Twelve Aeglogues Proportionable to the Twelve Monethes*," *ELH*, III (1936), 190–217, for an exposition of the background of calendar and season; the author's suggestion of Queen Elizabeth as Dido is less useful.

[86] See Parmenter, p. 191.

think, by Pope: "The addition he has made of a Calendar to
his Eclogues, is very beautiful: since by this, besides that general moral of innocence and simplicity, which is common to
other authors of pastoral, he has one peculiar to himself; he
compares human Life to the several Seasons, and at once exposes to his readers a view of the great and little worlds, in
their various changes and aspects." [87] The missing emblem
for Colin is explained by E. K.: "The meaning wherof is that
all thinges perish and come to theyr last end, but workes of
learned wits and monuments of Poetry abide for euer." [88]
This is clearly the implication of the whole eclogue and, as
summary, of the whole *Shepheardes Calender.* Shakespeare
found in Ovid the same commonplace and developed it in a
non-pastoral setting in his sonnets. The pastoral handling of
the theme enjoys an added richness, for, as the reply to Marlowe's "Passionate Shepherd" shows, time is the answer to the
pastoral ideal. But what if, in poetry, there is an answer to the
answer?

The five "moral" eclogues, "February," "May," "July,"
"September," and "October," are arranged in such a way as
to develop a climax, just as the plaintive eclogues were. In
this series the climax comes in the September eclogue, and the
succeeding and final one, "October," turns, as the plaintive
series did, specifically to the subject of poetry. If in the plaintive series the difficulty was to build out of the given state of
mind of the lovesick shepherd an expression which would do
justice to the emotion itself and yet reconcile with it the verve
of the poetry, the problem in the moral eclogues is to find a
function for poetry in the social, political, and cultural environment.

Far from being escapist, pastoral poetry was the most apt of
all the kinds for serious humanistic purposes. Because of

---

[87] "A Discourse on Pastoral Poetry," *The Prose Works of Alexander Pope,*
ed. Norman Ault (Oxford, 1936) , pp. 301–302.

[88] A. H. Gilbert, "The Embleme for December in the *Shepheardes Calender,*" *MLN,* LXIII (1948) , 181–182, gives reasons for thinking that *Merce non
mercede,* at the end of the book, is the misplaced December emblem. Whatever the case, we have the meaning of the December emblem preserved for
us in the Glosse, and it is the meaning that is here important.

the central concern with the relative value of wealth, power, riches, and the "contented mind," and because of its conventional machinery of shepherds, with their singing contests, debates, and complaints, the eclogue lent itself readily to indirect or slightly masked criticism of contemporary affairs. It had been so used by Virgil, and the Renaissance imitators of the greatest of Roman poets had developed the satirical, critical strain still further. Spenser's chief model in this series is Mantuan, especially his eclogues 7, 8, and 9. But he fuses with Mantuan's serious, satirical manner something from his own English Tityrus, Chaucer. It is not so apparent to us as it was to the sixteenth century that Chaucer is a very moral poet; Spenser was chiefly impressed with his use of fables. So "February," "May," and "September" utilize Aesopic or pseudo-Aesopic material, told in the manner of Chaucer. The fable gives a narrative interest to these eclogues; there is something more primitive and perhaps more solid in their stories than there is in the extended emotion of the plaintive series. For this reason, perhaps, as well as to produce further variety, Spenser has devised a characteristic style for these eclogues— rough, uncouth, non-lyrical, and full of dialect words. The matter is harsh, the meter is old-fashioned, suggesting the alliterative accentual verse of an earlier age in "February," the stolid fourteeners of the 1560's and 1570's in "July."

"February" tells the fable of the oak and the briar, after a dramatic introduction in the form of a quarrel between the young shepherd Cuddie and the old shepherd Thenot. There is a connection here with the time of year, for old age and winter are explicitly identified:

For Age and Winter accord full nie,
This chill, that cold, this crooked, that wrye.

The conflict of age and youth is very common in the pastoral mode.[89] It is simply another form of the central problem which makes pastoral—the problem of the values inherent in

---

[89] The reason is sometimes the differing attitudes of young and old toward love. See, for example, the conflict between Geron and Philisides in the old *Arcadia* (*Works,* ed. Feuillerat, pp. 68–72).

the good life. Here the quarrel is resolved by a story, the briar finding out when winter comes that it has been dependent upon the old oak. So the threat of winter and rough weather or old age, when times drives the flocks from field to fold, is the basic challenge to the pastoral ideal and must be faced. The fable in the February eclogue is simple, but its theme is central.[90]

The May eclogue first introduces what E. K. calls "some Satyrical bitternesse"; it is an attack on Catholic pastors, who are not true shepherds but deceitful and malicious, like the fox that devoured the kid. This involves of course the equation of shepherds–pastors–priests; more significantly, it poses the question of the relative value of the gay, irresponsible pastoral life and the conscientious tending of sheep. The month of May is utilized to give the shepherd Palinode an opportunity to urge participation in the pagan revelries of May Day and to have Piers, the spokesman for the serious, Protestant, point of view, reprove these sports as follies, fit for "Younkers" but reprehensible in men of elder wit. The connection between this subject of true and false pastors (a theme which Milton later developed, with even more satirical bitterness, in *Lycidas*) and the personal, direct, moral effect of these eclogues lies in the subject of friendship and trust. Palinode believes that tolerance and resignation are the only ways to deal with differences between shepherds:

> Let none mislike of that may not be mended:
> So conteck soone by concord mought be ended.

But Piers, who is given the advantage of being the teller of the fable, says that no peace or compromise is possible with that shepherd "that does the right way forsake." The story is told with more art and elaboration than the story of the

---

[90] The sources and significance of the fables in the moral eclogues are discussed by L. S. Friedland, "Spenser as a Fabulist," *SAB*, XII (1937), 85–108, 133–154, 197–207. I agree with Renwick, Parmenter, and Friedland (and E. K.) that the February eclogue is merely moral and general, on the subject of youth and age, not specifically allegorical, as Greenlaw and others would have it.

oak and briar; besides, in accordance with the climactic scheme of the series, the whole eclogue is more vigorous and outspoken. A link with a later moral eclogue, "September," is prepared in the lines (126–129) about the wolves in sheep's clothing. In the lines just preceding these, Spenser prepares for the theme of "July." By the time "July" is reached, the basic theme has been so clearly introduced, through the narratives of the preceding moral eclogues, that now it can be debated directly, taken out of the fable framework, and presented dramatically. Spenser chooses the old familiar 4–3–4–3 ballad measure, that of the versified psalms and of all matter to be committed to memory, the most familiar of Elizabethan verse forms.[91]

Thomalin, in a long speech, gives the conventional praise of shepherds derived from Mantuan, which we have already noticed. His emphasis is that the true shepherds are not ambitious, not aspiring, but humble and low. This serves as an image which works in several ways: Thomalin and Morrell represent, respectively, the valley and the hill, and the woodcut at the head of the eclogue naïvely shows them stationed at these two points while they hold their debate; Thomalin represents the Puritan ideal of a clergy unelevated, humble, and devoted to pastoral care, while Morrell represents the Catholic or Anglican clergy gloating in worldly pomp; most general and most significant of all, Thomalin represents the mean estate, the central theme of pastoralism, and Morrell embodies the aspiring mind. Their emblems summarize this contrast:

Thomalins Embleme.
  In medio virtus.
Morrells Embleme.
  In summo foelicitas.

So rich is the central doctrine of pastoral that the poet can find application for it pictorially, topically, and gnomically.

---

[91] Sixteenth-century attitudes toward this verse form are discussed in my article, "English Metrical Psalms in the Sixteenth Century and Their Literary Significance," *HLQ*, IX (1946), 249–271.

The ethical imagination of the Elizabethans was not narrow and compartmentalized but broad and versatile in scope. Feeling about a great moral commonplace could find its expression in picture, topical narrative, or satire, or in the posy of a ring.

"September," though it has been called "the least interesting and most difficult" (Herford) of the eclogues in *The Shepheardes Calender,* and even more harshly "a tedious though fluent stream of commonplace complaint" (Palgrave), is really the climax of the moral series.[92] Here the bitterness about bad shepherds is stronger than in any of the other eclogues; here the verse form is a hard, punching couplet. Hobbinol and Diggon Davy do not argue, but Diggon reports to Hobbinol the sad state of things in the country he has just visited, and Hobbinol provides the choral comment. It is again the pastoral assertion:

> Content who liues with tryed state,
> Neede feare no chaunge of frowning fate.

In this eclogue, as Friedland points out,[93] the technique of the fable is brought to its climax; here the fable is an integral part of the eclogue, not just appended for illustrative interest as in "February" and "May." The fable this time is a genuinely poetic idea. Spenser's source was Mantuan, as usual in the moral eclogues, but the idea, concisely expressed in Matthew 7:15, "Beware of false prophets, which come to you in sheep's clothing, but inwardly they are ravening wolves," appears often in the sermons of the time,[94] and its suggestions

[92] Variorum *Minor Poems,* I, 350–351. H. S. V. Jones, *A Spenser Handbook* (New York, 1930), p. 51, places "September" more accurately when he says it is the most persuasive statement of the philosophy of moderation and that "'September' points the moral to be drawn from the whole series." But he curiously finds this philosophy and moral to be the distinctive property of Gabriel Harvey. Harvey no doubt approved of it, but the significant point is that it is the central doctrine of pastoral. The *Calender* is organized as pastoral; a realization of this fact is different from saying, "We may conclude, then, that in the opinions of Harvey we find a principle of unity for the *Shepheardes Calender* as a whole" (Jones, p. 52).

[93] "Spenser as a Fabulist," p. 147.

[94] W. L. Renwick (ed. *The Shepherd's Calendar* [London, 1930], p. 213) quotes usefully from Thomas Cartwright.

are so wide that it provides the satisfactory image for the unification of the pastoral, religious, and social ideas in this
whole group of poems. The shepherd's life is always stressed
as one in which the characteristics of the mind and will are
important; the conditions for human existence are most favorable, and there are few dangers from pride or ambition, but
the goddesses still appear before a shepherd and demand that
he choose between them. A wrong choice is always possible.
The shepherd is still man seen simply, but his idyllic life is
now put upon a basis of moral responsibility, and the existence of evil is recognized.

Hobbinol's statement presents an awareness of human limitations and an acceptance of them, within the pastoral framework, as sad but valuable. Here is a link, in mood, with the
encompassing tone of the plaintive eclogues, and the moral
poems are finding their place in the unity of the whole.

The October eclogue, which E. K. placed among the moral
eclogues, has seemed to some students to belong by itself because it treats the subject of poets and their low state at the
present time instead of the problem of the good pastor. But
as I have shown, the plaintive series developed toward a self-
conscious emphasis on poetry, and it is only according to the
pattern that the moral eclogues should do so too. Herford,
who separates "October" from its group, says that "this noble
and pregnant piece is the very core of *The Shepheard's Calender.*" [95] It is interesting, by the way, to see how the critics
decide what is central in the book. Greenlaw, partly because
he reads the poems so heavily as historical allegory and propaganda, sees the moral eclogues together as "the core and
heart" of the *Calender.*[96] R. E. N. Dodge calls the Rosalind
story "the central theme of *S. C.*" [97] I have been trying to show
that there is not a core of something wrapped up in a cover-
ing of pastoral, but that the pastoral idea, in its various rami-
fications, *is* the *Calender.* H. S. V. Jones regards "October"
as the keystone of the arch structurally because he recognizes

[95] C. H. Herford, ed., *Shepheards Calendar* (London, 1907), p. xlv.
[96] Variorum *Minor Poems*, I, 603.
[97] *Ibid.*, p. 602.

only two kinds of eclogues, the plaintive-recreative and the moral.

The shepherd as pastor is responsible for caring for his flock; he has his reward in protecting them from the wolves. What, then, are the responsibilities of the shepherd as poet? Shall he be content "to feede youthes fancie, and the flocking fry" with his dapper ditties? Is he a mere entertainer? No, Piers replies, he can influence them morally. Here Piers is giving voice to the justification for poetry that runs through Elizabethan criticism from Sir Philip Sidney to Milton:

> O what an honor is it, to restraine
> The lust of lawlesse youth with good aduice:
> Or pricke them forth with pleasaunce of thy vaine,
> Whereto thou list their trayned willes entice.

But if the lowly are not grateful for instruction, then the poet should turn to heroic poetry, celebrating deeds of greatness and becoming the spokesman for the national spirit. This was the pattern followed by Virgil, who, being favored by Maecenas, was enabled to rise above the humble style of the pastoral and write the epic of Rome. Yet as Cuddie recalls this, he says that in these degenerate days the poet has no such prospect; he must make "rymes of rybaudrye" or resign in favor of the doggerel-monger Tom Piper.

This concern over the place of poetry is not so much professional as it is moral. True, some glances at the niggardly ways of patrons are taken over from Mantuan, but the primary concern is for the use and value of poetry, and the final conclusion is that it is holy. The Platonism which here enters the *Calender* [98] serves this purpose. It gives a theory of poetic inspiration which allies the poet with the priest. Their work is in essence divine. Love is a source of such divine inspiration, and even love poetry may provide it, as is the case with Colin. Cuddie, however, can approximate the high elevated style of truly inspired poetry only by imagining himself aroused by wine, and when he does we have, for a moment,

[98] See Osgood in Variorum *Minor Poems*, I, 371.

heroic poetry. But the feeling must soon subside and return within the scope of pastoral:

> But ah my corage cooles ere it be warme,
> For thy, content vs in thys humble shade:
> Where no such troublous tydes han vs assayde,
> Here we our slender pipes may safely charme.

The contrast between the style of this eclogue and that of the other moral eclogues is very striking. It is as if Spenser deliberately made the satirical eclogues rough and uncouth for reasons of decorum and effectiveness of the moral ideas, but culminated his series in an eclogue which not only showed that the poet is as directly connected with the divine in his business as the pastor is, but that his sounds, too, are closer to heavenly music than to the sounds of Tom Piper.

The three remaining eclogues, "March," "April," and "August," have not been taken seriously as a group by themselves, presumably because E. K. does not specify the members of his "recreative" category, "such as al those be, which conceiue matter of loue, or commendation of special personages." As Jones observes,[99] some of the plaintive eclogues come within this definition. But the three poems under consideration are not plaintive, and in examining the structure of the whole series they may well be considered separately. "March" is the most clearly recreative of all. It comes after the plaintive "January" and the moral-fabulist "February"; it is high time for some relief. Specifically, "March" is a comic eclogue. The tone is set by the loutish Thomalin, who is annoyed at his sheep for getting lost, fearful that something will happen to them if he even turns his attention long enough to tell a story, petulant about his pastoral duties. He has gone hunting on a shepherd's holiday and hears something stirring in a bush. Without knowing what it is, he shoots at it. Thomalin here is some sort of cousin of Lyly's Sir Thopas, the braggart hunter and fisherman. His quarry is the nimble laughing god, and Thomalin relates how with heavy earnestness he shoots all his bolts at Cupid and then

[99] *A Spenser Handbook*, p. 43.

falls to throwing "pumie stones" which Cupid easily and lightly catches. The point here is the contrast between the lubberly shepherd and the fleet god of love; the effect is remotely like that of Bottom and Titania. When Thomalin is wounded in the heel, and he is no Achilles nor was meant to be, a mock-heroic touch is added to the comedy of simple contrast. E. K.'s elaborate nonsense about the Achilles' heel is, I suppose, further pedantic contribution to the joke.

The sage and serious Spenser was no great humorist, to be sure; the comedy is feeble enough. But perhaps the commentators have been so intent upon connecting Spenser with Bion and Ronsard that they have missed the point. The verse form, which is that of Chaucer's *Sir Thopas,* should have given the clue. Are we to suppose that Spenser with all his worship of Chaucer never once saw the comic element in his master or tried to imitate it? [100]

The following eclogue, which has already received some attention in the discussion of the pastoral lyric, has been much admired. It is "the gem of the whole *Calender,*" according to B. E. C. Davis,[101] and it surpasses its only competitor, "November," in subtlety of versification and freshness of atmosphere. Structurally, it provides a transition to the moral eclogue of "May." The serious Protestant subject matter of "May" cannot be approached directly from the absurdity of "March," and the lyrical, religious-patriotic quality of the blazon for Eliza, queen of shepherds all, is the natural modulation. The adulation of Elizabeth is tactful and politic coming where it does, just before Spenser opens his case against deceptive Catholic pastors. Moreover, the dryness of pastoral doctrine is justified artistically only when it

---

[100] Drayton apparently saw Spenser's intention here and used the same verse form for his poem of "Dowsabell" in the eighth eclogue of *Idea The Shepheards Garland* (1593) . Mrs. Tillotson speaks of "a factitious and charming air of archaism" achieved by Drayton in using this meter, and her comments on the manner of Drayton's poem are excellent criticism (see *Works,* ed. Hebel, V, 11–12) . The most useful examination of Spenser's relation to Bion and Ronsard is Leo Spitzer's "Spenser, *Shepheardes Calendar, March,*" *SP*, XLVII (1950) , 494–505.

[101] *Edmund Spenser* (Cambridge, England, 1933) , p. 198.

can be used as the foil for lyric expression, just as the humble occupation of shepherds is felt to be saved by the fact that they have freedom and time to play upon their oaten pipes.

"August," which comes between two moral eclogues, the seventh and ninth, where the climax of the satirical bitterness is reached, also offers primarily a lyric interlude. The framework of the eclogue is the singing match, a conventional and traditional pastoral device which Hughes has shown Spenser derived not from the classics but from the Pléiade.[102] Whether the elements of this device, the challenge, the pledges, the election of the judge, and his decision, were "ripe for parody" or not, they serve Spenser adequately for the purpose of his poem—to introduce the roundelay, with its gay, popular rhythm and its well-known tune, and an art work of the opposite kind, a sestina.[103] The subject matter of both the roundelay and the sestina is painful love, so we have here a pair of miniature plaintive pieces, reflecting the mood of the first series and preparing for the reappearance in "November" and "December" of this motif. The scale or "distance" which I have pointed out so frequently in this discussion comes from the framing of complaint in the singing-match convention and, stylistically, from the contrast of two extremes, the roundelay and the more formal and lugubrious sestina. Again we can observe the subject matter and the technique turning together toward a focus on poetry.

It is not difficult to see, then, why *The Shepheardes Calender* occupies a most important place at the beginning of a great age of English poetry. Spenser's achievement must be evaluated in artistic terms; its magnitude can be understood only when justice is done to the shape and design of the *Calender,* to its realization and exploitation of the possibilities in the commonplace of pastoral, and to the concrete de-

---

[102] *Virgil and Spenser*, pp. 271–286.

[103] Herford's idea that the second part may be an afterthought (ed. *Shepheards Calendar*, p. xl) , because E. K. confines his glosses to the first part, does not carry much weight against the general considerations of the structure of this part of the *Calender*. Even if it should be true, the question of why Spenser thought the addition necessary might be answered on the basis I have just suggested.

tails of its marvelous experiments in style. Like the *Lyrical Ballads* in 1798 and *Prufrock and Other Observations* in 1917, it is a book which changes the course of English poetry, but like them also its importance lies not in what it does but in what it is.

Of comparable importance for the development of English poetry, though not of the same level of achievement, perhaps, are the eclogues included by Sir Philip Sidney in the *Arcadia*. The significance of these poems, their interest as poetry, has been well indicated by Theodore Spencer. I shall not attempt to add much to his analysis, but it may be useful to indicate how closely Sidney's eclogues correspond to those of Spenser in general purpose and method, aside from technical versification.

The eclogue of narrative, with beasts for characters and a moral conclusion, the pastoral fable, in short, is exemplified in Sidney's "As I my little flock on Ister bank." [104] In the old *Arcadia* this was sung by Philisides, supposedly Sidney himself, and the story is said to have come from the shepherd Languette, obviously Sidney's friend Languet. In the 1590 version it is moved up to the eclogues at the end of the first book [105] and attributed to an anonymous shepherd. The narrative is clearer in the moral allegory than Spenser usually is and lacks the suggestion of topical or historical significance. Its satirical bitterness is therefore less crabbed and the target at which the poem aims is more general.

Sidney attacks the problem of how to write English verse in a more academic way than Spenser does; his experiments are more radical and more extensive. The double sestina, "You gote-heard Gods, that love the grassie mountaines," which Theodore Spencer rightly calls the most beautiful of the poems in the *Arcadia,* was moved from the fourth book in the old *Arcadia* up to the eclogues in Book I. The significance of this poem, aside from the merits as poetry which Spencer and Empson have pointed out, is that it finds the

---

[104] *Arcadia* (1590), ed. Feuillerat, pp. 132–137.
[105] The disposition of the eclogues in 1590 does not have Sidney's authority but only that of the overseer. See the note following the dedication, p. 4.

perfect form for the complaint. The sestina, and especially
the double sestina, is well suited to this kind of poem because
the undertone of grief and despair is naturally provided by
the repetition of the end words. These words, always the same
but recurring in a new order, make a ground bass or undertone for the invention which rides above them. The reader's
attention is on the new words, the statements, while these
familiar repeated words exercise upon him an insistent and
continuing beat. The end words are grouped in pairs: mountains and valleys, morning and evening, forests and music.
The coda groups them within three lines, making the contrast operate from beginning and end of the line at the same
time.

Sidney's complaint poems also show a sharper psychological probing than Spenser's do; they depend less upon tone
and more upon the dramatic expression of the speaker's feelings. The passion mounts to a genuine climax, as in the striking line

And stop mine eares lest I growe mad with Musicke.

This is not surprising in view of Sidney's sonnets, and the
reader of the pastoral poems in *Arcadia* can also find the
conflict between reason and passion which is a major motif
in *Astrophel and Stella*.[106]

Sidney's eclogues are of course all recreative in purpose
with respect to the large plan of the *Arcadia*. They are a
shepherd's entertainments for a court, since serious political
and moral ideas are dealt with sufficiently in the romance.
Several of the comic pastorals, whose purpose is partly recreative, partly satirical, may be noticed. There is the comic pastoral contest of Nico and Pas, in which a dog and a cat are the
wagers instead of the usual mazer and lamb.[107] This has been
uncautiously identified as a satire on the convention itself,
but the real effect comes from having such preposterous fellows undertake a form which was still in good repute. If the

[106] See the beginning of the second eclogue, p. 339 in 1590 *Arcadia,* ed.
Feuillerat, p. 129 in old *Arcadia.*
[107] *Arcadia* (1590) , ed. Feuillerat, p. 344.

form were stale there would be little point to it. Dicus, the
umpire of the match, concludes with

> Enough, enough: so ill hath done the best,
> That since the having them to neither's due,
> Let cat and dog fight which shall have both you.

The old *Arcadia* makes the joke clearer: "But this Eglogue
of all other was counted the Sportefullest they yet had hearde,
and a greater Questyon, whether in deede had wonne ye
Wager. Dicus still demaunded Justice, that synce hee had
bene lawfully appoynted Judge, the Catt and Dogg mighte
bee sent for to Trye the Duello betuixt them." [108]
Another comic poem of Sidney's, placed first in the 1590
Arcadia, has been described as a sample of the kind of thing
Sidney was trying to replace by his experiments.[109] It may be
so, but I am dubious. The poem is in the old *Arcadia,* though
it is not the first one there; in the old *Arcadia* the "pleasant
fellow of my acquaintance" who made the verses is named;
he is "Alethes an honest man of that tyme." [110] The poem is
in fact a mock-blazon. Mopsa, the daughter of a loutish clown
and a splayfooted witch, inherits the perfections of both
parents:

> Like great god Saturn faire, and like faire Venus chaste:
> As smooth as Pan, as Juno milde, like goddesse Isis faste,
> With Cupid she fore-sees, and goes god Vulcan's pace:
> And for a tast of all these gifts, she borowes Momus' grace.

When it is remembered how the blazon continued to flourish
as a device in all the sonnet cycles, it seems misleading to suggest that because it is mocked here it is outworn.[111] The

---

[108] Feuillerat ed., p. 139.
[109] Spencer, "The Poetry of Sir Philip Sidney," p. 257.
[110] Feuillerat ed., p. 27. *Alethes* is Greek for truthful or realistic.
[111] The dialogue of Doron and Carmela in Greene's *Menaphon,* 1589 (ed.
G. B. Harrison [Oxford, 1927], p. 102), is a similar performance; it, too, has
been taken seriously by modern scholars as a satire on the type. As a mock-
blazon, it is funnier than Sidney's:

> Carmela deare, euen as the golden ball
> That Venus got, such are thy goodly eyes,

strength of the conventional blazon is what makes the mock-
blazon effective. As for Sidney's use of poulter's measure, the
poet no doubt felt it a suitable form for mocking verse, or
for the uncouth subject matter of this poem. The intention
of the whole is not serious but comic.

Fuller analysis of Sidney's eclogues in the *Arcadia* is unnecessary. Many of them are metrical experiments, and the
oddest are perhaps not the hexameters but the attempt to
reproduce Italian *sdrucciola* in English. Sidney failed to see
that triple rhyme in English is almost never capable of serious
effect. But the undeserved neglect under which Sidney's
poetry has suffered for so long is now in the process of being
remedied, and perhaps no apology is needed for placing him
for consideration next to Spenser.

The most elaborate single eclogue in English is probably
Spenser's *Colin Clouts Come Home Againe,* written in 1591
and published in 1595. It is especially interesting in contrast
with *The Shepheardes Calender* because in it Spenser aban-
dons the antique language which he had used in the *Calender*
and brings both content and style forward, out of the convention, toward direct and plain communication. Dodge remarks that the pastoralism here is more a point of view than
a set disguise,[112] but I have tried to indicate that in the important examples of pastoral poetry in the Elizabethan period
pastoralism was always a point of view. Renwick feels that
in *Colin Clouts Come Home Againe* there is a sort of oscil-
lation between the complete pastoral disguising and the
straightforward personal story, between Virgil and Words-

When cherries iuce is iumbled therewithall,
Thy breath is like the steeme of apple pies.

Thy lippes resemble two Cowcumbers faire,
Thy teeth like to the tuskes of fattest swine,
Thy speach is like the thunder in the aire:
Would God thy toes, thy lips and all were mine.

There were continental precedents for this sort of thing, of course. Berni's
Sonetto 2 was a burlesque on the conventional blazon of the mistress's beauties,
and there were imitations by St. Gellais and Du Bellay. See Janet G. Scott,
Les Sonnets Élisabéthains (Paris, 1929), pp. 17, 122.

[112] Variorum *Minor Poems,* I, 448.

worth.[113] Certainly *Colin Clout* seems more modern than the
eclogues in the *Calender;* it is more fluent, more informal,
more journalistic. But I should say that it is a continuation
and completion of some pastoral tendencies inherent in the
Calender rather than a new sort of thing. The friendly contest between the two shepherds is now moved into the past
and must be recounted rather than presented directly; this
is a way of framing the device of the singing match which
Spenser had already used in "August." Colin's contribution
to it is not the characteristic complaint or blazon he had already done in the *Calender,* but a pastoral-mythologizing
story of the love of two rivers. It therefore extends the area of
normal pastoral subjects; it is outside the expectation of listeners like Cuddie, who wonders

> Whether it were some hymne, or morall laie,
> Or carol made to praise thy loued lasse.

(This remark of Cuddie's shows again, I think, how naturally
the Elizabethans thought of pastoral songs in several fairly
definite types.)

Moreover, the principal subject of this eclogue, the relationship between a poet and his society, is a continuation and
extension of "October." In "October" the complaint was
that the artist was insufficiently appreciated by the public and
that the classical generosity of patrons could no longer be
depended upon. In the later poem a much deeper analysis
of the situation of the artist is attempted. His problem is
always to build Jerusalem in England's green and pleasant
land, and Colin first pays tribute to the fundamental beauty
and promise of English life.

The shepherd's attention is very naturally fastened on the
court, not merely because Sir Walter Ralegh had taken
Edmund Spenser to Elizabeth's court but because the court
is inevitably and logically the symbol and representative of
culture. The famous survey of the English court, with its
poets and ladies, is obviously of topical and historical interest.
But Colin's listeners immediately raise the question that is

[113] *Ibid.*

most important: What is the matter with life there, then?
It sounds admirable. At this point the great device of pastoral is brought into play: to contrast the simple, natural
goodness of the pastoral ideal, self-contained and unaspiring,
to the vanity and ambition of the world. And the other great
subject on which the pastoral convention served as a criticism
of life is also presented: is love to be found at court? Ah yes,
says Colin, love abounds there.

> For all the walls and windows there are writ,
> All full of loue, and loue, and loue my deare,
> And all their talke and studie is of it.

But it is very different from pastoral love. Among us shepherds love is a religion:

> So we him worship, so we him adore
> With humble hearts to heauen vplifted hie,
> That to true loues he may us euermore
> Preferre, and of their grace vs dignifie.

Among the courtiers it is otherwise:

> For with lewd speeches and licentious deeds,
> His mightie mysteries they do prophane,
> And vse his ydle name to other needs,
> But as a complement for courting vaine.

But I have displaced the order of Spenser's poem. He leads
from the abuses of the courtiers up to an assertion of the
shepherds' religion of love, and then proceeds from that to a
rhapsodic passage on love as the creator, as the great moving force in the universe. Then, to return to the pastoral level
for the close, Colin is again cast as the disappointed lover
of Rosalind, and he ends his discourse with the assertion
that he is only a "simple trophe of her great conquest."

The final effect of *Colin Clouts Come Home Againe* is not
that of satire, though the satiric elements in the poem are
prominent and strong. The poem is closer to *Fowre Hymnes*
than to *Mother Hubberds Tale*. But it may be well to consider here some aspects of the satiric element in pastoral and
of the susceptibility of pastoral itself to satire.

We have noticed how, in the moral eclogues of *The Shep-heardes Calender,* the contrast between good and bad shep-herds brought in an element of "Satyrical bitternesse," to use E. K.'s phrase. The tradition of the eclogue, from Petrarch and Mantuan through their vernacular imitators, authorized this. It has sometimes been called "impure pastoral," on the ground, I suppose, that the only pure pastoral was the sen-timental sort, bent on an escape from life rather than a criticism of it. But if my thesis is correct, that in the English Renaissance pastoral was inherently a criticism of life, it should not cause surprise that sometimes the criticism became explicit.

The satirical bitterness in pastoral did not always come out in the form of attack on courtiers or on bad parsons. There were other themes and attitudes in the pastoral complex which could be sharpened into satire. The shepherd's love complaint, for example, sometimes sees only too clearly the bitterness of love as the one bondage in a life of liberty.[114] Or, there may be a realization of the basic foolishness of love and disdain of the absurdity of the lover's behavior. Ethically, pastoral supports the contemplative life, and as such it is always vulnerable to the objection that virtue can consist only in action; from Aristotle to Milton there is always some stern voice which announces, "I will not praise a cloistered virtue." And even within the idealized pastoral world, it is not always possible to idealize women; the anti-feminist lit-erature of the Middle Ages is too well remembered, perhaps, or it may be that even the authors of pastoral literature could not strain their imaginations far enough to picture a woman who was wholly natural. Histor's attack on wives in Sidney's *Arcadia*[115] and the satyr's speech in Guarini's *Pastor Fido*[116] illustrate the point; these are not city ladies but Amaryllises and Daphnes, yet they are satirized for using cosmetics and

[114] Cf. Montemayor's *Diana* (trans. Yong, sig. B3^r) : "The mens endeauours are naturally disposed to spend their life time in sufficient content, & the womens beauties to take it from him, who liueth most assured of his libertie."
[115] Ed. of 1590, ed. Feuillerat, p. 138.
[116] Trans. Dymock (1602) , sigs. D2^v–D3^r.

making themselves wholly artificial. It is possible to find a
good deal in pastoral literature that would please the Wife
of Bath's fifth husband.

In "The Teares of the Muses" Spenser presents the Muse
Euterpe lamenting the decline of pastoral poetry:

> And arbors sweet, in which the Shepheards swaines
> Were wont so oft their Pastoralls to sing,
> They haue cut downe and all their pleasaunce mard,
> That now no pastorall is to bee hard.

This sad state of affairs, however, cannot be substantiated
from literary history. The shepherd swains flourished between the time of Spenser and Milton, so that the period has
been called the golden age of English pastoral. Spenser contributed a pastoral elegy on Sidney, "Astrophel," to the large
number of poetic tributes after Sidney's death; it is formal
and follows the conventions of the pastoral elegy, and it occupies itself with what appears to be an attempt to assure the
reader that Sidney's Stella was the lady he married, Frances
Walsingham, though the poet invents a death for Stella in
grief at Astrophel's demise. To fill out the volume in which
Colin Clouts Come Home Againe was published in 1595,
other poems about Sidney by Ralegh, Greville, and Matthew
Roydon were reprinted from *The Phoenix Nest* (1593), and
Spenser's friend Lodowick Bryskett contributed a pastoral
eclogue which is of more interest as pastoral than Spenser's
"Astrophel." Bryskett's eclogue and his other poem, "The
Mourning Muse," are both paraphrases of Bernardo Tasso,
the eclogue of the Italian's *Alcippo*.[117] The greatest interest
in the eclogue, however, derives from those passages which
look forward to Milton's *Lycidas*:

> Loe father Neptune, with sad countenance,
> How he sitts mourning on the strond now bare,
> Yonder, where th'Ocean with his rolling waues
> The white feete washeth (wailing this mischance)

[117] W. P. Mustard, "Lodowick Bryskett and Bernardo Tasso," *AJP*, XXXV
(1914), 192ff.

Of Douer cliffes. His sacred skirt about
The sea-gods all are set; from their moist caues
All for his comfort gathered there they be.[118]

Sidney was a favorite subject for pastoral elegy, and the eclogue in Davison's *A Poetical Rhapsody* (1602) by A. W., "made long since," according to the title, illustrates the pervasive influence of Spenser. The writer imitates Spenser's archaisms of language and his tricks of style. Sidney is referred to as "Willy," and Spenser himself is brought in as one of the shepherds.[119]

The most ambitious of Spenser's followers is Michael Drayton, who published in 1593 a group of eclogues modeled on *The Shepheardes Calender* and called *Idea The Shepheards Garland Fashioned in Nine Eglogs.* Drayton plans his series with the same objectives of variety in style and mood, contrast of type, and seriousness of aesthetic and moral purpose which characterized Spenser, and in many instances the imitation is more direct and specific. His second eclogue, for example, is a debate between age and youth, and his third is a panegyric on Elizabeth under the name of Beta, filling out the rest of her name from Spenser's Eliza in the April eclogue. His first and last eclogues are complaints, as are Spenser's.

Drayton republished his pastorals in 1606 and 1619. He is especially interesting to the student of the history of English poetry because of the revisions he made for the edition of 1606. Some of these, at least, were made before 1600, as the revised versions appear in *England's Helicon* of that year. Drayton, in revising, cuts down the religious imagery, transforms his style into something more balanced, epigrammatic, and classical. He removes some of the archaic language, but on the whole, instead of moving away from discipleship to Spenser, he clearly moves closer to his master. This is a significant point, and Drayton provides the natural link between the pastoral tradition of the Elizabethans and the more do-

[118] Sig. H3ᵛ. For a discussion of the relationship between Bryskett's poems and *Lycidas,* see Deborah Jones in *Thomas Lodge and Other Elizabethans,* ed. C. J. Sisson (Cambridge: Harvard University Press, 1933) , pp. 245–253.

[119] Rollins ed., I, 43–44.

mesticated and yet more classical school of the seventeenth
century with its Browne, Herrick, and Milton.

Yet Drayton must not be dismissed as a mere historical link.
His pastoral poetry deserves attention on its own merits.
Probably the eighth eclogue in *The Shepheards Garland* represents him at his best. It is based upon the same structural
principle as Spenser's "August," with two well-marked and
contrasting parts. The first part is a treatment of the theme
of the Golden Age, traditional enough in pastoral, but Drayton prefaces it with an interesting comment on contemporary
kinds of poetry:

> Shepheard why creepe we in this lowly vaine,
> as though our muse no store at all affordes,
> Whilst others vaunt it with the frolicke swayne,
> and strut the stage with reperfumed wordes.
>
> See how these yonkers rave it out in rime,
> who make a traffique of their rarest wits,
> And in Bellonas buskin tread it fine,
> Like Bacchus priests raging in franticke fits.[120]

This alternative of flamboyant stage poetry, as practiced by
the Marlowes, Kyds, and Shakespeares of the time, is rejected
by the shepherds, as is the poetry of the *Mirror for Magistrates* sort:

> My Muse may not affect night-charming spels,
> whose force effects th'Olympicke vault to quake,
> Nor call those grysly Goblins from their Cels,
> the ever-damned frye of Limbo lake.[121]

When Drayton proceeds to his description of the Golden
Age, he makes clear that it was the time when the pastoral
ideal governed mankind. His description of the Golden Age
is both pictorial-idyllic and moral; simplicity and beauty
went hand in hand with innocence. When the aspiring mind
destroyed the pastoral *otium* and the Golden Age was no
more, poets began to write of "slaughtering broiles and
bloody horror." The corruption of more recent times may
be seen by the absence of the natural and simple in life. Para-

---

[120] *Works*, ed. Hebel, I, 84.   [121] *Ibid.*, p. 85.

doxically, it is ages other than the Golden Age which put an undue and immoral value upon gold.[122] This position is sometimes misunderstood, since it seems almost like the position of the satirist. It is in reality no more than the criticism of life which inheres in pastoral itself. In the fifth eclogue, Drayton is more specific about the levels of poetry. Rowland, who represents Drayton himself, declines to sing heroic poetry, which is too high, or satire ("foul slander," as he calls it), which is too low, but he will sing pastoral, which is the mean.[123]

The second part of Drayton's eighth eclogue is the pleasant poem of "Dowsabell." For this, Drayton has imitated Spenser's trick in "March" of using Chaucer's Sir Thopas meter for comic effect. But the comic tone here mingles with one of sympathy and familiar recognition, for Dowsabell is a "naturalized" shepherdess, obviously an inhabitant of the Cotswold hills rather than of Arcadia. She is involved in the usual *pastourelle* situation, though she begins the wooing herself, and the conclusion is as pretty and naïve as the conclusion of Breton's "As it fell upon a day." The contrast between the two parts of the eclogue is therefore very effective; we have the seriousness of the pastoral judgment of life, with the Golden Age as criterion, and we have the precise, actual, identified situation in the Dowsabell lyric, treated with detached amusement.

Drayton is the most interesting of the followers of Spenser in pastoral, and he illustrates well enough the survival of interest in pastoral poetry, even though the style of it changed, on into the seventeenth century. But Drayton was not so popular among his contemporaries as some other writers of pastoral who might be mentioned. The popularity of the pastoral lyric has already been demonstrated in the discussion of *England's Helicon* (1600). The eclogue, too, had

[122] *Ibid.*, p. 87.

[123] Mrs. Tillotson, in discussing *The Muses Elizium* (Drayton, *Works*, ed. Hebel, V, 220), well remarks that "the bitterness of his own satires has found its solvent in pastoral." But she perhaps exaggerates the proximity of pastoral to satire; she cites a picture on the title page of Wither's *Vice's Executioner* to illustrate an identification of the satyr and the shepherd, but it should be remembered that the illustrative title page of Drayton's own 1619 volume keeps them separate.

its vogue, and it is worth observing that the anthology of 1602, finally called *A Poetical Rhapsody,* was originally entered in the Stationers' Register under the title *Pastoralles and Eglogues Odes and Madrigalles.*[124] Moreover, Davison in arranging his book offered first to the prospective buyer "two pastoralls, made by Sir Philip Sidney, neuer yet published" and added nine more poems of a pastoral sort, mostly eclogues, to his first section.

The popularity of pastoral in the nineties may well be illustrated by the contributions of the experimenter Thomas Watson and of the rhetorician Abraham Fraunce. In 1585 Watson published an *Amyntas* in Latin; two years later this was translated into English hexameters by Fraunce, and there were other editions of the translation in 1588, 1589, and 1596, besides inclusion of the translation in Fraunce's *The Countesse of Pembrokes Yuychurch* (1591 and later). Here we have a work which rivals, and perhaps surpasses, *The Shepheardès Calender* in popularity. Watson's contemporary reputation, as Greg points out,[125] comes largely from his fellow university poets, but this means that the critical audience of the time was impressed. In 1590 Watson published a pastoral elegy on Walsingham, called *Meliboeus,* and in the same year brought out an English translation by himself, apparently unwilling to let his work fall again into the hands of a Fraunce. In 1592 he published other eclogues called *Amintae Gaudia.*

Watson's work is elaborate manipulation of the pastoral devices, especially those of the *querulae* or complaints. It is in Watson that we see most clearly the connection between the pastoral mode and the vogue of the Petrarchan sonnet series. The influence of Petrarch came down indirectly through Italian pastoral poetry and drama, and Watson represents this stream. As Leicester Bradner says, "Quite naturally, we find Watson using the Latin eclogue as a medium for the expression of Petrarchan sentiment."[126]

124 Rollins ed., II, 4.
125 "English Versions of Watson's Latin Poems," *MLQ,* VI (1905), 125–129.
126 *Musae Anglicanae* (New York, 1940), p. 44.

Another minor pastoralist was Abraham Fraunce, a member of the Pembroke circle and therefore a follower of Sidney and an admirer of Spenser. At Cambridge he was a student of the philosophy of Ramus. After eight years of this pursuit he came to London and studied law at one of the Inns of Court. It is characteristic of him that he tried to combine all his interests in one production. He pursued the Cambridge fad of composing English hexameters; he was interested in the pastoral mode as exemplified in Sidney and Spenser; he had studied Ramist logic and English law. Therefore he published in 1588 *The Lawiers Logike,* a revision of an earlier book which he had apparently called *The Shepherd's Logic.* In it he included a translation into English hexameters of Virgil's second eclogue, the *Alexis,* together with a logical analysis of the poem, just as he gave logical analyses of the Earl of Northumberland's case and Sandford's crown pleas. He reprinted this translation, without the analysis, in his *The Countesse of Pembrokes Yuychurch* in 1591, a book which contained his version of Watson's *Amyntas* and a sequel, the funeral of Phyllis, together with the beginning of Heliodorus' *Ethiopian History.* In 1592 he published a third part, called *Amintas Dale,* consisting of "the most conceited tales of the Pagan Gods [from Ovid's *Metamorphoses*] in English Hexameters" enclosed in a pastoral framework in which the tales are told by the shepherds and shepherdesses of Ivychurch and explained by the sage Elpinus.

Fraunce is chiefly interesting, as Kathrine Koller has pointed out, for the evidence he offers of the application of the literary doctrines of the Penshurst group.[127] That this serious and civilized coterie maintained a continued interest in the pastoral long after the success of the *Arcadia* and *The Shepheardes Calender* is additional evidence of the intellectual respectability of the mode, even if Ben Jonson did dismiss Fraunce's experiments with the abrupt "Abram Francis, in his English hexameters, was a foole." [128]

---

[127] "Abraham Fraunce and Edmund Spenser," *ELH,* VII (1940), 108–120.
[128] *Conversations,* ed. R. F. Patterson (London, 1923), p. 6.

OVIDIAN POETRY

The Growth and Adaptation

of Forms

A TRADITION allied to the pastoral but developing in a different direction is the strain of Ovidian-mythological poetry which provided one of the most characteristic expressions of the Elizabethan mind. Pastoralism involved a set of values, and its natural bent was toward a serious criticism of life. The Ovidian tradition, on the other hand, emerged from the Middle Ages as heavy allegorical didacticism, evolved in the sixteenth century in an emancipated glorification of the senses and the imagination, and returned in the seventeenth century to philosophical interpretation.

The change may be most easily traced chronologically, but it should be remembered that this is to some extent misleading. A more truthful account would make distinctions between classes in the reading public, for example, between the court circle which tended to acquire Italianate tastes and the middle class which clung patriotically to its native tradition and looked for the useful and the uplifting in its art. But the line separating these classes is vague and shifting, and the historian can only warn the reader that it is there; his narrative would be too complex if he were to try to follow it.

As an example of the Ovidian narrative, let us take the story of Salmacis and Hermaphroditus, related by Ovid in just over a hundred lines in the *Metamorphoses*.[1] The tale is narrated by Alcithoë, who offers it for its novelty. The peculiar quality of the fountain of Salmacis—that it produces weakness and effeminacy in any man who bathes in it —is well known, she says, but the reason for this strange fact is a mystery. The explanation is that the nymph of the spring, Salmacis, fell in love with a beautiful youth, Hermaphroditus, and pursued him into the pool while he was bathing; her advances being repulsed by the shy youth, she prayed to the gods that the two of them might be merged into one. The prayer was granted, and Hermaphroditus, feeling himself become half feminine, prayed that all other men who bathed in the pool would undergo the same experience. This, too, was granted.

The order and disposition of events in Ovid is interesting and offers some hints of possible ways to elaborate the story. Hermaphroditus is introduced first. His birth, nurture, and travels are related briefly; he arrives at the pool; the wonderful spring is described; and then the nymph Salmacis is introduced. Her general character is sketched, her indifference to hunting, her vanity, her love of flowers; her wooing when she approaches Hermaphroditus is direct, not to say abrupt. But the youth, who knows not what love is, blushes and threatens to leave. To prevent this she departs, but spies on him from a bush as he feels the water, removes his clothes, and dives into the pool. The climax is the wooing in the pool which culminates in the prayer.

The tone of the narrative is, as always with Ovid, a mixture of sensuous delight, humor, preciousness, and airy sophistication. The details and imagery are pictorial, not dramatic: the nymph's eyes flash like a mirror reflecting the sun as she watches the naked youth, and his body in the water is like ivory or lilies in clear glass. His blushes are like ripening apples, painted ivory, or the red of the moon's eclipse. The similes, even when they apply to action, are primarily decorative: Salmacis clings to him like a serpent to the eagle which has seized it in its claws, or like ivy to a tree, or like the sea-

[1] *Metamorphoses*, IV, 285–388.

polyp to its victim. There is rhetorical heightening in the nymph's exclamation as she dashes to the pool and in the wooing and the prayers, but the rhetoric is controlled and kept in place by the speed and verve of the narrative.

A primary quality of Ovid's tale is its refinement. The sensuous details are never lush, and the reader's impression of the passion felt by Salmacis is dispelled through the rapid action and the continual intrusion of the setting and atmosphere:

> saepe legit flores. et tum quoque forte legebat,
> cum puerum vidit visumque optavit habere.[2]

The shape and proportion of the story are delicately controlled by the focus on the crystal pool, which constitutes the "purpose" of the story.

Possible variations on Ovid's treatment immediately suggest themselves; in fact, it is the presence, in the Latin version, of these alternatives with their execution so tactfully declined that gives the tale much of its grace and vitality. One might, for example, emphasize the weakening and enervating power of the pool; then the nymph Salmacis, the pursuer, becomes the cause of this quality; the tale could illustrate the devitalizing effect of lust and warn against it. Or, on the other hand, one could seize upon the beauty and reluctance of Hermaphroditus and the corresponding passion of Salmacis, to make the whole effect highly aphrodisiac. The wooing in the water and the final union of the two would then be a symbolic and appropriate conclusion. Or, again, there is an opportunity to characterize the two protagonists much more fully or to expand almost indefinitely the descriptive-pictorial aspects of the scene.

From a grave and sober point of view, of course, Ovid is a wanton poet. But from a very early period, there was a way out of this difficulty: his poems could be read as allegories. We have already seen how the story of Salmacis gives a natural opportunity for an allegorical reading. The medieval tradition, already well established by the time of Charle-

[2] *Metamorphoses*, IV, 315–316.

magne, read Ovid allegorically.[3] Various moralized Ovids, including the French *Ovide moralisé* and the Latin *Metamorphosis Ovidiana moraliter . . . explanata,* fortified the tradition, but even the texts of Ovid "plain" commonly included the notes of Regius, which gave an allegorical explanation. The fourfold method of interpretation (*Literaliter, Naturaliter, Historialiter,* and *Allegorice*) turned Ovid's storehouse of tales into an edifying compendium only slightly, if any, less useful than sacred scriptures, which were of course also allegorized. This tradition not only solved the moral problem about such erotic works as those of Ovid and King Solomon, it also stimulated the ingenuity of readers and expositors. Satiric attacks on this complicated method of reading Ovid had already been made by the early sixteenth century, but they were of little effect in driving out the vogue.[4]

It was this tradition of interpretation which the Elizabethans inherited, and its characteristics are thoroughly exemplified in the translation of the *Metamorphoses* by Arthur Golding in the 1560's. In his preface to his first four books, which he dedicated to Leicester as a New Year's gift in 1565, Golding defended himself with a theory of poetry based on the allegorical interpretation of Ovid. The pagan gods represented here, he claims, are really only types of people.[5] The transformations or metamorphoses represent the subjection of men to fleshly appetites and their consequent internal resemblance to beasts.[6] In view of this, the art of reading allegorically is a difficult but very rewarding one, according to Golding.[7] In the epistle to his complete translation, two years later, Golding illustrated the moral value of each of the fifteen books by giving an explanation of the principal

[3] See D. P. Harding, *Milton and the Renaissance Ovid* (Urbana, Illinois, 1946), chap. 1; Bush, *Mythology and the Renaissance Tradition in English Poetry*, chaps. 1, 2, 4, and 13; C. B. Cooper, *Some Elizabethan Opinions of the Poetry and Character of Ovid* (Chicago, 1914).

[4] Letter 28 of *Epistolae Virorum Obscurorum*, cited by Cooper, *Some Elizabethan Opinions*, p. 13.

[5] Sig. *ii^v.

[6] Sig. *iii^r.

[7] Sig. *iii^v.

myths related in it. For the fourth book he gives, among others, the significance of the Salmacis legend:

> The piteous tale of Pyramus and Thisbee doth conteine
> The headie force of frentick loue whose end is wo and payne.
> The snares of Mars and Uenus shew that tyme will bring too lyght
> The secret sinnes that folk commit in corners or by nyght.
> Hermaphrodite and Salmacis declare that idlenesse
> Is cheefest nurce and cherisher of all volupteousnesse,
> And that voluptuous lyfe breedes sin: which linking all toogither
> Make men to bee effeminate, vnweeldy, weake and lither.[8]

Golding's view of Ovid is thoroughly medieval; he makes everything support the couplet he printed on his title page:

> With skill, heede, and iudgement, this worke must bee red,
> For els too the reader it stands in small stead.

As a recent student has said, "Golding's attitude toward the *Metamorphoses* is essentially that of Theodulfus, who lived in the days of Charlemagne." [9]

Exactly contemporary with Golding's translation is the work of Thomas Peend, who began a translation of the *Metamorphoses* but did not publish it because Golding's version reached the market first. But Peend did publish, in 1565, *The Pleasant Fable of Hermaphroditus and Salmacis . . . With a morall in English Verse*. His choice of this part of Ovid was made, he says, because he was impressed by an account of how a man might lose himself.[10] Aside from this statement of purpose, Peend's only interpolation in the poem is an expansion of the pursuit of Hermaphroditus in the water. He compares the two characters to a little roach pursued by a voracious pike and to a hare pursued by hounds; this interpolation serves the purpose of leading up to a bitter remark about women.[11] The moral which directly follows the translation maintains the same doctrine Golding had

[8] Sig. a iij^r.
[9] Harding, *Milton and the Renaissance Ovid*, p. 22.
[10] Sigs. Aiii^v–iiii^r.
[11] Sig. A7^v.

held, the traditional one that Ovid, though seeming to tell a trivial tale, was in reality making a profound moral statement.[12] Hermaphroditus represents the youth who has just outgrown childhood, is innocent and ignorant of vice, and is just starting out into the world. The country of Caria to which he travels is the world. The nymph Salmacis represents all kinds of vice which are present in the world. The spring represents "the pleasant sport, that doth content the wyll." The young man, thinking everything innocent because he is himself so, is deceived into sin.[13] Hermaphroditus' fault is that he pursued his will, not reason.[14] Peend places particular emphasis upon the nature of the spring, and it is perhaps because of his allegorical reading of the story that he has made it a lake of considerable size.[15]

Peend fills out his book with an attack on women called "A Pleasant Question," in which he recites a list of lustful women, including many from Ovid and others from more modern times. His list of famous lovers includes Hero and Leander, Pyramus and Thisbe, Venus and Adonis, Romeo and Juliet. They all illustrate the viciousness of women:

> Such be the fond and frantike fits
>   which in the blinded brayne
> Of wanton women often times,
>   with swinging swey doth reigne.[16]

Some indication of the audience Peend was aiming at may be gathered from a glossary at the end of his book which gives the identification and story of the classical figures (and Juliet of Verona as well) who appear in his book, "That the vnlearned myght the better vnderstande these." But there is plenty of evidence that Golding's Ovid, which was

12 Sig. B1r.
13 Sig. B1v.
14 Sig. Biir.
15 Sigs. B2v–B3r.
16 Sig. B5v. Peend's attack, possibly because it is appended to another kind of poem, does not appear in F. L. Utley, *The Crooked Rib: An Analytical Index to the Argument about Women in English and Scots Literature to the End of the Year 1568* (Columbus, Ohio, 1944).

as deeply allegorical as Peend's selection, was read by men who knew their Ovid in Latin.[17]

This kind of moralizing of Ovidian myths did not of course cease with the 1560's. Sandys' seventeenth-century translation of Ovid also moralizes the tales. But in the second half of the sixteenth century there was a different approach to the material. The explanation of the Salmacis and Hermaphroditus story given by Abraham Fraunce in 1592 is a contrast to Peend's. Fraunce gives two versions, one an astrological one, that the person who is born when the planets Venus and Mercury are in conjunction is "giuen to inordinate and vnnaturall lust, noted by Salmacis. For these two planets are so repugnant, that they can neuer be well conioyned; sith Venus is all for the body, and Mercury onely for the minde." The other, given in Italian, professes to deliver a scientific explanation of the origin of hermaphrodites.[18] More sophisticated explanations of myths in the later sixteenth century stemmed from different Italian handbooks of mythology from those used in the mid-century. Chapman's "philosophical" reading of myth, for example, came largely from Natalis Comes.[19]

Now if we turn to a verse treatment of the same story, the *Salmacis and Hermaphroditus* published anonymously in 1602, we have an opportunity to see how different an approach a later Elizabethan could make to the same subject matter.[20] The title page of the volume carries a fragment of

[17] Another example of the moralized tale from Ovid, which might have been used to illustrate the same characteristics as that of Peend, is *The fable of Ouid treting of Narcissus, translated out of Latin into Englysh Mytre, with a moral thervnto, very pleasante to rede* (1560), by the printer Thomas Hacket. For a discussion see Bush, *Mythology and the Renaissance Tradition*, p. 48.

[18] *The Third Part of the Countesse of Pembrokes Yuychurch. Entituled Amintas Dale* (1592), sig. N4[r].

[19] See F. L. Schoell, "Les Mythologistes italiens de la Renaissance et la poésie élisabéthaine," *Revue de littérature comparée*, IV (1924), 5–25.

[20] The poem was attributed to Francis Beaumont by the bookseller Blaikelocke in 1640 and again in 1653. But the editor of the nineteenth-century reprint of the 1602 edition, "Dramaticus," in the *Shakespeare Society's Papers*, III (1847), 94–126, exposed Blaikelocke's methods and cast doubt on the attribution. The authorship therefore remains unknown.

Ennius, *Salmacida spolia sine sanguine & sudore* (Spoils of
Salmacis gained without blood or sweat) , quoted by Cicero [21]
and by Raphael Regius in his commentary; and the poem is
dedicated by the poet to the Muse Calliope as "the issue
of an idle brayne." The piece is obviously the work of a
sophisticated gentleman; the author speaks of his "sportiue
Muse" and expresses his intended effect upon the reader in
jocular terms:

> I hope my Poeme is so liuely writ,
> That thou wilt turne halfe-mayd with reading it.

One of the three complimentary verses prefixed to the work
maintains that the author has overgone Ovid's "inticing
rimes" with his "more mouing passion."

The poet does, in fact, elaborate Ovid in an Ovidian way,
interpolating myths to make more dazzling the beauty of the
two protagonists and involving the amorous gods much more
in the action. For example, Salmacis is courted by Bacchus
and Jove, and she would be the conquest of one or both of
these gods were it not for the jealousy of other divinities.
Hermaphroditus is so beautiful that he has aroused the feelings of Diana and of Phoebus. The scenery, too, is related to
a wider area of myth than it is in Ovid's story. The spring,
or "brook" as it is called here, is identified with that in which
Narcissus pursued his own image, and some of the traits of
Narcissus from the third book of the *Metamorphoses* are
transferred to Hermaphroditus. The roses are described as
getting their color from blushing at Hermaphroditus. He
has the eyes which formerly belonged to Cupid. The beautiful youth takes over some of the functions of Helen of Troy,
since he is brought to Salmacis' spring as the result of a
promise by Phoebus to the nymph to provide her with

> So louely faire, and such a well shap't boy,
> As ne're before his owne all-seeing eye
> Saw from his bright seate in the starry skye.[22]

---

[21] *De Officiis*, I, xviii, 61.   [22] Sig. D3ʳ.

What the anonymous poet sacrifices in speed and compression he compensates for in lightness of touch, delicacy of decoration, and intensity of erotic atmosphere. He begins with an invocation to Venus to temper his verses so that "euery Louers eye may melt a line." [23] An effect of lightness and grace is increased by the occasional insertion of reflective or even mildly satiric comment in the course of the narrative. For example, when Jove is wooing Salmacis he promises to make her a star in the heavens, but has to confirm his oath by the witness of Astrea. So he journeys to Astrea's palace; there he finds

> The dewe of iustice, which did seldome fall,
> And when it dropt, the drops were very small.[24]

Moreover, there is a crowd of attendants about the palace of Justice, and even Jove himself cannot get in without paying numerous fees.[25] But these more serious reflections are caught up in the decorated and sensuous texture of the whole, and they only serve to show the primary quality of the poem the more strikingly. The visual appearance of Astrea's palace is more significant than its meaning.[26]

Little dramas within the main narrative keep the extended tale from becoming too static and like a tapestry. The formalization is constantly broken down by coy, idyllic touches, such as this episode: Salmacis is almost successful in winning Hermaphroditus to her love, she is so beautiful, but he sees reflected in her eyes something more beautiful still, so she shuts her eyes and woos him "blindfold." When she opens her eyes she finds that the boy has stolen away. This little drama is resolved in a simile, which for once leads to a natural description instead of into further mythology.[27] In the climax of the narrative, the departures from the Ovidian source are less extensive, but there is a heightening achieved by a constantly reiterated participation of nature in the affair of the two lovers. As Salmacis hides, watching Hermaphro-

---

[23] Sig. B^r.   [25] *Ibid.*   [27] Sig. E^r.
[24] Sig. B$_3$^{v}.   [26] Sig. B$_4$^{v}.

ditus by the pool, for example, she touches her knee to the ground; Ovid has only

> delituit flexuque genu submisit . . . [28]

but the English poet embellishes it with

> Therefore she turn'd, and hid her in the grasse,
> When to the ground bending her snow-white knee,
> The glad earth gaue new coates to euery tree.[29]

And at the same time, when Hermaphroditus is merely dipping his toes in the lapping water according to Ovid,

> Then with his foote he toucht the siluer streames,
> Whose drowzy waues made musike in their dreames,
> And, for he was not wholy in, did weepe,
> Talking alowd and babbling in their sleepe.[30]

Finally, the conclusion of the poem shows further departures from the emphasis of Ovid. The English poet drops two of the similes about the clasping of Hermaphroditus by the nymph; he keeps only the image of the ivy and rejects those of the eagle and snake and the sea-polyp. Moreover, he allows time for Salmacis to make one more sophistic appeal to the boy, her argument being that it is contrary to nature to be solitary.[31] This lyrical profusion colors the end of the poem, and the original theme that the effeminizing quality of the spring was something dreadful and unfortunate is glozed over.[32]

The general effect of the *Salmacis and Hermaphroditus* of 1602 is one of irresponsible delight, with variety, color, and lightness of touch. The couplets are stiff enough to give a formal feeling and free enough to allow for fluent narrative. The mythological excursions along the way provide variety of interest and involve the gods and nature in the essentially simple story of the wanton nymph and the reluctant beautiful boy. There is a dreamy humor about the whole

---

[28] *Metamorphoses*, IV, 340.
[29] Sig. E2^v.
[30] *Ibid.*
[31] Sig. E3^v.
[32] Sig. E4^r.

affair, without burlesque or travesty. The frustration of the
gods who pursue Salmacis and then of Salmacis herself in
the pursuit of Hermaphroditus are effects which balance each
other neatly. Hermaphroditus is not made a lout; his character of youth and innocence and modesty is preserved by the
weaving around him of many decorative elements—the speech
of Salmacis, the participation of nature in all his actions, and
the ever-present gods who are themselves involved in just
such life as his. The world evoked by the poem, though elaborate and rather rich, is consistent in tone and constantly
suggestive of more imaginative details.

The contrast between these two versions, half a century
apart, of the story of Salmacis and Hermaphroditus provides
a framework for the examination of Elizabethan mythological-erotic poetry. The Hermaphroditus myth is, moreover, a
central one in the whole movement, because, as we shall see,
the characteristics of this Ovidian story and its near kin,
the story of Narcissus and Echo in Book III of the *Metamorphoses,* influenced the presentation of such other characters
in the genre as Adonis and Leander, just as the anonymous
author of 1602 was in turn influenced by the narrative and
poetic methods of Shakespeare and Marlowe. Before tracing
the change, however, it is desirable to recall some familiar
evidence of the taste on the part of the English aristocracy
for Ovidian-mythological poetry, painting, and shows.

In Marlowe's play, *Edward II* (1591), Gaveston is left alone
on the stage after being approached by several men who seek
service with him; he thinks they will not do and proceeds
to soliloquize on the surest way to catch the fancy of the king:

> I must have wanton poets, pleasant wits,
> Musicians, that with touching of a string
> May draw the pliant king which way I please.
> Music and poetry is his delight;
> Therefore I'll have Italian masks by night,
> Sweet speeches, comedies, and pleasing shows;
> And in the day, when he shall walk abroad,
> Like sylvan nymphs my pages shall be clad;
> My men, like satyrs grazing on the lawns,

Shall with their goat-feet dance an antic hay.
Sometime a lovely boy in Dian's shape,
With hair that gilds the water as it glides,
Crownets of pearl about his naked arms,
And in his sportful hands an olive-tree,
To hide those parts which men delight to see,
Shall bathe him in a spring; and there, hard by,
One like Actaeon peeping through the grove,
Shall by the angry goddess be transform'd,
And running in the likeness of an hart
By yelping hounds pull'd down, and seem to die;—
Such things as these best please his majesty.[33]

Here we have the other story of bathing in the spring and the erotic business of a spy on the bather. These motifs from the third and fourth books of Ovid became so intermingled and so pervasive that it is no wonder we find in *The Passionate Pilgrim* (1599) a couple of sonnets, IV and VI, in which Venus watches Adonis bathing as Salmacis had watched her beautiful youth. We have the same thing in another dramatic portrayal of the amusements of a lord, when the imposture is practiced on Christopher Sly in the Induction of *The Taming of the Shrew:*

> *Sec. Serv.* Dost thou love pictures? we will fetch thee straight
> Adonis painted by a running brook,
> And Cytherea all in sedges hid,
> Which seem to move and wanton with her breath,
> Even as the waving sedges play with wind.[34]

And Spenser had also described a tapestry in which Venus and Adonis figured, the goddess watching him with eager eyes as he bathed.[35]

The pioneer in the new kind of treatment of Ovidian material in English verse was Thomas Lodge, who published, in 1589, *Scillaes Metamorphosis: Enterlaced with the vnfor-*

---

[33] *Edward II*, I, i, 50–71. H. B. Charlton and R. D. Waller point out in their edition (London, 1933, p. 72) that this account differs significantly from the source passage in Holinshed.

[34] Induction, ii, 50–55.

[35] *Faerie Queene*, III, I, xxxvi.

tunate loue of Glaucus. Lodge was a member of Lincoln's Inn
at the time, one of those young men more interested in fashionable literature than in the law, and his poem combines
popular features of several traditions. The title page proclaims it "verie fit for young Courtiers to peruse, and coy
Dames to remember." The theme of disdain on the part of
the lady and constancy on the part of the lover, the standard
theme of the Petrarchan sonnet cycle, is prominent in the
poem. In addition, *Scillaes Metamorphosis* has a framework
of the love-complaint, and the general setting of the beginning of the poem, where the poet on the banks of the Isis
hears the sea god tell of his woes, is reminiscent of the complaints of the *Mirror for Magistrates.* Lodge clearly knew
Sackville's *Induction,* and he is adapting Ovidian myth to
styles familiar to readers of contemporary poetry.

The innovation in Lodge's poem is that it does not treat
the myth as an allegory. Scylla, when the tables are turned
and she is complaining in vain of Glaucus' indifference, is
attended by such figures as Fury, Rage, Wanhope, Despair,
and Woe, but the primary love situation itself is told for its
own sake, and the erotic and pictorial aspects of it are developed without moral purpose.

The complaint device mingles oddly with the mythological
subject matter. In the section which is supposed to develop
Glaucus' attractiveness, for example, the fact that the sea
god himself is forced by the form of the poem to tell of his
own effect upon others makes him seem a preposterous swag-
gerer.[36] And Lodge is usually uncertain whether to depend
upon descriptive poetry or upon rhetorical speeches for his
effect. What he does do is to seize the opportunity offered by
the first appearance of Scylla to give a fairly complete blazon
of the nymph's beauties, and to repeat the process when
Venus appears. He also sees the possibilities in the wooing
of a reluctant male by an ardent maiden. The poem suggests
a great deal more than it performs, and the passage from the
poem which has received the most attention, because of its
connection with Shakespeare, is also the best verse:

[36] Sig. B1ᵛ.

He that hath seene the sweete Arcadian boy
Wiping the purple from his forced wound,
His pretie teares betokening his annoy,
His sighes, his cries, his falling on the ground,
   The Ecchoes ringing from the rockes his fall,
   The trees with teares reporting of his thrall:

And Venus starting at her loue-mates crie,
Forcing hir birds to hast her chariot on;
And full of griefe at last with piteous eie
Seene where all pale with death he lay alone,
   Whose beautie quaild, as wont the Lillies droop
   When wastfull winter windes doo make them stoop.[37]

But Lodge is here, as elsewhere, interesting for what followed him rather than for what he did himself. The epitaph for his poem has been written in the severe lines of Knox Pooler: "The faults are not those of immaturity but of incompetence, of an imagination that can only work piecemeal. Lodge makes his stanzas as a coalheaver makes cartloads, successive shovelfuls with the same swing . . . Such is the work of a man writing without either the assistance of the control of the mind's eye or the mind's ear. There is not a ripple on the verse. The reader passes from line to line and from stanza to stanza with an indifference as unbroken as its own fluidity." [38]

The story of Hero and Leander, told by the sixth-century Alexandrian Musaeus, enjoyed a high reputation in the Elizabethan period. It was supposed to be the work, not of a sixth-century grammarian, but of the divine bard who was the master or perhaps the pupil of Orpheus. Scaliger considered the poem to be superior to Homer. The story, moreover, is prominent in Ovid. It is referred to in the *Amores* and the *Ars Amatoria;* it is the subject of two of the epistles in the *Heroides*. In the Renaissance there are translations into Latin and the continental vernaculars. Abraham Fraunce declared

[37] Sig. A3ᵛ.

[38] Introduction to *Venus and Adonis,* Arden edition (2d ed. rev., London, 1927), pp. xvii–xx. The relationship of Lodge's poem to Italian pastoral and the love complaints of Petrarchan poetry is well discussed by Bush, *Mythology and the Renaissance Tradition,* pp. 81–85.

in 1592 that "Leander and Heroes loue is in euery mans mouth," but he refers only to the epistles in Ovid's *Heroides* and to the Spanish version by Boscan.[39] He had used quotations from the Spanish poem to illustrate rhetorical figures in his *Arcadian Rhetoric* of 1588.

The treatment of the story by Christopher Marlowe is a fragment consisting of two books or sestiads, left unfinished and completed by George Chapman. The poem was entered in the Stationers' Register in 1593, the year of Marlowe's death, but the earliest surviving edition is of 1598. It was very popular in the nineties and the first few decades of the seventeenth century; the 1602 *Salmacis and Hermaphroditus* and most of the other Ovidian-mythological poems are heavily indebted to it.

Hero and Leander fits the requirements of the Italianate entertainment perfectly. In two passages we can trace specific resemblances between this poem and the description of courtly amusement in *Edward II*:

> He thus replied: "The rites
> In which love's beauteous empress most delights,
> Are banquets, Doric music, midnight-revel,
> Plays, masques, and all that stern age counteth evil . . ."[40]

> And when he sported in the fragrant lawns,
> Goat-footed Satyrs and upstarting Fauns
> Would steal him thence.[41]

The plot has many resemblances to the Salmacis myth. There is one specific reminiscence, when the beautiful Hero, in embracing her lover, is compared to the lascivious nymph of the spring:

> Therefore unto him hastily she goes,
> And, like light Salmacis, her body throws
> Upon his bosom, where with yielding eyes
> She offers up herself a sacrifice.[42]

[39] *Amintas Dale* (1592), sig. M4[r-v].
[40] *Hero and Leander*, I, 299–302, in *Poems*, ed. L. C. Martin, vol. IV of *Works and Life of Christopher Marlowe* (6 vols.; London, 1930–1933).
[41] II, 199–201.   [42] II, 45–48.

The story does not end in a metamorphosis, but the youth and naïveté of both of the lovers mean that the voluptuous effects in the narrative can be doubled. The plot of the tale is very simple, and the narrative can accordingly be rapid and yet highly decorated. Hero and Leander are neither human beings nor gods; they live in a world remote enough so that individuality, "psychology," and consistency of character are unimportant. The paradox of Hero as a "nun" in the service of the goddess of love, yet virginal and innocent, suggests immediately the Ovidian tone in dealing with the love affair. Marlowe had translated Ovid's *Amores*, and there are many echoes in the *Hero and Leander* of the manner and phrasing of these poems.

The tone is the result of a highly romantic or baroque decoration combined with gravely mocking asides. These comments are like those of Ovid in the *Amores* and the *Ars Amatoria*, but Marlowe uses them even more frequently. Sometimes they constitute a parody of sober philosophy, as in the passage explaining Leander's pity for Neptune; [43] at other times they are gravely comical displays of worldly wisdom; [44] and again the aside may be used as a sly apology for some device of style. [45] But the final effect is not ironic; these asides merely control the extent of the romanticism in the poem and subdue the excesses of lavish decoration.

The descriptive embellishment of the poem is largely pictorial; it has little to do with nature (some modern critics have complained because there is so little feeling for the sea), and it is not ordinarily atmospheric in the romantic sense. Passages like

> Far from the town, where all is whist and still,
> Save that the sea, playing on yellow sand,
> Sends forth a rattling murmur to the land, [46]

are less common than the more rapid and objective painting of the crystal floor of Venus' temple. [47] The mythology is used, in other words, for color; the emotional implications are only

[43] II, 215–218. [45] II, 273–276. [47] I, 145–156.
[44] II, 293–296. [46] I, 346–348.

sketched in, and the rapidity of the narrative leaves no room for extended pampering of the feelings. When Leander sinks to the bottom of the strait, for example, at the beginning of his swim, the explanation is that Neptune has mistaken him for Ganymede and is wooing him. But the description of the bottom of the ocean is pictorial, not emotional. It has none of the wistful mystery of "Full fathom five thy father lies"; it is a little self-contained picture:

> Leander striv'd, the waves about him wound,
> And pull'd him to the bottom, where the ground
> Was strew'd with pearl, and in low coral groves
> Sweet singing mermaids sported with their loves
> On heaps of heavy gold, and took great pleasure
> To spurn in careless sort the shipwreck treasure.[48]

Not all of the decoration is descriptive; some of it is narrative. The most obvious example is the myth at the end of the first sestiad, a story introduced to explain, at some length, why the Fates are not favorable to love. But in true myth fashion, one thing leads to another, and we learn also why scholars are always poor. This narrative has struck some critics as nonfunctional and destructive of the design of the poem. It is, however, consistent with the whole method of myth: it involves the gods in the same love difficulties experienced by men, and in its representation of the Fates as hostile to love it provides a premonition of the tragic conclusion of the tale. Marlowe offers it to a taste very much more interested in narrative for its own sake, for its decorative effect, than the modern mind readily comprehends. He introduces it with the primitive invitation: "Hearken a while, and I will tell you why." [49]

Another kind of decoration is the rhetorical. This would be more obvious if the poem were dramatic, but in the absence of profound characterization and of fundamental conflict, the decorative effect of the rhetoric is sometimes overlooked. Leander's sophistic speech of persuasion is an example. It is of no importance that these Ovidian arguments against

[48] II, 159–164.   [49] I, 385.

chastity seem inconsistent in the mouth of the Leander who
is later represented as being so naïve sexually that he, after

> Long dallying with Hero, nothing saw
> That might delight him more, yet he suspected
> Some amorous rites or other were neglected.[50]

The arguments against chastity must be introduced to
sharpen the contrast between Hero's beauty and her virginity. Moreover, this rhetorical decoration contrasts with,
and balances, the narrative decoration of the tale of Mercury's love.

Some modern critics boggle at the characterization of the
two lovers. The inconsistency in Leander, already mentioned,
is one charge; another is that the difference between Hero's
maiden bashfulness and her Salmacis-like lightness is not natural but exaggerated. To press these complaints is to ignore
the purpose and method of Marlowe. His characterizations
are not done in any psychologically realistic way; they are
subordinated to the nature of the poem as a whole, a myth;
they are done mythologically. Hero is portrayed by the details that the young Apollo courted her for her hair, that
Cupid mistook her for his mother, that Nature bestowed on
her so much beauty that it depleted the stock and there was
none left for half the world. Leander is described as having
hair that would have inspired the Grecian youth more than
the Golden Fleece, and cheeks and lips that exceeded in
beauty those of Narcissus. The purpose here is obviously
not to delineate the characters with any realism or verisimili-
tude; it is to relate them to the whole fabric of myth. The
intensification of their beauty is not done directly, for the
most part, but by exhibiting its effects upon others. Leander
can subdue the wild Hippolytus or the barbarous Thracian
soldier with his beauty, and the power of Hero is like that
of the moon on the tides:

> Nor that night-wandering, pale, and watery star
> (When yawning dragons draw her thirling car
> From Latmus' mount up to the gloomy sky,

[50] II, 62–64.

Where crown'd with blazing light and majesty,
She proudly sits) more over-rules the flood
Than she the hearts of those that near her stood.[51]

In a sense, therefore, Hero and Leander are not "characters" at all. They are merely focal points for mythological inventions. Marlowe's intention is to produce a world of directly apprehensible beauty, the mysteries of which are not referred to the reader's memories of his own vague emotions, or to an imagined but intangible experience, but to the standard and recognized pattern of mythological lore.

The design of the poem is so filled with this mythological decoration that the events of the narrative are sometimes compressed with what seems ludicrous rapidity. An action which the modern reader expects to be developed at some length is compressed into a couplet:

Thence flew Love's arrow with the golden head,
And thus Leander was enamoured.[52]

By this, sad Hero, with love unacquainted,
Viewing Leander's face, fell down and fainted.[53]

With that he stripp'd him to the ivory skin,
And crying, "Love, I come," leapt lively in.[54]

The climaxes are quite clearly not climaxes of action, any more than they are of character.

The speed of the poem is its essential characteristic. There is no time for lingering images; even the finest of them must drop their hold for the next in line. The problem therefore is one of variety and contrast. In the following passage there are three images; the modern reader will do violence to Marlowe if he focuses his attention on the second one and neglects the first and third:

But as her naked feet were whipping out,
He on the sudden cling'd her so about,
That mermaid-like unto the floor she slid,
One half appear'd, the other half was hid.
Thus near the bed she blushing stood upright,
And from her countenance behold ye might

---

[51] I, 107–112.   [52] I, 161–162.   [53] II, 1–2.   [54] II, 153–154.

A kind of twilight break, which through the hair,
As from an orient cloud, glimps'd here and there;
And round about the chamber this false morn
Brought forth the day before the day was born.
So Hero's ruddy cheek Hero betray'd,
And her all naked to his sight display'd;
Whence his admiring eyes more pleasure took
Than Dis, on heaps of gold fixing his look.[55]

The figures of the mermaid, the false twilight, and Dis in his counting room are of equal validity within Marlowe's system. They are all evocative, though of pictures rather than of emotion. The difference may perhaps be illustrated by a passage from Keats:

She was a Goddess of the infant world;
By her in stature the tall Amazon
Had stood a pigmy's height: she would have ta'en
Achilles by the hair and bent his neck;
Or with a finger stay'd Ixion's wheel.
Her face was large as that of Memphian sphinx,
Pedestal d haply in a palace court,
When sages look'd to Egypt for their lore.
But oh! how unlike marble was that face:
How beautiful, if sorrow had not made
Sorrow more beautiful than Beauty's self.
There was a listening fear in her regard,
As if calamity had but begun;
As if the vanward clouds of evil days
Had spent their malice, and the sullen rear
Was with its stored thunder labouring up.[56]

These two kinds of mythological poetry can not be qualitatively evaluated in relation to each other, their intent is so different.

Marlowe's poem created a vogue in the 1590's. His fragment was completed by George Chapman, in a style very different from Marlowe's own, and another version, on a far lower level, was published by Henry Petowe in 1598.[57]

[55] II, 313–326.

[56] *Hyperion: A Fragment*, lines 26–41, in *Poetical Works*, ed. H. W. Garrod (Oxford, 1939) , p. 277.

[57] For the bibliography of the Ovidian tradition, see the appendix to Bush, *Mythology and the Renaissance Tradition*, pp. 301–323.

The most famous of the Ovidian poems to appear is of course Shakespeare's *Venus and Adonis,* which came from the press of Richard Field in 1593. Shakespeare uses the same six-line stanza which Lodge had used for *Scillaes Metamorphosis,* not the couplets of Marlowe. His material comes mainly from the tenth book of Ovid's *Metamorphoses,* but as in other Elizabethan Ovidian poems, the legend has been modified by the Salmacis-Hermaphroditus story in Book IV and the Narcissus story in Book III.

The comparison between Marlowe's *Hero and Leander* and Shakespeare's *Venus and Adonis* is a critic's set piece. The two poems, close together in time and belonging to the same tradition, offer a chance to compare the genius of these two poets as their plays can never do. On the whole, the judgment in the competition has been in favor of Marlowe. It is well expressed in a recent illuminating essay by W. B. C. Watkins.[58] In commenting on the "natural imagery drawn from first-hand observation of the fields and woods," for which Shakespeare's poem is usually praised, Watkins remarks, "In attempting to combine a conservatory atmosphere and the out-of-doors, an ornate style and simplicity of observation, Shakespeare may have had in mind something more than merely another Ovidian poem, or something different, but he failed."

Shakespeare chose one of the most familiar of Ovid's stories for artistic treatment. It was common enough in paintings and tapestries, and it had been done in the poetical description of a painting by Lydgate and by Spenser.[59] Spenser's description is that of an appropriate decoration for his Castle Ioyeous. The room in which it hangs gives an impression of royalty and rich purveyance, as Spenser emphasizes, so luxurious that it conveys to visitors

The image of superfluous riotize,
Exceeding much the state of meane degree.[60]

---

[58] "Shakespeare's Banquet of Sense," *Southern Review,* VII (1942) , 710.

[59] For a discussion of the vogue of tapestries and their subjects, see Frederick Hard, "Spenser's 'Clothes of Arras and of Toure,'" *SP,* XXVII (1930) , 162–185.   [60] *Faerie Queene,* III, I, xxxiii.

As Mr. Hard points out, the tapestry is apparently in four panels, portraying the enamorment of Venus, her enticements, Adonis sleeping, and the metamorphosis of the slain Adonis into a flower. It is described by Spenser as

> A worke of rare deuice, and wondrous wit.

The lascivious aspects of the picture presumably derive from an identification with part of the Salmacis story,

> And whilest he bath'd, with her two crafty spyes,
> She secretly would search each daintie lim.[61]

Although Venus does all the wooing, the reluctance of Adonis is not stressed, and Spenser gives the impression that the goddess won him.[62] That the whole purpose of this tapestry was aphrodisiac is made explicit in the activities of the occupants of the room.[63] The attitude of Britomart and the Red Cross Knight toward these festivities, if not toward the arras, was one of proper disapproval.[64] Even the serious and moral poets, in the 1590's, drew their Ovidian pictures with some warmth. Such survivors of the allegorical tradition as Abraham Fraunce, writing for the Countess of Pembroke a series of tales from the *Metamorphoses* under the title *The Third Part of the Countesse of Pembrokes Yuychurch. Entituled Amintas Dale* (1592), gave a fairly lascivious version of the love-making of Venus.[65] Furthermore, Fraunce associates Venus and Adonis with Hero and Leander:

> Sometimes, louely records for Adonis sake, she reciteth;
> How Laeander dyde, as he swamme to the bewtiful Hero.[66]

---

[61] III, I, xxxvi. Spenser's source, according to H. G. Lotspeich, is Natalis Comes for everything except the transformation to a flower (Variorum *Faerie Queene*, Book III, p. 208).

[62] III, I, xxxvii.

[63] III, I, xxxix.

[64] III, I, xl.

[65] Sig. M2ʳ. The relevant lines are quoted by Bush, *Mythology and the Renaissance Tradition*, p. 145, n. 15. The best critical account of Fraunce is to be found in Kathrine Koller, "Abraham Fraunce and Edmund Spenser," *ELH*, VII (1940), 108–120.

[66] Sig. M2ʳ. This association is unusual, though the Venus and Adonis story is a common ornament for other Ovidian tales. It is represented on the sleeves of Hero's dress in Marlowe's poem (I, 11–14) and on the dress of Venus in

Venus and Adonis is a crude production in comparison with *Hero and Leander*. A much larger part of it is contained in the dialogue of the two characters, and the action is almost confined to the event of the horse and the breeding jennet. There is nothing like the variety of color, of surface finish, that Marlowe's poem exhibits. And curiously, Shakespeare's queen of love herself seems considerably less divine than the semi-human figures of Hero and Leander.

Marlowe had sensed that Ovid got some of his most telling erotic effects by utilizing reluctance, innocence, and naïveté; he therefore did not scruple to make Leander a novice, for all of his sophistic arguments against virginity. But Shakespeare, in trying to imitate this, betrayed something of his own provincial background. Instead of an erotic innocent, Adonis is something of an adolescent lout. He is from the country and very conscious that he hasn't been around. This makes the attempts to emphasize his beauty ridiculous, and the final impression Adonis leaves is not that of a creature of a world of myth but of a young fellow from Stratford ill at ease in the presence of a court lady.

> Faire Queene (quoth he) if anie loue you owe me,
> Measure my strangenesse with my vnripe yeares,
> Before I know myselfe, seeke not to know me,
> No fisher but the vngrowne frie forbeares,
>   The mellow plum doth fall, the green sticks fast,
>   Or being early pluckt, is sower to tast.[67]

Venus herself represents no ideal picture of physical love. She is dominated by the imagery, which most often and most significantly revolves around the hard and violent appetite of the hawk.[68]

The critics have often remarked that Shakespeare tempers the erotic atmosphere of the poem with references to the fields and open air. The description of the horse and the ac-

---

Lodge's *Scillaes Metamorphosis*. But the "louely records" are not, for Fraunce, simply ornaments; they are part of Venus' repertoire of erotic persuasion.

[67] *Venus and Adonis*, lines 523-528, in *The Poems*, ed. H. E. Rollins (Philadelphia, 1938), vol. 22 of *A New Variorum Edition of Shakespeare*.

[68] Lines 55-60, 547-558.

count given by Venus of the coursing of the hare, the images of the dive-dapper and the snail, of the lark mounting from his moist cabinet on high, are frequently admired for their own sake. The question of their appropriateness to an Ovidian poem is a more difficult one. Watkins suggests that in one respect Shakespeare is closer to Ovid than Marlowe is: that he "does not exclude any possible suggestion of the physically unpleasant from the portrayal of sensual beauty, though he fails to maintain Ovid's sense of proportion." [69] But it is a question of the particular nature of the physically unpleasant which is admitted into the myth. The "vultur thought" and the comparison with the ravenous appetite of animals are a criticism of the feelings of Venus, and that new world of joy evoked by the struggle of Marlowe's lovers is a very different thing. The associations in Shakespeare's mind become clearer from *Lucrece,* where Tarquin's thoughts as he proceeds to the rape are compared to the vulture, and this leads naturally to the sense of repletion and disgust when such feelings are satisfied, again in terms of the hawk:

> Looke as the full-fed Hound, or gorged Hawke,
> Vnapt for tender smell, or speedie flight,
> Make slow pursuite, or altogether bauk,
> The praie wherein by nature they delight; [70]

and we are reminded of the sonnet which begins "Th' expense of spirit in a waste of shame." Marlowe can indicate this fierceness of sexual appetite without his imagination being dominated by it. The lines

> Love is not full of pity, as men say,
> But deaf and cruel, where he means to prey,

are followed immediately by

> She trembling strove; this strife of hers (like that
> Which made the world) another world begat
> Of unknown joy. [71]

---

[69] "Shakespeare's Banquet of Sense," p. 728.
[70] *The Rape of Lucrece,* lines 694–697.
[71] *Hero and Leander,* II, 287–288; 291–293.

In the style of *Venus and Adonis* Shakespeare was no doubt influenced by two opposing models: the painting or tapestry, which would give him such visual details as Venus' lightness on the primroses (lines 151–152), Adonis' "bonnet" (line 339), and the horse,[72] and a rhetorical or dramatic tradition which would persuade him to put so much of his narrative into direct speech. There is not such an abrupt break between *Venus and Adonis* and *Lucrece* as the critics have usually made out.

If, as it is reasonable to suppose, Shakespeare had in mind the taste of the young Earl of Southampton when he chose a subject and style for his maiden effort, he was probably right in attempting something in the Ovidian-erotic tradition. It was courtiers like Southampton who fancied the genre most, and, as the references to Shakespeare's poem show, it was the young who were especially attracted to it. But considering how much of the rustic Englishman Shakespeare still had about him, it was a bold experiment. The rusticity shows through. The poet cannot escape from the barnyard, the hawking field, and the rabbit hunt. His senses are still coarsened, and the Ovidian theme is not quite strong enough to refine them for him. The catalogue of the senses, which Chapman was later to make into a structure for his Ovidian poem, is crudely handled here (lines 433–450). When Shakespeare decorates his discourse, it is either with description from nature or rhetorical involutions, and they are both to be used sparingly in this type of poem. The decoration which is suitable and functional is that of the fragment of myth. Marlowe's poem is rich in these decorations and Shakespeare's is poor in them.

Modern criticism of the poem has not been as successful as its auspicious beginning, with Coleridge, would suggest. Coleridge used the poem for illustrative material on two general subjects: the evidence of genius in a young writer and the celebrated distinction between fancy and imagination. These are of course relevant to the poem, and turned

[72] See A. H. R. Fairchild, *Shakespeare and the Arts of Design* (Columbia, Missouri, 1937), pp. 137–139, for a discussion of the horse passage.

back upon it with closer analysis they might have produced very fruitful results. But the critics have followed other courses, with the result that judgment on the poem is without an appropriate frame of reference; it varies from E. W. Sievers' "*Venus and Adonis* . . . is really the foundation of the entire structure of Shakespeare's philosophy of life" to John Bailey's "Much of it is rather empty and verbose, more is crude in taste, at once sensuous and sentimental, without reserve or reticence, dignity or manliness or morals." [73] Professor H. T. Price interprets very elaborately the imagery of *Venus and Adonis,* after the manner of G. Wilson Knight, finds the poem to be the expression of the most savage irony known to him in literature, and says in conclusion, "I am the only man of our days to say in print that he has really received from *Venus and Adonis* the joy that Shakespeare intended to communicate." [74]

Viewed from within the convention to which it belongs, Shakespeare's poem shows the difficulty of acclimatizing the new Ovidian poem in English. Marlowe had done it, but his success hung precariously on a skill and taste which even his greatest contemporary did not have in 1593. Considering the nature of Shakespeare's artistic development, it might be said that the failure of *Venus and Adonis* predicts the success of *A Midsummer Night's Dream.* Shakespeare was unwilling or unable to shed a basic English earthiness; had he done so he might have matched *Hero and Leander* but he might never have produced Bottom or Falstaff or Juliet's nurse. Tucker Brooke used to say that just as Keats wrote *Endymion* to de-cockneyize himself, Shakespeare wrote *Venus and Adonis* as the quickest way out of the mental climate of Stratford. It is fortunate for his later work that he did not succeed in getting completely out.

Whatever modern criticism may say about *Venus and Adonis,* in its own time "the younger sort," as Gabriel Harvey said, found in the poem a triumph of fancy and delight.

[73] Variorum *Poems,* ed. Rollins, pp. 486, 513–514.
[74] "The Function of Imagery in *Venus and Adonis,*" *Papers of the Michigan Academy of Science, Arts, and Letters,* XXXI (1945), 275–297.

There were at least ten editions in Shakespeare's lifetime, and the poem was, as Professor Bentley says, "probably Shakespeare's best-known composition between 1590 and 1616." [75] Some of its popularity was due to its erotic subject matter, and there are many allusions to prove that in the eyes of some contemporaries "Shakespeare's poems were the favorite reading of loose and degenerate people, and that, as a consequence, they led to looseness and degeneracy." [76] But of course the critics who objected to the salacious qualities of *Venus and Adonis* would also object to Ovid, even in the *Metamorphoses,* unless they happened to consider him an allegorical poet. It is amusing to hear a character in the Cambridge play of 1601, *The Return from Parnassus, or The Scourge of Simony,* praise *Venus and Adonis* and *The Rape of Lucrece* but suggest wistfully that Shakespeare would be a better writer

> Could but a grauer subiect him content,
> Without loues foolish lazy languishment.[77]

The greatest testimony to the vogue of *Venus and Adonis* comes not from allusions but from the many Ovidian poems of the next decade which borrowed from it and *Hero and Leander.* Even poets who considered Spenser the greatest English bard, as many of them did, turned to Marlowe and Shakespeare for models of the mythological poem.

Six months after the entry of *Venus and Adonis* on the Stationers' Register, on October 22, 1593, entry was made for *Procris and Cephalus.* Since this is presumably the same as the *Cephalus and Procris* which was published with an additional poem, *Narcissus,* in 1595, we have evidence that within a very short time Shakespeare's poem was imitated and referred to. In 1595, at any rate, *Cephalus and Procris* was already popular, for William Covell speaks of it in his *Poli-*

---

[75] G. E. Bentley, *Shakespeare and Jonson,* 2 vols. (Chicago, 1945), I, 41. *Venus and Adonis* did not maintain this position through the seventeenth century. See Bentley's list, I, 109, and his comment on I, 117, that "the poem's vogue was largely a sixteenth-century one."

[76] Variorum *Poems,* ed. Rollins, p. 456.

[77] Ed. by W. D. Macray (Oxford, 1886), p. 87.

manteia as one of the works "by the greedy Printers so made prostitute that they are contemned." [78] According to Nashe, it was not so much the greedy printer, in this case John Wolfe, as it was Gabriel Harvey who was responsible for this further attempt to please the younger sort.[79] The author of the two Ovidian poems contained in the volume was Thomas Edwards, about whom nothing is known except that Mrs. C. C. Stopes identified him with a courtier of that name.[80]

Edwards' poem on the Cephalus and Procris story from the seventh book of the *Metamorphoses* depends upon *Hero and Leander* for style and form. It is in couplets, tentative and awkward in comparison to Marlowe's, and the mythological decoration is in the Italianate manner. About forty specific borrowings from *Hero and Leander* have been traced.[81] But the wooing of Cephalus by Aurora while he is on his way to a boar hunt derives from *Venus and Adonis*. It is fairly typical of Edwards' work, and it shows quite clearly what struck contemporaries in Shakespeare's poem.[82] Together with this imitating of Marlowe and Shakespeare, Edwards pays specific tribute to Spenser and Sidney as the "Heroicke Parramore of Fairie land" and the *"Arcardian* knight, earthes second Sunne." [83]

Edwards' version of the Narcissus story, which appeared also in the volume, belongs with *The Rape of Lucrece* and other complaint poems and will be discussed in another section. In connection with *Venus and Adonis,* however, we may note here that Narcissus compares himself to Adonis [84] and Leander [85] and that in the envoy to *Narcissus* Edwards ap-

---

[78] Sig. Q4ʳ.

[79] *The Works of Thomas Nashe,* ed. R. B. McKerrow, 5 vols. (London, 1904–1910) , III, 89.

[80] "Thomas Edwards, Author of *Cephalus and Procris,*" *MLR,* XVI (1921) , 218.

[81] Douglas Bush, "The Influence of Marlowe's *Hero and Leander* on Early Mythological Poems," *MLN,* XLII (1927) , 212.

[82] *Cephalus and Procris. Narcissus,* ed. W. E. Buckley (London: Roxburghe Club, 1882) , pp. 12–13.

[83] *Ibid.,* p. 12.

[84] *Ibid.,* p. 43.

[85] *Ibid.,* p. 44.

parently calls Shakespeare "Adon," as he certainly calls
Marlowe "Leander." [86]

Seven months later, on May 17, 1594, the printer Richard
Jones registered another poem in the new erotic style. It was
*Oenone and Paris, wherein is Deciphered the extremitie of
love the effectes of hate the operacon of them bothe,* by the
young Thomas Heywood, just beginning his long and prolific
career.[87] In taking the subject of Oenone and Paris, from
Ovid's *Heroides,* Heywood was forcing somewhat the situation of the reluctant male wooed by the ardent goddess, but
he made his Oenone use the same kind of arguments and the
same salacious allurements that Venus had used. Heywood
also apparently alludes to Edwards' poem:

> Loe, howe Aurora with her blushing face
> Bewrayes her lust with Cephalus her louer.[88]

Paris cannot be made into the same kind of bashful boy
that the Narcissus-Hermaphroditus-Adonis figure is. Instead,
he becomes an apologist for the irresponsibility of lovers,
of the doctrine which Marlowe had expressed that love is
overruled by fate and is not a matter of the individual's
choice. Oenone stresses her immortality as a nymph, apparently to bring her closer to the pattern of Venus wooing the
mortal Adonis.

It is interesting to see Heywood, who became a dramatist
for the middle class, beginning his literary career with a poem
of the type generally calculated to appeal to young aristocrats. But his interest in Ovid seems to have been profound,
since he translated the *Ars Amatoria* and the *Remedia Amoris,* as well as the epistles between Helen and Paris which
Jaggard printed in *The Passionate Pilgrim* as Shakespeare's.

---

[86] *Ibid.,* p. 62.

[87] The unique copy has been edited by J. Q. Adams (Washington, D. C.:
Folger Shakespeare Library, 1943) . He presents the evidence for expanding the
initials T. H. of the entry to Thomas Heywood and points out, in his notes,
many parallels to *Venus and Adonis.*

[88] *Oenone and Paris,* lines 61–62. Adams does not notice this, and he over-
looks Edwards completely in the claim in his preface (p. v) that *Oenone and
Paris* is "the earliest known imitation of Shakespeare."

Moreover, Heywood continued to use this Ovidian material over again in his later works, both dramatic and nondramatic, for some years.

Oenone and Paris, like *Venus and Adonis,* is dependent upon dialogue rather than narrative for its structure. Heywood's style is fluent and even, without distinction but more than competent. His poem is capable of giving the pleasure that the anonymous "Elizabethanism" of much verse of the nineties can give.

The year 1595 saw the height of the Ovidian fad. During that year the earliest surviving edition of Edwards' two poems was published, and such varied additional poems in the mode as Richard Barnfield's *Cassandra,* Michael Drayton's *Endimion and Phoebe,* and George Chapman's *Ovid's Banquet of Sence* appeared. They illustrate well how individual Elizabethan poets, seizing the opportunity to profit by the fashion for a particular genre, could shape it to suit their own purposes, and they show how flexible these "kinds" were.

We have already seen that there were certain connections between the Ovidian-mythological tradition and the pastoral tradition. Pastoral poetry was often erotic, and the distinction between goddesses, nymphs, and shepherdesses, or between the beautiful young men of myth and the feigned shepherd of pastoral, was often not clear. Barnfield had published in 1594, for example, a volume called *The Affectionate Shepheard,* dedicated to Penelope, Lady Rich, and containing a selection of poems of various sorts. The first two, complaints or love lamentations, are put in the mouth of a shepherd, Daphnis; but the object of his love is a boy, Ganymede, on the model, as Barnfield said, of Virgil's second eclogue, to Alexis. The work combines an elaboration of the pastoral invitation, as seen in Marlowe's "Passionate Shepherd" and similar poems, with the erotic appeals to a reluctant boy which characterize the Ovidian poems. The volume also contains a "poem of good life," a sonnet, a complaint in the *Mirror* tradition, and a hexameter poem called "Hellens Rape, or a light Lanthorne for light Ladies," in the manner of Abraham Fraunce. It is typical of Barnfield's eclectic method. In the next year, 1595, he published a poem called "Cassandra" which is a purer sample of the Ovidian-erotic poem, but he included it in a volume with *Cynthia,* professedly the first imitation of Spenser's *Faerie Queene,* and some sonnets. Barnfield echoes Shakespeare, and in the story of the wooing of Cassandra by Apollo and her unhappy end as the mistress of Agamemnon he finds opportunity to attempt the effects produced in both *Venus and Adonis* and *The Rape of Lucrece.*

Drayton, who had alluded to *Venus and Adonis* in his *Piers Gaveston* of 1594 [89] and who had shown the influence of *Lucrece* in his *Matilda* the same year, produced his own contribution to the fashionable Ovidian mode in 1595, with *Endimion and Phoebe.* His poem is distinctive, however; he sees the mythological love affair in Platonic terms, and he manages to combine his Ovidian material with influences from the great French Protestant poet, Du Bartas. Drayton's first published work, *The Harmonie of the Church* (1591), might lead us to expect this, but the remarkable thing is that he managed to utilize the erotic convention which Marlowe and Shakespeare had made popular.

Endimion and Phoebe has for its subtitle *Ideas Latmus;* Drayton lavishes much more detail on the description of the place than either Shakespeare or Marlowe had done. He gives a Spenserian (or Chaucerian) tree catalogue and proceeds to embellish the arbor on Mount Latmos for the most extravagant feminine taste.[90] It is obvious that here the model for Drayton is not the poems of the Ovidian-erotic tradition but the descriptions in Spenser of the Garden of Adonis and the Bower of Bliss.

To be sure, there are connections with Marlowe, and the Ovidian source for the Endymion-Phoebe story, brief as it is, comes in the epistle in the *Heroides* written from Leander to Hero.[91] The characterization of Endimion is done in the Marlovian manner; [92] but in the wooing of the boy by the god-

---

[89] See J. W. Hebel, *MLN,* XLI (1926), 248–250.
[90] *Endimion and Phoebe,* lines 35–54 (*Works,* ed. Hebel, I, 130).
[91] *Heroides,* XVIII, 59–74.
[92] *Endimion and Phoebe,* lines 83–96 (*Works,* I, 131).

dess, though she catalogues her own beauties and offers him luxurious delights in the manner of the pastoral convention, the conclusion is

> If not all these, yet let my vertues move thee,
> A chaster Nymph Endimion cannot love thee.[93]

The very choice of the Endymion story indicated that Drayton was to treat mythological material from a Platonic viewpoint. The myth was commonly symbolized as the origin of a knowledge of astronomy; such an ordinary source of information as Cooper's dictionary gave

> Endymion, The name of a man, whiche founde the course of the moone: wherfore the poetes feigned that the moone loued hym, and descended downe to kisse him while he slepte.[94]

The love of the moon goddess for a mortal therefore signifies divine inspiration for Drayton.[95] The climax of the poem is reached when the goddess finally reveals her identity as the nymph whom Endimion had scorned for her sake. This demonstrates the validity of the Platonic love of physical beauty, provided that love is not enslaved to the physical body itself. The lover is rewarded with the knowledge of divine things.[96] The conclusion is that Endimion acquires power over nature and a knowledge of astronomy. Drayton depends upon Du Bartas for much of his lore about the divine nature of astronomy, and his Phoebe is not clearly distinct from Urania. But the poet finds hereby a method of relating poetry, astronomy, and divinity, and he shows by his philosophy of the mystic significance of the numbers nine and three that they are all intimately connected. There is no inconsistency, then, when Drayton breaks off his poem without giving Endimion's vision, which he says he will relate another time, and concludes with a tribute and dedication to three fellow-poets, Spenser, Daniel, and Lodge, and to his "Sweet Nymph

[93] Lines 223–224 (*Works,* I, 134).
[94] *Dictionarum Historicum & Poeticum propria locorum & Personarum vocabula,* appended to Thomas Cooper, *Thesaurus* (1565), sig. H2ᵛ.
[95] *Endimion and Phoebe,* lines 505–510 (*Works,* I, 142).
[96] Lines 633–646 (*Works,* I, 145–146).

of Ankor," Idea, the symbol of beauty and of his faith in the immortality of verse.

A more deeply philosophical poem than Drayton's is Chapman's Ovidian performance of the same year (1595), *Ovid's Banquet of Sence*. This, too, is neo-Platonic, depending primarily upon Ficino's commentary on Plato's *Symposium*. Chapman had already, in 1594, asserted his opposition to fleshly interpretations of the classic myths; in the "Hymnus ad Cynthiam" in *The Shadow of Night* he wrote that Cynthia loved "Endimion for his studious intellect." [97] A passage near the end of the poem may refer to contemporary Ovidian works, whether or not there are any specific references to Shakespeare in the poem:

> Thy virgin chamber then that sacred is,
> No more let hold, an idle Salmacis,
> Nor let more sleights, Cydippe iniurie:
> Nor let blacke Ioue possest in Scicilie,
> Rauish more maids, but maids subdue his might,
> With well-steeld lances of thy watchfull sight. [98]

Chapman also attacks the erotic poems of the Ovidian tradition in his sequence of ten sonnets attached to *Ovid's Banquet* called "A Coronet for His Mistresse Philosophie." He warns the writers of such poems that they stain the living substance of their glory. [99] But Chapman's approach to Ovid is far different from that of the interpreters of a half century earlier who saw only parables in the *Metamorphoses*. His *Banquet of Sence* is a poem for the learned and the intelligent; he admits, in the dedication to his friend Matthew

[97] Lines 490–494 (*Poems*, ed. P. B. Bartlett [New York, 1941], p. 41).

[98] Lines 509–514 (*ibid.*). Lines 162–165 have been taken to refer to the motto on the title page of *Venus and Adonis:*

> Presume not then ye flesh confounded soules,
> That cannot beare the full Castalian bowles,
> Which seuer mounting spirits from the sences,
> To looke in this deepe fount for thy pretenses.

But the motto was not, apparently, peculiar to Shakespeare; see Variorum *Poems*, ed. Rollins, p. 369. The reference more naturally refers to all those who use Ovid and classical mythology as a justification for their sensuality.

[99] Sonnet 1, lines 1–6 (*Poems*, ed. Bartlett, p. 83).

Roydon, that "empty, and dark spirits" among his readers "wil complain of palpable night," a prediction which has been amply fulfilled. But the enlightened, he hopes, will understand the poem and find in it a work "varying in some rare fiction, from popular custome, euen for the pure sakes of ornament and vtilitie."

Chapman portrays Ovid watching Corinna bathing in a fountain, the reverse of the old Salmacis situation. He hears her sing, and his sense of hearing is inspired; he smells her perfume; he sees her beautiful body; he receives a kiss from her and touches her—all for the rapture of his various senses. This "banquet" is in reality, as Chapman sees it, an education for the soul. "The sence is given vs to excite the mind," he says, and the mind conveys this excitement to the soul. The soul is incapable of direct apprehension of experience or of comment upon it; the flesh, as the servant of the soul, must aid.[100] Moreover, the flesh is glorified in that it has a direct communication with beauty, which is divine.[101] The effect which the agitation of the physical sense has upon the soul may best be illustrated by the account of the consequences of hearing music.[102] Chapman rejects the idea that heaven can only be gained by labors of the soul and by continence.[103] It can also be gained by means of the senses, which, when fully contented, procure a delight "That so the soule may vse her facultie." [104] He returns several times to the contrast between those who banquet the senses, as a means of freeing the soul, and those sordid men whose only motive is gain.[105] The truest wisdom is the pursuit of beauty, he argues, for all agree with the pastoral doctrine that "All wealth and wisdome rests in true Content," [106] and beauty joined with love has more force to bring about content than "thrones with wisdome" or "iudgments grauen in Stoick grauitie." [107] Chapman here touches upon commonplaces which I discuss in connection with the pastoral and with satire.

[100] *Banquet of Sense,* sts. 111–112 (*Poems,* ed. Bartlett).
[101] Stanza 52.
[102] Stanzas 21–22.
[103] Stanza 62.
[104] Stanza 63.
[105] Stanza 35.
[106] Stanza 53.
[107] Stanza 54.

The effect of the poem is difficult to describe, but it is specific and vivid. The style is vigorous, yet sometimes very delicate. Rich alliterative effects are mingled with interesting figures, so that the attention is held between sound and thought:

> Her sight, his sunne so wrought in his desires,
> His sauor vanisht in his visuale fires.[108]

Instead of the tapestry figure, Chapman presents us with the philosophical nude:

> And thus she sang, all naked as she sat,
> Laying the happy Lute vpon her thigh,
> Not thinking any neere to wonder at
> The blisse of her sweet brests diuinitie.[109]

Sometimes the conceits are startlingly "romantic":

> Shee lay, and seemed a flood of Diamant
> Bounded in flesh: as still as Vespers hayre,
> When not an Aspen leafe is styrred with ayre.[110]

Of course, the doctrine about the relation of the senses to the soul continually controls the erotic element in the poem. So it is not "Ovidian" in the manner of Shakespeare and Marlowe. And Chapman, who undertook to complete Marlowe's unfinished *Hero and Leander,* was far from feeling as Marlowe did about the decorative use of mythological inventions. To Chapman these additions are intellectual illustrations, not primarily visual or pictorial:

> And as a Taper burning in the darke
> (As if it threatned euery watchfull eye
> That viewing burns it,) makes that eye his marke,
> And hurls guilt Darts at it continually,
>   Or as it enuied, any eye but it
> Should see in darknes, so my Mistres beautie
>   From foorth her secret stand my hart doth hit:
> And like the Dart of *Cephalus* dooth kill
> Her perfect Louer, though shee meane no ill.[111]

---

[108] Stanza 40.   [110] Stanza 56.
[109] Stanza 12.   [111] Stanza 66.

The difference between this reference to Cephalus and the general atmosphere of Edwards' poem marks the divergence of Chapman from the fashionable Ovidian-mythological tradition.[112]

Marlowe's *Hero and Leander* appeared in two editions in 1598 and another in 1600. By 1600 six editions of *Venus and Adonis* had been published. The erotic-mythological poem, therefore, was in high vogue at the time when the eruption of satires in the last three years of the century took place. Such minor works as Nashe's *Choice of Valentines* and Marston's *Pigmalion,* though they had little of mythological interest about them, or little of any interest except the pornographic, were of course remotely derived from Ovid, and they tended to accent the salacious aspects of the whole genre. Hall made indecent poetry one of the main objects of his satire in *Virgidemiarum,* and Marston's preoccupation with lust is so pervasive that one wonders whether he has quite escaped from identifying himself with the object of his attack. In this situation we are provided with an interesting document by the ubiquitous John Weever, a poem in the manner of Marlowe written in the midst of the uproar of the satirists.

Weever's title, *Faunus and Melliflora or The Original of our English Satyres,* attempts to capitalize on the current interest in the suppression of the satires. But the account given of the origin of English satires is really only an inserted mythological story in an Ovidian poem, like the story of Mercury and the Fates in *Hero and Leander.* The *Faunus and Melliflora* itself is of some interest, because it has been generally overlooked in modern accounts and because it is probably the most slavish of all the imitations of Marlowe's masterpiece.

In his dedication Weever calls the poem "but a Shepheards lowly pastorall," but this is a blind; it is essentially an erotic poem, with no closer relative in the pastoral tradition than

---

[112] Janet Spens discusses the poem, not in the context of the Ovidian tradition, but in respect to Chapman's general philosophical system, in "Chapman's Ethical Thought," *Essays and Studies by Members of the English Association,* XI (1925), 158–160.

Daphnis and Chloe. It has prefixed to it several commendatory poems, one by Michael Drayton and one signed "T. H."
Another friend of the author who signs himself "I. F." antici-
pates the criticism that this poem will be considered a lascivious toy; he replies to it by saying

> Content thee Momus, thou hast lost thy sight,
> For this is neither vaine, obsceane, nor slight,

and by citing the precedent of Chaucer, who also wrote of
love and love's delights.

Faunus, the hero of the story, is a recognized figure in classical mythology and had become identified with Pan, but he
is treated by Weever as a "prince of Italie," [113] and his beauty
is elaborated as Leander's was. Melliflora, however, is new:

> Faire Melliflora, amorous, and yong,
> Whose name, nor story, neuer Poet sung.[114]

Her beauty, not Phaeton, caused the burning of half the
earth. She has shells on her slippers; she makes Freudian slips
of the tongue:

> And in my bed, *My,* vnawares out slipt,
> Her face bewraide how that her tongue had tript.[115]

In fact, she is constantly derived from Marlowe's Hero.
Faunus is "rude and raw," but a persuasive arguer against
vows of virginity. His robe, like Hero's, is stained with the
blood of those who have died for love of him.[116] Sexual excitement in the poem is treated in Marlowe's language:

> And fear'd such strife another strife would moue.[117]

> And still they striue, but who obtainde the day,
> Let him be iudge that er'e fought such a fray.[118]

In Book XIV of the *Metamorphoses* is the story of Picus,
who was turned into a woodpecker by Circe because he despised her love. Picus is the father of Faunus, and his transfor-

---

113 *Faunus and Melliflora*, sig. F^v.   116 Sig. B2^r.
114 Sig. B3^r.   117 Sig. C3^r.
115 Sigs. B4^v–C^r.   118 Sig. F1^v.

mation is used by Weever to allow Faunus to succeed to the throne. There is a boar hunt in this section of Ovid, too, and Weever utilizes a boar hunt in his narrative. But the boar is the one of the Venus and Adonis story. According to Weever, Adonis was not killed by the boar at all; the animal had already been dispatched by Faunus. Adonis died of love for Melliflora. And Venus, finding Faunus in the woods, took him for Adonis and wooed him in characteristic vein.

Here we have an eclectic performance, combining with some ingenuity those elements of Marlowe and Shakespeare which had proved to be so popular. In style and attitude toward the material Weever recognizes Marlowe as his model. The grave aside is utilized:

(Loue neuer loues to rest, but alwaies ranges) [119]

or

In womens mouths, No is no negatiue; [120]

and the description of costume is very elaborate.

It is curious indeed to see such a poem veering around to specific topical reference to the quarrel of the satirists, but Weever's position is clear by the end of the poem, when, after introducing translations of the first satires of Horace, Juvenal, and Persius as samples of the whole corpus of Latin satire to be translated, he then attributes the suppression of English satires to the sentence of Venus, and in a prognostication for the first year of the new century says that all the vices complained of by such writers as Marston and Hall have been remedied. Lascivious poetry has returned to Italy where it belongs, and, if it ever returns, satire can cope with it. Weever's intention is presumably to satisfy both tastes, for his book is neither one thing nor the other. It includes satire and opposes satire; it says farewell to the mythological-erotic poem and offers a highly spiced example of the type. Weever's journalistic shrewdness is evident.

[119] Sig. B4r.
[120] Sig. C2r.

II

Sweeping across all Elizabethan literature is the great pervading theme of the Fall of Princes. A heritage from the Middle Ages, this doctrine of the perilous turning of Fortune's wheel and of the all but inevitable disaster of the man who proudly climbed to high place in the world never completely lost its hold on the imagination and the moral convictions of men of the Renaissance. From Boccaccio to Lydgate to the group of men who gathered around William Baldwin in the middle years of the century to write the *Mirror for Magistrates* down into the seventeenth century the formula flourished. The ghost of an eminent person presented himself to the poet, told the story of his fall from glory, and begged for remembrance and pity. The poet wrote down the story partly, he says, to fulfill his promise to the ghost and partly to allow the world to note the warning conveyed by the narrative: it is the highest trees that are struck by lightning; the greater the height the farther the fall; all flesh is grass; the end of human glory is misery; and the only safe and wise attitude toward the finest this world can offer is that of contempt.

The warning was not simply moral and religious; it was also political. These poems were history teaching by example. The very title of the *Mirror for Magistrates* indicates the intention. Princes and those in authority were to be held in check by observing the tragic fate of their predecessors and by avoiding the sins which, the ghosts testified, had been responsible for their downfall. Policy could be hinted broadly or even indicated directly and explicitly. And the readers of this kind of poem were by no means confined to magistrates and councilors of state. The ordinary man could read and be edified. The extraordinary popularity of the genre throughout the Elizabethan period and its significance have been elaborately demonstrated by Professor Lily B. Campbell and Professor Willard Farnham.[121] As Mr. Farnham shows, much

---

[121] See Lily B. Campbell's edition of the *Mirror* and of *Parts Added to the Mirror* (Cambridge, England, 1938, 1946); her article "Humphrey Duke of

of the emphasis and direction of the *Mirror* narratives was absorbed into Elizabethan drama.

What is left for the nondramatic verse of the end of the century; what is the connection between the *Mirror for Magistrates* complaints and the New Poetry? The answer is that a revival of the complaint form, with new emphasis and character, took place late in the century, and that the *Mirror* tradition has interesting connections with the pastoral convention, with the Petrarchan love tradition, and with Ovidian-mythological poetry.

Pastoral poetry glorifies the mean estate directly, by praise and celebration of a life that renounces ambition and is content with its own peace of mind. Some of the complaints of the *Mirror* tradition had a comparable function in that they showed the disasters consequent to vaulting ambition. The two types thus converge from opposite directions; the arrogant prince and the humble shepherd are both figures illustrating one of the great commonplaces which stored the Elizabethan mind.

In general tone the *Mirror* poems had something in common with Petrarchan sonnets, which often resolved themselves into small and systematic complaints on the subject of love. The assumed speaker and listener relationship in the ghost-complaint may well have had something to do with the transformation and exploitation of this relationship in the sonnet cycles. At any rate, the pioneer in the new kind of complaint poem, Samuel Daniel, draws a connection between his sonnets to Delia and his *Complaint of Rosamond*.

Because of the special nature of the new complaint poems, their concern with love and chastity, the Ovidian tradition had an opportunity to influence and color the complaint. This works in various degrees in Daniel, Drayton, and Edwards; the result is peculiarly revealing of the variety of traditions and symbols which influenced poetic creation in the

Gloucester and Elianor Cobham His Wife," *HLB,* no. 5 (1934) , pp. 119–155; and her lecture, *Tudor Conceptions of History and Tragedy in A Mirror for Magistrates* (Berkeley, Calif., 1936) ; Willard Farnham, *The Medieval Heritage of Elizabethan Tragedy* (Berkeley, Calif., 1936) .

nineties. So eclectic was the Elizabethan mind that it could find satisfaction in a piece which combined the stern and sober warnings of the old wheel of Fortune and the titillating, decorative, luscious matter from the Italianate Ovidian tradition. To a modern taste the result is at least odd, and we sometimes wonder what happened to the principle of decorum so emphasized by the Elizabethans in their formal criticism.

My survey is intended to provide a context for about a dozen poems, a number of which are frequently discussed without any realization of the genre to which they belong. These poems raise a problem about the treatment of character, whether individual and precise or general and symbolic; and some modern critics, confused about this problem because of their neglect of the context, wander off extravagantly into the search for topical significances, so that Shakespeare's *Lucrece* becomes a political tract or a satire on Sir Walter Ralegh. Of more profit than such speculations is the study of the process by which a literary form became democratized, and, for the reader interested in poems as works of art, the study of the development of baroque tendencies in feeling and imagery, especially in the complaint poems of Drayton and Middleton.

The vogue of the new complaint poem was started by Samuel Daniel with *The Complaint of Rosamond* in 1592. What *Hero and Leander* was for the Ovidian poem, *Rosamond* was for the complaint.

Daniel published his *Rosamond* as an appendage to his sonnet cycle *Delia*, which he issued in 1592 to compete with a piracy of the previous year. His motive may have been to escape from the limitations of the love sonnet and try something which gave him a chance for more heightened and decorated style, yet produce a graver labor suitable for dedication to the Countess of Pembroke. In any case, we know it was Spenser's opinion that in writing the complaint Daniel was following his best gift:

> Then rouze thy feathers quickly Daniell,
> And to what course thou please thy selfe aduance:

> But most me seemes, thy accent will excell,
> In Tragick plaints and passionate mischance.[122]

The tradition of "Tragick plaints and passionate mischance" was indeed a flourishing one, but its subject matter was almost entirely political. The exception to this general rule was the tragedy of Jane Shore, written in the time of King Edward VI by Thomas Churchyard and included in the 1563 edition of the *Mirror for Magistrates*. Jane Shore, the mistress of Edward IV, was still alive in Sir Thomas More's day, and he included an account of her in his history of Richard III. More's apology for including her in a treatise of high matters of state was repeated by the chronicler Halle, and the chief source book for the *Mirror* thus gave justification to her inclusion.[123] The story of her rise from the rank of citizen's wife to that of king's mistress and her subsequent downfall and misery under Richard III was extremely popular in the Tudor period for several reasons. As a victim of Richard III, she could of course be viewed as a martyr. She was in addition, of course, a kind of Cinderella. Her paramour, King Edward, was from the point of view of romantic lovers the most interesting of English kings; Sidney bears witness to this in the seventy-fifth sonnet of *Astrophel and Stella*.

Daniel saw in the woman's complaint, exemplified by Churchyard's poem, an opportunity to temper the grim atmosphere of the fall of princes with pathos, description of physical beauty, and even some Italianate mythological decoration. He found a subject in Fair Rosamond, the mistress of King Henry II; her story was being told in verse about the same time by William Warner in his *Albion's England*.[124] There had been earlier complaint poems in which the ghost was a woman, but she was "bad" because she had violated the

---

[122] *Colin Clouts Come Home Againe*, lines 416–427.

[123] See Campbell, *Tudor Conceptions of History and Tragedy*, p. 20.

[124] Priority between the two cannot be decided, according to the authoritative and interesting account of the whole Rosamond legend by V. B. Heltzel, *Fair Rosamond* (Evanston, Illinois, 1947). But the treatments seem independent of each other, and, as Professor Heltzel says (p. 15), Warner's poem is a "versified *novella*," not a complaint.

code of courtly love or had proved faithless. The tale of Lydia in the thirty-fourth canto of *Orlando Furioso* is an example: Astolfo encounters Lydia's ghost in a cave which is the mouth of hell and listens to her complaint or confession of her betrayal of her lover. The derivation of the form from Dante, and ultimately from· Virgil, is obvious.[125] But the English background of Fair Rosamond was more appealing; her tomb at Godstowe nunnery had been destroyed by a zealous bishop, and she now enjoyed no fame or compassion. Daniel makes her ghost draw specifically the comparison between herself and Jane Shore.[126] Daniel drew a connection also between this work and his sonnets to Delia; they are both laments, and since the poet's success in softening a mistress' heart depends upon a woman's grace, he should be sensitive to the complaint of a beautiful woman. Moreover, Delia herself may read the story and breathe a sigh of pity for fair Rosamond, thus justifying both the subject and the poet. This indication that the poem was written to appeal to a feminine taste is supported by some other elements in it: mild satire on cosmetics, on court life, and on scandal. But more than anything else, there is the softening and sweetening of the effects of the old warning against pride and other sins of princes.

Rosamond's downfall was caused, according to her account, by nature, youth, and beauty. This provides the opportunity to describe these qualities, and the tone of sympathetic wistfulness makes these descriptions the most attractive part of the poem.[127] Beauty is supreme, even over monarchs and

[125] A poem in fourteeners called "Hecubaes mishaps. Expressed by way of apparition, touching the manifolde miseries, wonderfull calamities, and lamentable chances that happened to her vnfortunate selfe, sometime Queene of stately Troy" is a kind of vision-complaint poem in which the complaining ghost is a woman. But the piece, which is by Thomas Fenne and appears at the end of his *Fennes frutes* (1590), is only a curiosity. It seems to be prompted by Fenne's zeal to persuade the English that they were really not descended from Brutus or any other Trojan.

[126] *The Complaint of Rosamond,* lines 25–28, in *Poems and A Defence of Ryme,* ed. A. C. Sprague (Cambridge: Harvard University Press, 1930).

[127] Lines 113–127.

conquerors, so there is little emphasis on moral fault in the story of Rosamond. She is in distress rather because of her obscurity, both when alive and kept secretly in the labyrinthine castle by her royal lover, and now after death, forgotten and unpitied.[128]

What corresponds to the sophistic speeches of wooing in the Ovidian poems is here provided by the arguments of a waiting woman who is employed to overcome Rosamond's chaste scruples. Her logic is evenly matched with the innocent girl's purity, but the decision is reached by force of something akin to nature.[129]

On the day before the consummation of the love affair, Rosamond is presented with a handsome casket, which bears pictures on the lid and sides of Ovidian love stories, the pursuit of Amymone by Neptune and of the transformation of Io. These could have served as warnings to her, she says, but they did not. The place they fill in the poem is clearly one of pictorial embellishment.

Daniel was very moderate in his use of rhetoric to heighten the dramatic character of the situation or the expression of heavy emotion. He included a speech of the king, who returns to Rosamond's bower only to meet her funeral procession on the way, but the speech is only seven stanzas long and is interrupted in the middle. In 1594 Daniel inserted in the poem twenty-three additional stanzas, very much heightening the episode of the poisoning of Rosamond and giving the heroine an opportunity for an impassioned complaint as she lies on the bed, and an apostrophe to women to profit by her example.[130]

The serious elegiac tone of the complaint and its "sweetness" of style find their culmination in the finest stanza of the poem, which shows also Daniel's pervading intention, the establishment of beauty and dignity in the world "to preserue

[128] Lines 512–518.

[129] Lines 362–364.

[130] Sprague ed., pp. 197–201. Bush, *Mythology and the Renaissance Tradition*, p. 152, n. 31, says that this addition seems to be inspired by Shakespeare's *Rape of Lucrece*. If so, Daniel was imitating his imitator.

them from those hidious Beastes, Obliuion, and Barbarisme":[131]

> Then when confusion in her course shall bring,
> Sad desolation on the times to come:
> When myrth-lesse Thames shall haue no Swan to sing,
> All Musique silent, and the Muses dombe.
> And yet euen then it must be known to some,
>   That once they florisht, though not cherisht so,
>   And Thames had Swannes as well as euer Po.[132]

Rosamond was an immediate and lasting success. It provided Shakespeare with a new model for his "graver labour" which he promised Southampton in the dedication to *Venus and Adonis,* and it inspired a host of imitations through the nineties and after. In 1595 Daniel seemed to William Covell to be the most distinguished poet of whom Oxford could boast, comparable with Spenser of Cambridge. "Oxford thou maist extoll thy courte-deare-verse happie Daniell," he says, "whose sweete refined muse, in contracted shape, were sufficient amongst men, to gaine pardon of the sinne to Rosemond, pittie to distressed Cleopatra, and euerlasting praise to her louing Delia." [133] It is in the margin opposite this remark that he lists two of Drayton's complaints, *Piers Gaveston* and *Matilda,* with Shakespeare's "Lucrecia" and "Wanton Adonis" as all praiseworthy.

The next year, 1593, saw the appearance of three complaint poems. Thomas Lodge, who had already utilized some of the features of the complaint in the beginning of his *Scillaes Metamorphosis* (1589), followed Daniel in appending a complaint poem to a series of sonnets. To his cycle *Phillis* he added the complaint of Elstred, written in his usual six-line stanza and derived largely from the tragedies of Humber, Locrinus, Elstride, and Sabrine included in John Higgins' continuation of the *Mirror for Magistrates* of 1574. Lodge did not perceive the novelty which Daniel had introduced into

---

[131] Dedication of *Delia* to the Countess of Pembroke (*Poems*, ed. Sprague, p. 9).

[132] *Rosamond*, lines 722–728.

[133] *Polimanteia*, sigs. R2ᵛ–R3ʳ.

the form, or, if he did, he did not approve of it. For *Elstred* is a mere exercise in the old *Mirror* style, with constant complaints about fortune, and a sentimental conclusion added.

A more interesting example is the poem called *Beawtie dishonoured written vnder the title of Shores Wife,* by Anthony Chute, entered on the Stationers' Register June 16 by John Wolfe. The poet, apparently a protégé of Gabriel Harvey, offers this as the "first invention of my beginning muse" [134] and speaks of it as "funerall verse." [135] It is considerably more sophisticated than Churchyard's treatment of the story. Chute has observed Daniel's contribution to the form, and he tries to make the story pathetic and wistful in its effect. This is done by continued emphasis upon the heroine's beauty; the various causes of her downfall are given as malicious rumor, marrying without love, and the stroke of Fortune upon those who attain high place, but pervading all this is a sense that beauty has been dishonored, as the title suggests, and that this is the essence of the tragedy.

Jane Shore compares herself with Penelope,[136] a comparison which is a matter of importance in some of the later complaint poems. She is so beautiful that Death itself is reluctant to take her; [137] her wantonness, it is argued, is the natural result of such incredible beauty and the effect it produces upon others. The poem therefore seems to have more relationship with the Ovidian genre than it has with the old *Mirror* tradition; Mrs. Shore is not, like Elstred and the women in the *Mirror,* the victim of Fortune, but merely an example of the tragic end of beauty. The poem is naturally grouped with Edwards' *Cephalus and Procris,* which John Wolfe entered only a few months after the entry of Chute's poem. According to Nashe, both poems were "Pamphlagonian things," and when they failed to achieve a wide popularity, Gabriel Harvey, who had persuaded Wolfe to publish them, raged at the stupidity of the reading public.[138]

[134] Sig. A2ʳ.
[135] Sig. A3ʳ.
[136] Sig. C2ʳ.
[137] Sigs. G3ʳ and A4ᵛ.
[138] *Works of Thomas Nashe,* ed. McKerrow, III, 89–90, 102.

Chute's virtues are a subtlety and delicacy in handling the awareness of beauty and the sense of guilt; his heroine is more complex than Rosamond and consequently more interesting as a character. The verse sounds like the verse of a beginner, but of a gifted one.[139] His use of figures and descriptions from nature vaguely resembles that of Shakespeare in *Venus and Adonis*.[140]

It is possible that these complaint poems were popular at the ballad level as early as 1593. The first two ballads in Deloney's *Garland of Good Will* (a collection now extant in no edition earlier than 1631, but entered in 1593 and certainly published by 1596, when it is referred to by Thomas Nashe) are on Rosamond and Jane Shore, and the third refers to Elstred.[141]

The new vogue of women as the speakers of tragic complaints attracted the attention of Giles Fletcher the Elder, who, in adding a complaint to his sonnet cycle *Licia* (also published in 1593?), chose Richard III and asserted that women were too light to be Fortune's tennis balls. He mentions Shore's wife, Rosamond, and Elstred specifically and says they do not move a tragic emotion:

Nor weepe I nowe, as children that have lost,
But smyle to see the Poets of this age:
Like silly boates in shallow rivers tost,
Loosing their paynes, and lacking still their wage.
    To write of women, and of womens falles,
    Who are too light, for to be fortunes balles.[142]

---

[139] He is capable of lines like "Then where from silver streamed Isis lying, Sylent in Swans: and quyet in her brookes" (sig. A4ᵛ), which remind one of Daniel.

[140] Sig. Gʳ.

[141] A warning against the assumption that seventeenth-century editions of a ballad collection are guides to earlier editions of that collection is given by Rollins in Shakespeare Variorum *Poems*, pp. 546–548. The Jane Shore ballad was in existence in 1603, however; see Rollins, *Analytical Index to the Ballad-Entries (1557–1709) in the Registers of the Company of Stationers of London* (Chapel Hill, N. C., 1924), No. 1452; and the Rosamond ballad was printed in another book of Deloney's in 1607 (see *Deloney's Works*, ed. F. O. Mann [Oxford, 1912], p. 563). The entry of 1593 which Mann (p. 565) thinks may refer to the Jane Shore ballad is actually to Chute's poem.

[142] *Licia*, sig. L2ᵛ.

Old Churchyard, whose complaint poem had first been published thirty years before, now reasserted his place with a revised version, published in his *Challenge* in 1593. He praises Daniel's *Rosamond* as "excellently sette forth" and says that he has refurbished his old poem "not in any kind of emulation, but to make the world knowe, my deuice in age is as ripe & reddie, as my disposition and knowledge was in youth." [143] His additions, however, plainly indicated in the 1593 edition by quotation marks, make a new emphasis which shows the influence of Daniel. He adds four stanzas of blazon of his heroine's beauties, four stanzas on the nature of love and harmony, three stanzas on the services she did the people, and nine stanzas on the theme that love is fleeting and the young should be warned. The whole effect of the grim spectacle of the *Mirror* poem has been softened into pathos and sentiment. Curiously enough, the influence of the Ovidian tradition has worked upon the *Mirror* type to produce an anti-erotic, didactic tract.[144]

In the autumn of 1593 Michael Drayton was busy writing a legend in the new fashion. It was on the subject of Piers Gaveston, a royal favorite whose character had been displayed in Marlowe's tragedy *Edward II*. Drayton's poem was entered on December 3, 1593, and published the next year. Its connection with the Ovidian-mythological tradition is very apparent. Drayton even uses, for an extended simile, the story of Salmacis and Hermaphroditus,[145] which as we have seen was central in the Ovidian tradition. The most important influences on Drayton's poem are those of Daniel, Shakespeare, and Marlowe. He borrows romantic elements from all of them,. and in the structure of his poem, as Mrs. Tillotson points out, he has learned from Daniel's *Rosamond*.[146] Drayton's mind is full of the color and richness of *Venus and*

---

[143] *Churchyards Challenge* (1593), sig. S4ᵛ.

[144] The influence of the *Mirror for Magistrates* in the nineties is discussed in Farnham, *Medieval Heritage of Elizabethan Tragedy*, chap. VIII; I have discussed the Jane Shore tradition and its influence upon the stage in "*A Woman Killed with Kindness*," *PMLA*, LIII (1938), 138–147.

[145] *Piers Gaveston*, lines 853–858 (*Works*, ed. Hebel, I, 182).

[146] *Works*, ed. Hebel, V, 23.

Adonis as he writes; three specific passages refer directly to Shakespeare's erotic legend, and one refers to Marlowe's *Hero and Leander*.[147] Gaveston's descriptions of the loves of himself and Edward, their revelry and luxury, constitute the main burden of the poem; the treatment of sin and of fortune is curiously ambiguous, since they are obviously part of the story but seem submerged by the enthusiasm of Gaveston's description of his Italianate pleasures with the king:

> In pleasures there we spend the nights and dayes,
> And with our revels entertaine the time,
> With costly Banquets, Masks, and stately Playes,
> Painting our loves in many a pleasing rime.
>> With rarest Musick, and sweet-tuned voyces,
>> (In which the soule of man so much rejoyces.) [148]

The condemnation of his course of life is unmistakable:

> Nothing there was could be discerned in me,
> But beastly lust, and censualitie.[149]

Yet the conclusion is not so much a warning against doing as Gaveston and Edward have done as it is a romantic appeal for them as the creatures of love.[150]

Drayton apparently realized the failure of his poem to give a coherent impression, for in the edition of 1596 he adds stanzas to it which considerably strengthen the moral element. For example, at the end of a passage in which Gaveston has compared himself and the king to Hero and Leander, to the Gemini, and to the traditional vine and elm, Drayton inserts in 1596 three stanzas on the conflict between love and reason.[151] Clearly what has happened is that in 1593 Drayton was too much under the influence of Shakespeare and Marlowe, with their luxurious glorification of the senses in mythological narrative, to assert his own more Platonic and serious

[147] See J. W. Hebel, "Drayton and Shakespeare," *MLN*, XLI (1926), 248–250.
[148] Lines 1147–1152.
[149] Lines 1229–1230.
[150] Lines 1699–1704.
[151] *Works*, ed. Hebel, V, 31.

attitude. As he recovered from the reading of *Venus and Adonis* (perhaps aided by *Lucrece*) Drayton became more himself. The claim made by Hebel that Drayton's poem contains the earliest known allusion to Shakespeare's work is dubious; but it is certain that *Piers Gaveston* shows more clearly than anything else the immense effect produced on the minds of the sensitive by Marlowe's and Shakespeare's handling of Ovidian material.

Another indication of the influence of *Venus and Adonis* is that these three complaint poems of 1593, though they owe much to *Rosamond,* are all written in the six-line stanza of Shakespeare's poem rather than the rhyme royal which Daniel had used. After the publication of *Lucrece,* in 1594, when Shakespeare adopted Daniel's verse form, the situation changed, and it might be said that the example of *Lucrece* still further strengthened the influence of Daniel's new method in the complaint.

In choosing the rhyme royal or Troilus stanza of seven lines rather than the six-line stanza of *Scillaes Metamorphosis* and *Venus and Adonis,* Daniel and Shakespeare were merely following the general rule, enunciated for example by King James of Scotland and by Gascoigne, that this stanza was to be used for tragic matters, complaints, and testaments. Shakespeare's choice of verse form is therefore not necessarily dependent upon Daniel. But a sufficient number of parallels in wording can be found to justify the conclusion that Shakespeare learned something from his predecessor. More interesting than the similarities between the two poems are the differences.

Shakespeare chose not to keep the form of the complaining ghost, possibly because his material, the story of Lucrece from Livy and Ovid, would not fit very neatly into the form. Lucrece could not claim to be neglected in fame; she was a standard example of fidelity and chastity. Besides this, the single point of view of the victim as narrator, the standard form of the complaint, was too narrow for the interests of a poet who was already revealing that his imagination worked most effectively in a dramatic rather than in a narrative medium.

Lucrece is chiefly remarkable for the heightening of the legend by a very full exploitation of the rhetorical and pictorial possibilities of the tale. Shakespeare makes the story the occasion for passionate outbursts upon Time, Night, Opportunity, less for the evocation of these abstractions in concrete form than for the production of resounding rhetoric. This display of rhetorical resources, although so old-fashioned and traditional that Chaucer, in the *Nun's Priest's Tale,* regrets that he cannot practice it more successfully, had enjoyed a new revival in the mouths of Elizabethan actors. The company which comes to Elsinore to play to Hamlet is a good example; they have in repertory a scene which exploits the tragic passions at the fall of Troy, just as the painting in Lucrece's house evokes these feelings.

So the tale is heightened to present these passions; from the first line through the melodramatic approach to the rape to the declamations [152] themselves the piece is organic. The purpose in the declamations is not to enlist sympathy for the weak and wronged woman, as in Daniel's poem; it is to make the reader participate in these execrations. The feelings are directed outward from the character toward circumstance, fate, evil impinging on her. The curse upon Tarquin is delivered with such ceremonial enthusiasm that it is impossible to have that superior feeling of pity for Lucrece; instead, one joins in the execration with a kind of joy:

> Disturbe his howres of rest with restlesse trances,
> Afflict him in his bed with bedred grones,
> Let there bechaunce him pitifull mischances,
> To make him mone, but pitie not his mones:
> Stone him with hardned hearts harder then stones,
>   And let milde women to him loose their mildnesse,
>   Wilder to him then Tygers in their wildnesse.
>
> Let him haue time to teare his curled haire,
> Let him haue time against himselfe to raue,
> Let him haue time of times helpe to dispaire,
> Let him haue time to liue a lothed slaue,

[152] *Lucrece,* lines 876–889 (Variorum *Poems,* ed. Rollins).

Let him haue time a beggers orts to craue,
  And time to see one that by almes doth liue,
  Disdaine to him disdained scraps to giue.[153]

But finally, of course, this rhetoric palls and there must be the renunciation of it; unpacking the heart with words, like a very drab, must be relieved by a reversal toward action:

This helplesse smoake of words doth me no right:
  The remedie indeede to do me good,
  Is to let forth my fowle defiled blood.[154]

Just as Daniel used the mythological pictures on the small casket to reflect Rosamond's fate and to connect her story with another world out of time, Shakespeare uses the painting of the fall of Troy for the reflection of Lucrece's feelings. It has often been pointed out that this serves something of a dramatic purpose, too, since some time must be allowed to pass while the messenger goes to Ardea and Rome and Lucrece's husband and father return. Lucrece discovers the model of herself in Hecuba, symbolically. Hecuba is "a face where all distresse is steld"; Lucrece "shapes her sorrow to the beldames woes"; and because the painter has failed to give Hecuba a voice, Lucrece will rail for her.[155] The fall of Troy and Hecuba's woes, like those of Lucrece, were caused by lust; [156] and the traitor Sinon, who brought ruin to Troy, corresponds to Tarquin.

Though Shakespeare did not use the device of the ghost for his complaint, he thus found occasion for elaborate rhetorical performance. His problem was to universalize the passions implicit in the situation, not to particularize the individual character. And for that purpose he found most useful the declamation which Marlowe and Kyd had popularized upon the stage. The gentleness and sweetness of Daniel were not strong enough for him.

The imagery and the profusion of conceits are the consequence of this general purpose of the poem. Criteria of propriety cannot here be made from a narrative or descriptive

[153] Lines 974–987.
[154] Lines 1028–1029.
[155] Lines 1444; 1458; 1464–1470.
[156] Lines 1471–1477.

point of view; the function of the images is to maintain a tone from which the apostrophes can be launched. Therefore the modern reader must beware of imitating Polonius, who stops to praise the figure of the "mobled Queen" without seeing that it, the "threatening the flames with bisson rheum," and the "lank-o'er-teemed loins" are all devices for sustaining the level that was to move the actor to tears and Hamlet to wonder.[157]

The quality of *Lucrece* which enabled it to "please the wiser sort," as Gabriel Harvey noted, was presumably not its dramatic and rhetorical energy, though those characteristics might easily have led to the coupling of the poem with *Hamlet* in Harvey's mind. *Lucrece* is a graver labor because it celebrates chastity. Shakespeare is not interested in the philosophical and psychological nature of chastity, as Spenser was in the third book of *The Faerie Queene;* it is not an ideal which he celebrates as the clearest and finest manifestation of moderation. There is no temptation, no testing of Lucrece, except in the matter of honest fame; her good name and her husband's honor must be preserved, and her decision is a heroically simple one. The poem is an expansion of a simple situation in which a readily recognized and accepted ideal is outraged. The artistic qualities of the poem depend upon the contrast between guilt and innocence, and the dramatic and rhetorical means by which the contrast is emphasized. The old complaint had constantly behind it the moral imperative of shunning ambition, high place, and the vagaries of fortune in this world. The new complaint, as introduced by Daniel, substituted gentleness, sweetness, and pathos for this stern and grisly background. Shakespeare's contribution to the new mode was to show how ideals treated seriously could still provide a texture of considerable intensity for the complaint poem and could give it a vigor which the parade

---

[157] The discussion in Bush, *Mythology and the Renaissance Tradition*, pp. 149–155, quite rightly calls the poem one of the complaints and makes useful suggestions about sources, but in its discussion of the images it fails to make due allowance for the purpose and nature of the poem. Esther C. Dunn has a useful discussion of the dramatic structure of *Lucrece* in her *The Literature of Shakespeare's England* (New York, 1936), pp. 53–64.

of ghosts in the *Mirror for Magistrates* could no longer show.
The selection of chastity as the ideal no doubt owed much
to Spenser's celebration of it in his third book. The theme
was there elevated to one of the great moral virtues on a
heroic scale, implicit in a life of action, motivating knightly
conquests and presiding over a romantic world like a creative spirit. No poet writing in 1594 could fail to be influenced by the achievement of Spenser's publication four years
earlier. Nor could anyone fail to see the patriotic implications of any celebration of chastity, since the theme was like
a signpost pointing to the English throne. A new gravity,
therefore, was possible, and the practitioners of the complaint
form after 1594 show that the opportunities offered by this
"hybrid" were very popular.[158]

Michael Drayton exemplifies the force of this popularity
in his second legend, *Matilda. The faire and chaste Daughter
of the Lord Robert Fitzwater,* in 1594. The poem differs from
Piers Gaveston, written the year before, in that it uses the
rhyme royal of *Lucrece* rather than the six-line stanza of
Venus and Adonis, that it is more grave and moral, and that
it celebrates a heroine of chastity. Matilda appears as a ghost,
and she begs for rescue from oblivion by the poet, as the old
Mirror ghosts did, but she compares herself to Rosamond,
Shore's wife, and Elstred, maintaining that because she was
chaste she has better right to be remembered. She considers
that she is the equal of Lucrece.[159] In an argument to the
poem, prefixed to the 1596 edition, she is called "a second
Lucretia." [160]

---

[158] The discussion of the poem by E. P. Kuhl, "Shakespeare's *Rape of
Lucrece*," *PQ,* XX (1941), 352-360, tries to make of it something like a political tract. I sympathize with Professor Kuhl's attempt to account for the poem's
popularity, and I agree that it has serious and patriotic implications, but I
feel that a good deal of his searching after topical significances would have
been rendered unnecessary if he had placed the poem in its genre. Daniel's
Rosamond was also very popular.

[159] *Matilda,* lines 36-42; the reference to the stage is probably metaphorical,
as Mrs. Tillotson suggests (Drayton, *Works,* ed. Hebel, V, 33). See a similar
use of the stage as an imaginary setting in Middleton's *Ghost of Lucrece*
(1600), ed. J. Q. Adams (New York, 1937), sig. B2ᵛ.

[160] *Works,* ed. Hebel, V, 35.

Drayton invokes Queen Elizabeth as a source of inspiration in addition to the Muses, and the precedent or example of Spenser is cited.[161] Daniel's influence is still strong; in the vein of Rosamond, Matilda gives an elaborate catalogue of her own beauties. Its imagery and repletion of detail are extraordinary.[162] The theme of the poem is not, as in Shakespeare, the helplessness of chastity against night, opportunity, and smoking lust; it is rather the overwhelming power of love and beauty.[163] Matilda, like Rosamond, hangs precariously in the balance between the seductive appeals of the king and her own chastity, but unlike Rosamond she is saved by grace. And the actual decision is given in legal figures which remind the reader immediately of the conceits of the sonneteers.[164] The king is no villain of melodrama; he comes to her like Jove, in many shapes; when he is met with refusal, he thinks of doing away with her by knife or poison to rid himself of his lover's malady, but he again tries to woo her:

> But first, with lines hee bravely sitteth on,
> Words steep'd in syrop of Ambrosia,
> Sweet method, savored with invention,
> What can be said that Lovers cannot say?
> Desire can make a Doctor in a day.
>> Each sentence seem'd a sweet inchaunting charme,
>> A trumpet sounding gentle Loves alarme.[165]

As Mrs. Tillotson has well said, "It is as a love poem, not as a drama nor as a 'mirror' of chastity, that *Matilda* strikes us; John is no ravisher but a wooer as plaintive as any sonneteer, and his 'words steep'd in syrop of Ambrosia' are those of *Ideas Mirrour*." [166] In the circumstances, it is not inappropriate to the nature of the poem that when the king causes her to poison herself, she dies with a prayer for him, and after her death the king amply repents.

Almost immediately after the publication of Drayton's

---

161 Lines 61–63.
162 Lines 113–127.
163 Lines 183–189.

164 Lines 442–455.
165 Lines 694–700.
166 Drayton, *Works,* ed. Hebel, V, 32.

poem, Richard Barnfield, perhaps the most incurably imitative of all the imitative Elizabethans, dashed off a short poem
on Matilda called "The Complaint of Chastitie" and published it in *The Affectionate Shepheard* in November 1594.
Barnfield announces in his subtitle that "the Storie is at large
written by Michael Drayton." [167] He does see that the one
opportunity which Drayton left him was to make invective,
so four out of his ten stanzas are declamatory denunciations
of lust. In his volume of the next year, *Cynthia,* Barnfield
tried a longer complaint poem, in the six-line stanza, called
"Cassandra." The poem is without any distinction, but the
heroine reflects the current fashion. She is both the victim
of Fortune and a warning to girls.[168]

Another work of 1594 which is related to the general type
of the complaint of the chaste woman is the notorious *Willobie His Avisa,* which contains the earliest known reference
to Shakespeare's *Lucrece.* The poem has been the happy
hunting ground of those who read Elizabethan literature
chiefly to find mysteries and "topical significances" in it.
Viewed from the perspective of a survey of the complaint of
chastity type, *Avisa* is of considerable interest, and the problems of identification which have exercised the Shakespeare
biographers and the sleuths of the so-called "School of Night"
seem rather insignificant.[169]

---

[167] *Poems,* ed. M. Summers (London, 1936), p. 36:

[168] *Ibid.,* p. 84.

[169] There may be topical significances in *Avisa,* for all I know, but the
attempts to find them have so far been unconvincing. Henry Willobie was a
real person and the author of the poem; Leslie Hotson in *I, William Shakespeare* (London, 1937), has uncovered some details of his background. The
"Hadrian Dorrell" who was allegedly responsible for publication has eluded
search and may be a fiction of the author's. The most recent, and best, discussion of the topical problems is in Tucker Brooke, 'Willobie's *Avisa,"
Essays in Honor of Albert Feuillerat,* Yale Romantic Studies, XXII (New
Haven, 1943). The edition by G. B. Harrison (Bodley Head Quartos XV;
London, 1926), tries to make very elaborate connections of the poem with
events in the life of Sir Walter Ralegh. Harrison (p. 230) carries this idea so
far that he asks us to believe that Elizabethan readers saw a portrait of Ralegh
in Shakespeare's Tarquin! A useful survey of the commentary on *Avisa,* especially with respect to supposed connections with Shakespeare, is provided
by Marie Louise Edel in the Variorum edition of Shakespeare's *Sonnets,* ed.
H. E. Rollins, 2 vols. (Philadelphia, 1944), II, 295-313.

Willobie's poem is the celebration of an English counterpart of Lucretia. This is made evident by the commendatory
poem, "In praise of Willobie his Auisa, Hexameton to the
Author":

> In Lauine Land though Liuie bost,
> There hath beene seene a Constant dame:
> Though Rome lament that she haue lost
> The Gareland of her rarest fame,
>   Yet now we see, that here is found,
>   As great a Faith in English ground.

> Though Collatine haue deerely bought,
> To high renowne, a lasting life,
> And found, that most in vaine haue sought,
> To haue a Faire, and Constant wife,
>   Yet Tarquyne pluckt his glistering grape,
>   And Shake-speare, paints poore Lucrece rape.[170]

The standard types of chastity were Susanna and Penelope;
they were all right in their way, but they were not English.
Besides, this lowly English woman, daughter of a town mayor

---

[170] Harrison ed., p. 19. The equality of chastity and heroic deeds is a commonplace, and Penelope is most frequently cited, as in Harington's *Orlando
Furioso* (1591), XII, 52:

> Penelope is spending chaste her dayes,
> As worthy as Vlysses was of praise.

Penelope's eminence as a heroine of chastity in the Renaissance owed something to Petrarch's *Trionfo della Castita*. In one of the dialogues of John
Florio's *Second Frutes* (1591; sigs. Cc^r–Cc2^r), a character says, "So as we may
say in honour of beauty, as Petrarke wrote in the triumph of chastitie,

> The chastest there of all, the fayrest was of all,
> And onely for in worke she spent her dayes,
> Penelopes renoune doth match Vlisses prayse."

Some of the Susanna and Penelope poems became popular as songs; Orlando
di Lasso and Ferrabosco wrote Italian madrigals on Susanna, and English
words were given for them in Nicholas Yonge's *Musica Transalpina*, first set
(1588), Nos. 19 and 20. Modified versions of these words were set by William
Byrd twice, 1588 and 1599, and by Giles Farnaby in 1598. In each of his two
mentioned volumes Byrd also included a madrigal on Penelope, and he left
another in manuscript (E. H. Fellowes, *William Byrd* [Oxford, 1936], p. 165).
John Mundy in 1594 published another setting for the words of Byrd's 1588
madrigal.

and wife of an innkeeper, surpasses them.[171] Avisa's first temptation comes from a nobleman, and she recognizes that she is proving superior to her compatriots, Rosamond and Jane Shore, when she does not succumb to the blandishments of high station.[172] The emphasis throughout is on the triumphant defensive chastity of an innkeeper's wife. She is a country girl and thinks of London as a sink of sin.[173] The reason for making her an innkeeper's wife is the obvious one that she would thus be open to frequent solicitation, and the reason for the details of the background, which seem so concrete that commentators have supposed the tale to be fact not fiction, may well be simply to bring home the lesson of Avisa's example by convincing realism. She emphasizes that she is a busy housewife and has no time for foolish wantonness.[174]

Her attempted seducers represent various ranks and nationalities as well as temperaments; she contrasts with them as good native English yeoman or citizen stock. The nobleman; the "cavaliero"; "D. B. A. French man"; Dydimus Harconius, the stolid Anglo-German; and the Italianate author himself, with his name transformed to Henrico Willobego —all meet with the same firm refusal, though like her descendant, Pamela, Avisa seems to enjoy defending her virtue. Her motivating ideals are a Christian decency, an English patriotism, and solid loyalty to her own bourgeois class. The climax of the tale is the suit of Henrico Willobego, who tries on Avisa all the techniques of the young university graduate who is Italianate in his tastes and can practice the modern sonneteering vogue. He finally showers her with a collection of amatory epistles which are intended, as a prose introduction says, to represent "the vnrewly rage of vnbrydeled fancy, hauing the raines to roue at liberty, with the dyuers & sundry changes of affections & temptations, which Will, set loose from Reason, can deuise, &c."[175]

The poem illustrates the process of democratization of the

[171] Harrison ed., p. 22. [174] *Ibid.*, p. 127.
[172] *Ibid.*, p. 34. [175] *Ibid.*, p. 117.
[173] *Ibid.*, p. 83.

complaint form.[176] Just as the Jane Shore story led to the development of the Elizabethan bourgeois tragedy and its masterpiece, Heywood's *A Woman Killed with Kindness*,[177] the example of Roman Lucrece led to the creation of a realistic English paragon of chastity, Avisa, who will undertake to surpass Lucrece, or Susanna, or Penelope, or any champion whatsoever.[178] The case is not unlike that of the popular biography, drama, and fiction of the time: Heywood's *Four Prentices of London* (c. 1592) and Richard Johnson's *The Nine Worthies of London* (1592) are comparable examples. The stage and the press worked together for the purpose of illustrating both vice and virtue by the examples of women. Thus Heywood says, in his *Apology for Actors*, "Women likewise that are chaste are by us extolled and encouraged in their virtues, being instanced by Diana, Belphoebe, Matilda, Lucrece, and the Countess of Salisbury. The unchaste are by us shown their errors in the persons of Phryne, Lais, Thais, Flora, and among us Rosamund and Mistress Shore." [179] This democratic propaganda could perhaps be illustrated most fully from the ballads, but one example must suffice. In a pair of broadside ballads first registered on March 1, 1600, we have the wooing of a London maid by King Edward and her reply to him.[180] The maid's answer cites Rosamond, and her arguments are substantially the same as those of Willobie's *Avisa*.

In 1596 the challenge to the classical heroines of chastity

[176] The account of *Willobie His Avisa* in Louis B. Wright, *Middle-Class Culture in Elizabethan England* (Chapel Hill, 1935), pp. 476–478, rightly emphasizes the bourgeois intention and appeal of the work. Wright's plausible suggestion that the reason for the calling in of the book in 1599 may have been that it cast disparagement on the aristocracy deserves more attention than it has received from those who are bent on discovering topical satire in *Avisa*.

[177] See *PMLA*, LIII (1938), 138–147.

[178] According to "Hadrian Dorrell," Willobie also wrote a poem about Susanna which remained in his desk and was unpublished in 1596 (Harrison ed., p. 239).

[179] A. H. Gilbert, *Literary Criticism from Plato to Dryden* (New York, 1940), pp. 562–563.

[180] Rollins, *Analytical Index*, Nos. 823 and 827; *Roxburghe Ballads*, ed. William Chappell, I (Hertford, England, 1871), 181–185.

was taken up by one Peter Colse, who published *Penelopes Complaint: or, A Mirrour for wanton Minions.* He says in his dedication that "an vnknowne Author, hath of late published a pamphlet called Auisa (ouerslipping so many praise-worthy matrons) hath registred the meanest," and in his address to the readers he says his style is modeled on that of his overpatriotic and class-conscious predecessor.[181] A friend of the author, one S. D., contributed a Latin poem which draws an elaborate contrast between the obscurity and mean estate of Avisa and the fame and eminence of Penelope.[182] The complaint of Penelope itself is of no particular interest, aside from the attempt of the author to utilize her as a model of chastity. Penelope utters an execration against Helen and all such light women; she edifies her maids with a discourse on the perils of hot affection; and she points to herself as a symbol of virtue.[183]

The appearance of *Penelope's Complaint* caused a curious reaction on the part of the author of *Avisa* and his friends. In the editions published after 1596 appears an "Apologie, shewing the true meaning of Willobie his Avisa," signed Hadrian Dorrell and dated from Oxford, June 30, 1596. It is this document which has excited the imaginations of the critics who search for topical significance. Dorrell claims that some have applied this poem as they ought not, and he specifically accuses P. C. of suggesting that Avisa was one particular, actual woman. Now Peter Colse had made no such assertion; he had merely objected to Avisa on the ground of her class. Dorrell seems to misunderstand this, since he nowhere defends the proposition, not impossible to defend, that an inn-keeper's wife may be as chaste as a queen. Dorrell spends all

---

[181] Sig. A4ᵛ.

[182] Brooke ("Willobie's *Avisa*," p. 100) selects from this poem and translates one line in such a way as to force the conclusion that Penelope is actually Lady Horsey. But if this is to be applied to the rest of S. D.'s poem, then Lady Horsey must have been separated from her husband for a long time, repelled a hundred suitors, been celebrated by the Greeks and Romans, and so forth. Besides, if, as he thinks, the Cavaliero of Willobie's poem is Sir Ralph Horsey, the Lord Lieutenant of Dorsetshire, it was rather Sir Ralph than his lady who needed defense by Peter Colse.

[183] Sig. E2ʳ.

his effort to show that Avisa is merely an abstraction—that she represents chastity, not any individual: "He saith: the Author hath registred the meanest. I thought that Chastitie had not beene the meanest, but rather one of the greatest gifts, that God giueth to men to women." [184]

This confusion between a character as an individual and as an abstraction served a purpose for the Elizabethan mind. It enabled the theorist to accept the Aristotelian theory of imitation, for it explained how an artist could "imitate" a character he had never seen, and it satisfied his demand for moral utility. Sidney, for example, compares "right poets" to those more excellent painters, "who having no law but wit, bestow that in cullours upon you which is fittest for the eye to see: as the constant though lamenting looke of Lucrecia, when she punished in herself an others fault. Wherein he painted not Lucrecia, whom he never sawe, but painteth the outwarde beauty of such a vertue." [185] This entanglement of the virtue and its circumstances confused even some Elizabethans, like Peter Colse, and it is responsible for much modern wrongheaded searching after topical references. It is true that Dorrell gives a different explanation, or rather, explanations, of the name Avisa from the one he gave in the preface to the first edition, but it must be remembered that in etymological matters the Elizabethan habit was to give as many alternative explanations as possible, and to accept them all. (See, for example, their explanations of the derivation of the word *satire*.)

Also added to the later editions of *Avisa* is a poem signed "Thomas Willoby Frater Henrici Willoby nuper defuncti," repeating the emphasis upon the purpose of the original work as a defense of *English* chastity. The object is, he says,

> To proue him vaine, that vainely striues,
> That Chastity is no where found,
> In English earth, in British wiues,
> That all are fickle, all vnsound,

[184] Harrison ed., p. 239.
[185] *An Apologie for Poetrie*, ed. E. S. Shuckburgh (Cambridge, England, 1891), p. 11.

We framed a wench, we fain'd a name,
    That should confound them all with shame.[186]

The popularity of the complaint, after Rosamond and
Lucrece had graced it, is exhibited in a curious production,
evidently the work of a boy, which appeared in 1595. It is
Raptus I Helenae. The First Rape of Faire Hellen, by John
Trussel. Using the material of Colluthus, the fledgling poet
makes Helen a complaining ghost who tells of her rape by
Theseus. There are some verbal reminiscences of Lucrece,
and some of Rosamond as well. Helen curses the night, as
Lucrece does, and she blames her beauty and her youth in
the manner of Rosamond. The tone in general is one of
pathos, but a happy ending is provided when the proposal
arrives from Menelaus for a marriage which will shield her
from disgrace. Nevertheless, at the end she refers to her later
elopement with Paris and says she is being punished for her
sins.[187]

Another curiosity among the complaint poems is the *Narcissus* which Thomas Edwards appended to his *Cephalus and
Procris* and published in 1595.[188] Edwards uses the seven-line
stanza for this poem, and in the first stanza he may be glancing
at the other recent exercises in the style.[189] The curious thing
about this complaint is of course that it utilizes the Ovidian

[186] Harrison ed., p. 249. Hotson found evidence that Henry Willobie did
not die in 1596 but was alive in August 1597 (*I, William Shakespeare,* p. 69).
A way out of this apparent difficulty, and a correction of Hotson's errors about
the editions of *Avisa,* may be found in Brooke, "Willobie's *Avisa,*" p. 102.

[187] Sig. E3ᵛ. This poem, like Heywood's *Oenone and Paris,* has had rather
extravagant publicity as an imitation of Shakespeare. It is no more so than
all the other complaint poems after 1594. The conclusion that the "sonnet"
prefixed to the poem and signed I. T. is addressed to Shakespeare seems to
me highly dubious. Apparently young Trussel's chief patron was a certain
S. I., who contributed a commendatory poem and who collected the other
commendatory poems in order to encourage the youth to publish. I have not
seen the Rosenbach copy, described in the *New York Times* for June 22, 1931;
I have used a photostat of the copy in Marsh's Library, Dublin, which lacks
signature B. The missing portion could not have included more than forty
stanzas; 114 stanzas remain.

[188] *Cephalus and Procris* was in existence in 1593, for it was entered on the
Stationers' Register then. *Narcissus* is not mentioned in the entry, and it
seems to me likely that it was composed after the appearance of *Lucrece.*

[189] Buckley ed., p. 37.

subject matter of a somewhat different kind of poem. The method is rhetorical, but the subject of Narcissus' complaints and execrations must necessarily be his own beauty and indifference to love. Instead of the Ovidian flower, he is now a ghost, and he inveighs against his beauty and his fortune like any of the distressed women of the current fashion.[190]

The account of the complaint poem in the Elizabethan period may be brought to a close by some notice of Thomas Middleton's imitation of Shakespeare, *The Ghost of Lucrece,* a poem published in 1600 but apparently written a few years earlier.[191] Middleton's opportunity to use the material Shakespeare had already used arose from the fact that Shakespeare's *Lucrece* is not a complaint poem in the strictest sense but a narrative. Middleton presents the heroine as a ghost; her complaint is theatrical, and the imagery is very extravagant:

> Thou art my nurse-child, Tarquin: thou art he,
> In steede of milke, sucke bloud, and teares, and all,
> In liew of teats: Lucrece, thy nurse, euen she,
> By tragicke art seene through a Christall wall,
> Hath carued with her knife thy festiuall:
> Here's bloud for milke, sucke till thy veines run ouer,
> And such a teat, which scarce thy mouth can couer.[192]

Shakespeare in one line makes Lucrece a dove which is captured by the night owl; Middleton develops this into six stanzas, each beginning "Tarquin the Night-owl." Freed from the requirements of narrative, Middleton makes his complaint narrowly operatic and stilted. Frequent use of images from the theater reminds us that this is the work of a beginning playwright, and a few stanzas [193] show that this is the same writer whose *Micro-Cynicon Six Snarling Satyres* appeared in 1599 as part of the revival of satire led by Hall and Marston.

---

[190] *Ibid.,* p. 45.

[191] See J. Q. Adams' edition, pp. xix–xxiii, for evidence of date of composition.

[192] Sig. A6ᵛ.

[193] Sig. B6ᵛ. Adams calls attention to the relationship between this poem and Middleton's satires.

III

The influence of Ovid and the material of the old *Mirror for Magistrates* tradition combined in another way to produce a very popular form, the Elizabethan "heroical epistle." Here the model was not so much the *Metamorphoses,* although that continued to provide mythological decoration, as it was the *Heroides.* And in this form one poet became so preeminent that he had virtually a monopoly on the field. Drayton's *Englands Heroicall Epistles* (1597, 1598, and 1599) have been well characterized and analyzed by Mrs. Tillotson in the introduction and notes to the Hebel edition. The interesting thing about this kind of poem is that it derives its material, in part, from the *Mirror* tragedies, but not, like the legends or complaints, its form. The epistolary device is a development from Ovid; the letters appear in pairs, and the dramatic and psychological situation is exploited. It is also significant that the characters from English history, chosen from the chronicles or the *Mirror,* are always lovers.

The invention of the English form may be credited to Drayton, for, as has been pointed out,[194] he has no predecessors closer than *Willobie His Avisa* and Peter Colse's *Penelope's Complaint.* The reasons for its success and popularity are not difficult to see. Because of its comparative brevity, the epistle had a concentration which the narrative legend lacked; this brevity encouraged emphasis on the dramatic aspects of the situation; and the subject matter—historical characters at a specially significant moment of their relationship to each other—was suited to the taste of the public which applauded history plays in the theater and bought the versified chronicles of Daniel, which began to appear in 1595, for reading at home. Mrs. Tillotson reminds us that models of letter writing became more popular in the period, and these epistles of Drayton could be considered models. Moreover, the combination of amorous and patriotic interest in these poems worked so as to strengthen both elements: the lovers were more concrete and credible than the lovers in a sonnet cycle,

[194] *Works,* ed. Hebel, V, 97, n. 1.

and the historical material was dramatized by the epistolary device. Drayton took the historical background seriously, appending notes to each epistle explaining or elaborating the facts from the chronicles. None the less, he was careful to make his characters expert in the pleadings of love. Edward the Black Prince, for example, reveals himself as a philosopher of beauty.[195] Fortified realistically and historically by references to places, times, and other known historical characters, as well as by Drayton's notes explaining the chronicle material, the characters are nevertheless related to figures of myth and legend. Mary, Queen of France and sister to Henry VIII, associates herself and her lover, Charles Brandon, Duke of Suffolk, with Hero and Leander, urging him to swim the English Channel as Leander swam the Hellespont.[196] Queen Margaret, more extravagant still, says that William de la Pole is a divine lover

> Whose Angell-eye, by pow'rfull influence,
> Doth utter more then humane Eloquence:
> That if againe Jove would his Sports have try'd,
> He in thy shape himselfe would onely hide.[197]

And Owen Tudor, the founder of Queen Elizabeth's house, is a specialist in love:

> All Men to some one qualitie incline,
> Onely to Love is naturally mine.[198]

The relationship of these poems to the legends or complaints is easy to trace. The first two pairs whose epistles appear are Rosamond–King Henry and Matilda–King John; the third pair, Isabel and Mortimer, form part of the background of the Piers Gaveston story; and there is a pair of epistles between King Edward IV and Jane Shore. In the first epistle, Rosamond is contrasted with Lucrece by means of a gallery picture of the Roman martyr which she has to explain to her woman. Matilda, in turn, writing to King John,

---

195 *Englands Heroicall Epistles*, lines 45–56 (*Works*, ed. Hebel, II, 176).
196 Lines 15–18 (*Works*, II, 261).
197 Lines 43–48 (*Works*, II, 240).
198 Lines 157–158 (*Works*, II, 212).

says that Rosamond would have averted her tragedy had she
gone to a nunnery instead of staying in the labyrinth. Alice,
Countess of Salisbury, writing to Edward the Black Prince,
says that Rosamond and Matilda are the two examples for
women.[199]

Drayton has chosen pairs which give him great opportunity
for variety of character and situation. In almost every case
one of the lovers is a king or queen; the only pair that have
no connection with a crown are Surrey and Geraldine, a pair
whom Drayton chose because he liked the emphasis on the
poet as hero. The situations vary from simple absence to
separation because of imprisonment. In every instance there
is some dramatic revelation of the importance of the moment
at which the epistle is being written. As Mrs. Tillotson has
remarked, the expository problem is deftly handled; Drayton
is skillful at reconciling the requirements of the recipient of
the letter and of the reader of the poem. Most important of
all the qualities of the epistles is their success in delineating
character. Free from the most hampering characteristics of
narrative, less formal and stilted than the ghost's complaint,
the verse letter can sketch in traits of character almost as
swiftly as dialogue can.

Drayton used for these epistles a rhymed couplet which
seems developed from Marlowe but carried further, probably
under the influence of the Latin elegiac distich. His verse is
capable of epigram, of sententiousness, of rapid narrative,
and of consecutive and logical reasoning. Yet it remains lyrical
in nature; "the thoughts of the letter-writers seem to range,
but only to circle back to their obsessing emotion."[200] The
control of the form, it has been suggested, was good for Drayton and curbed his excesses so that these of all his poems
required the least revision when he republished them.[201] They
look ahead to the style of the seventeenth century and beyond. The Elizabethan decoration is still there, but it is in
place.

[199] Lines 49–58 (*Works*, II, 183).
[200] Mrs. Tillotson in *Works*, V, 99.
[201] *Ibid.*

Even in using details which were almost worn out, Drayton could achieve a kind of freshness by the formality of the couplet, the colloquialism of the diction, and the approach to a "metaphysical" quality in the conceit. King John is forced to use very familiar arguments against chastity in his letter to Matilda, but he produces the following epigram on the phoenix:

> Th'Arabian Bird, that never is but one,
> Is onely chaste, because she is alone:
> But had our Mother Nature made them Two,
> They would have done as Doves and Sparrowes doe;
> And therefore made a Martyr in desire,
> To doe her Penance lastly in the Fire:
> So may they all be rosted quicke, that bee
> Apostata's to Nature, as is shee.[202]

Drayton's epistles were the most popular of his poems, and he came to be called the English Ovid. This probably reflects a patriotic feeling which was in accordance with the poet's intention. He had provided heroic lovers for England, out of her own history and in her own tongue, which were a match for those ancient and legendary lovers whom Ovid had immortalized. His success is also an illustration of how in the 1590's various traditions, forms, and subject matter could intermingle to produce something new.[203]

---

[202] Lines 149–156 (*Works*, II, 151).

[203] Mrs. Tillotson cites some imitators of Drayton (*Works*, V, 97, n. 1), but none is very close to him, and none does what he distinctly did—apply the Ovidian epistolary form to English historical material.

III

THE SONNETS

Modes of the Search for Vitality

WHAT is the trait in Elizabethan poetry which more than any other marks it as Elizabethan? Most readers would probably agree from their experience that there is such a trait. One of Sir John Squire's parodies, if I remember correctly, is a poem which is supposed to be the work of "Almost Any Elizabethan" and begins "Aske me not for the semblance of my loue." J. W. Mackail, in discussing Chaucer, tells of encountering a puzzling passage in *Troilus and Criseyde:* "So strange is the accent, that one's first instinct is to think that Chaucer is at his favourite game of parody, as he parodies the contemporary lyric in Absolon's song in the Miller's Tale. But the note of the stanzas is Elizabethan; and whatever Chaucer's genius as a poet, he could hardly parody the style which English poetry was to adopt a hundred and fifty years later." [1]

The explanation is quite simple, as Mackail points out. What seems Elizabethan to us is the method and manner of Petrarch. Chaucer was translating one of Petrarch's sonnets to make a song for Troilus.

The story of the influence of Petrarch on English verse at the end of the sixteenth century is not something to tell statistically, or wholly chronologically, or mechanically as a matter of identification and tabulation of sources. It is a

---

[1] *The Springs of Helicon* (New York, 1909), pp. 15–16.

story of experiment and reaction, of refinement and excess and corrective discipline. The account must be critical and illustrative in order to show just how some of the strains of Petrarch became so prominent in the poetry of the period that they now represent for us the Elizabethan manner.

The following discussion begins with Thomas Watson as the pioneer experimenter and deals with the elements of variety and passion he tried to introduce by his importations from Petrarch. These elements, sorely needed by English poetry about 1580, indeed liberated poetic expression from some of the shackles in which it had been languishing, but they also opened new possibilities of eccentricity, extravagance, and artistic irresponsibility. Once we have observed that the object of these experiments was to promote variety, the analysis of moods, and metaphoric inventiveness, we can trace contributions by later and better poets than Watson, contributions which of course vary with the personality and gifts of the poet and with the particular stage in the development at which they were made.

Sidney, seeing the great possibilities in Petrarchan sonnets but fearful of their excesses in the hands of Englishmen childishly delighted by new variety or heedless of form, decorum, and probability, devised a dramatic method in the sonnet cycle which imposed a principle of selection on the details. Samuel Daniel, modest, serious, and tender, opposed the excesses of wit, ingenuity, and gaudy diction possible in the love sonnet by making Petrarchan models in a quiet, reserved style. Michael Drayton, on the contrary, accepted the role of chameleon, reveled in the Elizabethan love of novelty and variety, only to repent as time went on, revise his sonnets, and finally learn from Sidney's example how to control and direct his Elizabethan exuberance.

Spenser, for whom the problem was less acute, seeing that he had already solved so many of his own artistic problems in *The Shepheardes Calender* and part of *The Faerie Queene*, utilized an emblematic method he had learned long before, strengthened the role of the lady in the cycle, and succeeded in finding a particular tone to suit his individual conception of feminine beauty and virtue. Shakespeare, seizing upon the sonnet fashion perhaps because it gave him more immediate opportunities than the drama, developed out of the variety, emotional analysis, and passion of the Petrarchan mode a more serious and profound use of metaphor. In his achievement lies the most curious and the most valuable answer to the Elizabethan problem in this exotic form: how to record experience and the analysis of it simultaneously; how to achieve a combination of probability and strangeness; how to make the sonnet cycle seem to reflect actual life instead of the stiff and outworn situation of the distant lady and the despondent wooer, but to reflect life not so much in its external conditions as in its inward meaning and significance.

There was considerable feeling about 1580 that English poetry had exhausted the possibilities of its native tradition and needed new models and new spirit from the flourishing literature of the Continent. A program something like that of the Pléiade in France was wanted, by which the English language would be glorified by a systematic imitation and exploitation of the models and devices of French and Italian authors. This would amount, in fact, to a reintroduction of the Petrarchan mode into England; it would mean an emphasis primarily upon love poetry; it would arouse the wit and ingenuity of English writers; and it would contribute to a polishing and developing of style which no English poetry except *The Shepheardes Calender,* just published, had been able to boast.

The man to inaugurate this new movement was conveniently at hand. His name was Thomas Watson, and in 1579 he had just returned from seven or eight years' stay on the Continent, where he had been studying law, traveling, and learning the tongues.[2] He was an Oxford man, well grounded in the classics, and, from all the accounts of his contemporaries, a very pretty wit. His first published work was a translation into Latin of Sophocles' *Antigone* in 1581, but a Latin

---

[2] Biographical information on Watson of considerable interest is given in Mark Eccles, *Christopher Marlowe in London,* Harvard Studies in English, X (Cambridge: Harvard University Press, 1934).

epistle by Stephen Broelman to Watson while he was still in Paris, published as a commendatory poem to the *Antigone,* shows that some Petrarchan poems by Watson were already written but not published. These poems were apparently translations of Petrarch's sonnets into Latin, for when Watson's *Hekatompathia* was published in 1582 the annotator of the book (someone like Spenser's E. K.) said of a Latin translation of one of Petrarch's sonnets published there, "The Author when he translated it, was not then minded euer to haue imboldned him selfe so farre, as to thrust in foote amongst our english Poets. But beinge busied in translating Petrarch his sonnets into latin new clothed this amongst many others, which one day may perchance come to light." [3]

Watson's interest was obviously in the rhetorical and stylistic possibilities of his sources. He appended to the translation of *Antigone* a series of *pompae* or verse dialogues between the poet and emblematic figures like Justitia, Aequitas, and Rigor. He also included some *themata,* or poems expanding proverbs, one of which is an interesting prelude to the writing of love sonnets because it is on the theme *Amare simul et sapere vix cuiquam dari.* There are side notes to Watson's Latin text of the play, pointing out the nature of the speeches (e.g., *ironice*) and indicating the source of the images (e.g., *a navigatione, ab agricultura, a medicina*) .

We have, then, a young man well read in foreign authors, who had translated Petrarch's sonnets from Italian into Latin and Sophocles' *Antigone* from Greek into Latin. He had the applause of the learned; scholars from Oxford and Cambridge saluted his first published work, and even the learned William Camden graced it with a flattering testimonial.[4] He had now only to use his familiarity with European vernacular and neo-Latin poetry to create a model in his own tongue. This he did by publishing, in the next year (1582) , a collection of one hundred sonnets, derived from Petrarch, Serafino, Ronsard, and many lesser French and Italian poets,

---

[3] Sig. A3ᵛ.

[4] For identification of these writers and some comment, see G. C. Moore Smith, *Notes and Queries,* 12th series, VII (1920) , 422–423.

under the title of *The Hekatompathia or Passionate Centurie of Loue, Diuided into two parts: whereof, the first expresseth the Authors sufferance in Loue: the latter, his long farewell to Loue and all his tyrannie. Composed by Thomas Watson Gentleman; and published at the request of certaine Gentlemen his very frendes*. These "very friends" were the most lively and promising writers of the time. Besides the academic group which had contributed to *Antigone*, Watson now had as sponsors John Lyly, George Peele, Matthew Roydon, George Buc, and Thomas Achelow, all enthusiastic about his introduction of the Petrarchan love poetry into English and justifying him for turning to something lighter than Greek tragedy. This group apparently constituted the chief promoters of poetry in the 1580's, for in 1589 Nashe, writing his preface to Greene's *Menaphon* to the gentlemen students of both universities, says that Spenser, miracle though he is, is not the only swallow of the English summer, "but he being forborne, there are extant about London many most able men to reuiue Poetry, though it were executed tenne thousand times, as in Platoes, so in Puritans Commonwealth; as, namely, for example, Mathew Roydon, Thomas Achlow, and George Peele." [5] Watson had hopes that his book would find its way also to the hands of Sidney and Dyer, who were of course interested in just the sort of English Pléiade which Watson was exemplifying. The volume's commentary, or gloss, explains Watson's sources, the effects he is after, and often the justification for his images.

The most important "passions" or eighteen-line sonnets in Watson's book are those which exhibit the typical methods of Petrarch in developing the conceits for love poetry. Such, for example, are No. 5 and No. 40. They both express the "contrarieties" of the lover's position, they formulate the paradoxical symptoms which the lover is conventionally supposed to feel, and they provide the foundation for the metaphors of which sonnets are made. No. 5 is based on a sonnet of Petrarch, "S'amor non è, che dunque è quel ch'io sento?" [6]

[5] Nashe, *Works*, ed. McKerrow, III, 323.
[6] *Rime*, 132.

Watson's version begins: "If't bee not loue I feele, what is it then?" The climax of this dilemma is, characteristically, a metaphor, and the popular one of the lover as a ship at sea is used.[7] The commentator points out that the interest of the poem lies in the fact that "certaine contrarieties, whiche are incident to him that loueth extreemelye, are liuely expressed by a Metaphore." These contrarieties the annotator assumes will be unfamiliar to anyone who has not been in love, but will be only too recognizable if he has been. In introducing the fortieth "passion" he makes such a comment: "But to such, as Loue at any time hath had vnder his banner, all and euery part of it will appeare to be a familier trueth."[8]

The fortieth is a version of Petrarch's famous "Pace non trovo, e non ho da far guerra."[9] The contrarieties are paraded directly in a catalogue.[10] This sonnet of Petrarch had been translated by Wyatt as "I find no peace, and all my warre is done,"[11] and there is an imitation of either Wyatt's translation or the original poem in another sonnet in Tottel.[12] The annotator of Watson seems wholly unaware of the priority of Wyatt and Surrey in introducing Petrarchan motifs into English. In fact, when he thinks of an earlier translator and compares Watson's version with his, it is not a sixteenth-century poet that comes to his mind but Chaucer, translating No. 5.

Both John Lyly in his prose testimonial to the volume and the annotator in his glosses speak of the "variety" of Watson's devices. Apparently the book was meant to show the great range of conceits and contrarieties which could be assembled around the theme of love. Sometimes the structure of the poem is emphasized, as in No. 47, in which each quatrain is a catalogue, the first line of the second and third

[7] Sig. A3[r].

[8] Sig. E4[v]. In manuscript the *Hekatompathia* had been called "A Looking Glasse for Loouers"; see Mark Eccles, *Harvard University . . . Summaries of Theses* (Cambridge, 1932) , p. 248.

[9] *Rime*, 134.

[10] Sig. E4[v].

[11] *Tottel's Miscellany*, ed. H. E. Rollins, 2 vols. (Cambridge: Harvard University Press, 1928, 1929) , I, 37, No. 49.

[12] No. 301 (ed. Rollins, I, 248) .

quatrains following in meaning the first line of the first quatrain, and so on. This feature of the style is especially recommended to those inexpert in poetry: "The oftener it is read of him that is no great clarke, the more pleasure he shall haue in it." [13] The catalogue itself became a very popular one. Watson's version, a translation of Serafino's sonnet 103, begins,

> In time the Bull is brought to weare the yoake;
> In time all haggred Haukes will stoope the Lures;
> In time small wedge will cleaue the sturdiest Oake;
> In time the Marble weares with weakest shewres.

It was picked up by Kyd for part of a speech at the beginning of the second act of *The Spanish Tragedy*,[14] and it became so famous from its use there that it is quoted as a proverb to Benedick in *Much Ado about Nothing*.[15]

Watson's "passions" are in reality sonnets of the three quatrain or English type, with a couplet inserted between the first and second quatrains and another between the second and third.

The chief interest in the sonnets, if we follow the annotator, is the exploitation of conceits and figures, the wit; however, he does comment several times on a quality which he calls the "patheticall." Sonnet 18, for example, which he calls "perfectly patheticall," is one in which the speaker applies many terms of abuse to love, then suddenly recants with "Yet mightie Loue regard not what I saye," [16] and ends in a prayer. Again, the last two lines of No. 22 are added by Watson, says the annotator, "to make the rest to seeme the more patheticall." [17] In the gloss on sonnet 50, we are given the approach to the poems which presumably the poet intended, and which may serve as a method of analysis for all such Petrarchan sonnets. The annotator first gives the theme, then describes the poet's manner of conveying the theme:

---

[13] *Hekatompathia*, sig. F4ʳ.
[14] *Works of Thomas Kyd*, ed. F. S. Boas (London, 1901), p. 21.
[15] I, i, 263.
[16] Sig. Cᵛ.
[17] Sig. C3ᵛ.

In this Passion is effectually set downe, in how straunge a case he liueth that is in loue, and in how contrary an estate to all other men, which are at defiaunce with the like follye. And this the Author expresseth here in his owne person.[18]

The "I" in the sonnets is then a role for effectiveness; it is to make the sonnet more "patheticall." Watson observes to the friendly reader in his preface that he hopes the reader will excuse any faults escaped, "in respect of my trauaile in penning these loue passions, or for pitie of my paines in suffering them (although but supposed)." [19]

The opposites and paradoxes which Watson found in Petrarch had originally served a purpose. Petrarch wrote such sonnets as "S'amor non è, che dunque è quel ch'io sento?" and "Pace non trovo, e non ho da far guerra" in the tradition of certain Provençal lyric riddles. The strategy of such poems was to approach the realization of a state of feeling by stating its apparently contradictory attributes, emphasizing their incompatibility, so that the reader to some extent creates the poem by his own solution of the problem; he puts together the attributes and by doing so experiences something like the feeling which the poet has not attempted to present as a whole. Watson's commentator, however, is aware that the question of plausibility will arise and tries to answer it by saying that anyone who has been in love will recognize the symptoms which the poem displays.

The reason for the strong appeal of sonnets of this sort to the Elizabethan poet was that he was constantly trying to give to love poetry an intellectual and moral respectability; he was aware that to his audience this kind of verse might seem a "toy" because of its subject matter. The way to avoid this was to complicate the technique. Ingenuity and wit might persuade the reader that the states of mind offered in the poem were not so frivolous or immature. The problem was to make love seem an almost heroic subject, and to do it by the insistence upon the consuming nature of the experience. The lover within the poetry had to reflect the world outside him, had to make that world seem relevant to, and involved

---

[18] Sig. G[v].   [19] First A4[r].

in, what was after all only his own individual state of mind. This could be done by metaphors, especially those which were in conflict with each other and which portrayed the conflict in the physical world which was a familiar story from the science of the time. The contrarieties, then, could be read on two levels; they were of course most obviously an account of the lover's state of mind, but they were also reflections of the coexistence of opposites and logical absurdities in nature, and they served thereby to justify the lover's position and the practice of love poetry.

The love sonnet is paradoxically public and private. It pretends to care only for the lady addressed, yet obviously Petrarch's sonnets to Laura had made for him a fame which was comparable to the heroic renown of an Alexander or a Tamburlaine. The preëminence of Petrarch was a constant reproach to English poets, and the finest of all the many tributes paid to Spenser by his contemporaries is that one by Ralegh which declared that on the appearance of *The Faerie Queene*, "Obliuion laid him downe on Lauras hearse."

The handling of Petrarch's contrarieties was, however, no easy matter. A firm hold on the two levels at which they were to be read was necessary or the device became merely a formula and was patently absurd. An example of these troubles may be seen in a sonnet of Drayton's, one of those in *Ideas Mirrour* (1594), which the poet dropped when he reissued his sonnets in 1599.

> Those teares which quench my hope, still kindle my desire,
> Those sighes which coole my hart, are coles unto my love,
> Disdayne Ice to my life, is to my soule a fire,
> With teares, sighes, & disdaine, thys contrary I prove.[20]

Here the poet has succumbed to the temptation to make his opposites confront each other in the same line, summing up the contraries after each quatrain. The result is that the tears and sighs, for example, have no utility except as physical phenomena, and even their qualities of heating and cooling are not really established in the poem. The essential conflict

[20] Amour 32 (*Works*, ed. Hebel, I, 114).

which the poem states is not achieved; the poet is trusting to stock response, which is the constant danger in the Petrarchan sonnet.

The essential flabbiness of the poem struck Drayton himself, and he tries to remedy the fault by tightening up the style. In 1599, lines 3 and 4 became

> Icie disdaine, is to my soule a fire,
> And yet all these I contrary doe prove,[21]

and the rest of the sonnet was revised on the same principle. The title "To Contrarietie" was given to it. But even greater directness, point, and vigor of expression could not save it, and the poem was dropped after 1603. Another sonnet in the 1594 volume is equally based upon contrarieties, but Drayton did not reject it in later editions, and the qualities which sustain it may be discovered by a comparison with those of the discarded sonnet:

> When first I ended, then I first began,
> The more I travell, further from my rest,
> Where most I lost, there most of all I wan,
> Pyned with hunger, rysing from a feast.[22]

The firmness of the grasp of these contrarieties is evident. "Pyned with hunger, rysing from a feast" is a dramatized version of the situation; the line produces its effect both when considered from the point of view of the state of mind described and from the point of view of the objective reality or value of the metaphor. The weakness of some Elizabethan sonnets, then, which is often put down to the fact that the poets embraced the more conceited and ingenious of Petrarch's models and continued to repeat them, is in reality caused by something else. There were effective and ineffective ways of handling contrarieties, and the critic's business is to see the difference between them.

Another way of estimating the point at which hyperbole

---

[21] *Works*, ed. Hebel, V, 18.

[22] Amour 50 (*Works*, ed. Hebel, I, 123). The poem was retained, without any important revision, on through the edition of 1619, where it is sonnet 62 (*Works*, II, 341).

and extravagance in the sonnets got out of hand is to consult the satirists. Of course, this must be done with caution, for it is possible to parody even effective or successful poetry, and such parody is often a testimony to its success. But in the gulling sonnets of Sir John Davies we can find enough samples to show what the tendencies were. Four of Davies' parodies, Nos. 2, 4, 7, and 8, depend upon the too heavy and literal application of metaphor or an extension which makes the state of mind conveyed a ridiculous one by its association with the compared objective reality. The conceit that thoughts are like sheep, for example, is a common one; but Davies makes his ridiculous love poet extend the idea so that an unhappy thought is like a diseased sheep and the effect of one unhappy thought upon the general state of mind is like that of a scurvy sheep spreading infection among the rest of the flock (sonnet 2). Again, the popular use of legal conceits is parodied in sonnets 7 and 8 simply by the device of multiplying the legal terms used until the impression is given that the lover is a mere parrot escaped from a cage in the law courts. Pattern poems and rhetorical devices like *gradatio* (as used in Sidney's first sonnet) are of course ridiculed for their extravagance, but the most vulnerable spot in the sonneteers attacked by Davies is their misuse of metaphor. One may agree, for example, that a central metaphor of spiritual qualities as armor and protection is a valid conceit and can be worked out in some detail as it is by Saint Paul:

Stand therefore, having your loins girt about with truth, and having on the breastplate of righteousness; and your feet shod with the preparation of the gospel of peace; above all, taking the shield of faith, wherewith ye shall be able to quench all the fiery darts of the wicked. And take the helmet of salvation, and the sword of the Spirit, which is the word of God.[23]

But propriety and decorum can easily be violated by the sonneteer who tries to express the emotions of a lover in terms of the clothing worn by Cupid; so for ludicrous effect, Davies dresses the god of love in

[23] Ephesians 6: 14–17.

his hatt of hope, his bande of beautye fine,
his cloake of crafte, his doblett of desyre,
greife for a girdell, shall about him twyne,
his pointes of pride, his Ilet holes of yre,
his stockings of sterne strife, his shirt of shame,
his garters of vaine glorie gaye and flyte;
his pantofels of passions I will frame,
pumpes of presumption shall adorne his feete
and Socks of sullennes excedinge sweete.[24]

The new fashion of the Petrarchan sonnet cycle carried
with it, then, as many new problems as the old ones it solved.
If wit, ingenuity, and invention were furthered, the possibilities of absurdity were also increased. If the feelings were analyzed with greater precision, there was no natural control over
the contrarieties of feeling the poet could allege. If metaphor
emerged into life, it was also true that metaphor needed extremely delicate handling. Many of the versifiers who turned
out cycles of sonnets in the decade of the nineties were un-
worried by these problems; they were simply seizing upon a
new fad in an attempt to win notice. They may be disre-
garded here, for though it is a matter of curiosity that so
many sonnets should have been written, not only in England
but on the Continent too, it can hardly be a matter of surprise
that so many of them are so bad.

If the criteria of historical significance (i.e., influence) and
of intrinsic value be considered together, certainly the sonnet cycle of Sir Philip Sidney, *Astrophel and Stella,* is the
most important of Elizabethan sonnet cycles. It was written
sometime about 1581–1583, published in a pirated edition in
1591, and finally issued with the authorization and textual
supervision of Sidney's sister, the Countess of Pembroke, in
the 1598 folio edition of the *Arcadia.* It circulated in manuscript copies, several of which have survived, and it was
known to readers of poetry even before its first publication
in 1591. *Astrophel and Stella* shares with Spenser's *Shepheardes Calender* the honor of inaugurating one of the greatest ages of English poetry.

Sidney's sonnets, of course, derive much of their method

[24] *Poems*, ed. Clare Howard (New York, 1941), p. 226.

and technique from the influence of Petrarch and, to a lesser degree, of Petrarch's imitators in various languages. In fact, the vitality (as distinguished from the mere "manner") of the Petrarchan tradition is first established in English by these 108 poems. The verse in the *Arcadia* included some sonnets, and in general the poetry interspersed in that romance, exemplifying many various forms, may be considered the experiment and exploration for the achievement and discovery of *Astrophel and Stella*. In many ways, also, the critical theories of Sidney's *Apologie for Poetrie* are involved in his performance in the sonnets; to him poetry was his "unelected vocation."

Sidney could not discuss the problems of poetry without being, in the process, a literary craftsman and artist; no more could he practice the art of poetry without being critical at the same time. The most prudent approach to the sonnets, therefore, would seem to be through the critical comments in the poems themselves, combined with the relevant observations on the art of poetry contained in the *Apologie*.

There are some dozen sonnets in *Astrophel and Stella* which deal with matters of purpose and style.[25] We can digest from these a doctrine about love poetry, and perhaps by implication about all poetry; more significantly, we can use these ideas, properly understood, as a method of analysis of the cycle itself.

In the first sonnet of the series Sidney gives some indication of his general purpose. It is twofold:

> I sought fit words to paint the blackest face of woe,
> Studying inuentions fine, her wits to entertaine.

Accordingly, the sonnet works in two contrary ways: it is a picture of the feeling of the speaker, Astrophel, and it is a contrived entertainment for the lady, Stella, as the supposed audience of the poem. We may postpone for the moment the question whether or not the lady is assumed to be the *only* audience to whom Astrophel is speaking and consider first to

---

[25] I include in this count Nos. 1, 3, 6, 15, 28, 34, 35, 44, 50, 70, 74, 90, 94. Quotations from the sonnets, as well as their numbers, are taken from the 1598 folio *Arcadia*.

what degree the sonnets are consistent in painting the blackest face of woe. Curiously enough, whenever the statement is directly made in a sonnet that Astrophel is completely woeful, it is usually in connection with some further consideration, never simply for its own sake. For example, Nos. 23 and 27 describe a state of "dull pensiuenesse" and "darke abstracted guise," but the purpose is to contrast the causes conjectured by others for his mood with what he declares is the true reason. In No. 45 Astrophel's woe is mentioned, but for the sake of showing how much more Stella's pity is aroused by fiction than by fact and to plead that, accordingly, she regard him as fiction:

> Then thinke my deare, that you in me do reed
> > Of Louers ruine some sad tragedie:
> > I am not I, pitie the tale of me.

In several instances the paradox that Astrophel's woe appears in the form of pleasure is exploited. Sonnets 57 and 58 tell of Stella reciting or singing his plaints and transforming things of woe into experiences of joy. The mode of expression, therefore, not the content, determines the effect:

> Oft cruell sights well pictured forth do please.

In fact, there is very little anatomy of woe in the sonnets themselves, and Sidney seems consciously bent upon making them independent of the conventional lover's mood of despair.[26]

> Sonets be not bound prentise to annoy:
> > Trebles sing high, as well as bases deepe:
> > Griefe but Loues winter liuerie is, the Boy
> > Hath cheekes to smile, as well as eyes to weepe.[27]

[26] There is a statement in the beginning of the sixteenth book of Ariosto's *Orlando Furioso* proclaiming that even though the lover is totally unsuccessful in his suit to the lady, he should not mourn, because his heart and thoughts are highly placed. Harington, in commenting on the passage, is reminded of Sidney. He says that "the nobilitie, the beautie, the worth, the graciousnesse, and those her other perfections, as made him both count her, and call her inestimably rich, makes him in the midst of those his mones, reioyce euen in his owne greatest losses, as in his eighteenth sonnet which many I am sure haue read" (ed. 1591, p. 126).

[27] Sonnet 70.

To be sure, woe in poetry is not always indicated directly, and we should take into account those passages in which the emotion is attributed to something else but is actually that of the speaker:

> With how sad steps, O Moone, thou climb'st the skies,
> How silently, and with how wanne a face.[28]

But even this mood, in the sonnet in which it occurs, soon changes into wry satirical bitterness toward a world in which constancy is called stupidity and ingratitude is called virtue.

The words that paint the blackest face of woe are not then the words of these sonnets; they are something in the background, a stage property in the drama, as if they existed before the sonnets of *Astrophel and Stella* did and are here referred to only as a part of the action. We should not, therefore, try to identify the sonnets mentioned in sonnet 58 as some of the actual poems in the cycle:

> Now iudge by this, in piercing phrases late,
>   The anatomy of all my woes I wrate,
>   Stellas sweete breath the same to me did reed.

They are of a different order of reality.

What, then, is the point of Sidney's referring to his sonnets as anatomies of woe when in fact they are not, or of introducing some lost or nonexistent sonnets into his narrative? This is a question which can be answered with more confidence after we have examined such questions as the audience of the sonnets, the theory and practice of style, and the identity of Astrophel and Sidney.

The first sonnet declares that the poet's purpose was partly to entertain the lady with fine inventions. It is of course basic in the assumed situation of the sonnet cycle that the lady's interest in these productions be not merely a literary interest but a personal one, that she be moved by the poems to grant the poet her love. We have already noticed how, in sonnet 45, Stella is said to be moved more by literature than by life. Are the sonnets, then, to be considered primarily as things ad-

[28] Sonnet 31.

dressed to the lady; is she the only audience? No, for the poet speaks of other readers in sonnet 74:

> How falles it then, that with so smooth an ease
>   My thoughts I speake, and what I speake doth flow
>   In verse, and that my verse best wits doth please?

(The "wits" referred to here appear again several times in the sonnets. In sonnets 3, 23, 26, and 104 they seem to be courtiers, friends of the poet, critics and arbiters. He usually dissociates himself from them.) If there were no other readers, it would surely be unnecessary for the poet to protest that he was not trying to achieve fame by his sonnets:

> Stella thinke not that I by verse seeke fame,
>
> .   .   .   .   .   .
>
> Nor so ambitions am I, as to frame
> A nest for my yong praise in Lawrell tree:
> In truth I sweare, I wish not there should be
> Graued in mine Epitaph a Poets name.[29]

This reminds us of Sidney's remark in the *Apologie:* "But I, as I never desired the title [of poet], so have I neglected the meanes to come by it. Onely, over-mastred by some thoughts, I yeelded an inckie tribute unto them." [30] And in the *Certaine Sonets* appended to the 1598 *Arcadia,* there is a poem which presents the argument about the lover as poet. The lady has complained that he does not love her because he has not written love poems to her, and his answer is a comment on the nature of love poetry:

> Are Poets then the onely louers true?
>   Whose hearts are set on measuring a verse:
>   Who thinke them selues well blest, if they renew
>   Some good old dumpe, that Chaucers mistresse knew,
>   And vse but you for matters to rehearse.[31]

The situation would seem to be, then, that of the Poet Suspect. From the point of view of the lady as audience, the poet

---

[29] Sonnet 90.
[30] *Apologie,* ed. Shuckburgh, pp. 49–50.
[31] *Arcadia* (1598), sig. Rr6ʳ.

should be purely amateur, without ambition for fame, without delight in the practice of art for its own sake, but devoted only to her. Yet there is clear evidence that even Astrophel's poems were praised by "the best wits." From their point of view, the poet was interesting as an artist, and they cared little whether he used the lady merely as an excuse for "matters to rehearse" or not. They will be interested in the devices, the artifice, the decoration of his verse.[32]

We are now dealing with the problem of two audiences, the lady and the reader, with their different concerns. How does the poet mediate between their claims? It is in this respect that Sidney effected his greatest novelty, and in which he stands apart from almost all the other poets of his century. His criticism of most contemporary love poetry in the *Apologie* shows how he approached the problem.

> But truely many of such writings, as come under the banner of unresistable love, if I were a Mistres, would never perswade mee they were in love: so coldely they apply fiery speeches, as men that had rather red Lovers writings, and so caught up certaine swelling phrases, which hang together, like a man which once tolde mee, the winde was at North West, and by South, because he would be sure to name windes enowe,—then that in truth they feele those passions: which easily (as I think) may be bewrayed by that same forciblenes or *Energeia* (as the Greekes cal it) of the writer.[33]

Sidney here adopts the point of view of the mistress as audience, and he objects to extraneous decoration and rhetorical excess on the ground that they would not convince *her*. He is trying, that is, to preserve the validity of the dramatic framework of the sonnet series (or of any love poem) and to derive from it a principle of decorum. His method is the same as that by which he justifies the unities in drama: the traditional argument of probability. I do not think we need to pause to

---

[32] For an account of Elizabethan taste which may justify this description of the interests of the reader, see Geoffrey Tillotson, *Essays in Criticism and Research* (Cambridge, England, 1942), pp. 5–16. In my description of the reader's probable tastes and expectations I am also drawing upon the character of other sonnet cycles which appeared later in English.

[33] Shuckburgh ed., p. 57.

refute the suggestion that Sidney simply supposes the chief
function of love poetry to be the winning of an actual lady;
the whole weight of the *Apologie* indicates a more serious
evaluation of poetry. Why, then, should the first consideration in love poetry be efficacy of the verse from the assumed
point of view of the mistress? I think the explanation may be
found in his remark about similitudes: "For the force of a
similitude, not being to proove anything to a contrary disputer, but onely to explane to a willing hearer, when that is
done, the rest is a most tedious pratling." [34] His point is that
there must be an emotional ground, prepared beforehand, for
the decoration. This can be done, in love poetry, by a con-
trolling emphasis on the lover-lady relationship. If everything
is subordinated to the probable persuasiveness to the lady, we
have a principle of selection. The poet does not then catch
up any and all passions convenient in order to show his versatility, as Sidney's countryman caught up three of the four
winds. He is confined within the probable, the convincing,
and he has an emotion in the work which gives force to his
similitudes and saves them from being most tedious prattling.

Fundamentally, this theory has to do with the reader, the
poet's second audience. Sidney concludes that the reader, despite his natural interest in decoration, conceits, elaborate
artifice, and ingenuity, will finally be more affected by the
poetry if the lady, the other audience, and her assumed point
of view are made paramount. Concentration, force, probability, and control of the details are the results to be hoped for.

It is in the light of these principles, and in recognition of
the fact that Sidney does have a positive theory of love poetry
which embraces the problems of the double audience, decorum, and style that the sonnets in *Astrophel and Stella* on
"Pindar's apes" and contemporary practice in poetry should
be read. And we are here approaching the question of the
identity of Sidney and Astrophel.

What is the "role" of Astrophel? It is not, as we have seen,
primarily one of woe, despite what he says about his own
poems. It is rather one of energetic simplicity and force. He

[34] Shuckburgh ed., p. 58.

is independent of literary society and its standards; he is natural, unartistic, being dictated to directly by love. He is no pickpurse of another's wit, no reciter of Petrarch's long-deceased woes; he looks in his heart and writes. He constantly mentions the difference between himself and others. Distinctiveness, not variety of feeling, is thus important. And the reiterated emphasis upon this individuality is Sidney's way of manifesting "that same forciblenes or *Energeia* (as the Greekes cal it) of the writer."

In style and diction this means the utilization of the colloquial, which has often been remarked as a feature of the sonnets:

Then some good body tell me how I do . . .[35]

Fy schoole of Patience, Fy, your lesson is
Far far too long to learne it without booke . . .[36]

Guess we the cause, what is it thus? fie no
Or so? much lesse: how then? sure thus it is.[37]

It means also the turning of irony upon the character of Astrophel, managed by the introduction of some external opinion of him; such as Cupid's:

What now sir foole . . .
Looke here, I say . . .[38]

or the court ladies':

What he? say they of me, now I dare sweare,
He cannot loue: no, no, let him alone . . .[39]

or that of his friends:

Art not ashamed to publish thy disease?[40]

or that of his Muse:

Thus great with child to speake, and helplesse in my throwes
Biting my trewand pen, beating my selfe for spite,
Foole, said my Muse to me, looke in thy heart and write.[41]

[35] Sonnet 60.   [37] Sonnet 74.   [39] Sonnet 54.   [41] Sonnet 1.
[36] Sonnet 56.   [38] Sonnet 53.   [40] Sonnet 34.

Astrophel is therefore something of an exile from society; he is bored with news of foreign affairs and statecraft [42] and with the gossip of the court circle.[43] He is the bargainer, the arguer, the trapped man.

Accordingly, the old problem of those sonnets in *Astrophel and Stella* which reject the practices of contemporary poetry should be reconsidered. It has been customary to cite these sonnets in connection with the problem of sources; the old position, stated most forcibly by Sir Sidney Lee,[44] was that Sidney's sonnets were highly derivative and that these professions of originality were in themselves conventional. Later students, like Miss Janet Scott,[45] have found less dependence upon Italian and French poetry than Lee indicated and have concluded that the professions of originality are by and large justified, given the Renaissance understanding of the term originality. But consider for a moment that these protestations are Astrophel's, not Sidney's, and see what follows. In sonnet 6 he separates himself from some of the specifically named types of current poetry:

Some Louers speake when they their Muses entertaine,
 Of hopes begot by feare, of wot not what desires:
 Of force of heau'nly beames, infusing hellish paine:
 Of liuing deaths, deare wounds, faire stormes & freesing fires:
Some one his song in Ioue, and Ioues strange tales attires,
 Bordred with buls & swans, powdred with golden raine:
 Another humbler wit to shepheards pipe retires,
 Yet hiding royall bloud full oft in rurall vaine.
To some a sweetest plaint, a sweetest stile affords,
 While teares powre out his inke, & sighs breathe out his words:
 His paper pale dispaire, and paine his pen doth moue.
I can speake what I feele, and feele as much as they,
 But thinke that all the Map of my state I display,
 When trembling voice brings forth that I do Stella loue.

[42] Sonnet 30.
[43] Sonnet 51.
[44] *Elizabethan Sonnets*, with an Introduction by Sidney Lee, 2 vols. (Westminster, 1904) , I, xliii-xlix.
[45] *Les Sonnets Élisabéthains*, pp. 15-53.

This seems to assert that he eschews conceits, that he rejects mythological poetry and pastoral love poetry, that he does not practice the conventional love complaint. Instead, he merely states his love for Stella in trembling voice. If it is not too absurd, we might raise the question whether these last two lines actually apply to the *Astrophel and Stella* sonnets. Of course not. The tone of these sonnets is not trembling; it is a tone of considerable vigor and force. We here encounter the same phenomenon noticed before, that there seem to be some mythical or lost love poems behind the ones we are reading. They are the "stage property" sonnets. The author of these mysterious poems is not Sidney but Astrophel. Their existence is merely a way of sharpening still further this sense of individuality that marks the role of Astrophel. Astrophel is a poet who uses no art and keeps swearing that he uses no art. He simply speaks his mind; the process of writing verse is almost automatic, with Stella dictating. He paints the face of blackest woe, his voice trembles.

Sidney, on the other hand, uses very considerable art. To be sure, he disapproves of "Curtizan-like painted affectation" in the *Apologie,* speaking in his own voice.[46] But he quite readily makes a whole sonnet consist of one expanded figure; [47] he adapts, of course, Petrarch's long-deceased woes; and he is capable of all kinds of rhetorical cunning. Apostrophes to Virtue, Reason, Sleep, the Moon, Hope, Desire, Absence, Grief; sonnets on the exploits of Cupid; "concession" sonnets like No. 5, in which the speaker grants a whole series of objections of some Platonic critic, building up the whole thing by introducing every phrase with "True" or "It is most true," only to reassert his own case in the last line— it is clear that the most complex rhetorical and dramatic resources are utilized in the sonnets by Sidney, whatever may have been the nature of those mysterious sonnets by Astrophel.

The interplay between these two effects is a matter of pri-

[46] Shuckburgh ed., p. 57.
[47] Sonnets 9, 29, 36, 49, and 97.

mary importance for criticism. A naïve or romantic account will overlook the distinction between the two roles which I have called Sidney and Astrophel and proceed to the question of whether Stella is to be identified with Lady Rich. Presumably she is. But it makes no difference to the quality of the sonnets whether Stella is Penelope Devereux, Frances Walsingham, or an entirely imaginary lady.[48] The significance of the Astrophel-Sidney identification lies in the fact that it solves the problem of the relationship between poet, subject matter, and reader. The professions of "sincerity," of plainness, of lack of art, are directed to the lady; she is not only subject matter but also a reader, within the framework of the convention of the sonnet cycle. The role of Astrophel is of course directed at Stella. The reader, an outsider in this situation, must go around through the lady's position to approach the poet. How much of her presumed attitude does he share? Not her coldness to the lover, perhaps; the sonnets, if successful, will move the reader even though they fail in their professed purpose of moving the lady. If the reader is persuaded, if he shares the emotion attributed to Astrophel, then there is the emotional ground for the control of decoration and "similitudes." As we recall, the force of a similitude, or the value of decoration, is not to prove anything to a contrary disputer but only to explain to a willing hearer. For Stella, then, unvarnished plainness and simplicity. For the reader, who goes beyond Stella in his sharing of the speaker's feelings, all the similitudes and decoration that the emotion will maintain. But the reader must partly share Stella's position, and so far as he does he will believe in the artlessness and simplicity of the poet, and the great feat of hiding art by art will be achieved.

The impression of simplicity and directness, of occasional magic and frequent drama, which Theodore Spencer has shown to be the effect of Sidney's sonnets,[49] is related to this

---

[48] The bibliography of the subject is extensive. A summary of the controversy, with the most recent conclusions and references to the earlier material, may be found in an appendix to L. C. John, *The Elizabethan Sonnet Sequences* (New York, 1938).

[49] "The Poetry of Sir Philip Sidney," *ELH*, XII (1945), 251–278.

skillful maneuvering which I have tried to describe. To see more clearly how distinctive Sidney is in this respect, we might compare Drayton. Drayton says of his style the opposite of what Astrophel says of his:

> But see, for you to Heav'n for Phraze I runne,
> And ransacke all Apollo's golden Treasure; [50]

and this is quite consistent with his aim. He is approaching the reader directly and offering him variety instead of passion (i.e., emotional consistency) in the usual Elizabethan manner to which Sidney had objected. Again, Drayton says:

> Into these Loves, who but for Passion lookes,
> At this first sight, here let him lay them by,
>
> .   .   .   .   .
>
> My Verse is the true image of my Mind,
> Ever in motion, still desiring change;
> And as thus to Varietie inclin'd,
> So in all Humors sportively I range:
>   My Muse is rightly of the English straine,
>   That cannot long one Fashion intertaine. [51]

The strong autobiographical effect which Sidney's sonnets have produced may be explained by reasons of the art of poetry. It is perhaps no wonder that the pursuit ever since has been for the data behind the poems. This is a measure of their success.

The force and effectiveness of Sidney's sonnets is of course not dependent upon the general strategy of the cycle alone. The dramatic quality and the skillful shifts in tone through variety in diction have already been mentioned. The protestations of originality and the creation of an individual role for Astrophel are heightened by such a juxtaposition of the formal and the colloquial as is evidenced in the lines,

> And this I sweare by blackest brooke of hell,
> I am no pick-purse of anothers wit. [52]

[50] *Works*, ed. Hebel, II, 321.
[51] *Ibid.*, p. 310.
[52] Sonnet 74.

The contrast in diction is really only one of several kinds of internal contrasts, and the poems exploit to the full a series of paradoxes and the irony resulting from them. The paradox that Astrophel's verses please "best wits" but achieve nothing with the lady has already been mentioned. There is the further paradox, exploited in the second sonnet, of the lover's state of feeling:

> And now employ the remnant of my wit,
>> To make me selfe beleeue, that all is well,
>> While with a feeling skill I paint my hell.

It is a combination of sorrow and joy, and the last sonnet in the series sums it up:

> So strangely (alas) thy works in me preuaile,
>> That in my woes for thee thou art my ioy,
>> And in my ioyes for thee my only annoy.

Even the sonnets punning on the name of Rich have a function other than satirical; they exploit a paradox involved in the name and the quality.[53]

These dilemmas serve to give a structure to the sonnets, to make for them a system in which the feelings work two ways and have an object in the reconciliation of opposites. The most extended and pervasive conflict in *Astrophel and Stella* is the battle between Reason and Passion; aspects of this struggle provide the specific framework for about one-fifth of the sonnets, and these sonnets are disposed throughout the cycle in such a way that they influence most of the others.

The arguments of Virtue or Reason offer, of course, convenient material for the content of the sonnet. They can be catalogued and conceded, refuted, or twisted in a sophistic way so that they serve as a tribute to Stella. Rhetorically, this argument is more fruitful than any other for the purpose of the sonnets. The poet can treat the precepts of virtue with a tone of impatience,[54] resignation, triumphant superiority;[55] he can use them for his own position or against it.[56] Stella's

---

[53] Sonnets 24, 35, and 37.　　[55] Sonnet 10.
[54] Sonnet 4.　　[56] Sonnets 21 and 91.

charms can teach Venus chastity,[57] but Cupid is a difficult and recalcitrant pupil.[58]

Traditionally, this element in the sonnets has been interpreted biographically, and commentators who make no distinction between Astrophel and Sidney, their eyes upon the identification of Stella with Lady Rich, have tried to make a narrative of the course of Sidney's love for a married lady and his final resignation in favor of virtue. This involves bringing in, to close the series, two sonnets of resignation from the *Certaine Sonets* of 1598, "Thou blind mans marke, thou fooles selfe chosen snare" and the very eloquent "Leaue me o Loue, which reachest but to dust." Apart from the fact that the Countess of Pembroke herself, who presumably knew how the *Astrophel and Stella* series should be arranged, did not transplant these sonnets, a further argument against the practice is that the course and tendency of the series in no way leads up to them. The last four sonnets have absence as the theme, but the song which precedes them, the "Eeleuenth song," has in dialogue form a clear statement that there is, after all, no conflict between the speaker's love for Stella and reason:

> But your reasons purest light,
> Bids you leaue such minds to nourish?
> Deere, do reason no such spite,
> Neuer doth thy beauty flourish
> More, then in my reasons sight.[59]

In view of this, the renunciation sonnets cannot be part of *Astrophel and Stella*.[60]

In the tenth sonnet Sidney pleads with Reason to leave sense and its objects to Will, to devote himself to the pursuit

[57] Sonnet 42.
[58] Sonnet 46.
[59] *Arcadia* (1598), sig. Bbb2ʳ.
[60] The order of the sonnets in the Briton MS. gives no support to those who would see the cycle leading up to a renunciation of desire. There the last sonnet is No. 48, in which physical beauty strengthens virtue and "Where Loue is chastnesse, Paine doth learne delight." For the order of sonnets in this manuscript, see Bernard Quaritch's Catalogue No. 641 (London, 1946), item 503.

of poetry, philosophy, and astronomy. He refuses to do so, fights both love and sense, and is overcome by beauty, finally vowing to engage in Stella's service. This is a characteristic structure; it allows a conflict to be terminated by a compliment to Stella without ever really facing the nature of love and desire or the relationship between them. The sonnets of concession to Platonism such as Nos. 5 and 25 answer objections to love by finding an identification between Stella's beauty and virtue. According to sonnets 14, 42, and 48, the love Stella inspires is the opposite of unchastity. Yet in No. 47 the poet sees Virtue and Beauty as opposed to each other; and in No. 49, a developed conceit in which love rides and manages him as he does his horse, the saddle is fancy, the wand is will, the girths are memory, and the spur is sharp desire. In No. 52, a sonnet built on a legal conceit, Virtue overrides Love's claim to Stella by citing his ownership of her self while Beauty owns only her "eyes, her lips, her all"; the poet accordingly proposes a division of the spoils. In sonnet 61 the love is apparently sensual and dishonorable. The wish of sonnet 62 is that she not love him, if such a love imposes virtue upon him. Sonnets 71 and 72 summarize this phase of the problem; her beauty is the outward sign of inward virtue, and she uses her power over others, specifically the lover, to transform love to good.

But ah, Desire still cries, giue me some food.[61]

The most explicit poem in the whole series is the "Eight Song," in which Astrophel pleads with Stella, using the argument that the time and place are right. She replies, justifying her refusal in the evidence of her love, and the situation is resolved in the "Ninth song," a pastoral in which Astrophel expresses his woes in a semicomic manner. A couple of sonnets, Nos. 18 and 64, show a concern over the question of whether a slavery in love is not shameful to a man because it is not a life of action or heroic achievement. Yet in both instances the supposed shame is welcomed as a sign of sac-

[61] Sonnet 71.

rifice for love, and the only regret is that the sacrifice could not be greater.

Fundamentally, the debate between virtue and love is utilized in the cycle to give it drama. Sidney is especially fond of the sonnet in which some action appears; he is noticeably more interested in action for this purpose than Daniel or Shakespeare, for example. This is an especially valuable conflict because it is readily resolved into particular compliments for the close of a sonnet, and because it permits the paradox and resulting irony which Sidney was able to utilize, in conjunction with the drama of his shifts of style and effect, to give the effect of particularity to his work.

The question of whether the absence series at the end of the sonnets [62] is intended to follow narratively from the events described in the "Eight Song" is a difficult one. In the *Certaine Sonets* there is a sonnet which says that the speaker voluntarily undertook an absence because his love was bad for him:

> Finding those beames, which I must euer loue,
> > To marre my minde, and with my hurt to please,
> > I deemd it best some absence for to proue,
> > If further place might further me to ease.[63]

The result, however, is the familiar paradox: he must either live as a blinded mole or a burned fly.

If Sidney's aim was to achieve, in a series of sonnets, a reality and vitality which he thought contemporary love poetry lacked, to dramatize the situation of the lovers, and to give the impression of credibility of the emotion by an individuality of style, the aim of his first follower in the sonnet vogue might be said to be just the opposite. Samuel Daniel's sonnets were published, in part, as an appendix to the surreptitious edition of *Astrophel and Stella* in 1591: in the next year Daniel brought out his own edition, with his very influential complaint poem *Rosamond*. He dedicated his work to Sidney's sister, the Countess of Pembroke, and in the

[62] Sonnets 87, 88, 89, and 91.
[63] *Arcadia* (1598), sig. Ss^r.

versified form of this dedication which took its place in the edition of 1594, Daniel proclaimed that the countess was not only the patroness but the inspiration of the poems.

The love element in the sonnets is therefore merely conventional; it is an opportunity for Daniel to achieve the expression of a gentle melancholy characteristic of him, to celebrate the lasting power of verse against the ravages of time and barbarism, and to show that the themes and devices which had been used so much by the French and Italian sonneteers had as much grace and dignity in English as they had in other tongues.

The personality of the speaker and the conceits of his arguments, which Sidney had dramatized so vigorously, are left very quiet and colorless in Daniel's poems. Yet these sonnets have an attraction of their own, and the reader of Elizabethan poetry finds himself stopping over sonnets of Daniel's almost as often as over those of any of his rivals. The explanation is that Daniel has made his sonnets effectively lyric instead of dramatic. He chooses the form of the sonnet characteristic of Surrey, with three well-marked quatrains and a couplet. He polishes the conventional themes and situations; his diction is clear and formal; and his emotion is untempered by irritation, argument, or the sudden turn that marks individuality of feeling. Instead of speech, his poetry approaches incantation, but it eschews rhetorical decoration and is self-consciously modern. He even rejects the poetic practice of Spenser:

> Let others sing of Knights and Palladines,
> In aged accents, and vntimely words.[64]

Daniel's preference for the feminine ending, one which he outgrew and renounced in his later revisions of the sonnets, ties the versification of the sonnets to that of *Rosamond*. In the sonnets it provides a variety of movement and relieves the calm and even pace of his lines, especially at the beginning of a sonnet, where the tone is often hushed and incantational:

[64] *Poems,* ed. Sprague, sonnet 46.

Looke Delia how wee steeme the half-blowne Rose,
The image of thy blush and Summers honor.[65]

But loue whilst that thou maist be lou'd againe,
Now whilst thy May hath fill'd thy lappe with flowers.[66]

The simple eloquence for which Daniel strove is achieved
even in the process of making the declaration of indifference
to literary fame and artistic renown. The same protestation
by Sidney had a dramatic purpose; in Daniel's fourth sonnet
it serves to give piquancy to the plain and humble modesty
of his style.

Essentially, the love situation in Daniel's cycle is merely a
pretext for the poetry. The most common theme in the series
is the eternity of verse, which is asserted in seven of the sonnets.[67] The lady is a chaste goddess; [68] she reconciles chastity
and beauty; [69] and though the lover speaks of his "youth and
error," his "blush and error," and "this error" in referring
to his love, there is no such conflict between desire and reason as Sidney had utilized in his sonnets. It is quite clear that
the love in the *Delia* situation is a "spotless love" and a
"chast desire." [70] The despair of the speaker that he is unsuccessful in his love provides the justification for the elegiac
tone of the poems; it is serving the same purpose as the old
Mirror for Magistrates device of the complaining ghost serves
for *Rosamond*. There is no analysis of the despair, no real
attempt to show its nature or causes; the mood is sustained
because it is a fruitful one for reflective lyrics on the passing
of time and beauty, the appropriate one for Daniel's characteristically quiet and chastened style.

Daniel's apparent difference from the fashion of his own
time has called forth many explanations; he is said to have
derived his method and doctrine from the Countess of Pembroke, or he is supposed to have been less robust physically
and emotionally than a good Elizabethan should be. One recent account suspects that Fulke Greville seduced Daniel into

[65] Sonnet 31.
[66] Sonnet 32.
[67] Nos. 30, 34, 35, 36, 37, 46, 48.
[68] Sonnet 5.
[69] Sonnet 6.
[70] Sonnets 12 and 49.

a position which was hostile to poetry itself and loyal only to philosophical and scientific knowledge.[71] These theories are based upon a definition of the Elizabethan attitude which is too narrow. The usefulness, for the modern reader, of the conventions and types in Elizabethan literature is that they enable him to see how much variation there is in the response to these set conditions for art.

Daniel wrote his tract *A Defence of Ryme* to rebut the contentions of Campion, contentions which he did not fully understand. In the *Defence* he shows himself the same conservative, patriotic, and modest spirit that is evident in *Delia* and *Rosamond*. He is in favor of rhyme because it is sanctioned in English by custom and nature—"Custome that is before all Law, Nature that is aboue all Arte." [72] He is against vanity, and specifically the kind of vanity to which writers are most prone, that of overestimating or overvaluing purely literary effects: "It is not the contexture of words, but the effects of Action that giues glory to the times." [73] This is not the utterance of a treasonable poet, but of a modest poet. The Ciceronianism of the Renaissance, the delight in excessive decoration which could be observed in sixteenth-century Englishmen, seemed to Daniel harmful to that one learning, that "one and the selfe-same spirit that worketh in all. . . Eloquence and gay wordes are not of the Substance of wit, it is but the garnish of a nice time, the Ornaments that doe but decke the house of a State, & *imitatur publicos mores:* Hunger is as well satisfied with meat serued in pewter as siluer. Discretion is the best measure, the rightest foote in what habit soeuer it runne." [74]

On two things he was insistent: that the past which had produced his England must certainly be a worthy past, so its traditions should be followed, though in no pedantic or antiquarian way; and that the experimentation, reformation, and discovery of new principles which he saw contemporaries

---

[71] "Samuel Daniel and Fulke Greville," *TLS*, June 5, 1930, p. 475.
[72] *Poems,* ed. Sprague, p. 131.
[73] *Ibid.,* p. 144.
[74] *Ibid.,* p. 145.

engaged in were suspect because they sprang from "Selfe-loue, wherevnto we Versifiers are euer noted to be especially subiect." It behoves the poet to be modest, "for there is not the simplest writer that will euer tell himselfe, he doth ill, but as if he were the parasite onely to sooth his owne doings, perswades him that his lines can not but please others, which so much delight himselfe." [75] The modesty and self-critical temper of this passage are also evident in the style and effect of *Delia*.

Michael Drayton is an interesting example of a poet who took up the sonnet fad at its height but who retained his interest in it long after the vogue had passed. He was influenced initially, as all poets were, by the examples of Watson and Sidney. Barnes and Daniel also exerted their influence on him, so that Drayton's specific obligations can be traced more easily in his English forebears than in the continental sonneteers.

Though Drayton reflects Sidney's phraseology and his favorite conceits in the sonnets (or "Amours," as he called them) of *Ideas Mirrour* (1594), it is quite apparent that at that time he did not see what was Sidney's greatest contribution to the Petrarchan tradition. He produced a line like "Were not Invention stauld, treading Inventions maze" [76] in his seventeenth Amour, when he was trying to convey the impression of confusion and frustration which was part of Sidney's theme in his first sonnet, but he never dispels the confusion with the direct colloquial command as Sidney did in his last line. He may suggest Sidney in his comments on other poets and his statements of independence of them, "Some when in ryme they of their Loves doe tell," [77] but his statement of his own position is much more mild and modest.

Drayton tries for, and sometimes achieves, a pleasant verbal music. [78] This mellifluous manner, which perhaps owes some-

[75] *Ibid.*, p. 157.
[76] *Works*, ed. Hebel, I, 107.
[77] Amour 18 (*ibid.*).
[78] See, for example, Amour 22 (*Works*, I, 109).

thing to Barnes and Daniel, was not Drayton's only style. He could get a variety of movement and internal pause in his lines which sometimes sounds individual.[79] Drayton courted the ridicule of the satirists by developing his conceits sometimes rather fully and literally, throwing off the balance between metaphor and description and coming dangerously near to absurdity. His Amour 44, for example, in which he makes himself a forge, with his heart the anvil, his words the hammers, love the fuel, and his sighs the bellows, needs, for parody, only an additional touch by Sir John Davies, let us say, that the sonnets he makes are then horseshoes and the lady to whom he gives them is a sore-footed horse. His striving for freshness, as Mrs. Tillotson has remarked, is itelf conventional, though it is conventional only in the way he does it—by seeking new areas from which to draw images, such as bookkeeping, the alphabet, and celestial numbers.[80] He is still following Watson in the belief that the way to give love poetry the effect of originality is to provide ingenious rhetorical and metaphorical variety.

By 1599, when Drayton published his sonnets again under the title *Idea* in the volume with *England's Heroicall Epistles,* he had changed noticeably. By dropping twenty of his 1594 sonnets and adding nineteen new ones, he gave the effect of a new cycle. His development was partly due to the satirists of Petrarchan poetry and of Drayton's own poetry in particular; as Mrs. Tillotson puts it, "Clearly, in was in 1599, and partly thanks to the satirists, that Drayton found himself in the sonnet form." [81] But the satirists alone would not have brought about the change which finally enabled Drayton to publish, in 1619, a poem which has some claim (according to Rossetti) to be the finest of all the Elizabethan sonnets. The qualities of his masterpiece, "Since ther's no helpe, Come let us kisse and part," [82] Drayton must have learned by going back and studying *Astrophel and Stella;* in writing it

[79] Amour 26 (*Works,* I, 111).
[80] Amours 10, 11, and 8. See *Works,* V, 14.
[81] *Works,* V, 139.
[82] *Works,* II, 341.

he carried farther than Sidney had done the Sidneyan traits of particularization of the event, shift of pace and tone, dramatization by the use of colloquial language in a "poetic" context, and the convincing result from the lady's point of view which gives an impression of *energy* to the reader. In this sonnet we have the utilization of the direct speech of the lover, its colloquial reality reinforced by the actuality of the situation in "Now at the last gaspe" and the development of a beautifully controlled picture in the Cupid series. The dramatic surprise in the couplet is softened and made appealing by the feminine ending, and the poem succeeds on just the grounds which Sidney had alleged for this kind of poem. Drayton is no longer depending upon variety and decoration for his effect; he is producing a concentration and energy, a directness and probability, for a triumph toward which Sidney had showed the way.

The question of whether Drayton's shift in 1599 and later was caused by his rereading of Sidney, as I have suggested, or by his own experience in writing plays, as contended by F. Y. St. Clair,[83] cannot, perhaps, be answered conclusively. The statement of W. B. C. Watkins seems to me the best yet made: "Actually, the poets had prepared the way. Wyatt and Sidney, while continuing artificial conventions of thought and style, had rebelled against them in search of more immediacy, more intensity, more passionate realism of image and rhythm. In a sense Elizabethan drama was an inevitable expansion of a kind of poetry no longer content with pure lyric and narrative expression."[84]

Spenser's sonnets, called *Amoretti*, constitute, in part at least, an interruption to his great labor in *The Faerie Queene*. Sonnets 33 and 80 comment uneasily upon this diversion from the poet's major work. He wrongs the Queen, he says, by not finishing the poem that is intended to increase her praises, and he can only plead that he had been rendered

[83] "Drayton's First Revision of His Sonnets," *SP*, XXXVI (1939), 40–59.
[84] "The Two Techniques in *King Lear*," *RES*, XVIII (1942), 10. Watkins also gives a valuable analysis of the realistic and symbolical elements in "Since ther's no helpe."

incapable because of the fact that his mind "is tost with troublous fit" in love. In sonnet 80 he has finished six books and is composing the sonnets as a resting place, after which he will plunge into the completion of the epic with new strength and vigor.

In spite of this fact, however, there is clear evidence that the sonnets are intimately connected with Spenser's earlier work, and in a sense he would have had to write the sonnets, even if he had not been worn out with *The Faerie Queene* and if he had not had any personal reason in the period around 1594 to compose love poems. The *Amoretti* are connected with the first two of his *Fowre Hymnes,* which he said in 1596 were written "in the greener times of my youth." They even owe something to the schoolboy translations which Spenser did in 1569 for Van der Noodt's *Theatre.* Their verse form, a special one which links the quatrains together by repeating rhymes, was one which Spenser had used as early as 1580 in a dedicatory sonnet to *Virgil's Gnat.* These relationships must be borne in mind as well as the more obvious ones usually pointed out in discussions of the *Amoretti,* the connection between the sonnets and the *Epithalamion,* published with them in 1595, and with Spenser's own marriage to Elizabeth Boyle, which took place, according to the best modern guess, in 1594.

Spenser would have to begin, of course, with a knowledge of Sidney's *Astrophel and Stella.* Such a knowledge is obvious and does not need to be demonstrated. What is of interest here is the question of whether Spenser realized the main principles of the sonnet cycle as Sidney had practiced them, and if he did whether he cared to follow in the master's steps. In the very first sonnet Spenser emphasizes the Sidneyan point that the only reader he is concerned with is the lady herself.[85] This may or may not be a conscious adaptation of Sidney's device, but there are sonnets in the group which are obviously *not* addressed to the lady, such as son-

---

[85] The theory advanced by Sir Israel Gollancz that this sonnet was intended not for the *Amoretti* but for *The Faerie Queene* has, I think, been successfully refuted. See A. C. Judson in Variorum *Minor Poems,* II, 419–420.

net 33, for example, addressed to Lodowick Bryskett. The second sonnet proceeds, in Sidney's manner, to give an account of the origin of the love affair; in Spenser it is an "unquiet thought," just as in Sidney it is the result of knowledge of the lady for some time, not the first shot of Cupid's bow. But in style and general manner we notice immediately that Spenser is not of Sidney's school. Not only the difference in versification, which makes for a reflective, musical, flowing style in Spenser's poems as opposed to the dramatic qualities of Sidney's, but even the arrangement and general strategy of the series are different. Spenser was too much under the influence of his own earlier practice to submit himself wholly to the model of Sidney, even if he had wished to do so.

To give a sense of actuality to the whole series, Spenser relied upon the same device he had used in *The Shepheardes Calender*, that of a calendar which reflected the passage of time and an awareness of the seasons. Of course, if the sonnet series is to be taken as naïvely as some critics take it, this is merely a record of events as they happened and the calendar is no invention. But there is no external evidence to confirm the calendar, and the resemblance to the device used in Spenser's volume of 1579 should make us at least consider the possibility that this scheme is a device for structure. At any rate, it gives the series an undeniable sense of actuality. New Year's day appears in sonnet 4; the first day of spring comes in sonnet 12; sonnet 22 has reference to Lent, "This holy season fit to fast and pray"; in sonnet 60 we have passed a year since the beginning of the love and hence since the beginning of the action in the series; the new year comes round again in sonnet 62, and the second Easter since the beginning of the cycle is referred to in sonnet 67.

Sidney's occasional sonnets refer to tournaments or to the events which are being discussed by the public; their utility is rather to mark the difference between the lover's concern and the concerns of the rest of the world. In Spenser's use of the calendar we get an identification between the course of the lovers' relationship and the natural course of the seasons. This is in keeping with the general presentation of love in

Spenser; in contrast to that of Sidney, it is felt to be natural, growing, progressing. Love is not primarily a dramatic conflict.

The most vivid thing in Sidney's sonnet cycle is the personality of Astrophel. The lover is characterized very particularly to give a sense of reality to the poetry itself. But in Spenser it is not the lover who is portrayed most fully; it is the lady. Curiously enough, the lady whose name does not ornament the title of the series, as most of them do, is more elaborately presented,- both physically and spiritually, than any of the Delias, Dianas, Phillises, Lauras, or even Stellas of the time. We can tell from sonnet 74 that her name was the same as that of the poet's mother and the Queen, but she is addressed by no Petrarchan name in the sonnets.

Her spiritual qualities are detailed in a number of places; they make of her the real protagonist of the series. Sonnets 5 and 6 deal with her pride; it has been criticized by some as too "portly" or rebellious. The poet defends it as the shield of innocence:

> Was neuer in this world ought worthy tride,
> without some spark of such self-pleasing pride.[86]

Her eyes calm the storm that passion did begin,[87] yet her own freedom from the bondage of love, her own independence in contrast to the poet's, is presented as a "licentious blisse/ of her freewill." [88] Her character is a mixture of majesty and humility; she looks upon the earth and remembers that she is mortal.[89] Her greatest glory is her mind, "adornd with vertues manifold." [90] Her awareness of heaven and of earth and her power to attract the eyes of others but chasten the desires produced by these looks derive from these qualities of "pride and meeknesse mixt by equall part." [91] This balance produces a self-assurance which is the subject of a dialogue in sonnets 58 and 59. This ample characterization, however much or little it may owe to the personality of an Elizabeth

---

[86] Sonnet 6. [88] Sonnet 10. [90] Sonnet 15.
[87] Sonnet 8. [89] Sonnet 13. [91] Sonnet 21.

Boyle whom Spenser married, is certainly in part the product of the elaborate analysis of feminine qualities in Books III and IV of *The Faerie Queene.*

It has often been observed that in Spenser's series the lady is not a goddess but a saint; she is the consecration and the embodiment of spiritual qualities.[92] Nevertheless, her physical attributes are not neglected, and the special way in which these are portrayed and the combination of these qualities with the spiritual traits already noticed gives Spenser's *Amoretti* its own peculiar quality. The blazon of the lady's beauties appears in several sonnets, most notably in sonnet 15, "Ye tradefull Merchants," in which her features are compared to the riches of the earth. A warmer and more sensuous blazon is contained in sonnet 64, in which she is related not to gems but to flowers. The tone of this description and the general imagery remind the reader of Spenser's *Epithalamion:*

> Her goodly eyes lyke Saphyres shining bright,
> Her forehead yuory white,
> Her cheekes lyke apples which the sun hath rudded,
> Her lips lyke cherryes charming men to byte,
> Her brest like to a bowle of creame vncrudded,
> Her paps lyke lyllies budded,
> Her snowie necke lyke to a marble towre,
> And all her body like a pallace fayre,
> Ascending vppe with many a stately stayre,
> To honors seat and chastities sweet bowre.[93]

Much of the imagery and the general tone here come from the Song of Solomon. It has been well described as a tone of "sensuous and sedative suggestiveness." [94] Spenser seems to have hit upon a range of imagery which was at once decorative in the sense that it would be appropriate for pictorial presentation and sensually effective or "suggestive." This is

[92] Sonnet 61.
[93] Variorum *Minor Poems,* II, 245, lines 171–180.
[94] Israel Baroway, "The Imagery of Spenser and the *Song of Songs,*" *JEGP,* XXXIII (1934), 23–45.

important because it is an aspect of his whole view of love.
Allegorically, the same kind of thing is given in the account
of the birth, education, and residence of Amoret in *The
Faerie Queene*, Books III and IV. As C. S. Lewis has pointed
out,[95] the best understanding of Amoret comes from such
sonnets as No. 8 in *Amoretti:*

> More then most faire, full of the liuing fire,
> Kindled aboue vnto the maker neere:
> no eies but ioyes, in which al powers conspire,
> that to the world naught else be counted deare.

This divine element in the lady is manifest in her physical
beauties as well as in the qualities of her mind; the fact that
these beauties strike us as somewhat creamy and glittering
simply raises the question of Spenser's technique in description. "Her goodly bosome lyke a strawberry bed" is obviously
not a simile of a simple descriptive sort, even though the
catalogue here is one of delightful odors. Throughout the
cycle, as a matter of fact, the descriptions of the lady which
could be called emblematic or formal are quite frequent. In
sonnet 20 she is a lion; in sonnet 38 a dolphin; in sonnet 53
a panther; in sonnet 56 a tiger; in sonnet 71 a bee; in sonnet
67 a deer. This emblematic method, going back as it does in
Spenser's own work through the *Complaints* and *The Shepheardes Calender* to the poems in Van der Noodt's *Theatre,*
serves here as a means of emphasizing the physical beauties
of the lady and yet avoiding Ovidian suggestions of licen-
tiousness. The oddest example is that of sonnet 77:

> Was it a dreame, or did I see it playne,
> a goodly table of pure yuory:
> all spred with iuncats, fit to entertayne
> the greatest Prince with pompous roialty?
> Mongst which there in a siluer dish did ly
> twoo golden apples of vnualewd price:
> far passing those which Hercules came by,
> or those which Atalanta did entice.
> Exceeding sweet, yet voyd of sinfull vice,

---

[95] *The Allegory of Love,* pp. 341–346.

That many sought yet none could euer taste,
sweet fruit of pleasure brought from paradice
by Loue himselfe and in his garden plaste.
Her brest that table was so richly spredd,
My thoughts the guests, which would thereon haue fedd.

The commentary on this sonnet by Baroway [96] makes clear that the emblematic language in this case comes from the Song of Songs: "Patently, the 'siluer dish' cannot even remotely suggest the human breast. It is purely a metaphorical standard of superlative beauty, which, with the preceding 'pure yuory' and the succeeding and similarly symbolic 'twoo golden apples of vnualewd price' must be interpreted in the spirit of 'His belly like white yuory couered with saphirs' (Song of Solomon 5:14), or 'His legges are as pillars of marble, set upon sockets of fine golde' (Song of Solomon 5:15), or even more aptly, 'Thy nauel is lyke a round goblet wherein no mingled wine is wanting' (Song of Solomon 7:3)."

This obligation to the Song of Songs is interesting chiefly because it is a matter of technique; but not all of the emblematic method comes from the Jewish wedding song. Spenser is here adapting to the special requirements of the love sonnet a method which he had used for other purposes and on other material.

Spenser's particular qualities in the Petrarchan mode are, then, the emphasis upon the lady, in contrast to Sidney's (and Petrarch's) practice, the presentation of her spiritual qualities rather fully, and the employment of an emblematic method in the blazoning of the lady's physical beauties. There are also some remarkable qualities in his metrics. The easy and natural flow of the verse, which is partly caused by Spenser's rhyme scheme, he can occasionally fortify by a steady and clear logical progression. In sonnet 34, for example, the thought of the sonnet moves through the carefully articulated sections marked by "Lyke as," "so," "Yet," "Till then," with the turn of thought at each quatrain emphasized rhetorically; yet the linked rhymes push the movement on into the next section, and we have a balance of rhetorical organization and metrical organization. The effect of Spenser's metrical inno-vation in the sonnet (of course, he was not the first to try it, only the first to use it consistently) was to give more space; by uniting the rooms of which the little house is made he gives an impression of amplitude and freedom which the son-net of Sidney does not have. The "sad pensiuenesse" of Spen-ser's style is perhaps most effective when it is conveyed in very simple terms, anecdotally perhaps, as in

One day I wrote her name vpon the strand.[97]

Sometimes the calm tone resolves itself from a question, re-flective rather than impatient or dramatic:

What guyle is this, that these her golden tresses,
She doth attyre vnder a net of gold.[98]

Is it her nature or is it her will,
to be so cruel to an humbled foe? [99]

The sonnets marking the progress of the year are also com-monly moral and reflective, turning from the immediate sub-ject of love to the more general one of life.

In subject matter, Spenser's sonnet cycle differs from the usual Elizabethan one in that the love proceeds to a happy conclusion, though the last few sonnets pay enough acknowl-edgment to the tradition to establish a separation which is the source of lament. In general, the similarity in tone between the sonnets and the *Epithalamion,* supported by the absence of any such conflict of conscience as appears in Sidney's *Astrophel and Stella,* makes the *Amoretti* seem to be the cele-bration of a love affair which leads up to and implies mar-riage, rather than the more courtly love situation which lies behind the usual sonnet cycle. Spenser's opposition to both the code of courtly love and the Ovidian celebration of sex is apparent enough from Book III of *The Faerie Queene.* But we must not go too far; there is actually no mention of mar-riage in the *Amoretti.* C. S. Lewis, impelled perhaps by a

[97] Sonnet 75.   [98] Sonnet 37.   [99] Sonnet 61.

special purpose, has made out Spenser to be "the greatest among the founders of that romantic conception of marriage which is the basis of all our love literature from Shakespeare to Meredith." [100] Even if this is true, Edmund Spenser must not be read as if he were Coventry Patmore. And the sonnets are not properly read when they are used to support dubious interpretations of the meaning of *The Faerie Queene*.[101]

The sonnets of Shakespeare, a cycle without a title and published only in 1609, after the decline of the vogue, though probably written in the 1590's, have been the subject of so much speculation and argument that it is all but impossible for the modern reader to approach them with a fresh eye. Of all the poetry of the Elizabethan period, these sonnets have suffered most from the nineteenth-century obsession with the biographical relation between poet and poetry. Mountains of conjecture have been built up concerning the story in the sonnet cycle, the identification of the persons involved in the story, and the secret of Shakespeare's heart, which, according to Wordsworth, the poet here unlocked for the world to see. These mountains of conjecture are almost all trash. They have no scientific or historical validity; no single theory about the sonnets commands anything even remotely approaching assent from all "qualified" critics. Nor do these theories contribute in the least to the understanding or appreciation of the poetry as poetry. The reason is fairly simple. They begin at the wrong end; they peer around the poetry at what they suppose is some exciting tissue of life or fact behind it. They are looking for scraps of diary or personal letters, more interested in the man than in his work.

[100] *The Allegory of Love,* p. 360.

[101] An example is Janet Spens's *Spenser's Faerie Queene* (London, 1934), p. 105. The author maintains that the captivity of Amoret by Busyrane and her sufferings "represent the mental sufferings of the young wife in consequence of the too lustful element in Sir Scudamour's passion for her. This lustful element at once wounds and enflames her. Busyrane is simply this side of Sir Scudamour himself." She says this point is elucidated by the sonnets and cites 72 and 83 as evidence. But in any case, Spenser was the author of the original ending to Book III of *The Faerie Queene,* and the *Amoretti* and the *Epithalamion* alike glorify the sexual element sanctified in the phrase from the old marriage service, "With my body I thee worship."

Nearly a thousand pages are required, in Professor Rollins' Variorum edition of the sonnets, merely to present a selection and digest of all this commentary. Very few of these thousand pages deal with the poetry itself at all. They either assume that the poetry is not so important as the mystery or they assume that the qualities of the poetry are self-evident and require no comment.

A recent editor of the sonnets, a learned, bold, and imaginative scholar, famous for his good sense and his critical perspicacity as well as for his mastery of the technical aspects of Elizabethan scholarship, summed up his view of the poetic nature of Shakespeare's sonnets in a paragraph.[102] In it, he maintains that Shakespeare's style in the sonnets, though very rich, is essentially simple. "There is nothing recondite, exotic, or 'metaphysical' in the thought." Nor, he believes, is there anything very subtle or complicated in the versification. He takes sonnet 116 for an example. "In short, the poet has employed one hundred and ten of the simplest words in the language, and the two simplest rime-schemes, to produce a poem which has about it no strangeness whatever except the strangeness of perfection." Here is the sonnet in question:

Let me not to the marriage of true minds
Admit impediments. Love is not love
Which alters when it alteration finds,
Or bends with the remover to remove.
O, no! it is an ever-fixed mark,
That looks on tempests and is never shaken;
It is the star to every wand'ring bark,
Whose worth's unknown, although his height be taken.
Love's not Time's fool, though rosy lips and cheeks
Within his bending sickle's compass come;
Love alters not with his brief hours and weeks,
But bears it out even to the edge of doom.
    If this be error, and upon me proved,
    I never writ, nor no man ever loved.[103]

102 Tucker Brooke, ed., *Shakespeare's Sonnets* (New York, 1936), p. 7.
103 Brooke ed., p. 196. I quote throughout from Brooke's edition, though I use the numbers of the 1609 Quarto rather than those of his rearrangement.

If we take the last phrase of Brooke's summary and consider further, we may wonder if this strangeness of perfection is not, in part at least, analyzable.

The theme of the poem is the stability and permanence of love. The method of treating the theme is essentially formal and rhetorical. After the first statement, hortatory in form, "Let me not to the marriage of true minds admit impediments," the poet proceeds to explain his position by defining love: first negatively, saying what love is not ("Love is not love which . . ."), then positively, telling what love is ("it is an ever-fixed mark . . ."), then negatively again ("Love's not Time's fool . . . Love alters not . . ."). The poem itself, or rather the argument, is entirely contained within the three quatrains, and the final couplet is only a comment, triumphant because of the airtight logic of the preceding lines; it is a challenge, a defiance to the reader to escape the consequences of this rigorous definition if he can. But it should be noticed that the comment is personal in form ("upon *me* proved, I never writ . . .") just as the opening exhortation was personal ("Let *me* not" instead of "Let us not" or "Let no one"), thus providing a framework of subjective immediacy for the rather detached, academic, or universal character of the threefold definition which comprises the main part of the sonnet.

Two great concepts, Space and Time, are applied to the consideration of Love in the poem, and the final statement in lines 11–12 is a climax and summary of the earlier statements of Love's changelessness in the face of these two powerful forces for change.

Shakespeare's language proceeds from abstract to concrete: the first negative definition plays grammatically on the ideas of *alter* and *remove,* going from verb to noun and from noun back to verb in lines 3–4. It then moves on to an image in the second quatrain, a complex image based upon navigation: love is a kind of sea-mark ("A conspicuous object distinguishable at sea which serves to guide or warn sailors in navigation" [104]), and like any proper and dependable sea-mark it is

[104] *OED*, def. 2.

proof against storms (line 6). In fact, since this is the love of "the marriage of true *minds*," it is heavenly and most like the celestial sea-mark, the North Star. It can be used for navigational purposes (its height is taken), even though the mineral riches included in the substance of the star or its astrological influence on the people on earth below it may be mysteries hidden from human intellect. The figure of the lover as a ship at sea is a conventional one, from Petrarch on down, but the seriousness with which Shakespeare takes the associations implicit in his navigational image is very unusual.

The image in the third quatrain is also complex; it is emblematic rather than symbolic, and we seem to have moved from the seashore and the context of Elizabethan navigation into a gallery hung with an arras or painted cloth.[105] Shakespeare is fond of the phrase "Time's fool"; he uses it always in an ironical situation, as in Hotspur's dying speech:

> But thought's the slave of life, and life time's fool;
> And time, that takes survey of all the world,
> Must have a stop . . .[106]

and it appears in the couplet of sonnet 124:

> the fools of time
> Which die for goodness, who have liv'd for crime.

"Rosy lips and cheeks," the property of mock-love or fancy, which depends upon the eye and not the mind, are represented as coming within the compass of Time's bending sickle. This bold and fantastic image, related to one in sonnet 60, is a part of the negative definition which closes the poet's case, but the two lines which follow it gather up everything in their summary. "Bending" in line 10 and "alters" in line 11, it should be noticed, tie up this last negative definition with the first one and recall the "alters" of line 3 and "bends" of line 4.

---

[105] For the various roles of Time in Renaissance art and poetry see S. C. Chew, "Time and Fortune," *ELH*, VI (1939), 83–113.
[106] *I Henry IV*, V, iv, 81–83.

"Bears it out even to the edge of doom" has some kind of notion of space in it, since it is difficult to imagine an "edge" to time, and there is something in the line which suggests the straight, purposeful, and direct sailing of the mariner who guides his wandering bark by the polestar in the second quatrain. The finality and sonority of the summary in lines 11–12 permits a quite dramatic shift of tone for the couplet; but the method of the couplet, with its use of the word "proved" and its formula, "This conclusion can only be proved wrong at the cost of accepting an obvious absurdity," calls our attention again to the logical rigor of the sonnet's organization.

What happens in the sonnet, then, is that the logical organization, the concepts of space and time, the imagery, and to a considerable extent the versification, reinforce each other. The way in which the first line of each quatrain strongly contradicts the normal expectation of iambic pentameter is important in stressing the argumentative and positive tone of the quatrains. How skillfully, then, is the tone shifted to a deceptive quietness and modesty by the consecutive unstressed syllables in the middle of line 13,

If this be error, and upon me proved,

to culminate in a total effect, for the couplet, of almost glib certainty in

I never writ, nor no man ever loved.

The context of the sonnet is of some importance, for it follows 115, of which the second quatrain is:

But reckoning Time, whose million'd accidents
Creep in 'twixt vows, and change decrees of kings,
Tan sacred beauty, blunt the sharp'st intents,
Divert strong minds to the course of altering things.[107]

The vitality of sonnet 116 partly depends upon the recognition that the changes brought about by time are taken into account, even in the extreme statements of the permanence

[107] Brooke ed., p. 195.

and unchangeability of love. The poem belongs to a larger group, too, in which the subject of mutability and change extends through nature, the works of man, even to "strong minds," and is the grand theme for improvisation, variation, and commentary.

This analysis is intended to show that for all their apparent simplicity, the sonnets of Shakespeare have a rich and complex texture, and that this richness and complexity is not to be found in diction, versification, or subject, but in the metaphors. The perfection is a matter of metaphorical variety, logic, and development. A sensitive awareness of the metaphorical structure of Shakespeare's sonnets will reveal a good deal of strangeness, and if it is perfection, it is surely not the perfection of simplicity. Shakespeare's sonnets have never been so inadequately characterized as they were by his seventeenth-century editor, John Benson: "Seren, cleere and eligantly plaine, such gentle straines as shall recreate and not perplexe your braine, no cloudy stuffe to puzzell intellect." [108]

Shakespeare demonstrates the height and climax of the Elizabethan quest in the Petrarchan sonnet tradition: to find variety, passion, invention, and plausibility. His own particular way of developing the type to this climax was through a complexity of metaphorical elaboration—not "metaphysical," because it does not exist for its own sake but to play against the other factors, rhythmical, rhetorical, structural. They go beyond anything Watson, or perhaps even Sidney, had envisaged, but they are consequences of the same impulse that moved the pioneers of the English sonnet vogue. With this key Shakespeare unlocked—what? I should say that he unlocked the mysterious rooms in a poet's mind in which metaphor as a mode of thinking illuminates new worlds of experience and insight.

The sonnets are generally thought to have been written

[108] Quoted by Brooke, *Shakespeare's Sonnets*, p. 9, unfortunately with approval. I have shown in "No Cloudy Stuffe to Puzzell Intellect," *Shakespeare Quarterly*, I (1950), 18–21, that these statements were not originally meant to apply to Shakespeare anyway. They were lifted from a testimonial by one disciple of Ben Jonson to another.

in the nineties.[109] Yet there are sonnets which remind readers of such later plays as *Hamlet, King Lear,* and *Antony and Cleopatra.* This fact, combined with the obvious maturity of thought and feeling in some of them and with the references in some sonnets to the·advanced age of the poet, might be considered arguments that the sonnets were written later. But Francis Meres gives testimony that some of them were in circulation among the poet's private friends in 1598, and two of them, Nos. 138 and 144 of the 1609 text, were published in 1599 in *The Passionate Pilgrim.* The maturity of the sonnets and the resemblances between them and the late plays have been explained by Brooke ingeniously and plausibly: "Is not the best explanation of this the simple one that Shakespeare's development within the sonnet's scanty plot of ground far outspeeded his development as a dramatist? The poignancy and immediacy of the feelings he was driven to express in the Sonnets taught him early, I take it, to handle with finality those intenser and more private depths of soul which in his drama were mainly reserved for a later period." [110] If it is true, and it seems to be, that the "sonnet's scanty plot of ground" developed Shakespeare's mind and art faster than the drama did, the reason may well be not in the particular feelings, indeterminable as they are, which prompted him to write sonnets, but in the nature of the sonnet itself, its conventions, its technique, and its opportunities. We should be justified, then, in leaving aside all questions such as the identity of Mr. W. H.; the claims of Southampton, Pembroke, or Willie Hughes to be characters in the story; the original order of the sonnet sequence; and new light on the dark lady. We ought to concern ourselves with the themes, the imagery, the structure, and the temper of the sonnets themselves. For their life and their significance

---

[109] See Appendix II in Rollins' Variorum edition. I am not convinced by the arguments of Leslie Hotson for an earlier date. See his *Shakespeare's Sonnets Dated* (New York, 1949), pp. 1–36, and the extensive discussion which followed its publication; contributions to the discussion are conveniently listed in E. W. Talbert *et al.,* "Recent Literature of The Renaissance," *SP,* XLVIII (1951), 313–314.

[110] *Shakespeare's Sonnets,* p. 16.

comes not from their value as narrative but from their value as poetry.

There is much in Shakespeare's sonnets on the theme of the conflict between time and beauty. The cycle opens with a series which pleads with a fair young man to marry and beget children so that his beauty may not perish with him but may survive through "breed." This leads very soon to the introduction of another means of defying time and death —poetry. In its simplest form, this theme may be handled rhetorically, with some satisfactory image such as that of nature, flowers, the spring, readily associated with youth. A good example is No. 18, "Shall I compare thee to a summer's day?" The poet counters the light and delicate effects, achieved largely through imagery, in the first eight lines, by an insistent and sonorous metrical effect in the line which marks the turn of thought. The fragility and temporary quality of physical beauty, which is the idea of the first eight lines, is not allowed to overwhelm the bright and lovely aspects of it; the two are evoked equally, one by statement and the other by illustrations and images. The gaiety that is injected by the refused or qualified comparison in the first two lines is carried through, to swell into the confident tone of the last six lines. The "fair" becomes an abstract idea, but its concreteness is supported by the darling buds of May, the gold complexion of the sun, and, by implication throughout, the youth of the one addressed. The recurrence of And . . . and . . . and, but . . . nor . . . nor . . . so . . . so . . . at the beginning of lines gives the verse a rapidity of movement; the word "Rough" in line 3 is the only strong accent to begin a line. Moreover, the rhetorical pattern is carried on by this process, so we have the impression of smooth, quick, effortless persuasion, fitted to the lighthearted character of the poem.

Time is not usually treated so lightheartedly, however. Sonnet 55 is an example of the treatment of time in a tone of solemn dignity. The poem is extraordinarily rich in texture of sound combinations, and a detailed analysis would reveal how subtly the sound effects reinforce the imagery.

But, at the risk of making explicit what should remain implicit, we must examine the nature of the metaphorical thinking in this sonnet, if only to show how different it is from Spenser's *Amoretti* 69, which also uses the commonplace of poetry as a monument or memorial.

> Not marble, nor the gilded monuments
> Of princes, shall outlive this powerful rime;
> But you shall shine more bright in these contents
> Than unswept stone, besmear'd with sluttish time.
> When wasteful war shall statues overturn,
> And broils root out the work of masonry,
> Nor Mars his sword nor war's quick fire shall burn
> The living record of your memory.
> 'Gainst death and all-oblivious enmity
> Shall you pace forth; your praise shall still find room,
> Even in the eyes of all posterity
> That wear this world out to the ending doom.
>   So, till the judgment that yourself arise,
>   You live in this, and dwell in lovers' eyes.

In the first quatrain there is a competition regarding the brightness of material things, specifically monuments, and the memory of "you" embodied in these poems. The word "gilded" implies no disrespect for princes' monuments; it is a way of introducing brightness and color which the marble failed to do. By line 4 the poet has turned to deprecation of gravestones and has a homely image for them. The key or principle of all this is the idea of brightness. Why "sluttish" time? Because "unswept stone" suggests a negligent housemaid, too lazy to sweep. "Unswept stone, besmear'd with sluttish time" has therefore a transferred epithet in it, and the line resolves two modes of considering time and gravestones: the aristocratic connotations of the first line of the sonnet are destroyed by the association with "unswept" and "sluttish," and simultaneously the contrast of brightness between poetry and stone is insisted upon.

The programmatic or imitative quality of the second quatrain is obvious; the movement and the sound texture together mimic the violence and disorder of war and civil strife ("broils"). The speed and violence of the destruction are conveyed rhetorically by the suspended subject, "Mars his sword," which has no verb, or rather, is joined with "war's quick fire" in the act, impossible for it, of burning. The rhythmical turbulence of the ten monosyllables in line 7 is quieted by the simplicity and calmness of the eighth line, and there is a curious connection between "living" and the ambiguity in the meaning of "quick."

The third quatrain begins with another transferred epithet, or rather a hysteron proteron: "all-oblivious enmity" should be, in prose, "all-inimical oblivion," but the transfer has accomplished something by emphasizing the antagonism of time and forgetfulness. It is a semi-personification. Furthermore, the tenth line has in it a dim suggestion of the aristocratic atmosphere of line 1; the pacing forth is like the entry of a nobleman into a crowded place, and room is made for him. If this impression is really there and is not a mere critic's fancy, then some sort of revolution has taken place in the sonnet by which princes, represented in their gilded monuments, are deposed to the level of sluts, but "you," celebrated only by poetry, pace forth as the new cynosure. At any rate, the person addressed will find his place "in the eyes" of posterity; the sense is double: posterity will read the poems, and the eyes of posterity are in some sense the final repository of fame. This is made clearer and more explicit in the fourteenth line. Posterity "that wear this world out to the ending doom" is somewhat more complex than "bears it out even to the edge of doom" in No. 116; as time, war, and broils wear out the physical monuments on the earth, so posterity wears out the world itself. The universal character of the enmity of time is again suggested. The "ending doom" here is also taken seriously, for the figure of the couplet includes an actual judgment day. The powerful rhyme which outlives marble and the gilded monuments of princes is coextensive with posterity, and this makes the introduction to the couplet a logical one: *So,* till the judgment . . .

It should be observed that the first twelve lines are all in the future; the word "shall" occurs six times. The continu-

ing present of the couplet is therefore very strong by contrast: "So, till . . . You *live* in this and *dwell* in lovers' eyes."
The contrasts in the sonnet's statement, between permanence
and change, destruction and survival, frailty and power, are
thus strengthened by the grammatical structure as well as by
the metaphorical thought; an examination of the rhymes and
other features of sound would show further reinforcement.[111]

These analyses may perhaps suggest the kind of study which
might show how Shakespeare differs from, and surpasses, his
predecessors. His sonnets are "indirect" in the sense that their
poetry largely devotes itself not to the professed subject but
to something in the realm of metaphor. They are vehicles of
the imagination, and the imaginative play here is almost all
directed by metaphorical complexity. We will be entirely unable to understand their effect or their significance if we stop
with the stage of critical investigation which concludes with
a tribute to "their grand simplicity and unambiguousness,
the complete mastery of mind over words which cuts straight
to the heart of the idea and expresses the intensest or most
intricate emotions in language so inevitably right and eco-
nomical that—if the reader properly apprehends it—it seems
easy." [112]

Some of the most impressive and eloquent of the sonnets
are those which depend less upon a reflective situation for
their framework than upon an apparent display of the poet's
moods directly. It is especially true that, of these sonnets,
those expressing a mood of despair or disillusion, of melancholy over the failure of the world or of the human personality, remind us of passages in the tragedies. The ideas are

111 The annotations of editors who try to "explain" meanings by straighten-
ing out grammar or syntax are sometimes harmful to the perception of the
metaphorical richness characteristic of this and other sonnets of Shakespeare.
For example, Pooler, in the Variorum *Sonnets*, interprets "than unswept
stone" as "thán *in* unswept stone": "my verse will be a better memorial than
the inscription on your tomb"; this ignores completely the intended contrast
in brightness. Dictionary annotations run the same risk: the *OED* cites line 4
as the only authority for a figurative use of a general meaning for "sluttish":
"Dirty and untidy in dress and habits." See Variorum *Sonnets*, ed. Rollins, I,
150–151.

112 Brooke, *Shakespeare's Sonnets*, p. 9.

sometimes bitter in the manner of a Hamlet or a Lear. The motivation seems to be partly the same motivation that lies behind the satire of the 1590's, partly a more profound sense of the inevitable corruption of man in a world which is beyond his managing or even his understanding. Hamlet's awareness of the reasons for rejecting the world is reflected in No. 66, "Tir'd with all these, for restful death I cry." Yet the main burden of these sonnets of despondency is not that the fault lies in a corrupting world; they throw the principal emphasis upon the truant disposition of the speaker himself; that is to say, on the face of it they seem more psychological than satirical. Two of the most effective of these sonnets of mood are Nos. 29 and 30, "When in disgrace with fortune and men's eyes" and "When to the sessions of sweet silent thought."

Shakespeare's method in these sonnets may best be observed in No. 73. Here the professed subject is the poet's age, which is contrasted with the youth of the young man addressed in several other sonnets. But the resultant mood is the same mood of despair as that of the sonnets we have mentioned. The utility of that mood, some of its origins, and the way in which it unifies and makes effective the sonnet are worth analysis.

> That time of year thou mayst in me behold
> When yellow leaves, or none, or few, do hang
> Upon those boughs which shake against the cold,
> Bare ruin'd choirs, where late the sweet birds sang.
> In me thou see'st the twilight of such day
> As after sunset fadeth in the west,
> Which by and by black night doth take away,
> Death's second self, that seals up all in rest.
> In me thou see'st the glowing of such fire,
> That on the ashes of his youth doth lie,
> As the death-bed whereon it must expire
> Consum'd with that which it was nourish'd by.
>   This thou perceiv'st, which makes thy love more strong,
>   To love that well which thou must leave ere long.[113]

[113] Brooke, *Shakespeare's Sonnets*, p. 163.

The quatrains here are clearly divided, the first devoting itself to an image of trees in early winter or late fall, the second to an image of twilight and the beginning of night, and the third to the image of a dying fire. The relationship of these to the professed subject of the poem, old age, is fairly obvious, and it might be said that the sonnet is merely an application of these images to the idea. However, Shakespeare's method is not quite so simple as this, and the way in which the images are worked out and the way in which they influence each other are worth notice.

The indirectness of Shakespeare's method could hardly better be exemplified than in the first quatrain. Here the picture of the trees in winter is used to project a situation of the feelings, rather than the external attributes of age. "When yellow leaves, or none, or few": the uncertainty here is clearly deliberate. Yellow leaves as a symbol of age are obvious enough, even if we do not recall Macbeth's "My way of life is fall'n into the sere, the yellow leaf," but the curious effect produced here is by the alternatives of "yellow leaves," "none," and "few." Then the purely descriptive part of the image is extended, with "upon those boughs which shake against the cold" carrying us farther into the picture of winter and away from the relationship between the speaker and the image. If we stop at this point and ask of the first line, In what respect may this time of year be seen "in me," there is no answer, for the figure has left the speaker behind and developed in a purely descriptive direction. But then in line 4 the boughs themselves are made the subject of further metaphor, "bare ruin'd choirs," and then returned immediately to their first existence as boughs by the "explanation" of the choir figure, "where late the sweet birds sang."

The problem here is one of deciding just what the nature of this figure is. To what degree does the image of the speaker remain in the reader's eye: are those boughs which shake against the cold supposed to cause us to picture an old man's arms? When the boughs are momentarily transformed by the "bare ruin'd choirs," are we to evoke very fully the picture of the decayed monastery churches with their ruined choirs and, as William Empson suggests,[114] the choirboys themselves, and associate this with the feeling of the poet toward the young man addressed? The control of the associations is very difficult. In general, it seems safest to say that the connections between the picture, doubly metaphorical, of the winter boughs is only atmospherically and symbolically connected with "in me." There is nothing of an allegorical correspondence or even a conceit. It is this reticence about the application of the description to the subject that allows for further development in the following quatrains.

The image of twilight fading and being taken away by night brings the imagery closer to the subject, for the night is called "Death's second self," and the ambiguous "that seals up all in rest" applies to both night and death, the two selves. "Seals up" is another of those rural terms common in Shakespeare's figurative language; it applies to putting cattle away for the night.[115]

The third quatrain uses the image of a dying fire, and here there is a genuine conceit. The fire still burns, but on the ashes of what has been already burnt. This is like old age, which rests on the youth which has produced it. But an additional idea is that this is a deathbed, relating our associations to the night-death image of the preceding quatrain, and the idea of a bed of ashes inevitably suggests repentance and humiliation. Moreover, the ashes tend to choke the fire, though they represent former fire, former fuel. Therefore, we get a formulation of a favorite idea of Shakespeare's: "Consum'd with that which it was nourish'd by." The irony of process, as it might be called, has many expressions in these sonnets; it is an indication of the antique cast of Shakespeare's mind: "And time that gave doth now his gift confound." [116]

---

[114] *Seven Types of Ambiguity* (London, 1930) , p. 3.

[115] See T. G. Tucker, *The Sonnets of Shakespeare* (Cambridge, England, 1924) , p. 149. In some ways Tucker's edition is the most useful of all editions of the sonnets, especially for the kind of analysis which I have been attempting here. He is, however, insufficiently sensitive to ambiguities in meaning, and his comment will often dogmatize on a single meaning when two or more exist at once.

[116] Sonnet 60.

Sonnet 73 is clear in its general design. The three quatrains have a relationship to each other and a natural development. They proceed from the declining of the year to the declining of the day to a declining of the fire, bringing the metaphorical point closer to the subject as the poem progresses. But the relationship of the figures to each other is also a metaphorical one: the year and the day are both metaphors for a lifetime; the fire has to do both with the heat and life of summer and noonday as well as with the vital essence of life. The richness of the sonnet derives more from its metaphorical involutions than it does from the clarity of its structure.[117]

The group of sonnets devoted to the "dark lady" has given rise to much biographical speculation and conjecture, but their real significance to readers interested in poetry is that they provide an opportunity for the treatment of a love situation far outside the area of the usual Petrarchan sonneteer. The dark lady is connected in the poet's experience with his other love, that of a young man, and the contrast between the two is sufficiently apparent. The central poem of the series is No. 144, "Two loves have I, of comfort and despair." All aspects of the relationship of the three are worked out—jealousy, justification of the young man for his moral lapse, joking over the ambiguity of the situation, and, most of all, an analysis of the nature of the poet's love for the lady. It is a

---

[117] R. M. Alden (*The Sonnets of Shakespeare* [Boston, 1916], p. 183) called this "the finest example of the Shakespearian mode," presumably because of its structure, for Alden is so resistant to the metaphors in Shakespeare that he recoiled with horror at some of the more obvious images in sonnet 60, preferring to pretend that they are not there. John Crowe Ransom's essay, "Shakespeare at Sonnets," *Southern Review*, III (1937–38), 531–553, republished in *The World's Body* (New York, 1938), comments on and praises the three-quatrain sonnets above the others. Arthur Mizener's reply to Ransom in *Southern Review*, V (1939–40), 730–747, deals with the structure of Shakespeare's figurative language. The line in sonnet 73 which I discussed only briefly, "Bare ruin'd choirs, where late the sweet birds sang," offers an example of the difficulties of critics: Ransom says he deplores the coexistence of the images of the boughs shaking against the cold and of the bare ruin'd choirs; not only this but he also says, "I believe everybody will deprecate *sweet*" ("Shakespeare at Sonnets," p. 550). Tucker, on the other hand, does not deprecate it. He says, "The epithet is not idle; the choirs formerly rang with 'sweet' singing. The implication is 'I was a summer poet once'" (*The Sonnets of Shakespeare*, p. 149).

powerful lust, which sometimes disgusts him and sometimes amuses him, but as he works out its implications, especially in the metaphors of the sonnets, he is developing in a more mature way an element which shows in the imagery of *Hamlet, Lear,* and *Othello* and which receives somewhat more explicit treatment in *Troilus and Cressida.*

Sonnet 147 gives perhaps the clearest and most unified treatment of the nature of this kind of love:

> My love is as a fever, longing still
> For that which longer nurseth the disease;
> Feeding on that which doth preserve the ill,
> Th'uncertain sickly appetite to please.
> My reason, the physician to my love,
> Angry that his prescriptions are not kept,
> Hath left me, and I desperate now approve
> Desire is death, which physic did except.
> Past cure I am, now Reason is past care,
> And frantic-mad with evermore unrest;
> My thoughts and my discourse as madmen's are,
> At random from the truth vainly express'd.
> > For I have sworn thee fair, and thought thee bright,
> > Who art as black as hell, as dark as night.

Reason as a doctor or guide whose commands the speaker has not followed, to his cost, is a commonplace of Petrarchan poetry. But there could be no better illustration of how different Shakespeare is from the conventional mode of the sonnet cycles than this piece. The essential paradox of the sonnet is expressed in the couplet, and in this instance the couplet is more functional than it usually is in Shakespeare, since it justifies and explains the quatrains. Essentially, the disease is that of regarding the woman, who is physically dark and morally evil, as fair and bright. The first quatrain presents this paradox in terms of the patient who is ill of a fever and who preserves this fever by eating things not good for him and which he does not wholeheartedly like anyway. Then the situation of his sickness is given: the physician has renounced him, and he exemplifies in himself the proposition that desire is death. The disorder of his state is implied in the ambiguous grammatical structure of line 8: "which physic did except" means both that the science of medicine (i.e., Reason) forbade desire and also, with subject and object reversed, that Desire, his fever and ultimately his death, has refused to take the medicine which Reason prescribed. From fever, then, he proceeds to frantic-madness in which he says the opposite of truth.

What makes this sonnet different from the usual Elizabethan discourse on love as a sickness is the moral emphasis, both in the content and the imagery. And this moral bias is, characteristically in Shakespeare, expressed most fully in metaphors.

Sonnet 129 is a formal description of lust, with important distinctions among the stages of it: before satisfaction, during satisfaction, and after satisfaction. Its relation to madness is again emphasized, but instead of the medical metaphor which dominates sonnet 147, this time Shakespeare connects it with that phosphorus poison used for rats which he uses again in *Measure for Measure:*

> So every scope by the immoderate use
> Turns to restraint. Our natures do pursue,
> Like rats that ravin down their proper bane,
> A thirsty evil, and when we drink, we die.[118]

The sonnet is as follows:

> Th'expense of spirit in a waste of shame
> Is lust in action; and till action, lust
> Is perjur'd, murd'rous, bloody, full of blame,
> Savage, extreme, rude, cruel, not to trust:
> Enjoy'd no sooner but despised straight;
> Past reason hunted, and no sooner had,
> Past reason hated, as a swallow'd bait
> On purpose laid to make the taker mad:
> Mad in pursuit and in possession so;
> Had, having, and, in quest to have, extreme;
> A bliss in proof, and, prov'd, a very woe;
> Before, a joy propos'd; behind, a dream.
>   All this the world well knows; yet none knows well
>   To shun the heaven that leads men to this hell.

[118] I, ii, 131–134.

This anatomy of lust has some resemblances to the imprecations in *Lucrece,* but its main objective is different; it is, like sonnet 127, an attack upon the self-contradictory aspects of desire. The positive value against which this must be seen is a kind of self-sufficiency, which we will examine in other sonnets in a moment. The first definition, shocking in its suddenness and its reversed grammatical order, shows the environment in which the imagery is to be felt. "Spirit" is ambiguous, meaning both energy, vitality, life, and the more concrete sense of semen, the "thrice-concocted blood" of common Elizabethan reference. "Expense," "waste," and "shame" are all related; there is a double sense to "expense" and "shame." In a way, the first line and a half complete a whole epigram. Then the poem turns into a catalogue of the attributes of lust as pursuit, and then appears the paradox of its hatefulness and its irresistibility. The feverish violence of the dilemma is imitated in the movement and sound of the last quatrain:

> Had, having, and, in quest to have, extreme.

The couplet admits that the attributes are well known but any way of escape is unknown because of the "heaven" which entraps us on the way to it.

The sonnets in which the "fair friend" is involved in this relationship show some curious attitudes on the part of the poet. In one series, the moral lapse of the friend is excused by various sophistical arguments, such as the ones in Nos. 35 and 41. It is clear that the seducer is the lady, and she, as the "bad angel," continues to represent the attraction of that power which is fatal to self-containment and self-sufficiency. Sonnet 94 is the poem which shows most clearly this ideal of self-containment as the opposite of indulgence in lust. Its general argument and the figure in which it is expressed have a much more general application in the sonnets, and perhaps in the plays as well, than most commentators have recognized.

> They that have power to hurt and will do none,
> That do not do the thing they most do show,
> Who, moving others, are themselves as stone,

Unmoved, cold, and to temptation slow;
They rightly do inherit heaven's graces,
And husband nature's riches from expense;
They are the lords and owners of their faces,
Others but stewards of their excellence.
The summer's flower is to the summer sweet,
Though to itself it only live and die,
But if that flower with base infection meet,
The basest weed outbraves his dignity:
　For sweetest things turn sourest by their deeds;
　Lilies that fester smell far worse than weeds.

This sonnet evokes some of the concerns which are present in the relationship of Prince Hal and Falstaff, as well as the obvious implications for Angelo in *Measure for Measure*. But it belongs also with the group of sonnets about the fair young man's offense in the sonnet cycle; the important thing is not so much what particular context of event or situation calls it up to Shakespeare's mind (apparently there were several) but the general significance of this view of sin. We have two rival prose abstracts of the sonnet for purposes of comparison:

The best people are indifferent to temptation and detached from the world; nor is this state selfish, because they do good by unconscious influence, like the flower. You must be like them; you are quite like them already. But even the best people must be continually on their guard, because they become the worst, just as the pure and detached lily smells worst, once they fall from their perfection.[119]

The other considers the context to be much more specific:

You have your own free will, to be unchaste or not, and your beauty exposes you to the temptation of women. But consider yourself as sole inheritor from heaven of this beauty, and expected to keep it to yourself; those who share their beauty in sex must regard themselves as but its stewards. There is no reproach upon the flower for being self-contained. But infected flowers smell to heaven.[120]

[119] William Empson, *English Pastoral Poetry*, p. 89. Empson proceeds to give an extremely complicated account of this sonnet. Some of the connections he sees are in my opinion clearly right, but there is no control whatever on the associations he brings in. He tries to reconcile this sonnet to those of the propagation series (Nos. 1–17) and sees in the octet some reference to the parable of the talents (*ibid.*, p. 94).

[120] John Crowe Ransom, "Mr. Empson's Muddles," *Southern Review*, IV (1938–39), 329.

It might be possible to reconcile the differences between these two versions, and preserve what each of them has of truth, by examining first the structure of the sonnet. The first eight lines constitute a definition of the true and false heirs of "heaven's graces" or "nature's riches"—perhaps not exactly true and false heirs, but heirs who are real owners, lords, and masters, as distinguished from mere stewards, managers, or tenants. The inheritance is clearly one of physical beauty, "their faces," and its value is clearly considered to be very great, since it is inherited from heaven. Physical beauty is, however, to be regarded as the wealth of nature, "nature's riches," and this gives rise to the figure of the beautiful as either owners of this wealth or mere stewards of it. Perhaps the class distinction here has something to do with the aristocracy of the supposed addressee of the sonnets, but in any case there is the feeling about the responsible lord, who "husbands" natural wealth from "expense." This last word reminds us of its use in the first line of sonnet 129, "Th'expense of spirit." Whether a beautiful person is a lord-owner or a mere steward depends upon whether he makes use of his powers or refrains from doing so. The cautious vagueness of the first few lines, especially the second, conveys a sense of shame about the wrong to be committed "That do not do the thing they most do show."

The octave of the sonnet, then (for the image structure here is Italian, though the rhyme scheme is English), seems to urge the hoarding or at least husbanding of this beauty: the doctrine is the exact opposite of the argument in the first seventeen sonnets of the cycle. It needs some justification. This justification is provided by the device of a metaphor: the summer's flower. The self-sufficiency of a flower was of course established or fortified by a sacred text, "Consider the lilies of the field, how they grow; they toil not, neither do they spin," and it may well have been the recollection of this verse which brought into Shakespeare's mind the line from *Edward III* (whether by him or another) which ends the sonnet: "Lilies that fester smell far worse than weeds."

This connection between flowers and moral concerns is

almost an obsession with Shakespeare: "For canker vice the sweetest buds doth love" (sonnet 70), and many other such images. In *Troilus and Cressida* there is an association of lilies and lust; as Troilus waits impatiently for Pandarus to convey him to his consummation with Cressida, he says he longs to go

> Where I may wallow in the lily-beds
> Propos'd for the deserver.[121]

The complex of ideas, some of them of course proverbial but none the less a part of Shakespeare's mind, exhibits itself in a passage in *The Rape of Lucrece* which just precedes the execration against Opportunity.[122] Here are the motifs of the spoiled flower, the muddy fountain of sonnet 35, the hoarding or husbanding of riches, sweetness turned to sourness, and the moral interpretation of the spectacle of the garden. This passage is not a "source" for sonnet 94, nor does it help in the problem of dating. It is merely an illustration of the way in which, within the sonnet form and the situations provided in the Shakespearean series, the poet's metaphorical thinking could work itself out. He dreams of beauty self-contained, a Narcissus-like emblem fully justified of itself, and he sees it corrupted and in danger of corruption. It is this that he finds most villainous in lust, that it destroys that self-sufficiency. His model is the garden, which in turn gives an image of aristocracy in the independence and lordliness of the flower. But it illustrates also corruption at the heart of that beauty.

That Shakespeare himself aspired to the kind of refinement and beauty which he celebrates in his friend may be the explanation of some of the obscurities in the sonnets. The expression must be, in most cases, indirect, and the sonnets are not, so far as we know, literal autobiography. But sonnets 110 and 111 are commonly interpreted as having to do with Shakespeare's life as an actor, and it is difficult to see how they can be separated from something of the sort. Sidney's sonnets

[121] III, ii, 13–14.
[122] Lines 848–875 (*Poems*, ed. Rollins, pp. 186–187).

about tournaments and horsemanship reflect the same kind of aristocratic pride which is marked in the tone of the opening of the *Apologie for Poetrie:* Shakespeare's two sonnets on his profession and his habits reveal a shame in his failure to achieve an aristocratic detachment and refinement which he so praises, admires, and worries about in the friend.

> Alas! 'tis true, I have gone here and there,
> And made myself a motley to the view,
> Gor'd mine own thoughts, sold cheap what is most dear,
> Made old offenses of affections new.

This does not make apparent what the connection is between making one's self a motley to the view and selling one's affections. If the next sonnet in the series belongs with this, and it seems to, the explanation is given in lines 6 and 7:

> O! for my sake do you with Fortune chide,
> The guilty goddess of my harmful deeds,
> That did not better for my life provide
> Than public means which public manners breeds.
> Thence comes it that my name receives a brand,
> And almost thence my nature is subdu'd
> To what it works in, like the dyer's hand.

The point of all this is not whether William Shakespeare of Stratford thought that acting was a degrading profession or not; it is that the sonnets reveal an ideal of self-sufficient beauty, untainted by moral and social corruption, which is urged upon the fair friend. Moreover, this ideal is also described by its failure: the vulgarity of being a motley to the view is closely associated with the goring and selling cheap of one's own most precious thoughts and feelings; the habits of a public livelihood induce "public," or unrefined, manners, and they color the nature of the speaker himself. He considers it a plague. This moral-aesthetic revulsion may be seen elsewhere in the experience of artists. André Gide's Journals show evidence of much the same kind of self-condemnation.

This scrupulosity I have said was of the imagination; I

wished to make a distinction between it and a fastidiousness of taste. There is perhaps as much catholicity in the sonnets as in the plays, were we sufficiently at home in the form to see it. Some of the sonnets urging a lady for sexual favors pun upon the name *Will* and in general suggest, in their indecency, the tone of epigrams rather than of Petrarchan sonnets. This attitude toward sexuality is not the extravagant and pornographic one observable, for instance, in Barnes's *Parthenophil and Parthenophe;* instead, it is rather humorous, vulgar, ingenious, and cold. One of the sonnets, No. 151, is an elaborate joke, in Rabelaisian manner, on the phenomenon of tumescence, and No. 138 rings changes on the meanings of "lie" and "lie with." These sonnets exist right along with those which portray lust in the serious moral-aesthetic way we have illustrated, to the confusion and embarrassment of those who read the sonnets to try to see the personality of William Shakespeare behind them.

IV

SATIRE

The English Tradition, the Poet
and the Age

THE significant sources of satire are not literary or philosophical; they are social and economic. For the understanding of satire, and response to it, we need not so much an acquaintance with models and conventions, or an understanding of ideas and principles, as a knowledge of the social milieu from which the satire sprang. Literary theory may influence the style and form of the writing, and ideas, stated directly or implied, may form a large part of its content, but the vitality of the work comes from its connection with actual human behavior. Satire not only concerns itself with the way men live, it is prompted by attitudes which are themselves part of that living. In some kinds of poetry the form may be the most important creative agent; in satire the form is secondary to the social concern which gives the work its impetus and motive power. Therefore, the most fruitful approach to Elizabethan satire is not from classical models or Renaissance theory but from the social and economic scene in sixteenth-century England.

In looking at the second half of the century we are arbitrarily selecting only one section of what was a continuous process from the fifteenth century or earlier to the end of the seventeenth century and later. This process was one of profound social and economic change. Sometimes in the Elizabethan period it speeded up, and the effects were felt immediately. Some factors in the process were more gradual, and phenomena which seemed new to contemporaries were the results of changes which had taken place in the first half of the century.

Before 1550 an acceleration of technology had taken place which resulted in the growth of the English cloth industry to the point at which wool was no longer exported but consumed in the manufacture of cloth; indeed, this went so far that wool was imported for manufacture. Also in the first half of the century, an agrarian reorganization had already begun which continued throughout the Elizabethan period, undiminished by the constant outcry of reformers, preachers, patriots, and satirists against it.

After the middle of the century, significant new developments occurred, making the picture more complicated. These were partly technological, like the partial change from wood to coal for fuel, improvements in metallurgy, and the expansion of the manufacture of brass and copper. But they were also economic, since capital was needed to finance these industries as well as to handle the increased volume of foreign trade in the Elizabethan period. Perhaps most important of all was the rapid growth of London, its evolution into a metropolitan market, and the consequent tremendous development of the functions of the middleman.

Throughout the century there was the most spectacular rise in prices known to history. Its effects upon exploration and discovery, upon the relationship between classes of society, upon the growth of ideals of individualism and free enterprise cannot be exaggerated. To a contemporary Englishman the real causes of this phenomenon were hidden; he did not realize the significance of the flow of gold from America to Europe, or of the change from local to metropolitan market practices. To him, high prices were simply a hardship, and "every imaginable grievance was blamed— the growth of luxury in living, the pride of courts, the greed of merchants, the laziness of artisans, the cost of wars, the selfishness of peace, the lack of religion." [1] The strange chemical effect of the rise in prices has been described as "at once a stimulant to feverish enterprise and an acid dissolving all customary relationships." [2]

Even in the fifteenth century the three estates of medieval society were losing their cohesion, and during the next hundred years the emergence of a new class, the bourgeoisie, became more and more evident. Some legislation of the first half of the century reflected mercantile interests, and it might have been foreseen that from the time of the dissolution of the monasteries on, the middle class would gain in numbers and power. From the gentry younger sons were constantly augmenting its ranks, and from the yeomanry increasing numbers of men raised themselves to financial independence and political power. The Tudor sovereigns encouraged the development of the middle class, for it was on the bourgeoisie that the power and security of the two Henries and Elizabeth rested. The dynastic wars in the fifteenth century had of course prepared the way; the English middle class in its rise to power had only a weakened aristocracy to impede it. But this great historic change, like any historic change, was not easy. It exhibited stresses and strains in the social fabric which sometimes seemed to contemporaries to augur the collapse of the whole civilization they knew. The changes which a modern student of history observes with curious sympathy as signs of progress were viewed by contemporaries with alarm, indignation, rage. They confirmed the philosophers who held, as most of them did, that man was constantly degenerating.

The spectacle of the gentleman, the possessor of landed estates, becoming a business man, for example, strikes the modern student as an interesting evidence of the adaptability and energy of that astonishing English class. But it filled the Elizabethan historian, William Harrison, with dismay: "I am sorie to report it . . . that men of great port and countenance are so farre from suffering their farmers to haue

---

[1] E. F. Gay, "The Renaissance Conference," *HLQ*, IV (1941), 161.
[2] R. H. Tawney, *Religion and the Rise of Capitalism* (London, 1929), p. 137.

anie gaine at all, that they themselues become grasiers, butchers, tanners, sheepmasters, woodmen." [3]

The historian of British commercial and economic life finds the fall of Antwerp to Parma's forces in August 1585 the beginning of London's dominance as the great commercial and trade center on the Atlantic. But Thomas Nashe, in *Christ's Tears over Jerusalem* (1593), defends the thesis that ever since the fall of Antwerp, London has become the scene of the Devil's major efforts. He has assumed the form of Pride, and his sons in London are Ambition, Vainglory, Atheism, Discontent, Contention; his daughters are Disdain, Gorgeous Attire, and Delicacy. [4]

The displacement of a social institution means a tangle of loyalties, ethical considerations, and practical motives. The resources of monasteries, chantries, and ecclesiastical establishments which had been dissolved by Henry VIII and Edward VI furnished economic nourishment for the new men who were supporters of the Tudors. But the social effects of the dissolution, and to some extent even the moral and religious effects, were not always acceptable to the most fervent Protestants. Thomas Lever, for example, was a left-wing Protestant, but in his Paul's Cross sermon of December 14, 1550, he declared with vehemence that from the point of view of the common good the new situation was worse than the old. Formerly, he said, fifty tunbellied monks given to gluttony kept up their house and relieved the poor of the community, but now the single lay owner consumed the house and the neighborhood as well. [5] A Gloucestershire complaint of 1577 points out that in the old days there were many monasteries in the realm and much idleness, but now, though the idleness, thanked be God, had been remedied, the extensive relief of the poor which had been provided by the monasteries was provided by no one. [6] The uncomfortable suspicion that the disappearance of the monasteries left Prot-

[3] R. H. Tawney and Eileen Power, eds., *Tudor Economic Documents*, 3 vols. (London, 1924) , III, 172.

[4] *Works*, ed. McKerrow, II, 81.

[5] Sig. D7^v.

[6] W. H. Dunham and Stanley Pargellis, *Complaint and Reform in England* (New York, 1938) , p. 450.

estant England less charitable than the Catholic countries of the Continent appears over and over again in the writings of Protestants. In 1593 Nashe is writing:

> I haue hearde Trauailers of credite auouch, that in London is not gyuen the tenth part of that almes in a weeke, which in the poorest besieged Citty of Fraunce is gyuen in a day. What, is our religion all auarice and no good works? Because we may not build Monasteries, or haue Masses, Dirges or Trentals sung for our soules, are there no deeds of mercy that God hath enioyned vs? [7]

To be sure, during the reign of Elizabeth the principle of social obligation for the deserving poor was increasingly recognized; many legislative solutions were tried, houses of correction were established, and attempts were made to impose upon local authorities the difficult task of distinguishing between worthy indigents and sturdy beggars and to administer help to the former and discipline to the latter. The prime difficulty lay in administration of the laws, and while the slow process of learning how to deal with the problem went on, there remained much material for the preacher, the moralist, the social economist, and the satirist to seize upon. [8]

Everyone who considered the state of the country in the Elizabethan period concerned himself with certain striking phenomena of economic life; the contemporary analysis of the situation usually differs markedly from that of the modern economic historian, however, for the reason that the Elizabethan observer was not trained in the use of statistics and because all of these problems were colored in his mind by traditional ethical considerations. The enclosure of land for pasture is an example. It was a favorite theme for preachers; its effects on population seemed only too obvious locally, and an oversimplified view of the phenomenon imputed all

---

[7] *Works*, ed. McKerrow, II, 161.

[8] E. M. Leonard, *The Early History of English Poor Relief* (Cambridge, England, 1900), traces the stages in the development of care of the poor. Of the efforts of the Privy Council to insure the execution of the Poor Law of 1597 she says (p. 144), "It is the first time in which this interference seems primarily dictated by motives of humanity and not mainly by a desire to maintain order."

the blame for its inconveniences or hardships to the selfishness of landowners. The enclosure question is a pretty one, because it brings sharply into conflict the profit motive and the common good, as these were understood by the sixteenth-century mind. In John Hales's classic of the middle of the century, *A Discourse of the Common Weale of this Realm of England,* the Knight asks, with reference to the landowners who were enclosing, "Yf they find more proffite therby then otherwise, why should they not?" The question is of course important any time in the capitalist period, but it was particularly critical and embarrassing in Elizabethan England, for that time marked a mid-point between two sharply contrasting attitudes. As Tawney puts it, "The opinion of the practical man on questions of economic conduct was in the sixteenth century in a condition of even more than its customary confusion. A century before, he had practiced extortion and been told that it was wrong; for it was contrary to the law of God. A century later, he was to practice it and be told that he was right; for it was in accordance with the law of nature." [9] Hales's Doctor, who answers the Knight's question, has an admirable answer:

I can tell youe well inowgh why they should not, for they maie not purchace them selues proffitt by that that may be hurtfull to others. But howe to bringe them that they would not doe so, is all the matter; for so longe as they find more proffitt by pasture then by tillage, they will still enclose, and turne arrable landes to pasture. [10]

The problem of administration was indeed an acute one even after the basic situation which Hales deplored, the differential between wool and grain prices, had changed during the second half of the century. Wool was not being exported but was being manufactured into cloth in England, and it was the demand from a home industry which maintained the continuing pressure for enclosures. But Elizabethan observers were often not aware of these facts, nor did they recognize the significance of the tremendous growth of London as

[9] *Religion and the Rise of Capitalism,* p. 163.

[10] *A Discourse of the Common Weale of this Realm of England,* ed. Elizabeth Lamond (Cambridge, England, 1893), p. 50.

a metropolitan market, and the traditional complaints, based upon the assumptions of a more provincial economic organization, continued to be voiced.

In the development of London as a great market, the old customary relationships between producer and consumer broke down, but the ethical and moral principles which men had long felt should govern such relationships were still strong. The spread of the area on which a more populous and industrialized London drew for its food supply meant that the middleman, who had always existed, became an indispensable part of the economy. He alone could systematize supply and make the necessary contact between country field and city kitchen. But traditionally there was an objection to the middleman, and it was hard to find an ethical justification for him as medieval philosophy had found a justification for each man in his estate or calling. Thomas Lever's denunciation of all middlemen in 1550 shows the traditional bias. They are merchants of mischief, he says, who intervene between farmer and householder, landlord and tenant, craftsman and merchant. They are really idle vagabonds, living upon other men's labors; they are crafty covetous extortioners.[11] These objections to the middleman had some justification in the local and provincial picture, because there the middleman did not serve to store up corn against a period of dearth and level out the supply and the price level, and in times of dearth he seemed an unnecessary and costly appendage, if not an absolute parasite. It was hard for the Elizabethans to see that the ethical validity of the middleman was changed just because he operated in the London market instead of in the provincial towns.[12]

The increase in the price of grain brought hardship and of course complaint. It was, apparently, the result of several factors, among them the flow of gold from New Spain into Europe, the conversion of land from tillage to pasture, and,

[11] *A sermon preached at Pauls Crosse,* sigs. F4ʳ–F5ʳ.
[12] See N. S. B. Gras, *The Evolution of the English Corn Market,* Harvard Economic Studies, XIII (Cambridge: Harvard University Press, 1926), chaps. VI and VII.

perhaps most important of all, the growth of the London metropolitan market. The many causes alleged for the dearth are listed and summarized by William Camden, who very prudently does not try to decide among them.[13]

The Elizabethans looked for a more concrete and personal villain than these elusive economic factors, and they found him in the grain speculator, the "engrosser" as they called him. He is denounced from the middle of the century to the end. Hugh Latimer, preaching before King Edward VI in 1550, damns "regraters" and hoarders; he tells of a merchant who had spent a lifetime in business to clear a thousand pounds and can now make the same amount in a year merely buying and selling grain.[14] Harrison, who calls these speculators "bodgers" or "great occupiers," complains that they take the market completely away from poor men, but he can think of no remedy except prayer.[15] The engrosser had of course been the subject of attack for centuries; but the Elizabethans confused the middleman with the speculator, saw the increased importance of the middleman, and concluded that the monstrous vice of extortion was increasing. Every period of dearth and every increase in the price of grain brought the old complaint to life again.

Most familiar of all as a victim of satire was the usurer. He was so often the object of attack that his appearance and behavior became conventionalized, and he was recognizable on sight.[16] Both the authority of Aristotle and the precepts of Christianity were against making money by the mere lending of money, but of course business had long utilized credit and contracts involving the payment of interest. The cloth

[13] *Remains* (2d ed., 1614), sig. Dd^v.

[14] *Sermons by Hugh Latimer*, ed. G. E. Corrie (Cambridge, England: Parker Society, 1894), p. 279.

[15] Tawney and Power, *Tudor Economic Documents*, III, 77. Many other examples of satire on this subject are cited in Burton Milligan, "Sixteenth and Seventeenth Century Satire against Grain Engrossers," *SP*, XXXVII (1940), 585–597.

[16] For an elaborate annotation of the usurer's role in Elizabethan literature see two articles by Celeste Turner Wright, "Some Conventions regarding the Usurer in Elizabethan Literature," *SP*, XXXI (1934), 176–197, and "The Usurer's Sin in Elizabethan Literature," *SP*, XXXV (1938), 178–194.

trade was based upon credit transactions, and its great expansion in the sixteenth century necessitated a much larger volume of borrowing. New capital was called forth by the increase in coal mining and metalworking, and the building and equipping of vessels for foreign trade was done on borrowed money. The Elizabethan age saw a tremendous expansion of credit operations, and new classes and individuals were affected. Therefore the question of usury was constantly in the air. Again it was a question of distinguishing between lawful, legitimate interest and usury.

Attempts to control interest rates led to further abuses. The statute of 1572 limited interest to 10 per cent, but lenders avoided this by the device of making the borrower take his money in the form of overvalued commodities, which he then had to sell at a loss in order to get his needed cash. The attack upon "taking up of commodities," with frequent reference to such goods as brown paper and ginger, provided additional matter for the satirist.

The usurer's customers were not always borrowing to finance business. The increasing extravagance of the nobility meant that the usurers were called upon to finance conspicuous waste, which could itself be morally denounced. Tawney has compiled a list of the debts of some typical nobles in the last twenty years of the century: the Duke of Norfolk, £6,000; the Earl of Huntingdon, £20,000; the Earl of Essex, £22,000; the Earl of Leicester, £59,000; Sir Francis Willoughby, £21,000; Sir Percival Willoughby, £8,000; Sir Philip Sidney, £6,000; and so on.[17] These were largely debts incurred to meet current expenses, and the money was furnished by "usurers" of all classes, from the most disreputable sharks to leading citizens of the middle class like Sir Thomas Gresham. As Tawney puts it, "merchants, mercers, drapers, grocers, tailors, wine-merchants, innkeepers, goldsmiths, scriveners, as well as an indefinite number of 'citizens,' are all found making advances."[18]

[17] Thomas Wilson, *A Discourse upon Usury*, ed. R. H. Tawney (London, 1924), p. 32.
[18] *Ibid.*, p. 39.

The harassed gentleman under these circumstances could not of course continue to borrow indefinitely to pay current expenses; he had to find a way to improve his condition. One method was to tighten up on the tenants on his land and rack the rents. This, too, became a major source of complaint. To some observers the whole process seemed an endless chain of evil. As Nashe said, "The snake eateth vp the toade, and the toade the snayle: the Vsurer eateth vp the Gentleman, and the Gentleman the yeoman, and all three being deuoured one of another, do nothing but complaine one vpon another." [19]

Gentlemen who were courtiers had another resource—that of extracting from the Queen a patent or monopoly, like Walsingham's on the customs from exports, or upon raw materials, like Ralegh's patent on Cornwall tin. Another type of patent was that of the right to collect forfeitures under some one of the penal statutes.

These devices of the crown for rewarding its servants could of course bear heavily on the public, and they became the source of increasing scandal through the reigns of Elizabeth and the early Stuarts. Parliament had to be careful in its attacks on the monopoly system, because it came near the Queen's prerogative. Peter Wentworth, one of the boldest of the reformers, asserted that when Peter Bell, sometime Speaker of the House of Commons, made a speech against "Licences granted to four courtiers, to the utter undoing of six or eight thousand of the Queen's Majesty's subjects," he was sent for by the Council and so hardly dealt with that nobody in the House dared speak of anything important for "ten, twelve, or sixteen days." [20] In the last Elizabethan Parliament, however, the attacks on monopolies,[21] combined with popular petitions and street cries, proceeded to such a degree that the Queen herself had to intervene and in her "Golden Speech" of November 30, 1601, revoked all the

[19] *Works,* ed. McKerrow, II, 159, note.
[20] Dunham and Pargellis, *Complaint and Reform,* p. 272.
[21] One of the many examples is George Phillips' *The Life and Death of the rich man and Lazarus* (1600).

patents then in force. This action has been called "the acme of Tudor kingcraft." [22]

Other sources of conflict and criticism were social rather than economic, but even these were related to the fundamental economic situation of the time. The growth of foreign trade meant that foreign goods, clothing, food, and wine, which changed the traditional habits of Englishmen, were more widely consumed and displayed, to the intense annoyance of the traditional provincial Englishman and of the serious Puritan who saw all such luxuries as visible evidence of the sin of Pride. Even the reasonable and unprejudiced Doctor in Hales's dialogue, describing conditions about 1549, saw in the importation of foreign goods an economic and a moral danger.[23] This new luxury was not confined to the nobility, the gentry, and richer merchants by any means. Harrison informs us, and his testimony is weighty because his intention is *not* satirical, that by 1587 this taste for finery had descended even unto inferior artificers and farmers, who can now boast of plate, silk hangings, carpets, and fine napery.[24] Harrison's attitude of approval of this tendency is unusual, though it is possible to detect a little nervousness under his protestations, for to most observers this increased love of luxury would seem decadent and morally wrong. The sumptuary legislation which had, more or less, kept the classes distinguishable from each other in the Middle Ages was now invoked by a series of proclamations, but it was powerless against the mingling of the classes, the importation of novel fashions from abroad, and the enrichment of the English merchant class. What made satire possible was the continuance of the older feeling, crystallized in the sumptuary laws, that status should be defined, authentic, and permanent.

Robert Greene's pamphlet, *A Qvip for An Vpstart Courtier: or, A quaint dispute between Veluet breeches and Cloth-breeches. Wherein is plainely set downe the disorders in all*

---

[22] Dunham and Pargellis, *Complaint and Reform,* pp. 340, 345–350.
[23] *A Discourse,* ed. Lamond, pp. 125–126.
[24] Tawney and Power, *Tudor Economic Documents,* III, 69.

Estates and Trades, gives the same kind of attitude in 1592 that Hales had given for the beginning and Harrison for the middle of the Queen's reign. Velvet Breeches, the upstart courtier, comes originally from Italy, as a symbol of the new foreign styles; Cloth Breeches is native English, with no pretensions to fashion or style.[25] To settle the argument between them, all the estates and trades of the kingdom select a representative; from these representatives the jury is chosen. Since either the upstart courtier or the plain homespun has something against most other men, the challenges are many, but a jury is finally chosen and it reaches its decision in favor of Cloth Breeches.[26]

This contrast between the ancient, homely English, manorial culture and the ostentatious, Italianate, courtly civilization is the basis of much Elizabethan satire. The contrasting ideals are what was called "honesty," meaning a kind of rugged simplicity and practicality, and what was called "bravery," meaning refinement, bravado, the flourish of superiority. Some of the harshest vituperation comes from extreme Puritans, like Stubbes, but it is hardly satire and the religious difference is not so fundamental as the cultural one. Cloth Breeches in Greene's pamphlet doesn't like Puritans; to him they seem merely to "raise vp new scismes and heresies amongst your people." [27] Perhaps the most important contribution of the Reformation to the state of mind that produced satire in the second half of the sixteenth century was that it emphasized with new sharpness the moral responsibility of the individual. Elizabethan literature is full of this attempt to solve morally questions of politics, economics, and sociology, and the fervor seems to be a Reformation fervor. Under the Catholic dispensation there was perhaps more institutional tolerance and realization that human nature was

[25] A similar debate between the two kinds of breeches may be found in Francis Thynne's *The Debate betweene Pride and Lowliness* (1570). For a discussion, see Helen C. White, *Social Criticism in Popular Religious Literature of the Sixteenth Century* (New York, 1944), p. 35. The device is used also in the fourth verse satire of Samuel Rowlands' *The Letting of Humour's Blood in the Head Vaine* (1600).

[26] Sig. H3ʳ.   [27] Sig. G2ᵛ.

not going to reach perfection at one jump. The Elizabethan religious "settlement," significant as it was, did not settle in a psychological sense.

The ideas which stored the Elizabethan mind were not ideas uncongenial to satire. Mutability, the degeneration of man, the decay of the world and its approaching end, all cast a somber light on the activities of men.[28] Moreover, the survey of man as he was, in his actions and appearance, the record of his actual behavior, had as a background the strongly contrasting image of man *in posse* as the pride of creation. Hamlet's speech of wonder at what a piece of work is a man is not unique; in the dedication to his *Anatomie of Abuses* Philip Stubbes, an observer very unlike Hamlet, shows the same kind of picture of man.[29]

The possibility of satire, or the necessity for it, comes from holding this general characterization of man in mind and then observing his antics under high heaven, especially as he experiences the disruptive social and economic changes of the sixteenth century.

Theodore Spencer has illuminated the dilemma of the view of man as it produced tragedy, showing how the skeptical tradition represented by Montaigne viewed man as another animal and challenged the Platonic-humanistic glorification of man.[30] The same dramatic contrast, as he recognizes, produces satire, but for satire the observation of actual life and behavior is probably more important than the skeptical theory.

Some students of Elizabethan literature have stressed psychological factors as producing a sardonic, melancholy, and bitter spirit in sensitive Englishmen, especially in the last decade of the century.[31] There was, no doubt, a relapse in

[28] See D. C. Allen, "The Degeneration of Man and Renaissance Pessimism," *SP*, XXXV (1938), 202–227, for an attack on the idea of the "joyous Renaissance," and A. L. Williams, "A Note on Pessimism in the Renaissance," *SP*, XXXVI (1939), 243–246, for a needed comment on the relative importance of economic and philosophical factors.

[29] Sigs. ¶ 2r–v.

[30] *Shakespeare and the Nature of Man* (New York, 1942), chaps. I and II.

[31] See, for example, G. B. Harrison's essay prefixed to his edition of Breton's *Melancholicke Humours* (London, 1929); O. J. Campbell's "Jaques," *HLB*,

general enthusiasm and confidence after the excitement of the victory of the Armada had died down and the serious problems facing the country regarding the succession found part of their expression in the Essex conspiracy.[32] But the understanding of Elizabethan satire as a whole cannot be clear on any theory of psychological factors or temperamental changes. They merely reflect deeper currents of influence.

It is commonly said that satire is not an important form in Elizabethan literature.[33] Yet any reader of the great body of the literature of the age is aware of the fact that there is a satiric element inherent in almost all of it. The literary histories have generally looked for formal satire and, finding none of importance until the 1590's, have focused their attention upon Hall and Marston and Donne as the three examples of satire. Even then the feeling is that these poets are forerunners, of historical interest only, that satire did not emerge as a mature form until the time of Dryden.[34] But the question of form is a difficult one in dealing with the sixteenth century in any kind of poetry, and the view that sixteenth-century satire is only a precursor of later things needs some modification.

Perhaps after all it is a smug and complacent society which can departmentalize its experience so much that it finds an adequate separate form for its satire. Pope could try to regularize and improve Donne's satires, but in the very process is there not something destructive of satirical integrity? The Elizabethans saw the satirical in the shadow of the pastoral, in the obverse of the heroic, in the extravagance of love poetry. What motive was there to make them find a separate form for it? Furthermore, the models, the sources from which a convention and a tradition could be made, were mixed.

---

no. 8 (1935), pp. 71–102, criticizes Harrison but continues to keep the emphasis on psychological or temperamental factors.

[32] See E. K. Chambers, "The Disenchantment of the Elizabethans," in his *Sir Thomas Wyatt and Collected Studies* (London, 1933).

[33] See, for example, Hardin Craig, *The Enchanted Glass* (New York, 1936), p. 207, and T. S. Eliot, *Elizabethan Essays* (London, 1934), p. 181.

[34] R. M. Alden, *The Rise of Formal Satire in England* (Philadelphia, 1899), is the standard work and illustrates these tendencies.

Just as Spenser was at once trying to follow Chaucer and the humanist writers of pastoral in his *Shepheardes Calender,* so a writer of verse satire had not only Juvenal and Persius to follow, but Horace and, even more important, the author of *Piers Plowman.*[35] Langland, according to Robert Crowley, the first printer of the *Vision of William Concerning Piers the Plowman* (1550), "doeth moste christianlye enstruct the weake, and sharply rebuke the obstinate blynde. There is no maner of vice, that reigneth in anye estate of men, whiche this writer hath not godly, learnedlye, and wittilye rebuked." His importance as a model for satire, then, lay in the fact that he was a saint of the Reformation, attacking the works of darkness in a time when they prevailed. Crowley admits that the English in which the poem is written may be difficult, but he assures the reader "that it may be vnderstande of suche as will not sticke to breake the shell of the nutte for the kernelles sake."

Crowley's own satires, which he published under the misleading title of *One and thyrtye Epigrammes* (1550),[36] include attacks upon forestallers, usurers, and rent-raisers, as well as discussing the more general subjects of blasphemers, alehouses, flatterers, and common liars. In *The Voyce of the laste trumpet* (1550), Crowley admonishes twelve different classes of people, from beggars to women, in a series of "lessons." In a prose tract, *An informacion and Peticion agaynst the oppressours of the pore Commons of this Realme* (1548),

---

[35] Helen C. White, who has an illuminating chapter on the Piers Plowman tradition in her *Social Criticism in Popular Religious Literature of the Sixteenth Century,* says (p. 3) that Langland's poem is not a satire. But Elizabethan critics, who did not distinguish between the *Vision* and the apocryphal poems, uniformly name *Piers Plowman* as a model in satire. To Puttenham he is the only English model and is mentioned in the same sentence with Lucilius, Juvenal, and Persius as examples of satire (*The Arte of English Poesie,* ed. Willcock and Walker, p. 26). Meres mentions Piers Plowman first in the list of those English writers eminent for satire (*Francis Meres's Treatise "Poetrie,"* ed. D. C. Allen [Urbana, Illinois, 1933], p. 79). Milton, in attacking Hall, says that he "might have learnt better among the Latin, and Italian Satyrists, and in our own tongue from the *vision and Creed of Pierce plowman*" (*Works,* 18 vols. [New York: Columbia University Press, 1931–1938], vol. III, pt. i, p. 329).

[36] Ed. by J. M. Cowper, EETS, Extra Series No. XV (1872).

Crowley urges legislative remedy for the evils of enclosure, rent-raising, and oppression by the clergy. Crowley was "a Puritan of the narrowest school," in the words of his editor; [37] but his work as a satirist shows a motivation of great concern over the social abuses of the time and an inspiration from *Piers Plowman* of the proper way in which to attack them. There is some evidence, from the preface of John Parkhurst to his epigrams, that the *One and thyrtye Epigrammes* of Crowley were held in high esteem.[38]

The name Piers Plowman in the sixteenth century referred not only to the *Vision* but also to an apocryphal work, first printed in 1553, called *Pierce the Ploughmans Crede*. This is a Wycliffite tract in verse attacking the four orders of friars. It was published in the same volume with the *Vision* in Owen Rogers' edition of 1561; to the Elizabethans it was in the canon. In addition, there were other satirical tracts in the middle of the century with the name Piers Plowman attached to them. One of them, apparently a Protestant tract published in Mary Tudor's time, begins,

> I playne Piers which can not flatter
> A plowe man men me call
> My speche is fowlle yet marke the matter
> How thynges may hap to fall.

It protests violently against the suppression of the scriptures in English and attacks the priests and bishops from the point of view of the poor and ignorant, whom Piers, as plowman, represents. Here the role of Piers is identified as the Wyclif tradition, with its religious, political, and class implications. The pamphlet was felt to be still topical about 1590, for there was an attempt to republish it, as written by "the Grandsier of Martin mare-prelitte." [39] Another tract, *Pyers plowmans exhortation vnto the lordes knightes and burgoysses of the Parlyamenthouse*, printed by Anthony Scoloker,[40] is an at-

[37] *Ibid.*, p. xi.

[38] See H. H. Hudson, *The Epigram in the English Renaissance* (Princeton, 1947), p. 141.

[39] See Percy Simpson, *Proof-Reading in the Sixteenth, Seventeenth and Eighteenth Centuries* (London, 1935), pp. 69–70.

[40] *STC*, 19905 (1550?).

tack upon enclosures and a plea for relief. Apparently the reason for the role of Piers Plowman in this piece is the author's low rank, his concern with social and economic welfare, and his connection of this concern with Christian principles.[41] The author suggests remedies, and he presents the interesting picture of a naïve variant of John Hales. But the Piers Plowman role may also have something to do with his announced qualities of style:

> For I being altogether ignoraunt of the arte of rethorycke, haue not conningly set furth this matter, but onely layde before you the naked trueth in rude wordes, which onely bare truth if you substancially wyll ponder, I dout not but you shall then easely perceyue.[42]

The importance of the Piers Plowman tradition in English satire is that it emphasized the unity of religious and social concerns, strengthened and kept alive the medieval manner of considering society as a group of the various "estates" and trades which made it up, and gave prestige to a style that was uncouth, rough, or plain, devoid of rhetoric, and trying for simple truth and rugged honesty rather than for polished wit.

An example of the verse satire in the tradition of Piers Plowman is Churchyard's *Dauy Dicars Dreame* (1552), a poem which started a "flyting" between Churchyard and Thomas Camell.[43] Davy Dicar is a rustic spokesman for plain honesty and truth, like Piers, and Churchyard's verse is a series of "When" clauses ending with the conclusion,

> Then baelful barnes be blyth
> that here in England wonne,
> Your strife shall stynt I vndertake,
> your dredfull dayes ar done.

---

[41] Sigs. A2r-v.

[42] Sig. B2r.

[43] Davy Diker or Digger was a common type-name for the humblest type of worker, the navvy. In a list in which all the other crafts are represented by their common names, Gascoigne uses the proper name here: "When Davie Diker diggs, and dallies not" (*Works*, ed. J. W. Cunliffe, 2 vols. [Cambridge, England, 1907–1910], II, 171).

Conditions that must be remedied before this happy state of affairs is reached include bribery, flattery, covetousness, neglect of learning, pursuit of private profit, and the attempt to move from one's own class into another.[44]

The tradition of Piers Plowman continues on down into the seventies in Gascoigne's *The Steel Glas* (1576).[45] This blank verse satire, representing Gascoigne in his phase of moralist, is introduced by an allegorical application of the myth of Philomela to the kinds of poetry. After this prelude, Gascoigne arraigns the various classes of society in the medieval manner, proclaiming their faults and crying out for amendment. He finally calls up as spokesman Piers Plowman specifically:

> Therfore I say, stand forth Peerce plowman first,
> Thou winst the roome, by verie worthinesse.[46]

The defense of Piers as spokesman comes from the contrast with the practitioners of the same evils which disturbed the moralists and satirists at the middle of the century. Then the poet proceeds to order the priests to pray for Piers and to pray for others who do amiss. In answer to a supposed angry question from the priests about when their prayers will have an end, Gascoigne replies with a "When" catalogue longer and more elaborate than Churchyard's "When." It includes some thirty-six separate crafts or trades, each with its characteristic vice, and concludes that when all these things are reformed, then the priests may make holiday and pray only ordinary prayers. This reflects an essentially medieval method of classifying society, with the additional zeal of the Reforma-

---

[44] The *Dreame* and its sequels, with the contributions of the other parties who tried to make peace between Churchyard and Camell, were collected and printed under the title *The Contention betwyxte Churchyeard and Camell, vpon Dauid Dycers Dreame, sett out in suche order, that it is bothe wyttye and profytable for all degryes* by Owen Rogers in 1560. A bibliography of the items in the controversy is given in Robert Lemon, *Catalogue of Printed Broadsides in the Society of Antiquaries* (London, 1866), pp. 7–10.

[45] I do not mean to suggest that it stopped in the seventies. In 1580 was published a book by R. B. called *The ploughman's complaint of sundry wicked livers in verse* (STC, 1061); I have not seen a copy.

[46] *Works*, ed. Cunliffe, II, 170.

tion concern about personal honesty and moral responsibility.[47] The suggestion might be made that the emphasis on diminished quality in the work of craftsmen and artificers reflects the decreased power and authority of the guilds over their members as well as the natural and inevitable consequences of production on a larger scale.

Gascoigne is portrayed, in the authoritative biography of him by Professor C. T. Prouty, as essentially a conservative, conscious of the fact that he was the eldest son of a knight and disgusted because all his own ventures turned out so badly, with perhaps a sullen and wistful feeling that in earlier days knights' sons fared better.[48] This is perhaps true, and the poet's attack on those who complained at racked rents rather than on the landlords themselves seems unusual, but fundamentally Gascoigne is merely following in the tradition of the *Piers Plowman* kind of satire. The epilogue to *The Steel Glas* contains a verse attack on women, especially for the extravagance of their dress.[49] But he breaks off his satire on women

> Since al the hands, al paper, pen and inke
> Which ever yet this wretched world possesst
> Cannot describe this Sex in colours dewe.

The continued influence of the medieval social tradition in satire, and of the method of Langland, is manifest in the satire of Spenser, *Prosopopoia or Mother Hubberds Tale,* begun perhaps about 1580 but substantially written and first published a decade later, in 1591. Spenser, as we should expect, makes his satire a more ambitious performance artistically than the works we have been considering. And for an

[47] The method was widely used in the Elizabethan period by moralists and preachers like William Perkins, whose *Treatise of the Vocations* covers approximately the same ground covered by the end of *The Steel Glas*. See Helen C. White, *Social Criticism in Popular Religious Literature*, pp. 190–192. For a discussion of Perkins as one of the most important spokesmen on the bourgeois code of ethics in the Elizabethan period, see Louis B. Wright, *Middle-Class Culture in Elizabethan England*, pp. 170–187, and "William Perkins," *HLQ*, III (1940), 181–183.

[48] *George Gascoigne* (New York, 1942), p. 251.

[49] *Works*, ed. Cunliffe, II, 173–174.

artistic model Spenser turned most characteristically to Chaucer. The beast-fable device offered him an opportunity to survey the various estates of society with critical and satirical purpose and at the same time to provide a narrative continuity and interest that the cruder devices of Churchyard and Gascoigne lacked.

The context out of which the poem takes its occasion is the social one: the time of the telling of the story is a time of plague, when commonly men examined themselves to see how much their miseries were the result of their sins; and, even more importantly, the action of the fable is motivated by the social unrest of the period which we have seen analyzed by preachers, poets, and economists. The adventures of the Ape and the Fox, in devastating the flocks of the husbandman, in appropriating to their own selfish uses the endowment which was intended for priests to use in the true service of Christianity, in perverting the function of courtiers by following the fantastic tastes of the court and rejecting the prayers of poor suitors for help, and finally in stealing and misusing the very symbols of government itself—all represent, by the method of fable, the abuses which were seen by social reformers as the crying disgrace of the times. The Fox and the Ape represent those traits of human nature which are forcing social institutions out of their true function. The Fox is the crafty beast of the Reynard cycle, unscrupulous in his methods and clever in his ability to circumvent simple and honest people. The Ape is the symbol of man as a beast, desecrating the form of his body which is the image of God by dressing up fantastically, parodying in a grim fashion the essential qualities of humanity—dignity, responsibility, love of God and of fellow man. The final episode, in which the Ape and Fox steal the Lion's regalia and proceed to ruin the country with their misrule, is of course the culmination of the plan of the poem. The problem of government, that is to say, the problem of the solution of the social problems so apparent in the sixteenth century—enclosures and maintenance of agriculture, control of prices, stabilization of the class structure, maintenance of the quality and output of manufactured goods—this problem or series of problems seemed to most serious Elizabethan observers to require primary moral qualities on the part of rulers and magistrates which were strikingly less common than they used to be.

> For not by that which is, the world now deemeth,
> (As it was wont) but by that same that seemeth.[50]

Spenser's device here is genuinely allegorical; it takes qualities out of the persons attacked and personifies them (the Ape and the Fox), and can therefore produce the satiric effect more indirectly but more "morally." That the Ape represents apish qualities which may, and do, seduce courtiers from their true function and quality is made clear in the section on the court.[51] In contrast to this, there is the sketch of the ideal courtier, who yields true courtesy to everyone:

> But not with kissed hand belowe the knee,
> As that same Apish crue is wont to doo.[52]

The economic and financial activities of the two kinds of courtier are consonant with their manners. The ideal courtier will study affairs of state, and especially domestic economy, to relieve the distressed:

> For he is practiz'd well in policie,
> And thereto doth his Courting most applie:
> To learne the enterdeale of Princes strange,
> To marke th'intent of Counsells, and the change
> Of states, and eke of priuate men somewhile,
> Supplanted by fine falshood and faire guile.[53]

The most serious of the crimes of the Fox and Ape at court was to deceive and frustrate the common man who was "supplanted by fine falshood and faire guile" and came to court to get remedy for his wrongs. The court was supposed to be the seat of appeal against the injustices of the time, and the courtier's greatest crime against his calling was to prevent or

---

[50] *Mother Hubberds Tale,* lines 649–650 (Variorum *Minor Poems,* II).
[51] Lines 655–854.
[52] Lines 730–731.
[53] Lines 783–788.

distort its use for this purpose. Spenser emphasizes this point with the most elaborate rhetoric in his poem.[54] The reason for the prominence of the satire on the court in the *Mother Hubberds Tale* is of course the conviction, natural to Spenser, that the court should be the true source for relief and remedy for the social dislocations of the age.

Modern commentary on *Mother Hubberds Tale* has concerned itself mostly with individual or special satire in the poem, trying to identify the elements of attack upon Burleigh or James VI, in order to account for the fact that there is a considerable body of evidence that Spenser's poem was "called in."[55] The precise interpretation of the specific satire in the poem is difficult, but the more general satire in the first 900 lines is clear enough, and the commentators would at least agree that Spenser is a defender of Leicester's Puritan party and an attacker of Burleigh, especially after the poet's unfortunate experience at court in 1590.

A minor satirist who was a follower of Leicester, a Puritan, and a humble representative of the medieval tradition in satire coming down from *Piers Plowman* is Edward Hake, whose *Newes out of Powles Churchyarde* survives in a revised edition of 1579, dedicated to Leicester, but was first published in 1567, an edition now lost. Hake was an understeward of the Borough of Windsor. His verses, in the monotonous fourteeners characteristic of the time, make no claim to literary importance; in fact, Hake says in his "To the Reader" that he knows as well as any of his critics "what is lackinge (as well in the inuention as in the verse of the booke) that shoulde carye away commendation amongst the better sort of english Poetes of our tyme"—namely, practice and reading, neither of which he has. The interest of Hake's book, then, comes from the subjects on which he felt moved to write satires. He first attacks the lawyers who obstruct justice by furthering their own greed for money rather than by serving poor litigants, who buy country estates and set up as gentlemen, racking tenants and driving them off their

---

[54] Lines 892–906.
[55] See Variorum *Minor Poems*, II, 568–585.

lands. Doctors are more interested in wealth than in healing the sick. Merchants venture across the seas for all kinds of vain luxuries with which the people are corrupted, for the profit of the merchant. The merchant himself loads his table with all manner of luxurious food, his wife and daughter are clothed with an incredible extravagance, while the poor and needy suffer more every day from the merchant's depredations. The country is teeming with false bankrupts or sharpers, who defraud their creditors and conceal their assets. Hake deplores the bull- and bear-baiting, the profanation of the Sabbath, the prevalence of bawds and whores, and then he returns to the subject of "brokers" who lend money upon commodities and make an outrageous profit. It is clear that in his moral indignation he never moves very far from the economic and social phenomena of the time, bringing to bear upon them a Christian, Protestant, common-man indignation.

II

Although the most prevailing ideas concerning the nature of satire, its purpose and function, current in Elizabethan England were native and associated with the vogue of *Piers Plowman,* there was a certain amount of theory of satire derived from the classics and from Italian critics of the Renaissance. The appearance of formal satire, on the classical model, in the last decade of the sixteenth century was not so abrupt or sudden as has been supposed. A primary reason why it did not appear sooner may be found in the suitability of the *Piers Plowman* style to the principal subjects of satire in the period, the social and economic changes brought on by the rise in prices, enclosures, and the emergence of modern capitalistic practices. Nondramatic satire, with Horace and Persius and Juvenal as models, had to make its way slowly; when it did finally emerge, the method of these satirists seemed to lead so inevitably to flytings and libels that authority had to step in, in 1599, and suppress satires.

What appears to be the first definition of satire in English is the work of Thomas Drant, prefixed to his metrical version of Horace's satires published in 1566.[56] Drant attributes his definition to "Priscus Grammaticus" ("an early Grammarian," probably Diomedes, according to Miss Randolph); it reads:

> A Satyre is a tarte and carpyng kynd of verse.
> An instrument to pynche the prankes of men.

Then Drant proceeds to give several of the etymological explanations of the name, all of which have something to do with critical ideas about how satire should be written. Satire comes from the Arabic, he says, and means a glaive: a sword or sharp cutting instrument. Or, he says, it comes from satyrs, the rough and shaggy wood gods; this impression was widespread among Elizabethan writers. Sometimes they apparently make no distinction between the two words at all: illustrative title pages representing the kinds of poetry represent satire by the figure of a satyr. Furthermore, satire comes from Saturn, and the melancholy, sullen disposition of those who are saturnine in temperament; as Saturn is pictured cutting down time with his scythe, so satire cuts down sin, says Drant. Or, again, satire comes from Latin *satur:* full, satiated, since the author must be full of "fostred arte" to teach his lessons to the world. Drant says that the masters of satire are Lucilius, Horace, Juvenal, and Persius.

A theory of satire which endorsed the practice of it in the native English tradition could be derived from Horace. In the fourth satire of Book I, the main points are the unpoetic nature of satire, its impersonality and objectivity, and its educational or didactic value:

> insuevit pater optimus hoc me,
> ut fugerem exemplis vitiorum quaeque notando.[57]

By example, too, Horace might be used to support the satire of the Piers Plowman tradition. The first of his satires, on the universal greed and desire for riches that makes men envy

---

[56] The definition is reprinted and discussed by M. C. Randolph in "Thomas Drant's Definition of Satire," *Notes and Queries*, CLXXX (1941), 416–418.

[57] I, iv, 105–106.

each other and wear themselves out in an endless search for wealth, suggests just the kind of complaint about the shifting of the estates and the breaking down of old ideals of moderation made by the preachers and moralists of the mid-sixteenth century. In Drant's translation, even when he is sticking close to his original, the medieval survey of society by trades appears.[58] Often the Roman picture found an easy and convincing Elizabethan equivalent, as in the second satire, in which spendthrifts are described squandering their estates and borrowing money, and usurers taking advantage of them. It is the Elizabethan gallant who appears in Drant's rendition of Horace's

> nomina sectatur modo sumpta veste virili
> sub patribus duris tironum.[59]

> Thunbrydled brutes, the younckers that
>   are paste the cure and charge
> Of Tutors graue, lyke lustye laddes
>   do loue to roue at large,
> To roiste and reuell wyth the beste,
>   in suits of silkes to flaunte:
> The harde headed fathers they denye
>   such spences vaine to graunte.[60]

Drant suppresses the second half of Horace's satire, on sexual offenses, and in part substitutes for it a greatly expanded version of Horace's remarks about the extremities of fashion.[61]

It is evident that however well known Horace was to Elizabethan writers, the distinctive qualities of his satires, their urbanity, their tempered and humorous tone, milder and less indignant than the style he found Lucilius had set for him, did not carry over into sixteenth-century English practice. The only approach to it is in the epistles of Wyatt, and they are a mixture of the influence of Horace and of Alamanni.

[58] *A Medicinable Morall* (1566), sig. A2^r.
[59] I, ii, 16–17.
[60] Sig. B^r.
[61] Sigs. B2^{r-v}.

Horace's theory of satire, as expressed largely in the fourth satire of Book I, and to some extent in I, x, and II, i, had an influence in Elizabethan England, both directly and indirectly. The critical doctrine of satire in the *De Poeta* of Minturno depends upon Horace and quotes him frequently.[62] Minturno adds to the theory of Horace a principle which was important for the development of Renaissance satire. He develops it most clearly in his treatise on vernacular poetry, *L'Arte Poetica* or *Della Poetica Thoscana*. As infirmities and wounds are the concern of medicine, he says, so the passions and troubles of the mind are the concern of satire. You cure one with bitter medicines, the other with harsh words.[63] This conception of satire as a function comparable to that of medicine is reflected in Drant's title for his first edition of the translation of Horace, *A Medicinable Morall*. It is in the background of all the satire of the period, and we see it in the mind of Shakespeare's Jaques when he proposes to set up as a satirist:

> Give me leave
> To speak my mind, and I will through and through
> Cleanse the foul body of th'infected world,
> If they will patiently receive my medicine.[64]

The satirist was accordingly viewed as a kind of barber-surgeon, lancing the sores of the commonwealth and causing pain but procuring health. Thus Marston, threatening the faults which he is satirizing, uses the metaphor of a series of surgical operations:

> Infectious blood, yee goutie humors quake
> Whilst my sharp Razor doth incision make.[65]

The Cambridge student Ingenioso, studying Juvenal, comments on his style and method:

[62] *Antonii Sebastiani Minturni de Poeta . . . Libri Sex* (Venice, 1559), pp. 420–425. A good account of Minturno's critical principles is given by Bernard Weinberg, "The Poetic Theories of Minturno," *Studies in Honor of Frederick W. Shipley* (St. Louis, 1942), pp. 101–129.

[63] *L'Arte Poetica* (Venice, 1584), sig. L14ᵛ.

[64] *As You Like It*, II, vii, 58–61.

[65] *Scourge of Villanie* (1598), sig. E5ᵛ, satire 5.

I, Iuuenall: thy ierking hand is good,
Not gently laying on, but fetching bloud,
So surgean-like thou dost with cutting heale,
Where nought but lanching can the wound auayle.[66]

The metaphor of the state as a human body is influential in all the thinking of the time, and the satirist as a kind of physician administering harsh cures is only a logical extension of the figure.[67]

The first use of the Latin satirists as models in English was experimental. The author, Thomas Lodge, had already indicated his interest in satire and had tried to further the practice of it. He had published an attack upon usury in 1584, and even earlier, in his *Reply to Gosson*, he had pleaded for satirical writers for the stage, who would decipher the abuses of the world in the person of notorious offenders. In both the *Alarum against Usurers* and his volume called *Scillaes Metamorphosis* in 1589 he had included satirical poems, "Truth's Complaint over England" in the former and "The Discontented Satyre" in the latter. Lodge was regarded by his contemporaries as an experimental writer. In *The Return from Parnassus* he is said to have "his oare in euery paper boate." [68] In 1595 Lodge published a miscellaneous volume containing eclogues, satires, and epistles. Called *A Fig for Momus*, the volume defied Lodge's detractors, who he said had unjustly taxed him with faults, among them that of servile imitation. He further remarked that the satires were "rather placed here to prepare, and trie the eare, then to feede it: because if they passe well, the whole Centon of them, alreadie in my hands shall sodainly bee published." For his experiment, Lodge had devised a form which was to have a future in English satire: he follows Spenser in using the pentameter couplet

---

[66] *The Pilgrimage to Parnassus with the two parts of The Return from Parnassus*, ed. W. D. Macray (Oxford, 1886), p. 80.

[67] See M. C. Randolph, "The Medical Concept in English Renaissance Satiric Theory: Its Possible Relationships and Implications," *SP*, XXXVIII (1941), 125–157. Miss Randolph concludes that in Renaissance thought there is a satiric catharsis, both of victim and of satirist. For the role of Jaques as a satirist, see O. J. Campbell, "Jaques," pp. 71–102.

[68] Macray ed., p. 85.

for satire in verse. Whether or not he actually had a hundred satires ready for publication, whether he had written them some time before 1595,[69] the experiment seems to have been unsuccessful from a popular point of view, for we do not get the whole "centon" of them published, nor does *A Fig for Momus* appear in a second edition.

Lodge denied that under the name of certain Romans he was attacking specific individuals; he was only, he said, following the laws of that kind of poem. His retort to the person who objects to seeing himself pilloried under a Latin name is the standard one of the satirist: "If any repine thereat, I am sure he is guiltie." But Lodge felt that his greatest originality was in the epistles: "For my Epistles, they are in that kind, wherein no Englishman of our time hath publiquely written." His satires, too, are epistolary in form and style. His model for method was Horace, though he drew upon Juvenal, and occasionally Persius, for content and detail.[70]

The introduction of the classical satirists was perfectly natural. They had been for a long time in the Latin curriculum of the English grammar school.[71] But the temper of English satiric writing did not all at once shed the influence of the social satires and complaints which had flared up all through the century on the subjects of usury, enclosures, and the state of the poor, and which had taken *Piers Plowman* as the model for English satire.

Lodge himself was active as a writer of prose pamphlets attacking some of the social monstrosities of the times. He published *An Alarum against Usurers* in 1584, and in 1591 a

[69] S. H. Atkins has argued, from attempted identifications of the individuals referred to in the satires, that Lodge must have written them between 1577 and 1580. See his letters in *TLS*, June 1, 1933; August 16, 1934; and February 7, 1935.

[70] The older critics, Gosse and Saintsbury, were essentially right in calling Lodge a Horatian satirist; Alden, in *The Rise of Formal Satire*, p. 95, disputes them because he finds that the second satire depends heavily upon Juvenal XIV and the fourth on Juvenal X. But there is nothing of the temper or tone of Juvenal in Lodge, and many smaller passages could be culled to show his dependence on Horace.

[71] See T. W. Baldwin, *William Shakspere's Small Latine and Lesse Greeke*, 2 vols. (Urbana, Illinois, 1944), II, 497–548, for discussion of editions and use in school.

tract called *Catharos. Diogenes in his Singularitie* (running title, *A Nettle for Nice Noses*). The latter pamphlet is in dialogue form and consists of fables moralized for their satirical effect, drawn from *The Dialoges of Creatures Moralized* and of tirades against usury and lechery from the *Somme des Pechez* of the contemporary Franciscan, Jean Benedicti.[72] In the year after the publication of *A Fig for Momus* he issued what Alice Walker calls the most interesting, the most vigorous, and the most successful of his prose pamphlets, *Wits Miserie, and the Worlds Madnesse* (running title, *Incarnate Deuils*). This again draws its material largely from the *Somme des Pechez,* but the interest of the work comes from the portraits of contemporary types, concisely and penetratingly done; they suggest the method of seventeenth-century "characters," but they profess to be incarnations of the various devils whom Lodge enumerates. Vivid examples are the devil as merchant [73] and the rustic who tries to keep up with courtly fashions.[74]

Lodge learned from Nashe, as Miss Walker points out, the trick of making a satirical prose pamphlet lively and readable, and it may be that the experiment of verse satire did not catch on readily because many of its functions were served by the prose tracts. The reader to whom satire appealed could turn to the Martin Marprelate tracts, to Greene's cony-catching pamphlets, or to the lampoons of Nashe and Harvey. Lodge refers to Nashe as the "true English Aretine," [75] and his influence and example were powerful. Had he expressed himself in verse satire instead of prose pamphlets, the experimental beginning made by Lodge, with its proper form the pentameter couplet, might have flourished in the mid-nineties.

As it is, Lodge's four satires in *A Fig* (numbered, through an error, 1, 3, 4, and 5) are too mild for their purpose and too general. The most effective passages are those which are

[72] See Alice Walker, "The Reading of an Elizabethan," *RES,* VIII (1932), 264–281.
[73] Sig. B3ʳ.
[74] Sig. C3ᵛ.
[75] Sig. Iʳ.

reflective and philosophical.[76] Lodge is more concerned, in *A Fig for Momus,* with friendliness, good counsel, solidarity among writers, than he is with anatomizing the body politic or operating on its visible sores. (Even the eclogues are addressed to friends, to Spenser, Drayton, and Daniel, for example.) He has felt the quality of Horace more than that of Juvenal and Persius, and his chief distinction as a writer of verse satire must be that he is one of the first in English to use for the purpose the heroic couplet.

The spectacle of the English boor assuming the refinements of the Italian Renaissance, of the fantastic effects of the artificialities of court life, of the extravagance of manners and lack of manners, became a major subject for writers of the nineties. In the nondramatic verse medium the most important satirists were John Donne, John Marston, and Joseph Hall. Their work, however, is not separated from the dramatic activities of the time, and Ben Jonson, with his "comical satires," merely carries into the theater the castigation of excesses and frumperies which were the concern of earlier satirists.[77]

Of Donne's five satires, three survive in a manuscript which bears the date 1593, but Sir Herbert Grierson has argued convincingly that this cannot be the terminal date for the poems and has shown that they belong somewhere in the period 1593–1597.[78] The first satire attacks the ostentatious figures on the London streets through a portrait of the "fondling motley humorist" who pays court to them. There are the bright parcel-guilt captain, with forty dead men's pay, the brisk perfumed pert courtier, fine silken painted fools, many-colored peacocks, all decorating the urban scene and enticing away from his companion, the speaker, the absurd fop who

[76] See, for example, the concluding lines of satire 1, sig. B2ᵛ.

[77] Interesting expositions of the background of Elizabethan satire which show the connection between nondramatic satiric poetry and Jonson's comedies are L. C. Knights, *Drama and Society in the Age of Jonson* (London, 1937), and especially O. J. Campbell, *Comicall Satyre and Shakespeare's Troilus and Cressida* (San Marino, Calif., 1938).

[78] *The Poems of John Donne,* ed. H. J. C. Grierson, 2 vols. (Oxford, 1912), II, 100–105.

flatters them. The value against which this picture is seen is one of simplicity, of nakedness:

> At birth, and death, our bodies naked are;
> And till our Soules be unapparrelled
> Of bodies, they from blisse are banished.
> Mans first blest state was naked, when by sinne
> Hee lost that, yet hee was cloath'd but in beasts skin.[79]

But the fop judges everyone by the amount of finery he wears upon his body.[80] This is the old sumptuary theme, but the situation of the satirist has changed in that now he does not try to reform the prevailing habits of Englishmen in dressing above their stations; he ridicules the superficial fool who takes seriously such tokens as costume.

The second satire attacks the extravagances of love poetry, especially of those verses which it was fashionable for the young men at the Inns of Court to write, larded with their newly acquired legal terms and plagiarizing freely from men of true wit. But the literary foibles of these young men satirize themselves, Donne feels, and he proceeds to the more serious charges against lawyers of social parasitism and of larceny.[81]

The third satire is the most famous of the collection, but it is not really a satire in the ordinary tradition. It is rather an epistle on the subject of finding the true religion. Its satiric touches come from the characterizations of those who refuse to make the effort to find truth in religion, or who make the search wrongly on narrow sectarian lines. The poem is no doubt central in Donne's personal development. Its thesis is that the Elizabethan courage which expressed itself in war, traffics, and discoveries, a bold defiance of the dangers of unknown countries and distant shores, the stout maintenance of the point of honor in duels, should be devoted to the greatest venture of all and the most significant—that search for truth which would determine the real future, not the fading, short-lived future of the world.

---

79 Satire I, lines 42–46.
80 *Ibid.*, lines 27–32.
81 Satire II, lines 61–112.

The imagery of the poem is largely sexual, and underlying the satire is a picture of the amorous proclivities of the Elizabethan gallant. Thus, for the current love of the world Donne chooses the metaphor:

> So the worlds selfe, thy other lov'd foe, is
> In her decrepit wayne, and thou loving this,
> Dost love a withered and worne strumpet.

For the various sects in religion he presents characters who have eccentric and stubborn sexual preferences. Crantz, the Puritan, loves only the Geneva religion,

> plaine, simple, sullen, yong,
> Contemptuous, yet unhandsome; As among
> Lecherous humors, there is one that judges
> No wenches wholsome, but course country drudges.[82]

Graius, the Anglican, will take only that religion which is handed him by his governors, like those that marry solely at the decision of their guardians. Phrygius is driven to indifference by the rival claims of the sects,

> as one,
> Knowing some women whores, dares marry none.[83]

His opposite, Graccus, sees no essential difference between them and loves all alike, promiscuously.

The effect of the third satire lies in this extended conceit, that the love of God is visible in Elizabethan society only as one of several kinds of "lecherous humours." The most famous and eloquent passage, in which Truth stands on a huge hill, craggy and steep, is not satirical at all, but hortatory. Donne was actually exhorting himself, as he continued to do even after taking Anglican orders in 1615, to find the true church.[84]

Donne's fourth satire has a more obvious classical model

---

[82] Satire III, lines 51–54.

[83] *Ibid.*, lines 63–64.

[84] His sonnet "Show me dear Christ, thy spouse" (*Poems,* ed. Grierson, I, 330) has the same theme. It was written after 1617 but not published until modern times. See Grierson, II, 235.

than the others; it is an adaptation of Horace's encounter with the bore.[85] Donne's pest is a hanger-on at court, a gossip, and an informer. He is also an English ape, a fantastic in language, a monster in dress and manners.[86] The poet escapes him by paying a crown, but he sees even stranger things spawned by the court:

> hast thou seene,
> O Sunne, in all thy journey, Vanitie,
> Such as swells the bladder of our court? [87]

But the satirist declares that he cannot cleanse all the sins of the court; it is too big a task for him:

> Preachers which are
> Seas of Wit and Arts, you can, then dare,
> Drowne the sinnes of this place, for, for mee
> Which am but a scarce brooke, it enough shall bee
> To wash the staines away.[88]

The fifth of Donne's satires is the least brilliant. It satirizes the corruption and inefficiency of law courts and complains at the bribing of officials and the misery of suitors. Donne addresses Sir Thomas Egerton, the Lord Keeper, who was now beginning, the poet says, to "know and weed out this enormous sinne." There is a reminiscence of Juvenal in one passage:

> O Age of rusty iron! Some better wit
> Call it some worse name, if ought equall it;
> The iron Age *that* was, when justice was sold; now
> Injustice is sold dearer farre.[89]

Donne exhibits the nervous and angry temper which might have made a successful satirist, and perhaps Grierson's comment is just: "a satiric art which is wonderfully vivid and caustic but still tentative—overemphatic, rough in style and verse, though with a roughness which is obviously a studied and in a measure successful effect." [90] But Donne's observations do not extend far into the fabric of contemporary so-

---

[85] Horace, *Satires*, I, ix.
[86] Satire IV, lines 18–26.
[87] *Ibid.*, lines 166–168.
[88] *Ibid.*, lines 237–241.
[89] Satire V, lines 35–38.
[90] *Poems*, ed. Grierson, II, xi.

ciety; he is mainly concerned with city and court types, and the general impulse which motivated English satire in the native tradition was lacking in Donne. He was too impressed, philosophically and imaginatively, with the degeneration of the world to make much of an art of satirizing it. *The Progresse of the Soule* is not in reality a satiric poem. It projects a standard of values in which satire becomes useless. Moreover, it is only by date of composition that Donne's satires come under our consideration at all. They were not published until after the poet's death in 1631; accordingly, the audience which they reached in the sixteenth century must have been limited to a few privileged aristocrats and friends of the poet.[91]

Joseph Hall professed to be the first English satirist.

> I First aduenture, with fool-hardie might,
> To tread the steps of perilous despight:
> I first aduenture: follow me who list,
> And be the second English Satyrist.

So the young Cambridge man, later to be distinguished as the Bishop of Exeter and then of Norwich, the antagonist of Milton, and a writer and philosopher so stern in his moralizing that he was known as "our English Seneca," made his bow to the public. His volume, *Virgidemiarum Sixe Bookes,* was published in two parts, the first three books "Of Tooth-lesse Satyrs" in 1597, and the last three books "Of Byting Satyrs" in 1598.[92] Hall's first three books are divided according to subject, and the title page describes them as "1, Poeticall; 2, Aca-

---

[91] An example of the friends is the satirist Everard Guilpin, who imitated Donne's first satire in the fifth satire of his *Skialetheia* (1598), and who may have Donne in mind in his third satire. See R. E. Bennett, "John Donne and Everard Gilpin," *RES,* XV (1939), 66–72. An example of the aristocrats is Lady Bedford, who received from Ben Jonson a manuscript of Donne's satires; see Jonson's epigram no. 94. Donne's relationship to the melancholy of his time and the significance of the satiric element in his work as a whole are discussed in Theodore Spencer, "Donne and His Age" in *A Garland for John Donne* (Cambridge: Harvard University Press, 1931), and in Arnold Stein, "Donne and the Satiric Spirit," *ELH,* XI (1944), 266–282.

[92] The first three books were reprinted, with corrections, in 1598 and again in 1602; the last three books were reprinted in 1599. For bibliographical details see the edition by A. Davenport (Liverpool, 1949), pp. lx–lxix.

demicall; 3, Morall." In his satires on moral and social subjects, Hall remains within the tradition of the English satire.
The novelty of his collection consists in his conscious attempt
to imitate the style of Juvenal and Persius and in his placing
the satires on literary and academic subjects in the beginning
of his book. Hall gives a defense of his work in the "Defiance
to Enuy" and in "A Postscript to the Reader." His defense of
the matter of his poems is the familiar one which Lodge and
others had used: if you complain of being attacked, you are
guilty of the vices satirized and had better keep quiet; if you
are not guilty of these vices, then you have no cause for complaint. The poet is more self-conscious about the style: he is
imitating Juvenal and Persius, he says, in default of any more
recent models, and he is afraid the learned will see the difference between his poems and his Latin models. There is
throughout Hall's work a consciousness of an academic audience, but he has also tried to reach a more popular level of
readers, and he fears criticism for "perhaps too much stoup-
ing to the lowe reach of the vulgar." [93] In defense he will de-
clare that "the English is not altogether so naturall to a
Satyre as the Latin" [94] and challenges anyone who does not
agree to try to translate one of Persius' satires into English.
Moreover, he complains that the public these days is not so
willing to grant poetry which is hard and obscure the necessary reading to get at the idea within: he is using the traditional image of the nut and the kernel. Hall announces that
aside from the classics he has come across only Ariosto's satires "and one base french Satyre" as models. None the less, he
is strongly under the influence of Spenser, and there are several indications that he knew Rabelais. [95]

Hall's novelty, it has been suggested, lay not only in his
conscious attempt to imitate Persius and Juvenal in English
and to find a style in English suitable for satire, but also in
his effort to emphasize literary and academic subjects. This

[93] *Poems,* ed. Davenport, p. 98.

[94] *Ibid.*

[95] See Huntington Brown, *Rabelais in English Literature* (Cambridge:
Harvard University Press, 1933), pp. 71–72, for a discussion. Hall's later prose
satire in Latin, *Mundus Alter et Idem,* is indebted to Rabelais also.

aim was more important than that of style. He says, for example, that his first satire "doth somewhat resemble the sour and crabbed face of Iuuenals, which I indeauoring in that did determinately omit in the rest." Hall has the self-importance of the literary undergraduate and is especially concerned to impress the reader with what he can do. He even boasts that he has written pastorals which are inferior to nobody's except Spenser's:

> Speake ye attentiue swaynes that heard me late,
> Needs me giue grasse vnto the Conquerers?
> At Colins feet I throw my yeelding reed:
> But let the rest win homage by their deed.[96]

The attentive swains are Cambridge men, and Hall's satires must be read against the background of certain academic quarrels of the time. They are connected with the Harvey-Nashe controversy, the Martin Marprelate controversy, and the issues concerning the New Poetry which appear in the Spenser-Harvey letters. This is the first body of English satire in which literary criticism is a major element, and it is usually considered that the best of Hall's satires are those on literary subjects.

The principal attack made by the Cambridge satirist is upon indecent poetry. This is the subject of the second satire in Book I, it is picked up again in the last satire, No. 9, of that book, and it continues over into the "Academicall" section by being treated in the first satire of Book II. Puritanical objections to lewd poetry were of course no new thing; they go back in the sixteenth century to the reign of Edward VI and before. Another Hall, John Hall, had fulminated against the love songs of Wyatt and others as early as 1550, calling them "songes of baudry & abominable wicked comunication," and *The Court of Venus,* to which John Hall objected, continued to be listed among trivial and ungodly books on down to 1601 and later.[97] From the point of view of the strict and godly,

---

[96] *Poems,* ed. Davenport, p. 10.

[97] In Arthur Dent's *Plaine Mans Path-way to Heaven.* See quotation in L. B. Wright, "The Reading of Our Colonial Ancestors," *ELH,* IV (1937), 89, n. 7.

any kind of love poetry might be called bawdy, either Petrarchan sonnets or, with more justice, the Ovidian-mythological poems of Marlowe, Shakespeare, and others. So it is difficult to decide just what is the target of the satire in *Virgidemiae*. In part the satire is certainly general,[98] and it is not a single example or single writer the author has in mind.[99] In the ninth satire of his first book, however, Hall seems to glance at specific poets, and they are those who were the enemies of Gabriel Harvey and the academic group in the Martin Marprelate, Harvey-Nashe, and related quarrels. The opening of the poem seems to allude to the notorious crowning of Robert Greene on his deathbed:

> Enuy ye Muses, at your thriuing Mate,
> Cupid hath crowned a new Laureat:
> I saw his Statue gayly tyr'd in greene,
> As if he had some second Phoebus beene.[100]

And the writers of this poetry are assumed to be as dissolute as their verses.[101] Formerly, writers of epigrams were blamed for being too licentious, though they only glanced at indecencies and passed on. Now, however, in this new poetry, it is different:

> But Arts of Whoring: stories of the Stewes,
> Ye Muses will ye beare and may refuse?
> Nay let the Diuell, and Saint Valentine,
> Be gossips to those ribald rymes of thine.[102]

The reference in the last two lines is to Thomas Nashe, whose *Pierce Penilesse his Supplication to the Diuel* had begun the Nashe-Harvey quarrel, and his unpublished but notorious pornographic poem, *The Choice of Valentines*.[103]

[98] See especially his second satire (*Poems*, ed. Davenport, pp. 13–14).
[99] "Now is Pernassus turned to the stewes," he writes (*ibid.*, p. 13).
[100] *Ibid.*, p. 19.
[101] *Ibid.*, p. 20.
[102] *Ibid.*
[103] See S. M. Salyer, "Hall's Satires and the Harvey-Nashe Controversy," *SP*, XXV (1928), 149–170, and A. Davenport, "An Elizabethan Controversy: Harvey and Nashe," *Notes and Queries*, CLXXXII (1942), 116–119. The identification of Nashe was first made by Konrad Schulze, *Die Satiren Halls* (Berlin, 1910), pp. 263–264.

Hall adopts, for the first satire of his second book, the general subject and the name Labeo for a bad poet from Persius' first satire. Incompetence on the part of practicing poets and the degeneration of public taste which permits their monstrous productions to be popular constitute the Latin satirist's theme. The English academic, irritated by the success of professional men of letters in the nineties, complains that there is so much writing done now that the price of paper has gone up and there is a shortage of goose quills for pens. The worst of it is that the truly learned and judicious men, in the universities, of course, do not write, but the professional poets flood the market. Labeo is conjured to "write cleanly, or write none." [104] He is in part a portrait of Nashe, and the source of his inspiration, as seen by Hall, comes from the most disreputable continental authors. As an example of the triviality of modern professional authors, Hall brings up the case of George Peele, whose *Tale of Troy* had been issued as a miniature book. This is a feat that surpasses Strabo of antiquity, who wrote an *Iliad* in a nutshell, says Hall sarcastically, and he compares it to the art of a London blacksmith who made trappings for a flea.[105] The general picture of Peele as a pismire struggling with the heavy load of his tiny Troy book is more ridiculous when seen in the light of Nashe's praise of Peele in his preface to *Menaphon:* "the chiefe supporter of pleasance now liuing, the *Atlas* of Poetrie." [106]

Hall's position was in reality one of defense: the issue was between the lively professional wits of the time and the graver, more learned rhetoricians of the university. And Nashe, a Cambridge man himself, which made it all the worse, had espoused the cause of the wits of the town and disparaged the somber academics in an epistle addressed "To the Gentlemen Stvdents of both Vniversities." "Giue me the man," cried Nashe, "whose extemporall veine in any humour will excell our greatest Art-maisters deliberate thoughts;

---

[104] Sig. C7ᵛ.
[105] The sources of this passage are discussed in A. Davenport, "Interfused Sources in Hall's Satires," *RES*, XVIII (1942), 210–211.
[106] *Works*, ed. McKerrow, III, 323.

whose inuentions, quicker then his eye, will challenge the prowdest Rhetoritian to the contention of like perfection with like expedition." [107] Even as critics Nashe will not give the palm to the learned: "Oft haue I obserued what I now set downe: a secular wit that hath liued all dayes of his life by What doe you lacke? to be more iudiciall in matters of conceit then our quadrant crepundios, that spit *ergo* in the mouth of euery one they meete." [108] The Ramist logic at Cambridge, the Puritan practice of educating primarily for the clergy and sending men out from their fellowships as quickly as possible to serve parishes (the professed aim of Sir Walter Mildmay, the founder of Hall's college of Emmanuel), the pedantry of the academics and their scorn of hack writers, all irritated Nashe into a defense of the literary renaissance which began about the time of his preface. The New Poetry was the result, as he saw it, of the encouragement of letters by the great university men of the preceding generation or two, but their successors were now sorry fellows and were no longer capable of stimulating wit and expression.

To Hall, therefore, the answer was to glance frequently at Nashe's remarks (and the references in his satires to Nashe's preface are very frequent, especially in the first satire of Book VI) and to pillory the extravagances and absurdities of the popular poetry of the nineties for which the brash and cocky Nashe had become the apologist. In Book VI, satire 1, Hall gives another picture of Labeo, and this one also is rather a composite than a satiric sketch of any one writer.[109] He then goes on to relate how the typical English poet of the nineties stumbles through an apprenticeship in pastoral poetry, following Mantuan and Virgil and Theocritus, or else is trained up in "Venus chamber," writing love poems to his mistress with extravagant and absurd compliments in them—all as a preliminary to his heroic poetry, before his Muse learns to manage her weapon or "dance a sober Pir-

---

[107] *Ibid.*, p. 312.
[108] *Ibid.*, p. 314.
[109] *Poems*, ed. Davenport, pp. 87–96.

rhicke in the field, / Or marching wade in blood vp to the knees." [110]

The principal features of contemporary poetry which Hall deplored were the popularity and bombast of the new blank verse which Marlowe had introduced to the stage; the older, more standard complaints of the ghosts of princes, invoked to narrate their tragic histories for the benefit of the present age, as in the *Mirror for Magistrates* and its many imitations; the sonnet cycles with their Petrarchan conceits; baroque treatments of holy subjects in profane literary conventions; and the absurdities of such quantitative metrical experiments as Stanihurst's translation of Virgil. Essentially, his point of view is one hostile to popular poetry; he thinks the Muses belong in academic groves and can only be sullied by being brought into the theater or the street.

In the third and fourth satires of Book I, Hall denounces the drama of the nineties. His basic objection is to its vulgarity:

> Shame that the muses should be bought and sold,
> For euery peasants brasse, on each scaffold.[111]

Hall was aware that much of the work of Marlowe, Peele, Greene, and Kyd came from the disreputable atmosphere of the taverns, and he pictures the drunken poet erupting his verse as a dunghill warmed by the sun spouts "filthy smoke and stinking steames." Mingling of clownage and royal dignity on the stage was no mere violation of a rule of literary

[110] This passage has caused much controversy, partly because most students have tried to find a single poet whom the description of Labeo fits. S. M. Salyer, "Hall's Satires and the Harvey-Nashe Controversy," pp. 158–160, is forced to the conclusion that, since Labeo is Nashe, Hall must be referring to lost poetical works by him—a dubious and unprofitable conclusion. Sidney H. Atkins, in *TLS* for July 4, 1936, and July 25, 1936, supported an identification of the Labeo of Book VI with Drayton and the use of the name for the generic bad poet in the earlier satires; he had to fight off two commentators who thought Labeo was Shakespeare (and Bacon), July 11 and July 18, and his Drayton identification, originally suggested by Singer, was rejected by Mrs. Tillotson (Drayton's *Works*, ed. Hebel, V, 138, n. 5). Schulze, *Die Satiren Halls*, p. 275, considered Labeo to be "the typical poet of the Shakespearian period," at least in the references after line 234.

[111] *Poems*, ed. Davenport, p. 15.

decorum for Hall; he disliked the essential democracy of the theater:

> A goodly hoch-poch, when vile Russettings,
> Are match't with monarchs, & with mighty kings.
> A goodly grace to sober Tragike Muse,
> When each base clown, his clumbsie fist doth bruise
> And show his teeth in double rotten-row,
> For laughter at his selfe-resembled show.

In satire 4 Hall scorns the writers of romantic legends in rhyme, but he comes close enough to a description of Spenser that he specifically mentions him in order not to be misunderstood:

> But let no rebell Satyre dare traduce
> Th'eternall legends of thy Faery Muse,
> Renowned Spencer: whome no earthly wight
> Dares once to emulate, much less dares despight.

He abuses the sonneteer, in satire 7, perhaps again because he thinks that the love poetry of a courtly Sir Philip Sidney might be of interest to the world, but the vaporings of a professional poet could not be.

Hall's section of "Academicall" satires is in reality a survey of the vices of the various professions. He portrays in satire 2 the contemporary pride in houses which reflects the ambition of members of all of the professions to set up as country squires, and the ostentation of new buildings, which Harrison the historian commented on as a feature of the age, is brought up against the consideration that the final result is futility. The lawyer is attacked in satire 3 and the doctor in satire 4. In satire 5 it is the parson who practices simony. They are all motivated by greed, and their practice belies the ideals and very reason for their professions. Satire 6 is an epigram against the squire who employs for the education of his children a "trencher-chaplain" and pays him, for all his trouble and humiliation, "five markes and winter liuerye." The seventh, which completes the book, is a more elaborate satire on the astrologers.

The "Morall" satires begin with a poem on the model of Juvenal, with a description of the Golden Age. In the times of our ancestors men lived simply and were happy. They were not subject to the passions of pride and greed. But now, and especially in England, the situation is quite reversed. Man, who was formerly hail fellow with the beasts, now aspires to be a god. But the result is that he succeeds only in being a fantastic in food and clothing.[112] Hall's point of view, which with respect to luxuries was shared by many contemporary observers, is consistent with his position in the literary satires. The new shifting of classes was something to view with alarm:

> Lo the long date of those expired daies,
> Which the inspired Merlins word fore-sayes:
> When dunghill Pesants shall be dight as kings,
> Then one confusion another brings.[113]

The symptoms of pride are not new, but they nevertheless deserve castigation: the pride shown in ostentatious monuments (satire 2) ; the vulgarity of lavish entertainment by mere citizens (satire 3) ; the modern desire to display everything— good deeds, wealth, possessions (satire 4) ; the vanity of periwigs (satire 5) ; the monstrous thirst of drunkards (satire 6) ; the absurdity of the gallant who swaggers in a vain attempt to conceal the fact that his new-found bravery of dress has stripped him of the price of a dinner (satire 7) . The "Morall" satires of Hall concern themselves with the manifestations of those profound social changes which characterize the age, judged from the conviction that the older hierarchical arrangement of society was more orderly, more stable, and inherently more virtuous.

The second installment of Hall's satires, the three books first published in 1598, are called "Byting" satires as distinguished from the "Toothlesse Satyrs" of the first three books. Hall probably meant by the adjective "toothless" that the satires of the first three books attacked only vices, not particu-

---

[112] *Ibid.*, p. 35.
[113] *Ibid.*

lar persons, even though it now seems clear that some of his literary references, at least, had particular persons in mind. Hall's adjective "toothless" was unlucky in any case, for it was easy enough for his antagonist John Milton to write many years later, "if it bite neither the persons nor the vices, how is it a Satyr, and if it bite either, how is it toothlesse, so that toothlesse Satyrs are as much as if he had said toothlesse teeth." [114] The biting satires are intended to be more violent and vigorous in style, as Hall several times points out. Appended to the 1597 volume is a short poem called "The Conclusion of all." It begins:

> Thus haue I writ in smoother Cedar tree,
> So gentle Satyrs, pend so easily.
> Henceforth I write in crabbed oke-tree rinde.

This seems to indicate that Hall planned to publish satires which were much rougher than these. His opening to Books IV–VI, in 1598, called "The Authors charge to his Satyrs," declares that the poet will not have them published until after his own death, and this, together with the printer's remarks before the errata,[115] has led some authorities to suppose that the publication was a piracy. But this is not likely, since Robert Dexter was the publisher in 1597 and 1598, and the 1598 printer, Richard Bradocke, was the same one used for the "Corrected and amended" 1598 edition of the first three books. Apparently the trouble with the style of the first three books was that the reader did not recognize himself in the satires—they were not on subjects that hit home directly and clearly enough.

> Ech points his straight fore-finger to his friend,
> Like the blind Diall on the Belfrey end.[116]

---

[114] *An Apology* . . . in *Works*, Columbia ed., vol. III, pt. i, p. 329.

[115] "After this impression was finished, vpon the Authors knowledge, I had the viewe of a more perfect Copy, wherein were these additions and corrections, which I thought good to place here, desiring the reader to referre them to their places." This appears in the 1598 edition of the last three books and has nothing to do with the problem of the 1602 edition, as Alden supposes (*The Rise of Formal Satire*, p. 98).

[116] *Poems*, ed. Davenport, p. 50.

Moreover, his satires had apparently been criticized as too academic.[117] But he promises that his style will be sharper and his victims more definitely fixed so that they cannot evade the charges against them.

> Those tooth-lesse Toyes that dropt out by mis-hap,
> Bee but as lightning to a thunder-clap.[118]

This is the true function of satire as it was in antiquity:

> The Satyre should be like the Porcupine,
> That shoots sharp quilles out in each angry line,
> And wounds the blushing cheeke, and fiery eye,
> Of him that heares, and readeth guiltily;
> Ye antique Satyres, how I blesse your daies,
> That brook'd your bolder stile, their owne dispraise.[119]

The interesting and significant fact about Hall's biting satires is that they are aimed more directly than the toothless satires at the major social and economic vices of the time. In hitting closer home he turned to the subjects which had formed the content of English satire from the first publication of *Piers Plowman* in 1550 on down to the end of the century. The thunderclap that followed the lightning was a series of attacks upon the commercial practices of the new business class and of landlords (Book IV, satire 5, and Book V, satire 1), on the discontent with one's own estate which made for shifting from one class or occupation to another (Book IV, satire 6), to the decline of "housekeeping," i.e., hospitality and charity (Book V, satire 2), and to the practice of enclosing commons (Book V, satire 3, and *passim*). The two satires in Book VI, which concern themselves with Labeo and with the ceremonies of the Roman church, are exceptional. The main weight of the satire in the last three books is on the social and economic revolution which was taking place under the Elizabethans' eyes but beyond their understanding.[120]

[117] *Ibid.*, p. 54.
[118] *Ibid.*, p. 51.
[119] *Ibid.*, p. 83.
[120] This directly contradicts the statement of Alden, *The Rise of Formal Satire*, p. 123: "Grouping the objects satirized by Hall under the usual heads,

The depopulation of the land of course struck the satirist in a moral light and he scourges the plowman for his discontent with his difficult lot.[121] The restless energy and the economic motives that prompted exploration, discovery, and colonization also offended the Stoic resignation of the future English Seneca.[122] The adventurer Fortunio, who sells his lands to search for gold in Guiana but comes home with only one miserable captured pinnace for booty, is even more foolish than the alchemist Raymundus,[123] who despite continued failures devotes all his pots and pans to gold.[124] And planting colonies appeared to Hall to be merely a part of the vicious process of enclosing.[125] The acquisitive instinct seemed to him apparent in every aspect of Elizabethan life; that vice, and the pride that went with it, he lashed unmercifully. He was probably conscious that the villain was the new middle-class Englishman, but it reminded him of an older and more familiar villain:

> If Mammon selfe should euer liue with men,
> Mammon himselfe shalbe a Citizen.[126]

Hall's invitation, in his prologue, to "follow me who list,/ And be the second English Satyrist" was soon accepted, by a young Oxford man at the Inns of Court, John Marston. In 1598, shortly after the appearance of the three books of biting satires which completed *Virgidemiae,* Marston published *The Metamorphosis of Pigmalions Image and Certaine Satyres.* The book was dedicated "To the Worlds Mightie Monarch,

---

we find private morals distinctly predominant. Without exception (save in the case of alchemy and one or two others, excluded for obvious reasons) the vices and follies in these satires are those of classical satire." Alden's "usual heads" are arbitrary classifications, and he so completely ignores the English tradition of social satire that he puts usury, lack of hospitality, and the various manifestations of avarice and greed in the category of private morals.

[121] *Poems,* ed., Davenport, p. 70.

[122] *Ibid.,* p. 71.

[123] See *Poems,* ed. Davenport, p. 210, for refutation of the claim that Raymundus is Ralegh. I had reached the same conclusion independently before Davenport's edition appeared.

[124] *Ibid.,* p. 60.

[125] *Ibid.,* p. 78.

[126] *Ibid.,* p. 69.

Good Opinion," and was signed only with the initials W. K., letters which Marston was later to expand into the pen name W. Kinsayder. The name apparently comes from the word "kinsing," the act of castrating an unruly dog. Marston is a name which could be considered a punning variant, "Marstone."

The poem on Pygmalion and his image which opens the book is an example of the lascivious poem on the model of Ovidian mythological poems, which had become popular in the nineties and had exhibited such specimens as Shakespeare's *Venus and Adonis* and Marlowe's *Hero and Leander*. A versified address "To his Mistress" preceding the poem showed the reader what to expect:

> My wanton Muse lasciuiously doth sing
> Of sportiue loue, of louely dallying.

Following the *Pigmalion,* Marston inserts a piece called "The Authour in prayse of his precedent Poem" in which he satirizes his own poem. I will, says the poet,

> Censure my selfe, fore others me deride
> And scoffe at mee, as if I had deni'd
> Or thought my Poem good, when that I see
> My lines are froth, my stanzaes saplesse be.[127]

Modern commentators have usually felt that Marston is not to be taken at his word here and have concluded that he first wrote the poem seriously, then outgrew it and published it as if he had written it with satirical intention. But though the poem itself does not show satiric exaggeration of the features of the Ovidian poem, many of the images used by Marston clearly betray a satirical bent. There are slurs on "the subtile Citty-dame" (stanza 10), the "peeuish Papists" (stanza 14), and the foolishness of sweet youths who solemnly protest that love is above lust and scorn it (stanza 19); but the principal indication of the satirical purpose of the poem lies in the author's attitude toward the reader. As he approaches the more salacious parts of the narrative he ridicules the reader's

[127] Sig. C2ʳ.

expectation which he has been carefully building up. He supposes that his reader is following him with a "wanton itching eare" (stanza 33), and he flatly tells the "gaping eares that swallow vp my lines" (stanza 38) to expect no more. This point of view toward the reader could hardly have been maintained if Marston had ever taken his own material seriously.

There is, in all his satire, a mixture of contempt for the vices he is attacking, contempt for the reader, and contempt for himself, which gives a particular character to his work. It is not simply a personal trait of Marston as a writer; it is a state of mind which is reflected in a good deal of the literature of the turn of the century. The attitude, which the Elizabethans called "malcontent," is clearer in Marston than it is elsewhere, but Shakespeare's Hamlet and Jaques share in it, as do many other characters in drama and poetry. Some definition of the attitude is necessary.

The psychological differences between men, according to sixteenth-century authorities, all arise from the disposition in individuals of the four humours of blood, phlegm, choler, and melancholy, and from the qualities of hot, cold, moist, and dry pertaining to these humours. Now the intellectual, the man of learning and reflection, is most inclined to the latter humour and its qualities, because the traits of mind which make him an intellectual are those fostered by these qualities. "Amongst the foure humours which we enioy," says Juan Huarte, "there is none so cold and drie as that of melancholie, and whatsoeuer notable men for learning, haue liued in the world (sayth Aristotle) they were all melancholike." [128] It is therefore to be expected that the scholar would be of melancholy disposition. The characteristics of the melancholy man, according to Dr. Timothy Bright, include "hollownes of eye, and vnchearefulnes of countenance . . . painefull in studie, and circumspect, giuen to fearefull and terrible dreames: in affection sad, & full of feare; hardly moued to anger, but keeping it long, and not easie to be reconciled: enuious, and ielous, apt to take occasions in the worse part, and out of

---

[128] *Examen de Ingenios. The Examination of mens Wits . . . translated by R. C.* (1594), sig. E6ʳ.

measure passionate, whereto it is moued." [129] The melancholy man is frequently very witty and addicted to the practice of wit.[130] The most striking feature of the melancholy man, however, is the alteration of his affection by the humour which rules him. Envy, jealousy, and passion, as Bright indicates, are the chief emotional manifestations of melancholy, and these distorted feelings alter the whole judgment and attitude of the mind. Melancholy people see everything as worse than it is, "suspitious least it be a matter of farther feare, and not indifferently weighing the case, but poysing it by their fantasticall feare, and doubt at home." [131]

The melancholy man is of course the most natural satirist, because his temper, his intellectual bent, and his conscientious habits all move him in that direction. The comic element in satire is also possible to him, because, as Bright puts it, he sometimes feels "his present calamitie, is of a mixed cause, compounded of some ioy, which riseth of confidence of remedie or reuenge, which causeth a dilatation of ioy, entermeddled with contraction of griefe: so a man that hath receaued a displeasure of his enemy, and assured howe he may be euen with him, will laugh, though he haue indignation at the displeasure, vpon hope of requittance: whereof riseth a certaine ioye mixed with griefe, that forceth out a Sardonian, bitter laughter." [132]

The existence of a familiar psychological type in the medical books does not of course do much to explain the character of a particular writer, but contemporary references to Mars-

---

[129] *A Treatise of Melancholie* (1586), sig. H6ᵛ.

[130] Sig. Iᵛ.

[131] Sig. I3ʳ.

[132] Sig. K4ᵛ. The foregoing account is of course simplified. I have tried to give the main outlines of the description of the melancholy man from Elizabethan sources. More elaborate and technical treatments of the subject will be found in Lily B. Campbell, *Shakespeare's Tragic Heroes; Slaves of Passion* (Cambridge, England, 1930); O. J. Campbell, "Jaques," pp. 71–79; L. C. Knights, "Seventeenth Century Melancholy," *The Criterion*, XIII (1933–34), 97–112, and appendix B in *Drama and Society in the Age of Jonson;* Lawrence Babb, "Melancholy and the Elizabethan Man of Letters," *HLQ*, IV (1941), 247–261; and G. B. Harrison, essay on Elizabethan melancholy appended to his edition of Nicholas Breton, *Melancholicke Humours* (London, 1929).

ton, such as those in the Parnassus plays and one by Davies of Hereford, show that he was regarded, in his verse satires, as a malcontent. "There could be no better illustration of the malcontent's bitter and strident invective than his *Satires* and his *The Scourge of Villainy*," says Babb.[133] It is an interesting detail that the man who was to be the great anatomist of melancholy, Robert Burton, was a contemporary of Marston's at Brasenose College, Oxford.[134]

Marston differs from Hall in that his malcontent role was not, like Hall's satiric position, founded upon a Stoic doctrine. Marston does not have, like Hall, a set of values based upon academic life, upon ancient simplicity and decency, and upon a moral earnestness which wished to correct the faults visible in a changing society. Instead, the malcontent despised himself as much as he despised the objects of his satire. One of Marston's characters, for example, is in reality a "haughty malecontent" himself, although he masks it in humble blandishment.[135] Another, in the same satire, is Bruto, who like Shakespeare's Jaques is a returned traveler and declaims against the age when he comes home.[136] Marston makes explicit the fact, essential to an understanding of his satire, that he is a part of what he is attacking. The position of the superior and aloof satirist he leaves to Hall.[137]

Between the third and fourth satires of his *Pigmalion* volume Marston inserted a flyting against Hall which he called "Reactio." The principal basis of the attack is Hall's first book and the literary criticism contained in it. Hall's objections to poetry on divine subjects and on the fall of princes are held up to scorn.[138] Hall's conservatism Marston calls want of imagination, as if the critic were trying to remove from poetry what is its essence, fiction. Attacking the modern spirit of adventure and discovery is also an academic stuffiness which

[133] "Melancholy and the Elizabethan Man of Letters," p. 259.
[134] For biographical details, see R. E. Brettle, *MLR*, XXII (1927), 7–14, 317–319.
[135] Satire 2 in *Pigmalion*, sig. D4^r.
[136] Sigs. D5^{r-v}.
[137] Sigs. C8^v-D^r.
[138] Sig. E4^v.

Marston lashes.[139] We might deduce from this that Marston's positive values were to be found in Elizabethan literature, a nest which Hall was only fouling, or in the feats of men like Ralegh, whom the Cambridge satirist insolently ridiculed, but one has the suspicion that if Hall had praised either of these things, Marston would have taken the other side. Hall made a convenient target for his follower, especially after the publication of the *Pigmalion* volume, because, according to Marston, Hall caused a hostile epigram to be pasted into every copy of *Pigmalion* that came to the stationers in Cambridge. Marston inserted an additional satire in the 1599 edition of *The Scourge of Villainie,* specifically mentioning the incident, to justify him for his many attacks on Hall.[140]

Of much greater interest than the details of the Hall-Marston quarrel, with its involvement of other writers like Weever and Guilpin, is the matter of the principal subjects of Marston's satire. It has been noticed by all his critics that Marston is particularly interested in lust. He returns to it again and again, so that the subject overshadows in his two books all of the more standard satiric themes. Hall had attacked Labeo, the indecent poet, but Marston seems obsessed by the subject of lechery in life as well as in literature. In the third satire of the *Pigmalion* volume he characterizes the age as a background for his character Lucian, an *inamorato:*

> O age! in which our gallants boast to be
> Slaues vnto riot, and lewd luxury![141]

His imitation of Juvenal's *Difficile est Satyram non scribere* (satire 2 in *The Scourge of Villainie*) shows the world itself as enveloped in lust.[142] And in the third satire Marston contrasts the trivial subjects which Hall chose for his satires with

---

[139] Sigs. E5^v-E6^r.

[140] See A. Davenport, "Some Notes on References to Joseph Hall in Marston's Satires," *RES,* IX (1933), 192–196, and "The Quarrel of the Satirists," *MLR,* XXXVII (1942), 123–130; Morse S. Allen, *The Satire of John Marston* (Columbus, Ohio, 1920), pp. 162–166.

[141] Sig. Dviii^r.

[142] Professor Bush finds in the last two lines of this passage a reference to Marlowe (*Mythology and the Renaissance Tradition,* p. 180, n. 9).

the monstrous lecheries, perversions, and debaucheries he un-
masks.[143] And again he asks, "Shall I with shadowes fight?"—
meaning such subjects as Roman ceremonials, which Hall
had treated—or "base channell rogarie?" Obviously not. His
theme is the "maggot-tainted lewd corruption" of which his
own Pigmalion is an example in poetry and of which there
are countless examples in the society around him.

In "A Cynicke Satyre" Marston calls for "a Man, a man, a
kingdome for a man," but Circe has turned them all to swine,
and the poet replies to the contemporary who offers him an
example of a man,

> Mean'st thou that sencelesse, sensuall Epicure?
> That sinck of filth, that guzzell most impure? [144]

And in the poem called "Inamorato Curio," which attacks the
fantastic behavior not only of lovers but of poets of love,
Marston lapses from the mode of satire into something like a
prayer:

> Returne, returne, sacred *Synderesis*,
> Inspire our truncks, let not such mud as this
> Pollute us still. Awake our lethargie,
> Raise us from out our brain-sicke foolerie.

Marston's preoccupation with lust was not confined to his
satires; it remains the predominant subject of his plays. As
Theodore Spencer pointed out, in his penetrating essay on
Marston,[145] "It is not easy to explain why, in the first years of
the seventeenth century, lust should have seemed to make
such a large scar on human nature, and to have been, in the
minds of sensitive people, a more ominous barrier to a good
life than ever before. Dante, in both his *Inferno* and his
Purgatorio made it the least of important sins; according to
Shakespeare, for a while at least, and to Marston for most of
his literary career, it did more harm than all the other sins
put together." The answer, no doubt, lies partly in the age

[143] Sig. C8r.
[144] *The Scourge of Villanie*, sigs. F2r-v.
[145] "John Marston," *The Criterion*, XIII (1933–34), 581–599.

and partly in the man. If Marston was a melancholy man, and he seems to have been, for he invokes the spirit of melancholy as his aid, it was natural to him to feel the attraction of physical desire more sharply than other men. As Bright says of melancholics,

Passionate they be out of measure, whereto a vehement obiect & of long continuance vrgeth them: this causeth them to be amorous . . . If the melancholie be sanguine adust, then may it supply the want in the obiect, and cause an internall amorous disposition, with such dotage, that maketh no discretion where the affection is bestowed.[146]

The melancholy man as satirist, then, felt within himself the urges which he saw being gratified at large in society, and his own impulses gave strength and vigor to the violent disgust which his malcontented disposition inspired in him. There is nothing strange about the fact that the three principal satirists of the nineties, Donne, Hall, and Marston, all became divines; it is a typical Elizabethan situation.[147]

In addition to the personal factor, there is a consideration of the social significance of lechery which was more apparent to the Elizabethans than it is to us. The solidity and strength of the state were of almost incredible concern to thoughtful men in the sixteenth century. Prognostications, astrology, the threat of invasion in '88, the conspiracy of Lopez, and, later, the Essex uprising—all are sources of this concern and to some extent symptoms of it. And both Roman and Biblical history stressed the connection between private morals and the overthrow of empires. Therefore, a writer like William Covell, in his *Polimanteia, or The Meanes lawfull and vnlawfull, to Iudge of the Fall of A Common-Wealth* (1595), was on familiar ground when he quotes authority to show "that three sorts of sins are noted in the holie scripture, which principally cause the ruines & changes of a common wealth. *Impietie* ruinating the Church: *Iniustice* corrupting the Com-

---

[146] *A Treatise of Melancholie* (1586), sigs. I3ʳ⁻ᵛ.

[147] O. J. Campbell finds from a study of Marston's plays, especially *What You Will,* that Marston came to reject the validity of the malcontent scholar's attack upon life. See *Comicall Satyre,* chap. VI.

mon wealth: and *Lecherie* destroying the familie, with which *Pride* is intermedled, & their seuerall harmes redound vnto al: for this cause *Intemperancie & Pride* mixt, is noted by the Poet to bee most speciall for the subuerting of a state: *Nam cetera regna Luxuries vitijs odijsque superbia vertit.*" [148] This connection between sexual practices and the social and political health of the state is implicit also in some of the speeches in *Hamlet*.

From the point of view of literary history, Hall and Marston are interesting for quite different reasons. Hall was highly praised in the eighteenth century; in fact, the most thorough and enthusiastic criticism of him ever written is that by Thomas Warton in his *History of English Poetry*. Hall's versification, more smooth and regular than that of Marston, satisfied the eighteenth-century ear: "The fabric of the couplets approaches to the modern standard," said Warton. Moreover, his aloofness, his Stoic values, his academic point of view, seemed to a neoclassic age to represent the correct point of view for satire. In Warton's words, "The indignation of the satirist is always the result of good sense." In short, Hall was felt to be a precursor of modern satire in the heroic couplet, and, as such, he could be called "a neglected writer of real genius." [149]

Marston is more difficult to read than Hall, in spite of his protest in the address "To those that seem the iudiciall peruser" prefixed to *The Scourge of Villainie* that he is not one who believes that those are bastard satires "which are not palpable darke, and so rough writ, that the hearing of them read, would set a man's teeth on edge." His own theory of satire is that the content should be rough, not the style. But his abruptness, his jerky use of allusion, his violence of pitch, sometimes leave the reader floundering. Hall can be understood if there is sufficient annotation,[150] but as one modern critic says, "Marston, in cultivating obscurity, is obscure not

---

[148] Sig. E3ʳ.

[149] Warton, *History of English Poetry,* ed. W. C. Hazlitt, 4 vols. (London, 1871), IV, 367–368.

[150] See the edition by Davenport.

only to the unlearned, who cannot follow his allusions; he is equally incomprehensible to those who understand his allusions but do not find that they lead anywhere." [151]

To a reader who is interested in the dark and murky despair of the late Elizabethans, who reads *Hamlet* not as a romantic nineteenth-century play but as an Elizabethan tragedy, Marston's satire is more interesting than Hall's. It has some of the flair and insolence of Nashe, who is perhaps the satirical genius of the period; it is directly related to the satire in Jonson's great comedies. The better the temper of the years around 1600 is understood, the more valuable Marston's satires will seem. But in a way, Marston has made criticism of his poetry impossible, because the reader who responds adequately to the poet's tone and attitude is in no position to praise or blame. The dilemma Marston presents him is a neat one, and no doubt judgment on the poet's work can only be resolved in it: "Hee that thinks worse of my rimes then my selfe [i.e., than I do], I scorne him, for he cannot, he that thinks better, is a foole."

To a sober Elizabethan the combats of satirists were disruptive of good order. The Martin Marprelate controversy and one of its sequels, the squabbling between Harvey and Nashe, had illustrated the unseemly violence to which such quarrels could go. And now Marston had started just such another melee by the bitterness of his reply to Hall and the general scurrility of his style. Marston's friend Edward (Everard) Guilpin, in his *Skialetheia or A Shadowe of Truth, in certaine Epigrams and Satyres* (1598), composes his last satire as an attack upon "opinion": opinion is the opposite of reason; it is what sways the multitude but should not enslave the philosopher; it accounts for the variable reputation of writers when their work remains what it always was. Guilpin is, like Hall, a product of Emmanuel College, Cambridge, and he shows his preference for the philosopher's detachment rather than the professional poet's dependence upon public favor:

[151] Arnold Stein, "The Second English Satirist," *MLR*, XXXVIII (1943), 278.

> Thus doth opinion play the two edg'd sword,
> And vulgar iudgments both-hand playes afford,
> Then who but fooles, and empty caske like minds,
> Would be engross'd with such fantastique winds?
> Let Players, Minstrels, silken Reuellers,
> Light minded as their parts, their aires, their fethers,
> Be slaues t'Opinion.[152]

Guilpin maintains that the ideal is the superiority of Epicte-
tus to any man's criticism or opinion. He is, in fact, deploring
the public controversy between Marston and Hall.[153] But the
differences between them are vulgar and taking sides in this
way is unworthy of a philosopher.[154] Marston replies to Guilpin in an added satire in the 1599 edition, the one called
"Satyra Nova," containing his final respects to Hall. He picks
up Guilpin's idea that opinion is to be scorned and says it is
only opinion which has given Hall any importance whatever.

> Opinion mounts this froth vnto the skies
> Whom iudgements reason iustly vilefies.[155]

Other Cambridge men felt as Guilpin did. William Covell,
a fellow of Queen's College, had already in 1595 protested
against carping and, speaking with the voice of England to
her daughter Cambridge, had urged that she reconcile her
two sons Harvey and Nashe.[156] Now John Weever, a former
student of Covell's,[157] issued a volume of epigrams in which
he declined to "cast in Enuies teeth defiance" as Hall had
done or dedicate his poems to Detraction in the manner of
Marston.[158] In the next year (1600), he published *Faunus and
Melliflora, or the Original of our English Satyres*. The volume consists of an Ovidian-mythological poem, heavily indebted to *Hero and Leander, Venus and Adonis*, and Sid-

---

[152] *Skialetheia*, sig. E1ᵛ.
[153] Sig. E1ᵛ.
[154] Sig. E2ʳ.
[155] *The Scourge of Villanie*, ed. G. B. Harrison (London, 1925), p. 102.
[156] *Polimanteia*, sigs. Q4ʳ⁻ᵛ.
[157] See *Epigrammes in the Oldest Cut & Newest Fashion*, ed. R. B.
McKerrow (Stratford, 1922), pp. 60, 117.
[158] *Ibid.*, p. 11.

ney's *Arcadia*,[159] followed by translations of the first satire of
Horace, the first satire of Juvenal, and a fragment of the first
satire of Persius; this is followed by a conclusion in which
Venus condemns satires, and the volume ends with a verse
"prophesie of this present yeare, 1600," in which he says that
those attacked in satires have reformed, and concludes that it
is just as well that satires have ceased, for they created more
evil than they cured.[160] In telling how it is that satires are the
enemies of love, Weever mentions specifically Hall's and
Marston's satires. He is willing to praise them both, within
their limits, but he objects fundamentally to satire as a type.[161]

At the end of *Faunus and Melliflora* Weever describes how
Venus journeyed to England on hearing the report that satires
attacked "her proceedings and her deitie"; it is decreed:

> That all the Satyres then in England liuing
> Should sacrifisde be in the burning fire,
> To pacifie so great a goddesse ire,
> And from their Cyndars should a Satyre rise,
> Which their Satyricke snarling should despise.
> All which perform'd, she left our English shore,
> Neuer I hope to trouble vs any more.[162]

This is a reference to the burning of the satires in 1599, an
event which is recorded in the Stationers' Register.[163] On
June 1 an order suppressing satires and epigrams, Nashe's

---

[159] The indebtedness of some passages from Weever to the *Arcadia* was
pointed out by Charles Crawford in his edition of *England's Parnassus*
(Oxford, 1913), p. 388. The "untraced" passages attributed to Weever in this
anthology come from *Faunus and Melliflora*.

[160] Sig. I4ᵛ.

[161] Sig. F3ʳ. The account of *Faunus and Melliflora* in Davenport, "The
Quarrel of the Satirists," pp. 123–130, is distorted, presumably because Davenport did not see the book, the unique copy of which is in the Huntington
Library, but only "rotographs of the relevant passages" (p. 123). He maintains
that in this book Weever shifts his allegiance from Marston to Hall. Actually,
as the whole work shows, Weever attacks both. He is following in the steps of
his old tutor, to whom in the next year he dedicated the *Mirror of Martyrs*,
a poem in defense of Sir John Oldcastle. Davenport has now published an edition of *Faunus and Melliflora* (Liverpool Reprints No. 2, 1948).

[162] Sig. I2ʳ.

[163] Edward Arber, ed., *A Transcript of the Registers of the Company of
Stationers of London, 1554–1640*, 5 vols. (London, 1875–1894), III, 677–678.

and Harvey's books, unauthorized plays and English histories was issued, and provision was made for collecting such books already in print and bringing them to the Bishop of London to be burned. On June 4 there is a list of books so burned and some others which were "stayed."

The motives behind this action of the Archbishop, the Bishop, and the Privy Council were obviously various. One purpose was to stop forgery of the licensing officers' names; another was to prevent the publication of dangerous books and plays, like Heyward's history and Shakespeare's play of *Richard II,* which had played a part in the Essex uprising; the third was to suppress pornography; and finally the authorities were trying to stop the publication of the more scurrilous kinds of satire and epigram. Hall's satires, though included on the first list, were not burned, whereas the books of Marston and Guilpin were part of the bonfire.

The authorities who supervised publication, then, were interested in curbing the excesses of satire. The censors were not, of course, completely successful, and the satirical spirit which had been manifest in nondramatic poetry continued to flourish on the stage. Marston and Dekker were involved with Jonson in the famous Stage-Quarrel, and in the theaters satirical attacks and counterattacks were all the fashion. As the young men from the city reported to the prince at court in Shakespeare's play, "there was, for a while, no money bid for argument unless the poet and the player went to cuffs in the question." [164]

Laymen continued to try to pacify the satirists, even after the episcopal decree. In 1601 appeared *The Whipping of the Satyre,* a versified reproof of the vainglorious satirist, epigrammatist, and humorist. The preface is signed W. I., but the identity of the author is obscure.[165] He attacks Marston, Nicholas Breton, and Jonson, maintaining that satirical violence is both un-Christian and un-English. The correction of sins should be done lovingly, he thinks, and the laying open of

---

[164] *Hamlet,* II, ii, 371–373.
[165] Davenport, in "The Quarrel of the Satirists," p. 129, argues inconclusively for the identification of W. I. and John Weever.

abuses harms the commonwealth by causing dissension. The true function of the poet is to celebrate heroic actions, and his contribution is rightly a positive one, not negative. In the same year appeared two answers, one from Breton called *No Whippinge, nor trippinge: but a kinde friendly Snippinge,* which agrees that satire is no proper form for poets and urges them all to turn to religious themes. An argument in defense of the satirist appeared, called *The Whipper of the Satyre his pennance in a white Sheete: or, The Beadles Confutation.* The author's argument is simply that satire does, by making vice loathsome and exposing it, advance the cause of virtue. He did not apparently know of the prohibition against the publication of satires:

> Meane time, good Satyre to thy wonted traine,
> As yet there are no lettes to hinder thee.[166]

The minor satiric productions of the period, both before and after the prohibition of the publication of any more such works, reflect the same basic concerns as those we have been noticing. The epigram writers, too, deal with these subjects and reflect these attitudes in part; the epigram can, of course, and most often does, treat social foibles, manners, trivial hypocrisies, and affectations, but it occasionally joins the longer satire in dealing with the major social and economic maladjustments of the time.

The subject of usury, for example, is treated in the first satire of T. M.'s *Micro-Cynicon* (1600) —the "Snarling Satires" which had been condemned in the proclamation; in John Lane's *Tom Tel-Troth's Message* (1600), E3ᵛ; in Harington's epigrams 214 and 228; in Bastard's *Chrestoleros* (1598), epigrams II, 19, and V, 9; and in Samuel Rowlands' *Letting of Humour's Blood in the Head Vaine* (1600), satire 2. Enclosures provide the subject for Bastard's epigrams III, 22, and IV, 20. The extravagance and prodigality of the Elizabethan young man are portrayed over and over again, for example in *Micro-Cynicon,* satire 2; *Tel-Troth,* E4ᵛ; Rankins' *Seauen Satyres Applyed to the Weeke* (1598);

[166] Sig. B5ʳ.

the "wandering satire," C^r ff.; and Nicholas Breton's *The Fooles-Cap* (1600), B3^v. The lechery attacked by Marston and the love poetry which both Hall and Marston considered an incentive to it are excoriated in *Tel-Troth*, F2^r, Rankins' satire 5, Guilpin's "Satyre Preludium" to *Skialetheia* (1598), and Rowlands' epigram 16. The railing humour and the disposition of the malcontent are satirized in Guilpin's epigrams 7 and 52 and Sir John Davies' epigram 34; Rankins had already attacked the state of mind as long ago as 1588 in his prose tract *The English Ape*. It is apparent, then, that the major subjects of complaint continued to occupy the minds of observing Englishmen during the last years of Elizabeth's reign. It should be remembered also that, as in other literary forms, the older models did not die out as the new ones came in. Some satirists still practiced the devices of the *Piers Plowman* tradition and medieval satire. The old formula of a catalogue of "whens," for example, is illustrated in Bastard's epigram 43 of Book VI, in Harington's epigram 83, and in Breton's "Pasquil's Prognostication" in the volume called *Pasquils Passe and Passeth Not* (1600). Some writers regarded Spenser as a better model in satire than Juvenal and Persius or Hall and Marston, and Lane's *Tom Tel-Troth* and Cyril Tourneur's *The Transformed Metamorphosis*,[167] both 1600, derive from *Mother Hubberds Tale*. The obstacles put up by the lord bishops and the Stationers' Company may have driven some satirists, like Marston, to the stage for an outlet, but the flow of nondramatic satire continued nevertheless.

If, as the satirists claimed, their function was salutary for the commonwealth, and if, as the opponents of satire argued, the uninhibited practice of it was indecent and disorderly, what judgment can be made between the two parties? Whitgift and Bancroft would probably have admitted that it was in the tradition of English Protestantism to smite sin hip and thigh and that even the most respected preachers had used

---

[167] Tourneur's remarkable piece, which gives some indication of the qualities which appeared in his later tragedies, is discussed by Allardyce Nicoll in his edition of Tourneur's works (London, 1929), and by K. N. Cameron, "Cyril Tourneur and *The Transformed Metamorphosis*," *RES*, XVI (1940), 18–24.

the weapon of satire. How, then, were the satirists and epi-grammatists in the wrong? It is, finally, a question of the proper point of view for the satirist, the ground on which he stands, and this subject is one of the themes of a master-piece by Ben Jonson of just this date, *Every Man Out of His Humour.* The conflicts between satirists themselves, between satirists and authority, between the malcontent and the normal member of society, form the background of Jonson's play, and it might be said that the whole story of Elizabethan satire culminates in Jonson's comedy.

The classic analysis of *Every Man Out* is C. R. Baskervill's seventh chapter in *English Elements in Jonson's Early Comedy.*[168] In it the connection between Jonson's play and the nondramatic satire of the nineties is made very clear, with a wealth of illustration. The principal characters are related to their types as they appear in earlier English roles.[169]

Baskervill's purpose is to show Jonson more deeply im-bedded in the English tradition than scholars had previously thought, and the case is proved beyond question. But the emphasis may be somewhat different if the play is approached from the satires, rather than the satires being used as a back-ground for the play.

The problem about satire as it faced the writers at the end of the century was primarily a problem of point of view. Should the satirist be detached and impartial, "academic," like Hall? If so, he lost something in force. Moreover, as Hall himself showed, such a position might amount to mere con-servatism, a rejection of what modern literature had accom-plished, a rejection merely on the basis of taste. The "Re-actio" of Marston, inspired in tone by Nashe, was sound. But Marston raised the question of the validity of the malcontent as a satirist. It could be suspected that his objections to the world rested not merely on taste, as Hall's did, but on some-thing equally irresponsible and peculiar, temperament. There

---

[168] Austin, Texas, 1911.
[169] The chapter on *Every Man Out* in Campbell's *Comicall Satyre* empha-sizes critical theory in the background of the play. It is, accordingly, useful as a supplement to Baskervill's discussion.

were too many signs that he was himself involved in what he was attacking. The problem was merely illustrated by Marston and Hall; they did not, of course, invent the dilemma of the satirist.

Jonson analyzes the problem by presenting three different characters who fill the role of the satirist; they are contrasted with each other as to function and validity, and a solution is reached which indicates Jonson's opinion of the true role and justification of the critic of society.

Asper, who takes part in the induction and frame of the comedy, is "an ingenious and free spirit, eager and constant in reproofe, without feare controuling [i.e., attacking] the worlds abuses." He attacks all public vice, unmasking it and lashing it. His victims are strumpets, ruffians, brokers, usurers, and lawyers. His satiric activities are necessary, he feels, because the power of conscience is not strong enough to inhibit the sins which are practiced.[170] The vices of the time are summarized in these three words: extortion, pride, and lusts.

Macilente, who operates within the play itself, is the intriguer who brings about the purging of the various humours in the satirized characters. In contrast to Asper, Macilente has a special motive for satire: he is incited by envy, he is something of a malcontent.[171] Jonson describes him as "a Man well parted, a sufficient Scholler, and trauail'd; who (wanting that place in the worlds account, which he thinks his merit capable of) falls into such an enuious apoplexie, with which his iudgement is so dazeled, and distasted, that he growes violently impatient of any opposite happinesse in another." His opening speech makes clear that he is incapable of feeling the Stoic content which the age preached as the desirable state of mind; "this vnproportion'd frame of nature" galls him, and reflection only strengthens his bitterness. Being motivated by Envy, even resembling, as Baskervill shows, the traditional

---

[170] Induction, lines 32–36.

[171] See Baskervill, *English Elements in Jonson's Early Comedy*, p. 159. Campbell, *Comicall Satyre*, p. 60, seems to think that Macilente is normal psychologically, but the distinctions he makes are not clear to me, and Jonson's characterization of Macilente prefixed to the play seems to support Baskervill's interpretation.

figure of Envy in allegory, he is the special opponent of Pride. He is, therefore, the undoing of Fastidious Brisk. But his hatred for Sordido, the farmer who is essentially a grain hoarder, is equally strong.[172] He is not more gentle to extortion than he is to pride. He is a man to be feared, as Carlo Buffone points out: " 'Ware how you offend him, he carries oile and fire in his pen, will scald where it drops: his spirit's like powder, quick, violent: hee'le blow a man vp with a jest." [173] Macilente's personal motivation for satire, for scourging and correction, does not invalidate his satire; Jonson makes this clear by showing the spectators within the play, Mitis and Cordatus, in agreement with him about the vices of the others, even though they realize that his motive is envy or a malcontent spirit.[174] Moreover, there is one of the characters, Carlo Buffone, whom he does not envy but hates, and this example of his attitude is also shared by the spectators within the play and outside it.

Carlo Buffone is described by Jonson as "a publicke, scurrilous, and prophane Iester . . . His religion is his rayling, and his discourse ribaldry. They stand highest in his respect, whom he studies most to reproach." As a mere railer and buffoon, he is of course a monster; [175] he has no respect for any honorable or reverend personages, and "he will preferre all Countries before his natiue, and thinkes he can neuer sufficiently, or with admiration enough, deliuer his affectionate conceit of forraine Atheistical policies." Even Carlo, however, can be the instrument of serious satiric attack. He is used ironically, for example, in the scene in which he gives Sogliardo his indoctrination on how to be an accomplished gentleman. The dramatic interest is not in whether Carlo believes this policy or not but in the ironic description of the way to succeed.

We have, then, three alternatives: the ordinary irresponsible railer, the malcontent or envious person, and the detached critic. Of these, the Carlo Buffone type is impossible because of his insensitivity to real worth, his lack of patri-

172 I, iii, 65–88.   174 See Induction, lines 147–198.
173 I, ii, 214–216.   175 Induction, line 365.

otism, and his devotion to "atheisticall policy." The Asper type does not achieve a correction of the abuses in society because he is detached from it. And the Macilente type has the shortcoming of a reprehensible motive. So Jonson shows his solution in the purging of Macilente's own humour and the transformation of this malcontent into one with the impersonality of Asper, suggested by the identity of the actor playing the two roles. In the first version of the comedy, Jonson had Macilente purged of his envious humour by being brought into the presence of the Queen. This conclusion, which Jonson altered because of its unpopularity (apparently rather a question of decorum than anything else), he nevertheless defended as appropriate and probable. He was, in reality, only applying the standard correction of the malcontent state of mind; it could be overcome by traditional patriotism. So long as attack on public vices was consistent with patriotic feeling, it was legitimate; when it worked the other way, so as to produce antagonism to the very basis of English society, it became a vice like those it was attacking. In the revised ending, Macilente is purged of his humour only because there is nothing left for him to repine at, the other humours all having been cured.

The play, whatever it may lack in comic and dramatic vitality, is a major piece of criticism. It arraigns the engrosser, the prodigal, the gallant, the uxorious man, the lecherous woman, the fantastic adventurer who practices the Elizabethan form of life insurance in reverse (not only for himself but for his dog and cat), the braggart, and other caterpillars of the commonwealth. But the most significant achievement of the play is its presentation of a complete examination of the grounds for, and the validity of, satire. It is in this sense, especially, that Jonson was writing a comedy, not filled with the romantic nonsense of cross-wooing among dukes and duchesses, or with the immortal paradoxes of character to be found in the plays about Sir John Falstaff, but "thus neere, and familiarly allied to the time." [176]

[176] III, vi, 200.

V

POETRY FOR MUSIC

The Nature of the Medium

Is poetry produced by ideas, by the reaction of sensitive minds to profound generalizations about life? It would seem so, from our consideration of pastoral. Is poetry the result of some discipline of wit and invention, of the development of metaphor, under the compulsion of a restricted form, such as we found in the tradition of the Petrarchan sonnet? Or is it a growth from the milieu, determined and directed by the social and economic environment, as was suggested by our survey of Elizabethan satire? Poetry is of course the result, in greater or less degree, of all of these. The poet in *Timon of Athens* says:

> Our poesy is as a gum, which oozes
> From whence 'tis nourish'd,

but he tells us nothing about the things which nourish it most successfully.

Among these formative and nourishing elements in the Elizabethan age, music is not the least important. Especially in the last decade of the sixteenth century there occurred a flowering of the English musical genius comparable in significance and value with the achievements of that period in drama and poetry. Never since have the English had so much to boast of in comparison with continental creativeness in music as when they could point to Byrd, Morley, Gibbons, Weelkes, Wilbye, Dowland, and Daniel. It was a fortunate time; the composers drew upon the poetry, and poetry was in turn nourished by music.

The English lyric was, in the age of Shakespeare, a mode of poetry which lived in intimate relationship with music; it was not merely "lyrical" by tradition or form. And the song which was its sustaining element was something vital in the life of the English people. Just as the Elizabethan drama owes much of its vigor to a popular tradition of folk play, pageant, and festival, matured and refined by infusions of classical structure, character types, and rhetoric, so the Elizabethan lyric was the result of the mingling of a tradition of ballad singing, street cries, and dance songs with a more sophisticated courtly kind of composition, the madrigal, imported from Italy and fostered, as so many of the new styles were, by self-conscious patriotic experimenters who were well aware of the needs of their own art and how those needs could be satisfied from foreign sources.

What no experimenter or reformer could do, however, was to provide a native tradition. The English were apparently as inveterate singers in the sixteenth century as the Italians of later times are supposed to be. Erasmus commented on the English aptitude for music and love of it. The evidence of contemporary descriptions is that the plowman sang in the fields, the journeyman shoemaker at his bench, and the peddler along the roads. All kinds of people, from the cooper who made a song of his street cry to the sovereign on the throne—everyone fancied himself as composer, performer, or both. Henry VIII composed songs, and his daughter Elizabeth was a capable performer on the virginals. Music was a part of education, and a serious part; Richard Mulcaster, the great master of the Merchant Taylors School and the teacher of Spenser, insisted that his pupils know how to sing and read music and even to perform upon instruments. The schoolmaster's prefatory verses to Tallis and Byrd's *Cantiones Sacrae* of 1575 expound his view of the value of music in promoting a sound mind in a healthy body. In the science of the day, the organizing principle of the universe was harmony; the spheres produced an exquisite music as they revolved, and the order and relation of one celestial body to another were governed by a harmonic principle. And, because human life was only a smaller model of the cosmic system, political and social institutions, even the personal relationships between men, were also governed by the same musical power. It was thought to be true, therefore, in a very literal sense, that the man who had no music in himself was fit for treasons, stratagems, and spoils. It is insisted throughout the discussions in Castiglione's *Courtier* that music is not optional in the education of a courtier but compulsory. The Count undertakes to show, in the First Book,

how it hath bene the opinion of most wise Philosophers that the world is made of musick, and the heavens in their moving make a melody, and our soule framed after the very same sort, and therfore lifteth up it self and (as it were) reviveth the vertues and force of it with musick.[1]

Since Alexander the Great, Socrates, Epaminondas, and Achilles were all practitioners of music, who can say that the art of music is not proper for the soldier or the philosopher? [2]

This is of course theory, and a culture may have a very insistent belief in an art without producing anything remarkable in it. The phenomenon to be accounted for is the sudden appearance, in the last years of the century, of a considerable number of English composers, some of the very first rank. The Elizabethan age was the great age of English music as it was the great age of English poetry, and the connection between the two is no accident.

Preëminent among Elizabethan composers, for both sacred and secular music, was William Byrd of the Chapel Royal. Something of his musical career must be sketched in order to show how his work, especially in the madrigal, was undertaken in collaboration with the poets and how the triumphs in composition had something to do with Elizabethan triumphs in lyric poetry. Byrd was rewarded in a characteristic way by the Queen for his services to her: he received, together with his old master Thomas Tallis, an exclusive license to

[1] Tudor Translations ed. (London, 1900), p. 89.
[2] *Ibid.*, p. 90.

print music of all kinds and also ruled paper for the purpose
of writing or "pricking" music. After the death of Tallis in
1585 Byrd held this monopoly alone, and most of the printed
music books of the period came out under it. Byrd was therefore in a central position, but his real contribution to English secular music depends rather upon his own compositions
and their effect upon the public than upon his importance
as the monopolist of music printing.[3]

In 1586 there appeared from the press of Joseph Barnes at
Oxford an anonymous volume called *The Praise of Musicke*,
citing all kinds of ancient authorities in support of the position that music was allowable and praiseworthy not only in
civil matters but also in church. Two years later there appeared from the same publisher a Latin work entitled *Apo-
logia Musices Tam Vocalis Quam Instrumentalis et Mixtae;*
this book was by the learned John Case. Possibly the English
work was by Case also, but proof is lacking. In any event,
Case's defense of music so pleased William Byrd that he composed a madrigal, to words by Thomas Watson, called "A
gratification vnto Mr. John Case, for his learned Booke,
lately made in the prayes of Musick." The song was published as a broadside.[4]

Watson, whose significance as a pioneer in the introduction of Petrarchan sonnets into English will be remembered,
and whose contributions to pastoral are of some importance,
seems to have been one of the first to realize the possibilities
for lyric poetry of the music of his time. He was not quite
the first, however, for the collection called *Musica Transalpina*, a set of Italian madrigals with English words substituted for the originals, was brought out by Nicholas Yonge,
a lay clerk and musician of St. Paul's Cathedral, in 1588.
Yonge explains that the translations were done "fiue yeeres
agoe by a Gentleman for his priuate delight, (as not long

[3] For information on Byrd and authoritative appraisal of his music, see
Fellowes, *William Byrd*.

[4] The only surviving copy is that of the Cantus Secundus part in the
Cambridge University Library. See Fellowes, *Byrd*, p. 162. Watson's words were
printed, from a manuscript copy (Rawlinson MSS. Poet. 148), by Joseph
Haslewood in *British Bibliographer*, II (1812), 543–544.

before certaine Napolitans had been englished by a verie honourable personage, and now a Councellour of estate, whereof I haue seene some, but neuer possessed any) ." [5] The publication of them, he says, was instigated by a group of "Gentlemen and Merchants of good accompt (as well of this realme as of forreine nations)" who were accustomed to resort to his house daily to sing the Italian songs which Yonge kept importing every year from Italy. Included with the Italian madrigals in Yonge's volume were two by Byrd, settings to two stanzas of Ariosto, which like the rest were translated into English.

From this evidence we may conclude that the vogue for Italian madrigals was already flourishing among citizens and gentlemen of London; but in the same year, 1588, Byrd issued his own volume of English madrigals, *Psalmes, Sonets, & songs of sadnes and pietie, made into Musicke of fiue parts,* dedicated to the Lord Chancellor, Sir Christopher Hatton, and bearing on its title pages Hatton's crest of the golden hind. As a result of this publication the vogue of madrigal singing flourished in the court circles, and happily enough, in the burst of patriotic pride and enthusiasm following the defeat of the Armada, the taste for such music could now be gratified by English compositions, with English words, inferior to nothing proud Italy could boast. In the next year, 1589, Byrd published another volume, *Songs of sundrie natures, some of grauitie, and others of myrth, fit for all companies and voyces;* he began the dedication to the Lord Chamberlain with the remark that he had observed "that since the publishing in print, of my last labors in Musicke, diuers persons of great honor and worship, haue more esteemed & delighted in the exercise of that Art, then before."

The influence on Byrd of the vogue of the Italian madrigal was strong, for he admits that the songs of the 1588 volume were originally for a single voice singing the words and instruments providing the harmony, but that he had rewritten them so that they "are now framed in all parts for voyces to sing the same." The result was that for ten years the

[5] Sig. Aij^r.

polyphonic madrigal, with the various voices singing independent melodic lines and the words used in such a way that
they were "interpreted" by the music rather than understood
by the hearers, was to triumph over the simpler song or air
for one voice and accompaniment.[6]

Although the words always came first in the composition
of a madrigal, and much ingenuity was devoted to the musical interpretation of the meaning of the words, we nevertheless find that the translations made by Nicholas Yonge's
anonymous friend acquired some independent existence as
English poems. Some of them were taken over and set by
other composers. No. 32, for example, was a madrigal by
Orlando di Lasso which was provided with English words
beginning "The nightingale so pleasant and so gay"; these
words were taken over by Byrd and set to new music in his
1589 volume.[7]

The influence of the madrigal upon English verse has been
insufficiently appreciated by the reader of Elizabethan lyric
poetry. Considering the music to be merely a "setting" of the
words, a comment upon them, the literary historian commonly regards the music as simply an evidence of the popularity of the poem or a tribute to it. There is of course no
external evidence that a poet actually called to mind the devices of madrigal music when he sat down to write a lyric.
All we can do is to point out the fact that the parallel between poetry and music is here most striking and to name
some of the ways in which musical influence on the poetry
seems possible. The first of these ways has to do with meter
and rhythm; the second way is connected with melody and
harmony.

[6] The account of this musical situation is rather clearer in Bruce Pattison's
chapter in V. De Sola Pinto's bibliography, *The English Renaissance* (London,
1938), than it is in the various accounts of Fellowes, in *The English Madrigal*
(London, 1925), and *Byrd*. Pattison contends that Byrd's 1588 volume is the
culmination of the older tradition, derived from the Netherlands, and that
the contents of that volume are "disguised as madrigals." Fellowes is inclined
to regard Byrd as a pioneer of the later single-voice song, the "ayre."

[7] Other examples of words from *Musica Transalpina* set by English composers are No. 30, set by George Kirbye in 1597 and again by Michael East in
1606, and No. 25, set by John Bennet in 1599.

The heavy jog trot and monotonous emphasis of the four-teener verse of the sixties and seventies gave way in the last two decades of the century to a versification of subtle variety and delicacy. Why this phenomenon took place has always been something of a puzzle to literary historians. But the recent work of Bruce Pattison has made it clear that music was of prime importance, and in the development of rhythmic variety we can find the most illuminating examples in the work of the madrigalist composers and of the poets who composed their verses in madrigalian terms. The nature of this influence has been described by Pattison: "The fact is that, despite the independence of the voices, there is a sort of basic regularity behind madrigals. The Elizabethans clearly realized the difference between metre and rhythm. In poetry there is a regular pattern that continues in the mind throughout the reading—the metre; but this implicit pattern is not always evident in the actual sound of the verse, which gains its interest from innumerable tiny variations from the fixed metre. The metre is subconscious most of the time, once the poet has set the mind ticking the right pattern; the rhythm is the tune counterpointed on that subconscious pattern by the natural stresses and quantities of the words. The madrigal, too, has metre behind its rhythmic fluidity." [8]

The actual illustration of this important fact can only be made by hearing the music itself. Perhaps the simplest and most obvious example to begin with is William Byrd's famous madrigal of the ballet or dance type, "Though Amarillis daunce in greene." [9] A metrical and rhythmic analysis of the poem without the music might or might not reveal the fact, made abundantly clear by the musical setting, that we have here two distinct rhythms, a four-beat measure and a three-beat measure. They occur in the piece separately and seem to have some symbolic significance for the two girls mentioned in the first verse: to some extent Amarillis is the four-beat meter and Corinna is the three-beat. But they occur simultaneously in some passages, and the counterpoint be-

[8] *Music and Poetry of the English Renaissance,* pp. 106–107.
[9] It is available in a recording by the English Singers.

tween them leads to the comic conclusion of the poem, "Hey hoe, chill loue no more."

More subtle examples can be found everywhere in the literature of the English madrigal school. Pattison remarks about the music, "Excessive fluidity of rhythm, leaving the mind in real doubt as to the metre behind the variations, or emphatic cross-rhythms in all the parts together, have usually some textual significance." [10] Clearly so. Yet the reader of the poetry, as distinguished from the musician, is most interested in the reflection that the composer who so read the words cannot have been the only such reader, and, further, that the poet who saw his words being treated in such a fashion, with complexities of meaning and attitude conveyed by complexities of rhythm, could not fail to profit by the musical example and thereafter to exploit the same methods in his verse.

The second way in which the relationship between music of the madrigal and English lyric verse seems very close has to do with melody and harmony. By these elements the composer interpreted the mood and feeling of the words, and the style of the madrigal composers was so naïvely and literally imitative that we may perhaps be able to draw some conclusions about the weight and power of Elizabethan stock poetic words in a sensitive ear.

The subject matter of the madrigal was most commonly Petrarchan love situations, and these of course had become highly standardized. The effect for poetry was baneful in that it deadened the effect of words describing feeling or sensation. These descriptive words were resharpened by the musical setting. John Wilbye, for example, uses simultaneous major and minor thirds to enforce the meaning of "my voice is hoarse with shrieking," and when he interprets the words "change me" he has the two upper parts rise a sixth and the two lower parts fall a sixth.[11] It was conventional to set a syllable to a single note of music; but when this principle

---

[10] *Music and Poetry*, p. 107.

[11] Fellowes, *English Madrigal Composers*, p. 217; Pattison, *Music and Poetry*, p. 107.

was violated, there was almost always picturesque or illustrative intention behind it.[12] Chromatics were used increasingly to express poignant levels of emotion, and the words of the madrigal lyrics sometimes call attention to this feature and invite its use.[13]

In general, Morley's *Plaine and Easie Introduction to Practical Musicke* (1597) gives the best account of the nature of the madrigal. It is, he says, "next unto the Motet, the most artificiall and to the man of understanding most delightful." The music, he observes, is usually made upon songs and sonnets, such as Petrarch and other modern poets have excelled in. "If therefore you will compose in this kind you possesse yourselfe with an amorous humour . . . so that you must in your musicke be wavering like the wind, sometime wanton, sometime grave and staide, otherwhile effeminat, you may maintaine points and revert them, use triplaes and shew the verie uttermost of your varietie, and the more varietie you shew the better shal you please." [14]

Morley goes into considerable detail in his rules for "dittying," and his precepts can show us a good deal about the attitude of the Elizabethans, whether composers or mere readers, toward the emotional significance of the words of a lyric. In general, Morley says, there are two principal moods, grave and gay. "You must therefore if you haue a graue matter, applie a graue kinde of musicke to it; if a merrie subiect you must make your musicke also merrie." The two dimensions of emotional expression in music are harmony and rhythm. In exploiting the harmonic possibilities, "when you would expresse any word signifying hardnesse, crueltie, bitternesse, and other such like, make the harmonie like vnto it, that is, somewhat harsh and hard but yet so that it offend not. Likewise, when any of your words shal expresse complaint, dolor, repentance, sighs, teares, and such like, let your harmonie be sad and doleful." The use of accidentals is recommended to

---

[12] Pattison, *Music and Poetry*, p. 108, gives a list of words so treated.

[13] *Ibid.*, p. 109.

[14] Morley, *Introduction*, Shakespeare Association Facsimiles No. 14 (London, 1937) , p. 180.

"make the song as it were more effeminate & languishing" in contrast to what he calls the "natural motions" of thirds, sixths, and so forth, which produce effects of "crueltie, tyrannie, bitternesse and such others." [15]

Rhythmic imitation is just as important: "If the subject be light, you must cause your musicke to go in motions which carrie with them a celeritie or quicknesse of time . . . if it be lamentable, the note must goe in slow and heauie motions." But the extreme of the imitative principle went beyond this propriety of emotion; Morley tells his pupil, "You must haue a care that when your matter signifieth ascending, high heauen, and such like, you make your musicke ascend: and by the contrarie where your dittie speaketh of descending lowenes, depth, hell, and others such, you must make your musicke descend." [16] This imitation of the subject itself, as distinct from its emotional association, was in part an attempt to make the words in this kind of polyphonic piece understandable.

There was no question in Morley's mind about the importance of the words. It was the composer's duty to respect their quantity and accent: "We cause no sillable which is by nature short be expressed by manie notes or one long note, nor no long sillable bee expressed by a short note." The Elizabethan composer was not bound, as the modern composer is, to a system of barring which automatically places an accent upon the first beat of a measure; the accent came where it would naturally appear on the word. Morley is even fussy about punctuation by the use of rests: "You may set a crotchet or minime rest aboue a coma or colon, but a longer rest then that of a minime you may not make till the sentence bee perfect, and then at a full point you may set what number of rests you will." The only exception to this is an imitative device when the words, as they often do in Petrarchan poems, include the term "sigh" or "sighs." Then, according to the master, "when you would expresse sighes, you may vse the crotchet or minime rest at the most, but a longer then a

15 *Ibid.*, p. 177.
16 *Ibid.*, p. 178.

minime rest you may not vse, because it will rather seeme a breth taking then a sigh." [17]

Morley takes a somewhat Platonic-Christian view of music. It is quite clear that the rapture or transport provided by song at its highest is dependent in his opinion on the words. In discussing the motet, which is the highest kind because it is on a divine subject, he declares that "this kind of all others which are made on a ditty, requireth most art, and moueth and causeth most strange effects in the hearer, for it will draw the auditor (and speciallie the skilfull auditor) into a deuout and reuerent kind of consideration of him for whose praise it was made." But if the words are not understood, he goes on, or if the notes alone are sung "as it were a musicke for instruments, [it] will in deed shew the nature of the musicke, but neuer carrie the spirit and (as it were) that liuelie soule which the dittie giueth." [18]

This emphasis upon the interpretive value of the music and upon the general moods evoked by lyric poetry may account in part for the peculiar impersonal nature of the Elizabethan lyric, its clarity, its bird-song simplicity, its limpid freshness for all the conventionality of its themes. Critics have been puzzled to account for this quality in Elizabethan lyric verse. A representative statement of the problem is that of Agnes M. C. Latham in the introduction to her edition of Ralegh: "The typical Elizabethan poem contains no jot of personal emotion . . . it is baffling and beautiful: baffling because it is beautiful and nothing else. Thought is not permitted to distort it nor feeling to betray it into incoherencies." [19]

It may well be that this quality of the Elizabethan lyric derives from the fact that it owes its birth to music, that the music which was felt to adhere to it sharpened the emotional stress, and that the Elizabethan reader of lyric verse felt the compulsive power of these "impersonal" emotional states more vividly than we do. The "beautiful and nothing else"

[17] *Ibid.*
[18] *Ibid.*
[19] *The Poems of Sir Walter Ralegh* (London, 1929), p. 13.

attribute of the Elizabethan lyric may mean only that the poetry is waiting for music to give it tone and emphasis. As for feeling which might betray the words into incoherencies, a mood which is expressible by music is of necessity a coherent mood. John Addington Symonds commented on this quality of Elizabethan lyrics and saw the connection with music. He wrote, "We feel that they have arisen spontaneously from the natural and facile marrying of musical words to musical phrases; they are the right and fitting counterpart to vocal and instrumental melody; limpid, liquid, never surcharging the notes which need them as a vehicle with complexities of fancy, involutions of thought, or the disturbing tyranny of vehement passions." [20]

Thomas Watson showed his continued interest in the madrigal and an understanding of its nature when he brought out a volume like Yonge's in 1590 under the title, *The first sett, of Italian Madrigalls Englished, not to the sense of the originall dittie, but after the affection of the Noate.* The title means that Watson was not trying to translate the Italian words but to supply English words which would suit the "affection of the Noate," the feeling or color of the music. In other words, he was doing the reverse of what the composer usually did.[21]

Watson chose mostly madrigals by the Italian master Luca Marenzio, but he, like Yonge, included two English madrigals by William Byrd, advertised on the title page as "two excellent Madrigalls of Master William Byrds, composed after the Italian vaine, at the request of the sayd Thomas Watson." These two madrigals are six-part and four-part settings for

---

[20] *In the Key of Blue* (London, 1893), p. 269.

[21] Watson's volume was reprinted, with discussion, by F. I. Carpenter in *Journal of Germanic Philology*, II (1898–99), 323–358. Carpenter's comments on the relationship of Watson's poems to the Italian sources show that he neglected to observe, or else did not understand, the words on the title page. He says that Watson shows a very imperfect knowledge of Italian. But Watson was not trying to translate "to the sense of the original dittie." His knowledge of Italian must have been at least as good as Spenser's. See Mark Eccles, *Christopher Marlowe in London* (Cambridge: Harvard University Press, 1934), for Watson's travels in Italy, and recall the use made of Italian sources in *Hekatompathia*.

the verses to Queen Elizabeth, "This sweet and merry month of May." The next year, 1591, an opportunity was offered to use the song in an entertainment for the Queen. But because the affair was in September, the May Day element was inappropriate, so Watson wrote new words to be sung to the six-part arrangement of Byrd.[22] This new version of Watson's lyric was published in *England's Helicon* with a title suggesting the earlier version: "The Nimphes meeting their May Queene, entertaine her with this Dittie." [23] Francis Pilkington took these new words and composed another song to them which he published in 1605 as No. 20 in his *First Booke of Songs or Ayres.*

The interrelations between the lyrics and music of the Elizabethan age are thus numerous and complex. It is not difficult to trace them through the external connections and to see how often poets wrote for composers, or in turn wrote new words to existing music, even in the difficult medium of the madrigal.

The great flowering of the English madrigal took place in the four years 1597–1601.[24] In the first of these years, 1597, Nicholas Yonge issued his second volume of *Musica Transalpina,* encouraged by the friendly reception accorded his first one. Among the madrigals included was one by Giovanni Croce with English words supplied for it which were to become famous under a setting of Thomas Morley and to be the foundation of the famous set of madrigals composed by the leading musicians of the time (with the exception of Byrd) and issued in 1601 under the title *Madrigales The Triumphes of Oriana, to 5. and 6. voices: composed by diuers seuerall aucthors. Newly published by Thomas Morley, Batchelor of Musick, and one of the gentlemen of her Maiesties honorable Chappell.* The words which Morley

<hr />

[22] *The Honorable Entertainement gieuen to the Queenes Maiestie in Progresse, at Eluetham in Hampshire, by the right Honorable the Earle of Hertford* (1591) , sigs. B4^{r-v}.

[23] Rollins ed., No. 26.

[24] Cf. Fellowes, *English Madrigal Composers,* p. 191: "In 1596 no important madrigalian work was published; but 1597 and the four years that followed it represent the richest period in the history of the English School."

took from Yonge are extraordinarily well suited to musical treatment, and the variety in movement and stress makes the poem interesting prosodically.[25] The last two lines of the poem appear to have been prescribed for the ending of each of the contributed madrigals, for all of the twenty-three "diuers seuerall aucthors" used these two lines, or a very close variant, for their conclusions. Morley and Ellis Gibbons contributed two apiece. Daniel Norcome and George Kirbye composed their madrigals to the same words, "With angel's face and brightness," but as Dr. Fellowes has shown, the editor substituted new words, "Bright Phoebus greets most clearly," and then, possibly because Kirbye protested, had to publish another edition with Kirbye's original words.[26] This is an illustration of the Elizabethan composer's proprietary concern with the words for his music.

Though the madrigal was a form popular among such city men as those Nicholas Yonge gathered about him at his house, though it was composed and published for amateur singers, and though there is considerable evidence that musical education was widespread enough in Elizabethan England so that many people could sing at sight parts in a complicated polyphonic composition which would severely test most professional singers at the present time, yet the form remained a sophisticated one, and the amount of its effect upon lyric poetry is difficult to measure. One can only speculate about the influence upon the ear of the poet of hearing interpretations of verse by music so sensitive, imitative of every suggestion of color or emotion in the words, free and inventive in the matter of rhythm, as were the madrigals. The musicians respected scrupulously the natural accent of the words, but they did more. They solved, in an extraordinary and unexpected way, the vexed problem of quantity in English verse which had been pestering the theorists of metrics for so long.

The controversy, it will be remembered, started with the group of humanists assembled at Cambridge around Sir John

---

[25] *English Madrigal Verse,* pp. 150–151; Fellowes does not, apparently, recognize that Morley was adopting the words from Yonge.

[26] *English Madrigal Composers,* pp. 247–249.

Cheke and Dr. Thomas Watson (Bishop of Lincoln, not to be confused with the other Thomas Watson who translated Italian madrigals) and found the first important expression of theory in Roger Ascham. In opposition, the first clear statement of the principles of accentual prosody in English was made by George Gascoigne in 1575; five years later, the Spenser-Harvey letters show that there were two schools of classical versifiers, the group around Sidney, which tried to follow some rules laid down by Archdeacon Drant, insisting on strict application of Latin principles to English verse, and the more moderate position maintained by Gabriel Harvey, which held that whatever Latin rules might say about quantity of a vowel because of position, the second syllable of an English word like "carpenter" was naturally short, not long. But Harvey, despite his good sense in realizing that the poet was not free to alter the quantity of a syllable "an inch longer or bigger than God and his Englishe people haue made him," [27] failed to see that he was really scanning accentually. In the period after Harvey, such experimenters with classical prosody as Stanyhurst and Abraham Fraunce compromised, without realizing that they were doing so, between the demands of the natural English pronunciation and the old Latin rules. What was needed was some substitute for the classical precepts; they were too narrow; they allowed only two degrees of quantity in any syllable when in English there are patently more than two; in fact, the rules were suited only to a language with settled and phonetic orthography, like Latin. But there is of course quantity in English as well as accent, and the most mature prosody will take it into account. It is here that the influence of music on the Elizabethan lyric poet frees him from a humanistic tyranny and opens up the possibility of exploitation of the quantitative resources of English without violence to the basic nature of the language.

The madrigal illustrated not only rhythmic freedom but complexity, for the individual voices often "follow an independent rhythmic outline regardless of what any other voice

[27] "Of Reformed Versifying," *Elizabethan Critical Essays,* ed. G. Gregory Smith, 2 vols. (Oxford, 1904) , I, 117.

may have been doing." [28] This meant that in any individual part, words would be repeated, dropped, summarized, developed into imitative interpretive renditions. The influence of this must have been felt by the poets, who could see that without any artificial application of classical metrics to English words the desired results could be obtained. Sidney had realized that the ancient quantitative system of prosody was "more fit for Musick, both words and tune observing quantity, and more fit lively to expresse divers passions, by the low and lofty sounde of the well-weyed silable." [29] The poet, listening to the quantitative commentary of music on his verses, or hearing perhaps some kind of musical phrase in his head while he wrote the lyric, learned to exploit the quantitative effects inherent in English without the application of a foreign and inhospitable set of rules. The problem of quantity in English verse was solved not by Gabriel Harvey or Abraham Fraunce or even by Sidney but by Campion and Ben Jonson.

Before we leave the madrigal for a consideration of the "ayre," we should stop for a moment to inquire what lyric heritage comes from the madrigal books themselves. What poetry as such can be found in the words, apart from the music? It is often insisted by the specialists in Elizabethan music that the words and the music cannot be separated; but the Elizabethans sometimes took the words out of the part-books and published them as poems in such collections as *England's Helicon* and *A Poetical Rhapsody*. The titles of Byrd's volumes, with their promise of pieces for every mood, suggest the catholicity of the madrigal. Many of the madrigals are pastoral, some are Petrarchan, and a good many are simply country English in their carefree gaiety. The special kind called the "ballet" contained a fa-la refrain and was a dance song. Thomas Morley was especially distinguished at this kind, and his familiar "Sing we and chant it" is typical.[30] On one side the imaginative creation of the poets of the madrigals

---

[28] Fellowes, *The English Madrigal*, p. 56.
[29] *Apologie*, ed. Shuckburgh, p. 60.
[30] Fellowes, *English Madrigal Verse*, p. 134.

is that of a world of morris dance, Barley-Break, the bower in the close alley, wanton dallyings, and savor-scenting May. But at the other limit of the madrigal were those serious ones which approach the motet in gravity of subject matter. John Wilbye, who was fond of setting words of this sort, chose, among others, the following doleful cry:

> O wretched man, why lov'st thou earthly life,
> Which nought enjoys but cares and endless trouble?
> What pleasure here but breeds a world of grief?
> What hour's ease that anguish does not double?
> No earthly joys but have their discontents;
> Then loathe that life which causeth such laments.[31]

The Petrarchan appeals that constitute so much of the matter of the madrigals were sometimes put into juxtaposition with a larger picture of Elizabethan life, as in the remarkable poem set by Thomas Weelkes, "Thule, the period of cosmography," with its Marlovian evocation of exploration, commerce, and natural wonders.[32]

The madrigal, with its complicated and elaborate tangle of voices, with the words occurring in the different voices at different times, or rather the different voices saying different words at the same time, was primarily music for the singers and not for the listener. This was especially true as far as the words were concerned, since one who was not looking at the book could often not make out what the words were. In fact, it was possible to write a successful madrigal to nonsensical words or to do as Robert Jones did and make a musical setting for the tags used to mark the division of a book.[33]

Contrapuntal music, for all its interpretative devices, was always capable of smothering the text. This fact rendered the madrigal generally incapable of being used on the stage, and performance of a madrigal was of course dependent upon the presence of the number of singers for which the piece was composed. From the point of view of the poet, there is no

---

[31] *Ibid.*, p. 244.
[32] *Ibid.*, p. 222.
[33] Pattison, *Music and Poetry*, p. 121.

question that the one-part song with lute accompaniment, usually called the "ayre," was more useful than the madrigal, because it allowed the words to be understood, it was usable in the theater, and it had closer connections with the popular ballad and folk tune.

Sir Frederick in Castiglione's *Courtier* expresses an opinion which shows that some reservation about the madrigal, or prick-song as it was called, was felt even in Italy and in courtly circles. And the Italian sources drawn upon by Lodowick Bryskett for his *Discourse of Civil Life,* though endorsing sacred music as part of the education of a gentleman, had reservations about the value of the madrigal.[34] Moreover, the madrigal type of composition was not suited to verse composed in stanzas, for usually the imitative characteristics of the music would be absurd when applied to any stanza other than the one for which the music was originally composed.

Toward the end of the nineties, accordingly, a school of lutenist composers began to publish songs which were a development from the older type which had flourished before the vogue of the Italian madrigal. Much of the impulse to this was popular, but there was also support from the learned, who felt that the Greek combination of music and poetry could best be achieved by the "ayre." The lyrics of Campion and Jonson, with their neoclassic tendency, exploit quantitative values in English verse to a greater or less degree with the time values suggested by, or evocative of, a single melodic line. Campion, in his preface to the reader in *A Booke of Ayres* published by Philip Rosseter and himself in 1601, goes as far as he can toward the true classical manner with the remark that "the Lyricke Poets among the Greekes, and Latines were first inuenters of Ayres, tying themselues strictly to the number, and value of their sillables, of which sort you shall find here onely one song in Saphicke verse, the rest are after the fascion of the time, eare-pleasing rimes without Arte." As we shall see, this scornful and overmodest dismissal of such lyrics as "When thou must home to shades of underground" and "Follow your saint" does not do justice to the quantita-

[34] Sig. V₁ᵛ.

tive element in them, but the one purely classical experiment, "Come, let us sound with melody, the praises," is not a great success.

Campion also objects to the imitative character of the madrigal, "where the nature of euerie word is precisely exprest in the Note, like the old exploided action in Comedies, when if they did pronounce Memeni, they would point to the hinder part of their heads, if Video, put their finger in their eye. But such childish obseruing of words is altogether ridiculous, and we ought to maintain as well in Notes, as in action a manly cariage, gracing no word, but that which is eminent, and emphaticall."

John Dowland's *First Booke of Songes or Ayres of Four Partes with Tableture for the Lute* in 1597 provided some of the copy for the great lyric-pastoral anthology *England's Helicon* in 1600. But there are many other songs which escaped the editor of that volume. Furthermore, it is clear that songs of this type were written earlier, before the madrigal vogue, for some of those which appear in the published books at the end of the century have survived also in manuscripts of earlier date.[35]

The quality of these lyrics demands some sort of explanation. It is of course in part the result of the close relationship between words and music, but this explanation does not go far enough. In music more than in anything else the popular tradition and the courtly refinement of Elizabethan England enriched each other. The effect of this happy harmony has often been noticed in the drama of the period, but it is even more remarkable in the music.

The contribution of the dances and May games to the rhythms of English lyric poetry has been much underestimated.[36] From Wyatt to Shakespeare it is a positive force, in-

---

[35] An example is Dowland's famous "Lachrymae," found in William Ballet's manuscript of lute music in Trinity College, Dublin, dated 1594.

[36] It is emphasized by Baskervill, who remarks, "It is important to keep constantly in mind the conventionality of dance with song, for the surviving songs themselves can only rarely be expected to show a connection with dance, and more rarely still is the method of performance described" (*The Elizabethan Jig*, p. 10).

ducing poet after poet to find words, even when there were already several sets, to bring new life to the tune. As William Webbe said in 1586, "neither is there anie tune or stroke which may be sung or plaide on instruments, which hath not some poeticall ditties framed according to the numbers thereof, some to Rogero, some to Trenchmore, to downe right Squire, to Galliardes, to Pauines, to Iygges, to Brawles, to all manner of tunes which euerie Fidler knows better then my selfe." [37] The most popular dance tunes of course acquired ballads to them, and these dance-ballad tunes were taken up by the courtly composers. "Walsingham" was arranged by Byrd and Dr. John Bull for virginals, and Byrd made a setting of "Sellengers Round." Even indecent ballads and peddler's songs provided material for serious composers; Byrd did an arrangement of the "Carman's Whistle" and Dowland did a peddler's song.[38]

John Selden comments on the character of the court with respect to dancing under Elizabeth: "At a solemn Dancing, first you had the grave Measures, then the Corrantoes and the Galliards, and this is kept up with ceremony, at length to French-more, and the Cushion-Dance, and then all the Company Dance, Lord and Groom, Lady and Kitchin-Maid, no distinction. So in our Court in Queen Elizabeth's time Gravity and State were kept up." [39] Perhaps the Queen's own taste had something to do with this. The Earl of Worcester wrote to the Earl of Shrewsbury in 1602, "We are frolic here in Court; much dauncing in the Privy Chamber of country dances before the Queens Maiesty, who is exceedingly pleased therewith. Irish tunes are at this time most pleasing, but in winter, Lullaby, an old song of Mr. Birds, will be more in request as I think." [40] Shakespeare's song for Ariel, "Come

[37] "A Discourse of English Poetrie," *Elizabethan Critical Essays,* ed. Smith, I, 272.

[38] See John Murray Gibbon, *Melody and the Lyric* (London, 1930), pp. 43, 49, 98.

[39] *Table-Talk,* ed. Edward Arber (London, 1868), p. 62.

[40] Quoted by Wilhelm Bolle, "Die gedruckten englischen Liederbücher bis 1600," *Palaestra,* XXIX (1903), 261.

unto these yellow sands," is said to be based on a country-dance rhythm.[41]

One of the songs in Morley's *First Booke of Ayres* (1600), is "It was a lover and his lass," the words of which appear in *As You Like It*. Since the earliest known edition of Shakespeare's comedy is that of the First Folio (1623), there has been considerable controversy over whether the song was set by Morley for Shakespeare or whether the playwright had nothing to do with these words at all but simply lifted them for use in his play.[42]

The lutenist composer's method of setting made it possible for a poem of several stanzas to be set each stanza to the same music, but this occasionally produced an effect of limitation upon the poet who was writing for music. The words to several of the lute songs can be shown to follow a pattern determined by the musical necessity, so that a given line in the second stanza, or third, will imitate the corresponding line of the first stanza.

Perhaps as good an example as any of the carefully molded words in the songs of Dowland is one which was printed in *England's Helicon*, "Come away, come sweet Loue."[43] Dowland's setting is an emphasis upon the combination of calm, unhurried descriptive pleasure and a somewhat wanton urgency of the aubade appeal. The first two lines are sung to the same strain of music, and then at the middle of the stanza the time changes from four-beat to three-beat with the words "And sweet." The words "rosy" (for "Roseate" in the text, Fellowes' emendation), "rueing," "staying," and "dying" in the successive stanzas have a melismatic turn which gives an especially plaintive effect to the poem at these points, and the words "souls," the first syllable of "beauty's," the last syllable of "entertain," "hopes," the first syllable of "beauties" again, and finally "Love" all fall upon an accidental (F sharp in the

---

[41] Gibbon, *Melody and the Lyric*, p. 118.

[42] The two sides of the case are presented by Ernest Brennecke, Jr., and J. R. Moore in "Shakespeare's Musical Collaboration with Morley," *PMLA*, LIV (1939), 139–152. There is not sufficient evidence for a positive conclusion.

[43] Rollins ed., No. 120. See Fellowes, *English Madrigal Verse*, pp. 413–414.

modern transcription, and the song is in the key of F) which emphasizes the poignancy of the feeling just before the close. The rhythmic variation in the poem is notable, and the undulating motion of the melodic line is seductive in just the way suggested by the tone of the words.[44]

Dowland also set the farewell tournament lyric of Sir Henry Lee, to words by George Peele; [45] the music changes from a three-beat rhythm in the first part of the stanza to a four-beat rhythm for the last two lines, accenting the gravity and solemn character of the concluding words. In Dowland's second book of ayres in 1600 appeared the famous "Lachrymae," which seems to have become the most popular blues song of the early seventeenth century.

> Flow, my tears, fall from your springs!
>   Exiled for ever let me mourn;
> Where night's black bird her sad infamy sings,
>   There let me live forlorn.
>
> Down, vain lights, shine you no more!
>   No nights are dark enough for those
> That in despair their lost fortunes deplore.
>   Light doth but shame disclose.
>
> Never may my woes be relieved,
>   Since pity is fled;
> And tears and sighs and groans my weary days
>   Of all joys have deprived.
>
> From the highest spire of contentment
>   My fortune is thrown;
> And fear and grief and pain for my deserts
>   Are my hopes, since hope is gone.

[44] See the appreciation by Germaine Bontoux, *La Chanson en Angleterre au temps d'Élisabeth* (Oxford, 1936), p. 658.

[45] For the occasion of the tilt and the versions of the poem, some of which are in the first person instead of the third, see E. K. Chambers, *Sir Henry Lee* (Oxford, 1936), pp. 135ff. The original music for the occasion on November 17, 1590, was probably not by Dowland but by the musician Hales who sang the song.

Hark! you shadows that in darkness dwell,
  Learn to contemn light.
Happy, happy they that in hell
  Feel not the world's despite.[46]

The music for the five stanzas is in three sections: A repeated,
B repeated, and C. In the setting of the third line of stanzas 3
and 4 the words "and tears and sighs and groans" are separated thus by rests, representing sighs, as Morley pointed out;
therefore, the words to the corresponding stanza must of
necessity fit this requirement, so we find "And fear [rest] and
grief [rest] and pain [rest]." The pattern of the tune is that
of the pavan, a slow and stately dance. Peter Warlock, in his
learned and delightful book *The English Ayre,* quotes passages from seven plays of the period which refer familiarly
to the song, so it must have been known to every Englishman.
Byrd and Giles Farnaby both made arrangements of it for
the virginals.[47]

The intimate connection between music and the Elizabethan lyric is fortunately exemplified for us by one great artist
who wrote both his music and his words: Thomas Campion
was fully aware of his unique position, for he said to the
reader of his *Two Bookes of Ayres,* "In these English Ayres,
I haue chiefely aymed to couple my Words and Notes lou-
ingly together, which will be much for him to doe that hath
not power ouer both." [48]

Before he published any of his English songs, Campion was
known as a poet in Latin. He had written Ovidian mythological-erotic poems and a series of Latin epigrams published
in his *Poemata* in 1595.[49] Apparently there was a close connection between the words to his ayres and his Latin epigrams, for the preface to Campion and Rosseter's *A Booke of
Ayres* (1601), usually conceded to be written by Campion,
begins with the statement, "What Epigrams are in Poetrie,

[46] Fellowes, *English Madrigal Verse,* p. 421.
[47] Warlock, *The English Ayre,* pp. 35–36.
[48] *Works,* ed. Percival Vivian (Oxford, 1909), p. 115.
[49] See Leicester Bradner, *Musae Anglicanae,* p. 52.

the same are Ayres in musicke, then in their chief perfection when they are short and well seasoned."

Self-conscious in the attempt to unite poetry and music, Campion was also a theorist of prosody, publishing in 1602 his notorious *Obseruations in the Art of English Poesy,* which drew forth Samuel Daniel's *Defence of Rhyme.* Campion's teaching has been much misunderstood; the older view, represented by his editor Vivian, that Campion failed to understand the difference between quantity and accent and that in his actual practice, "what was accentual verse when read, became quantitative verse when sung," [50] has now been modified. Miles Kastendieck, who brought a scholarly training in both music and poetry to the study of Campion, has successfully shown that Campion's theory was based upon a recognition of the presence of both accent and quantity in English, and that his application of principles of music to prosodic theory made a new and remarkable achievement rather than the confused and reactionary document which earlier critics had seen in the *Obseruations.* Campion was merely the culmination of a movement, which had begun as early as Sidney, of seeing music and poetry together, but Sidney had not the benefit of the great English musical renaissance on which to draw. His tendency toward the conclusions Campion reached is evident from a passage in the old *Arcadia:*

> Discus said that since verses had their chief ornament in music, those that were justly appropriated to music agreed with music. Since music stood principally upon the sound and the quality, to answer the sound [the poets] brought words, to answer the quality they brought measure, so that every semi-breve or minim had its syllables matched accordingly with a long foot and a short foot, and without wresting the word, did kindly accompany the time, so that either by the time a poet should know how every word should be measured unto it, or by the verse as soon find out the full quantity of the music.[51]

[50] *Works,* ed. Vivian, p. lxi.

[51] Quoted by M. M. Kastendieck, *England's Musical Poet, Thomas Campion* (New York, 1938), p. 90. For a more elaborate version of this passage, and identification of Sidney's version of Drant's rules, see W. Ringler, "Master Drant's Rules," *PQ,* XXIX (1950), 70–74.

When Campion stuck to the rules of classical versification, as in "Come let us sound the praises," he had to confine himself to notes of only two different time values in the music. He must have realized that in English there are more than two units of length for a syllable, and in his setting of the poems which he called "ear-pleasing rhymes without art" he utilized this fact. The relationship between the versification and the music in Campion is difficult to explain for the reason that he wrote both, and quite possibly there was interaction between them in the process of composition. "As he composed both words and music . . . it is scarcely accurate to say his verse derives unusual rhythms from the music or that his music succeeds admirably in following the quantities and stresses of the words: both poetry and music often owe delightful rhythmical effects to a just appreciation of the time values of syllables, in attending to which he felt he was in the tradition of the classical lyric." [52]

It is not merely in the matter of rhythmical freedom and variety that Campion's musical method in poetry is significant. He knew that the movement of poetry and its sounds are inextricably entwined. He comments in the preface to the *Two Bookes:* "The light of this will best appeare to him who hath paysed our Monasyllables and Syllables combined, both of which, are so loaded with Consonants, as that they will hardly keepe company with swift Notes, or give the Vowell conuenient liberty."

It is this scrupulous care and sensitiveness to the movement of the line, the inflectional effects suggested by music, and the concern for the convenient liberty of the vowel that has made some of Campion's ayres among the most successful lyric poems in the language.

> I care not for these Ladies
> That must be woode and praide,
> Giue me kind Amarillis
> The wanton countrey maide;
> Nature art disdaineth,
> Her beautie is her owne;

[52] Pattison, *Music and Poetry,* p. 131.

Her when we court and kisse,
She cries, forsooth, let go.
But when we come where comfort is,
She neuer will say no.[53]

The theme, a common one of the contrast between court and country in the matter of love, is treated with extreme simplicity. Yet Campion has managed some subtle effects within the poem, largely as a result of seeing the words in terms of a melodic line. There is a pretty contrast between the feminine endings of lines 1, 3, and 5 and the masculine endings of 2, 4, and 6; in the music they are quantitatively (in terms of time) equivalent. The last two lines, being the epigrammatic conclusion of the whole, are an example of the skillful use of rhythmical and quantitative devices which the music can support. The penultimate line is a foot longer than normal, and the music of the last line plays sportfully in the climax which has been so provocatively built up.

In great contrast to the gaiety of "I care not for these Ladies" is the fourth ayre in the collection; its verse is as simple, but the emotions illustrated are far different and the methods used show Campion in a different light. The first stanza runs:

Followe thy faire sunne, vnhappy shadowe,
Though thou, though thou be blacke as night,
And she made all of light,
Yet follow thy faire sun, vnhappie shadowe.[54]

The contrast between the attitude involved in the word "shadowe" in the first line and in the fourth is strongly emphasized by the music. In the first line it is represented by two eighth notes after a succession of steady quarter notes. At the end it is set to a dotted quarter slurred to an eighth note for the first syllable and a half note for the second.[55] The

---

[53] *Works*, ed. Vivian, p. 7.

[54] *Ibid.*, p. 8. I have included the repetition in line 2 because it is significant in the musical development of the stanza.

[55] I use Fellowes' modern transcription (*The English School of Lutenist Song Writers*, 16 vols. [London, 1920–1932], Pt. I, vol. IV, p. 15); he has halved the note values, but this represents Campion's intention.

melody is in the minor, but in the first instance the shadow is represented as trivial, in the second as pathetic. The line "And she made all of light" is set to an ascending chromatic scale, a note to a syllable, suggesting the emergence from the "blacke as night" as if one were climbing a ladder.

Campion is not always so simple as in these two examples. His remarkable utilization of the convenient freedom of the vowel is perhaps best shown in No. 20. The delicacy of the manipulation of vowel sounds is so extraordinary that one feels that here is an ear even more sensitive than Tennyson's:

> When thou must home to shades of vnder ground,
> And there ariu'd, a newe admired guest,
> The beauteous spirits do ingirt thee round,
> White Iope, blith Hellen, and the rest,
> To heare the stories of thy finisht loue
> From that smoothe toong whose musicke hell can moue;
>
> Then wilt thou speake of banqueting delights,
> Of masks and reuels which sweete youth did make,
> Of Turnies and great challenges of knights,
> And all these triumphes for thy beauties sake:
> When thou hast told these honours done to thee,
> Then tell, O tell, how thou didst murther me.[56]

The correspondence of "smoothe toong" and "O tell" indicates the careful attention of the poet to quantity; the notes are long (half notes in modern transcription) in comparison with the context. The felicity of sound arrangement in "White Iope, blithe Helen" and elsewhere are beyond praise. But it should be observed that Campion saves the poem from monotonous ease and smoothness by appropriate but slightly "metaphysical" epithets twice in the course of the two stanzas: *"finisht* loue" and *"banqueting* delights." [57]

The degree and quality of this "metaphysical" trait in Campion is perhaps best exemplified in No. 14 in the *Booke of*

[56] *Works,* ed. Vivian, p. 17.

[57] Campion's double control over music and words enabled him to provide another ditty, a religious one this time, for this melody. The two versions are compared and commented upon by Pattison, *Music and Poetry,* p. 133.

Ayres; it is really a development of the regular Elizabethan habits with conceits, the treatment of figures by amplification, and other devices.

> Blame not my cheeks, though pale with loue they be;
> The kindly heate vnto my heart is flowne,
> To cherish it that is dismaid by thee,
> Who art so cruell and vnsteadfast growne:
> For nature, cald for by distressed harts,
> Neglects and quite forsakes the outward partes.
>
> But they whose cheekes with careles blood are stain'd,
> Nurse not one sparke of loue within their harts,
> And, when they woe, they speake with passion fain'd,
> For their fat loue lyes in their outward parts:
> But in their brests, where loue his court should hold,
> Poore Cupid sits and blowes his nailes for cold.[58]

Campion exploits a kind of irony possible only for the poet who is writing for music and has control over the musical setting of his words. The phrase "For their fat love lyes in their outward parts," for example, seems to be a complex figure, startling in the context of the conventional cheeks, heart, blood, and flame. But the music to the poem reveals that "For their fat loue" corresponds to "Who art so cruel" in the first stanza, an ascending chromatic passage followed by an octave leap downward; moreover, this is the second time the musical phrase has appeared: it was first used for "The kindly heate" and "Nurse not one sparke." It might be said that the first occurrence of the musical passage produced an effect of wistfulness, but when it is repeated and insisted upon, the feeling becomes inevitably bitter.

The discussion in the opening chapter of Rosemond Tuve's recent book, *Elizabethan and Metaphysical Imagery,* uses Campion as an example of the Elizabethan poetry which "would come nearest to modern expectations" in utilizing

[58] *Works,* ed. Vivian, p. 13. The poem was reprinted, not quite accurately, in Davison's *Poetical Rhapsody,* 1602 (ed. Rollins, No. 153), and was set again by Robert Jones in his *Ultimum Vale* (1608). See Fellowes, *English Madrigal Verse,* p. 517.

imagery to assist in representing a state of mind or to show just how the writer felt. Even Campion, Miss Tuve argues, does not really do this, and she contrasts with three of his best-known lyrics the opening lines from Eliot's *Preludes*. Campion's images, she maintains, are "not sensuous in function, but they lead the poem toward generalized reflection rather than toward the more exact understanding of the writer's emotion as peculiar to him"; and "clearly, Campion with his emphasis on conceptions and on 'art' and on the ear does not think of poetic imitation as the *representation* of an emotional experience." [59]

Apart from the question of whether modern expectation is for purely sensuous effects from imagery as Miss Tuve supposes, the general question of the emotional effects intended in an Elizabethan lyric may need clarification. It is no doubt true that the states of mind Campion was intending to reproduce by his lyrics were not states of mind or emotions "peculiar to him"; he was drawing upon the great Renaissance storehouse of commonplaces, and his intent was probably no more autobiographical than that of any other Elizabethan poet. To say, however, that for him poetic imitation was not thought of as the *representation* of an emotional experience is to be dangerously misleading. The effect of the combination of music and words was to make the experience as vivid as possible; the marriage of diction and ayre was to result in an intensification of the feelings projected. Their particularity it is difficult to assess; but surely we are not to follow the direction of "generalized reflection" in reading these lyrics— rather the reverse: the intensification of the emotional weight of each line, each phrase, each word in the poem as a melodic line can interpret, intensify, and reveal the verse which it sets.

Most striking of all the many examples in Campion of the lines inviting music as their interpreters, standing aside for the music to carry the effect, evoking and stimulating the melodic, harmonic, and rhythmic resources of music, is the poem which is usually cited only as the most interesting example of Campion's experiments in classical versification:

[59] *Elizabethan and Metaphysical Imagery* (Chicago, 1947), pp. 15–17.

Rose-cheekt Lawra, come
Sing thou smoothly with thy beawties
Silent musick, either other
    Sweetely gracing.[60]

One of Campion's lyrics became so popular that it appears as a broadside ballad and is current in many different forms. Campion never published it himself, but it appeared in Richard Alison's *An Howres Recreation in Musicke* (1606) along with other lyrics of Campion, set as a madrigal. Its popularity is no doubt partly accounted for by the standard, old-fashioned nature of its sentiment—the vanity of earthly joys and the imminence of fate. It begins:

What if a day, or a month, or a yeare
Crown thy delights with a thousand sweet contentings?
Cannot a chance of a night or an howre
Crosse thy desires with as many sad tormentings? [61]

The prosodic skill shown in this popular song combines oddly with the subject matter. But Campion was interested in popular motifs, and two of the songs from the later books of ayres exploit these very successfully. One is based on a fairy charm:

Thrice tosse these Oaken ashes in the ayre,
Thrice sit thou mute in this inchanted chayre;
And thrice three times tye vp this true loues knot,
And murmur soft, shee will, or shee will not.[62]

---

[60] Cited as an example in *Obseruations* (*Works*, ed. Vivian, pp. 50–51).

[61] *Works*, ed. Vivian, p. 353. The argument by Swaen against Campion's authorship is successfully refuted by Vivian (*ibid.*, p. 378), in so far as Swaen's argument from the date of the Scottish Metrical Psalter is concerned. There is, however, some question about the statement made by Vivian (p. 378) that in Alison's *An Howres Recreation* "the poem is signed 'Thomas Campion M. D.'" No such attribution or signature is present in any of the five part-books of Alison in the Bridgewater-Huntington copy. One suspects that the statement about the signature really depends upon Edward Arber's edition in *An English Garner*, 8 vols. (Birmingham, 1877–1890), VI, 396. If so, the earliest printed attribution to Campion of "What if a day" is by Alexander Gil in *Logonomia Anglica* (1619), sigs. S2^{r-v}.

[62] *Works*, ed. Vivian, p. 169.

As Kastendieck points out, the "uncertainty expressed in the words finds its counterpart in the undulating melody of the piece," [63] and the modal nature of the composition fits the ancient, superstitious atmosphere which Campion has evoked in the words.

The other ayre is almost too well known to quote. It is the famous "There is a garden in her face," perhaps the best known of all Campion's songs. Its popular derivation is in the "cherry ripe" part of the poem, when the music imitates a London street cry and the accompaniment strikes a chord before each cry and then is silent.[64]

Campion is the finest of the Elizabethan poets who wrote for music, and the reason is the obvious one that he was a composer at the same time. But he is in reality only an extreme example of the general situation in the late Elizabethan lyric. The lyric's shape and quality and its curious Elizabethan freshness are all determined by its close kinship to music.

The songs in the Elizabethan drama carried on the popular tradition. Characters in the plays sing snatches of ballads and of psalms; Shakespeare's Sir Hugh Evans even combines Marlowe's "Come live with me" and the vaguely remembered first line of the 137th Psalm, "When we did sit in Babylon." In general, the songs in the plays came to be used functionally and to represent not only periods when action without words is taking place, as in the selection of the caskets in *The Merchant of Venice,* but also as emotional and dramatic symbols in the play. Shakespeare's songs are the matchless flowering of the popular tradition. Even love songs in his plays capture and domesticate Petrarchan motifs to the atmosphere and manner of the fairs, the May games, and the tavern. Shakespeare makes a duke commend a song which he describes as a favorite of the folk:

> O fellow! come, the song we had last night.
> Mark it, Cesario; it is old and plain;
> The spinsters and the knitters in the sun,

[63] *England's Musical Poet*, p. 145, where the music is printed.
[64] See Kastendieck, *England's Musical Poet*, pp. 155–156.

And the free maids that weave their thread with bones,
Do use to chant it: it is silly sooth,
And dallies with the innocence of love,
Like the old age.[65]

The use of country dancing measures, the frequency of refrains, and the predominance of images drawn from rural life and pastimes mark Shakespeare's lyric tendency in the plays.

It was of course inevitable that the Elizabethan drama should be full of music. The earlier masters of court entertainment, John Heywood, John Redford, William Cornish, and Richard Edwards, were musicians as well as poets and producers. William Byrd wrote songs for such plays as *Gismond of Salerne,* produced in 1567/8 at the Inner Temple, and for *Ricardus Tertius* by Thomas Legge, acted at Cambridge in 1579. There was a vogue in the eighties for masque-like plays combining elements of myth, song, and atmosphere, and in the nineties Peele developed from the merely decorative use of song to a nearly consistent exploitation of songs for dramatic purposes. By the middle of the decade there is elaborate use of song in Munday's *John a Kent and John a Cumber.*[66]

The madrigal was not generally used on the public stage, though in the private theater of Blackfriars and presentations at court it was a special feature. The public theater stuck to the ayre or the traditional song, and if several musicians sang, it was likely to be a catch or a round. Ben Jonson and George Chapman, as writers for the Children of the Chapel playing at Blackfriars from 1597 to 1603, were able to utilize the talents of the boys who had been especially trained in music and who were only secondarily actors. Two of Jonson's finest poems, "Slow, slow, fresh fount" and "Queen and huntress, chaste and fair," were set as three-part madrigals by Henry Youll.[67]

[65] *Twelfth Night,* II, iv, 42–49.
[66] See J. R. Moore, "Theater Songs at Shakespeare's Time," *JEGP,* XXVIII (1929), 172.
[67] See E. S. Lindsey, "The Music in Ben Jonson's Plays," *MLN,* XLIV (1929), 86–92, and W. M. Evans, *Ben Jonson and Elizabethan Music* (Lancaster, Pa., 1929).

In the split experienced by lyric poetry in the early seventeenth century between the tendencies represented in general by Jonson and those represented by Donne, there is not so much a repudiation of the Elizabethan manner as there is an extension of its latent possibilities. Because of the close relationship between music and poetry in the Elizabethan period, Jonson was able to find a quantitative element in English and make his best lyrics classical without pedantry and without violence to the nature of English. The happy blending of classical restraint and form with a native earthiness and freshness sometimes to be found in Jonson are the result of the Elizabethan experiments and successes we have been considering.

The lyrics of Donne, on the other hand, owe not so much to music, though the poet seems to have considered them songs, as they do to the rhythm of speech. On the stage, "spoken verse had freed itself from the tyranny of metre over rhythm," [68] and Donne's break with Elizabethan tradition was in building his stanzas from a speech rhythm. What he gained in force and intensity was worth it, considering the comparable vigor of Donne's mind, but the verses of the lesser Metaphysical poets show that it was not a method for everyone.

The son of one of the contributors to Morley's *Oriana* volume of madrigals was a poet; he also profited from the intimate Elizabethan union of poetry and music. The heritage of John Milton shows nowhere more clearly in his work than in his appreciation of Henry Lawes, the musician, and his own constant awareness that whatever else it may be, poetry is also song.

[68] Pattison, *Music and Poetry,* p. 146.

VI

HEROIC POETRY

The Great Choice

O F ALL that the Renaissance gained from the revival of learning and the study of the ancients, probably the most important idea was the conception of the hero and the relationship of the hero to society. Plutarch's *Lives,* as everyone knows, profoundly influenced the mental outlook and the values held by Montaigne and by Shakespeare. But this is only an example of a fact which had much wider implications. Theories of education, doctrines of morality, attitudes of nationalistic patriotism, all derived from a central cluster of ideas about the hero.

The justification of poetry also rested upon the value of the hero and the heroic. Preëminent among the kinds of poetry, the heroic was the most patently and clearly an answer to the attacks made by the enemies of the secular imagination. The classical commonplace of Alexander's envy of Achilles because the Greek champion had a Homer to give him immortality never lost its point for sixteenth-century Englishmen. There is evidence that Queen Elizabeth was jealous of the Duke of Ferrara because he and his ancestors had been celebrated in heroic verse by Tasso. The primary ambition of every serious English poet was to provide such a glorification, not only of the particular person of Elizabeth or one of her nobles, though that was important, but even more of the qualities and virtues which could be represented and symbolized in her. Elizabethan hopes and fears for poetic art revolved about the practical possibility of heroic poetry in modern times. The poet's aim was to hold up for emulation and guidance the qualities which should move young men and inspire their actions.

The epics of Homer and Virgil had long been considered morally edifying and instructive; the narratives of ancient heroic deeds glorified ancient virtues. Even more, the reader was supposed to extend the context of useful doctrine in the poetry. He could disregard the presumed intention of the author and bring the moral home to his own present circumstances by making the story apply to himself. As Plutarch said, "The poet's statements can be given a wider application . . . what is serviceable should be taken over and made to apply to like situations." [1]

Renaissance commentary of Aristotle did not understand that the father of criticism had stressed the goodness of the hero in epic only because he thought it important to the pleasure-giving function of poetry: that "the desired pleasure could not be derived from a poem which holds up low ideals of life and conduct." [2] Instead, the critics assumed and emphasized that goodness of character in the epic hero was necessary for didactic reasons, in order to furnish an example for the reader to imitate. Hercules, Ulysses, and Aeneas became models, and their actions and motives could be translated into terms of modern life.

The superior virtue which is always attributed to the great men of an earlier generation was supposed, in the Renaissance, to result from the fact that these ancestors were educated on epic poetry. Lodowick Bryskett gives a typical account in his *Discourse of Civil Life* (1606): "But if that auncient kinde of musicke, framed and composed wholy to

[1] "How the Young Man Should Study Poetry," *Moralia,* 34 B, trans. F. C. Babbitt, Loeb Classical Library, 14 vols. (1927–1939), I, 179.

[2] R. C. Williams, "The Purpose of Poetry, and Particularly the Epic, as Discussed by Critical Writers of the Sixteenth Century in Italy," *Romanic Review,* XII (1921), 2. There is a good survey of Renaissance doctrine on the epic in the first chapter of H. T. Swedenberg, *The Theory of the Epic in England, 1650–1800,* University of California Publications in English, XV (Berkeley, 1944).

grauitie, were now knowne and vsed, which kinde was then set forth with the lerned and graue verses of the excellent Poets, we should now also see magnificall and high desires stirred vp in the minds of the hearers." [3]

The most important element in an epic was therefore the character of the hero; the disposition of the epic events and the style were secondary. The adventures of the hero were regarded as events designed to show his wisdom, prudence, and self-control. Lawrence Humphrey, in dedicating his treatise on nobility, *The Nobles,* to Queen Elizabeth in 1563, points out how the adventures of Ulysses in the *Odyssey* teach us the value of wisdom and learning: because he was guided by Minerva or wisdom, says Humphrey, the hero was able to drink Circe's enchanted cup, to hear but not approach the Sirens, to visit and depart from the Lotus-Eaters—nay, even to journey to hell and return safely.

To be sure, the full-blooded heroes of classical epic sometimes indulged in displays of wrath or lust which could hardly be considered virtuous from a modern point of view, and some of the critics are forced to admit that the actions of the epic protagonists are not always good. Giraldi and Trissino condemn the use of vicious actions in heroic poetry. [4] But the more usual way out of the difficulty was to adopt from Plutarch the device of throwing the responsibility on the reader. The bee gathers honey from flowers, even among the thorns, said Plutarch, and the young man should do the same with poetry. [5] To William Fulbecke, the author of *A Booke of Christian Ethics* or *Morall Philosophie* (1587), the moral ambiguity of the Troy story was only too evident; he therefore warns the reader in the strongest terms that he is to emulate the bee and not the spider. [6]

When it was possible to transform the hero and remove the

---

[3] Sigs. T4^v–V^v. The best account of the relationship between Giraldi's *Three Dialogues of Civil Life* and Bryskett's *Discourse,* as well as the bearing of these on Spenser, is to be found in John Erskine, "The Virtue of Friendship in *The Faerie Queene,*" Variorum *Faerie Queene,* Book IV, pp. 291–293.

[4] Williams, "The Purpose of Poetry," p. 18.

[5] *Moralia,* 32 F, trans. Babbitt, I, 171.

[6] Sigs. A6^{r-v}.

moral ambiguity, the Renaissance did so, not trusting the average reader to take the honey and reject the poison. The most remarkable example of this transformation is Hercules. To the Renaissance, Hercules was a man very different from the one visualized by the modern historical sense. He is pictured for the twentieth century, by Edith Hamilton, as "what all Greece except Athens most admired." [7] He is incredibly strong, completely confident that he cannot be defeated, rash and hotheaded but abnormally penitent, and generally stupid. "His intellect was not strong. His emotions were . . . It would have been ludicrous to put him in command of a kingdom as Theseus was put; he had more than enough to do to command himself." [8] Yet to the sixteenth century Hercules was a moral hero, a champion against tyranny, and a model for any young aristocrat to follow. For the Renaissance stressed, not the twelve labors or the other feats familiar to us, but a legend in which the hero is shown deliberately choosing the kind of life he will lead.

The story of Hercules' Choice, or The Hero at the Fork in the Road, was actually developed in antiquity. It derives from a sententious passage in Hesiod's *Works and Days:* "Wickedness can be had in abundance easily: smooth is the road and very nigh she dwells. But in front of virtue the gods immortal have put sweat: long and steep is the path to her and rough at first; but when you reach the top, then at length the road is easy, hard though it was." [9] A dramatization of this idea needed only the joining of the two roads at a fork, the presence of the protagonist at the division point so that a decision must be made, and two spokesmen to urge the advantages of the rival paths. All this embellishment was invented by the sophist Prodicus, according to Socrates in Xenophon's *Memorabilia.*[10] As Socrates remembers the story,

When Heracles was passing from boyhood to youth's estate, wherein the young, now becoming their own masters, show whether they will

[7] *Mythology* (New York, 1942), pp. 224–225.
[8] *Ibid.*, p. 226.
[9] Lines 286–292.
[10] II, i, 21–33, trans. E. C. Marchant, Loeb Classical Library (1923), p. 95.

approach life by the path of virtue or the path of vice, he went out into a quiet place, and sat pondering which road to take. And there appeared two women of great stature making towards him. The one was fair to see and of high bearing; and her limbs were adorned with purity, her eyes with modesty; sober was her figure, and her robe was white. The other was plump and soft, with high feeding. Her face was made up to heighten its natural white and pink, her figure to exaggerate her height. Open-eyed was she; and dressed so as to disclose all her charms. Now she eyed herself; anon looked whether any noticed her; and often stole a glance at her own shadow.

These two ladies are Pleasure (or Vice, as she is called by her enemies) and Virtue. They urge to Hercules the claims of the two paths in life, and he decides, of course, to follow Virtue.

Very early this subject became a favorite one for pictorial representation, and the long history of the theme in art has been elaborately traced by Erwin Panofsky in *Hercules am Scheidewege.*[11] Before the end of the third century Philostratus remarks that the picture is a common one.[12]

The subject, of course, is one which is similar in many ways to the Judgment of Paris; the moral significance of both tales was seen in antiquity. Athenaeus, about A.D. 200, sees the two legends in the same light: "And I for one affirm also that the Judgement of Paris, as told in poetry by the writers of an older time, is really a trial of pleasure against virtue. Aphrodite, for example—and she represents pleasure—was given the preference, and so everything was thrown into turmoil. I think, too, that our noble Xenophon invented the story of Heracles and Virtue with the same motive."[13]

Now the Elizabethans may not have read these Greek authors, but there can be no doubt that they knew the story of the Choice as a most familiar legend, not only from pictorial representations, of which the modern reader can get an idea by examining the rich stock of illustrations at the end of Panofsky's work, but also from their reading. Cicero's *De*

[11] Leipzig: Bibliothek Warburg, 1930.
[12] *Life of Apollonius of Tyana*, VI, x, trans. F. C. Conybeare, Loeb Classical Library, 2 vols. (1922), II, 33-34.
[13] *The Deipnosophists*, XII, 510, trans. C. B. Gulick, V, 295.

Officiis, one of the most popular manuals of conduct and morality to come down from antiquity, contains a reference to the legend in the first book.[14] Cicero's reference is particularly interesting to the student of Elizabethan heroic poetry because it emphasizes the idea that the clarity of the choice before Hercules was an especial mark of his heroic nature: "For we cannot all have the experience of Hercules, as we find it in the words of Prodicus in Xenophon . . . [Cicero then summarizes the story.] This might, perhaps, happen to a Hercules, 'scion of the seed of Jove'; but it cannot well happen to us; for we copy, each the model he fancies, and we are constrained to adopt their pursuits and vocations." [15] There was another account by which Hercules was less divine and subject to the same education by imitation as any modern young nobleman. It is well represented in Heywood's *Apologie for Actors.*[16]

Even the twelve labors of Hercules, as interpreted by medieval mythographers, illustrate the hero as a moral figure. Fulgentius discusses three of Hercules' feats immediately after his moralization of the Judgment of Paris; a typical example of his interpretation is that of Hercules' victory over Antaeus as the conquest of fleshly lust. According to Natalis Comes, the stories about Hercules serve to encourage the strenuous life, and Hercules himself represents nothing other than that virtue and strength of mind which casts out all vices and conquers all voluptuous desires.

For the purpose of moral instruction, of course, it made no difference whether there were several heroes of the name of Hercules or only one; the traditions of the Libyan Hercules, the Cretan Hercules, and the Theban Hercules were merged into one. Lilio Gregorio Giraldi, the Italian humanist, published a *Vita Herculis* composed of the various legends of the hero collected from classical and later sources, with the different symbolic and moral interpretations which had been given

[14] *De Officiis* was studied in Latin at school, and the popular translation by Nicholas Grimald was printed nine times between 1553 and 1600.
[15] I, xxxii, 118, trans. Walter Miller, Loeb Classical Library (1913) , p. 121.
[16] Sig. B3r.

to them; he also summarized the story of Hercules' Choice.[17]

To the Elizabethans, Hercules was a figure in early history who was particularly interesting because he was supposed to have liberated England from a tyrant, the Albion from which the country took one of its early names. This notion is given prestige by appearing in William Harrison's *Description of England* which was the introduction to Holinshed's *Chronicle*.[18]

The knowledge of the Choice was continuous throughout the period. It appears in Lawrence Humphrey's *The Nobles or of Nobilitye* in 1563, in a comment on the pronouncement, "To me the good is Noble, poore or riche." Some receive nobility from their ancestors, whom they should imitate, says Humphrey, while others acquire it by following the path chosen by Hercules.[19] Anthony Munday padded the dedication of his little volume of crime stories, *A View of Sundry Examples*, in 1580, with what he called "a proper discourse of the choyse of Hercules," taken from Cicero, and went on, preposterously enough, to identify "the simplenesse of my capacitie, the meanesse of my learning . . . the lack of eloquence" with the plain appearance of the Lady Virtue.

Hercules making his decision was quite naturally a popular subject in the emblem books. He appears in Geoffrey Whitney's *Choice of Emblemes* (1586), standing not in the desert but on a Palladian stage, with houses on either side of the street and a temple in the distance.[20] So firmly fixed was the idea that Hercules was a representative of virtue that Thomas

[17] See Isabel E. Rathborne, *The Meaning of Spenser's Fairyland* (New York, 1937), chap. 2, "Gods and Heroes"; for the influence of material of this sort on Elizabethan writers, see the review of C. F. Wheeler's *Classical Mythology in . . . Ben Jonson* (Princeton, 1938) by A. H. Gilbert, *PQ*, XIX (1940), 92–96.

[18] Ed. of 1596, fol. 4a.

[19] Sig. K4ʳ.

[20] Page 40. The source is emblem 44 in Hadrian the Younger, *Les Emblesmes* (Antwerp, 1567), "La fourchée de Vertu & de Vice"; this volume was sometimes issued with Plantin's French edition of Sambucus' emblems. Henry Green, in his edition of *A Choice of Emblemes* (London, 1866), does not identify the source, but he finds parallel Hercules emblems in Gilles Corrozet's *Hecatomgraphie* (Paris, 1543) and the French translation of Peter Costau's *Pegma* (Lyons, 1560).

Fenne characterized him with a hyperbole like the one Jonson charged to Shakespeare: "Hercules was alwayes a freer of Countreyes from tyrannie, a reformer of wrongs, a helper of the afflicted, and neuer in his life did iniure or hurt anie prince, people or Commonwealth, without iust cause of shamefull villanie." [21] The plainness of Lady Virtue and the gaudiness of Lady Vice led to allegorical interpretations of the two figures beyond their obvious significances. In Thomas Bradshaw's *The Shepherds Starre* (1591), for example, Hercules is the Protestant champion, and his two paths are the old and the reformed religion. When Corydon quotes a wise senator in his land who maintains that of the two religions there is only one end, "and that the one is but a little the farther way about, both may come to one home," [22] he is answered by Amaryllis with the fable of two ladies at the fork in the path. The idea that the path of pleasure was an easy one was so standard that when he encountered a contradiction of it while translating Ariosto, John Harington immediately thought of the Choice of Hercules story: "Whereas in the eight staffe the way was said to be vnpleasant, (though that seeme contrarie to the saying of Hercules two wayes of vice and vertue) yet no doubt but euen in this way of pleasure, there be many ill fauoured and daungerous passages." [23] Milton, in *The Reason of Church Government*, thinks of the function of poetry as something connected with this traditional picture: "Teaching over the whole book of sanctity and vertu through all the instances of example with such delight to those especially of soft and delicious temper who will not so much as look upon Truth herselfe, unlesse they see her elegantly drest, that whereas the paths of honesty and good life appear now rugged and difficult, though they be indeed easy and pleasant, they would then appeare to all men both easy and pleasant though they were rugged and difficult indeed." [24]

[21] *Fennes Frutes* (1590), sig. Aa3ʳ.
[22] Sig. C3ᵛ.
[23] *Orlando Furioso* (1591), p. 54.
[24] *Works,* Columbia ed., vol. III, pt. i, p. 239.

The picture of Hercules at the fork was closely associated in the sixteenth-century mind with the basic idea of the pictorial representation of abstractions. For example, in Vincenzo Cartari's treatise on classical iconography, translated into English by Richard Lynche in 1599 as *The Fountaine of Ancient Fiction. Wherein is liuely depictured the Images and Statues of the gods of the Ancients, with their proper and perticular expositions,* the discussion of the ways in which the ancients represented such qualities as Truth and Virtue in statuary is followed immediately by an elaborately descriptive version of the Choice of Hercules story,[25] with references to Xenophon and Cicero.

There is something quite Spenserian in Cartari's luscious landscape painting, and it is no surprise to the reader accustomed to *The Faerie Queene* to follow on to the conclusion that Hercules, having made the choice of the stony path of Virtue, "& so attained to that delicious & beautifull medow, which his choice so elected, afterwards purchased vnto him euer-liuing fame and glory, registered by time in the brasse-leaued booke of endlesse perpetuitie."

When Edmund Spenser came to progress from his apprenticeship as a pastoral poet to his maturity as the writer of *The Faerie Queene,* he was of course well aware of the moral concerns proper to the writer of epic. More specifically, he knew the tradition of Hercules as the type of moral hero conquering the temptations of the flesh by probity and uprightness of mind. However much the machinery of his narrative may owe to Arthurian romance, the basic conception of the meaning and value of a knight's achievements came from the implications of such stories as that of the Choice of Hercules. In the third canto of Book II, Bragadocchio, the type of the false knight who pretends to honor and fame but lacks the understanding of the fundamental moral basis of chivalry, is given a little lecture by Belphoebe which consists of the first lesson in heroic living. It is, quite naturally, a version of the lines from Hesiod which were the source of the Prodican story of Hercules:

[25] Sigs. T2r-v.

Who so in pompe of proud estate (quoth she)
  Does swim, and bathes himselfe in courtly blis,
  Does waste his dayes in darke obscuritee,
  And in obliuion euer buried is:
  Where ease abounds, yt's eath to doe amis;
  But who his limbs with labours, and his mind
  Behaues with cares, cannot so easie mis.
  Abroad in armes, at home in studious kind
Who seekes with painfull toile, shall honor soonest find.

In woods, in waues, in warres she wonts to dwell,
  And will be found with perill and with paine;
  Ne can the man, that moulds in idle cell,
  Vnto her happie mansion attaine:
  Before her gate high God did Sweat ordaine,
  And wakefull watches euer to abide:
  But easie is the way, and passage plaine
  To pleasures pallace; it may soone be spide,
And day and night her dores to all stand open wide.[26]

Spenser certainly found a similar treatment in Tasso, whose account of the palace and garden of Armida in the sixteenth book of *Jerusalem Delivered* furnished him with so much for the description of the Bower of Bliss; Tasso's version of the Choice of Hercules is part of the speech by the sage to Rinaldo after his return from Armida.[27]

Hercules was not only a moral but also a political hero. He freed the western kingdoms of tyrants, and he was able to do this because of the choice he had made at the fork in the road. Spenser, bearing Hercules in mind, begins his legend of Justice with an introduction of his hero Artegall in the great tradition: even in ancient times when virtue was held in the

[26] *Faerie Queene*, II, III, xl–xli. Chapman, in his translation of Hesiod, calls attention to the relationship between this passage and the pseudo-Virgilian epigram on the Pythagorean letter Y, a piece which he also translates. The letter Y is, of course, a representation of the fork in the road. See Edwin Greenlaw, "Two Notes on Spenser's Classical Sources," *MLN*, XLI (1926), 323–326.

[27] Book XVII, st. 61, trans. Edward Fairfax (1600). The adaptation of this classical statement of Simonides to Christian purposes by Tasso is discussed by C. M. Bowra, *From Virgil to Milton* (London, 1948), pp. 153–154.

highest esteem, he says, the seeds of vice began to spring up and flourish at the expense of the good,

> But euermore some of the vertuous race
> Rose vp, inspired with heroicke heat,
> That cropt the branches of the sient base,
> And with strong hand their fruitfull rancknes did deface.

> Such first was Bacchus, that with furious might
> All th' East before vntam'd did ouerronne,
> And wrong repressed, and establisht right,
> Which lawlesse men had formerly fordonne.
> There Iustice first her princely rule begonne.
> Next Hercules his like ensample shewed,
> Who all the West with equall conquest wonne,
> And monstrous tyrants with his club subdewed;
> The club of Iustice dread, with kingly powre endewed.

> And such was he, of whom I haue to tell,
> The Champion of true Iustice Artegall.[28]

Moreover, in Spenser's myth Hercules had a positive connection with Britain in that he was the slayer of Albion, who appears, because of his relationship to Neptune, as a guest at the wedding of the Thames and the Medway.[29] The significance of these reminiscences of the Hercules legend in *The Faerie Queene* is that they help to show how the heroic ideal projected in Spenser's poem was formed. The Renaissance was forced to find some justification for a life of achievement which would not do too much violence to the traditional values associated with the life of contemplation. The contemplative ideal needed redefinition, or at least description which would dissociate it from the idle life of monks. The worry in a passage of Fulbecke's, in which the author tries to show what the contemplative life is not, illustrates how readily he seized upon the image of a man at the fork

---

[28] *Faerie Queene*, V, i, i–iii. Bacchus and Hercules are also celebrated as liberators in Petrarch, *Trionfo della Fama*, I, 93.

[29] *Faerie Queene*, IV, xi, xv–xvi. There is also a reference to the quelling of Albion by Hercules in *Faerie Queene*, II, x, xi.

in the road. You cannot, he insists, be Hercules by standing still.[30] And Grimaldus Goslicius, as he cites the Hercules story,[31] explicitly rejects the idea that the quiet and retired life can be virtuous.

But if the life of virtue is the life of action, this fact must somehow be shown. The actions themselves may not make the meaning explicit. In pastoral, where the freedom from ambition, the ideal of self-sufficiency, and *otium* are celebrated, virtue is demonstrated negatively, by showing how many of the evils of active life are avoided in the retired, obscure life of shepherds. But the representation of action may lead the reader to think that action is of value for its own sake; he may be more interested in the events than in the virtue they are supposed to represent.

To show the meaning clearly and explicitly, the heroic poet used allegory. According to Tasso, heroic poetry consisted of two elements, the Imitation and the Allegory. Imitation is nothing but the pattern and image of human action; allegory is a glass and figure of "human life"; that is to say, the passions, feelings and motives not as they reveal themselves in action but as they are "hidden and inward" in the mind.[32] Dante's *Divine Comedy* and Homer's *Odyssey* are throughout, Tasso says, figures of the contemplative life. The *Iliad* and the *Aeneid* are rather more patterns of action, of civil life, but even here there is a mixture of civil life and contemplation. "But since the Contemplatiue Man is solitarie; and the Man of Action liueth in ciuill companie, thence it commeth that Dantes and Ulysses in their departure from Calipso are fained not to be accompanied of the armie, or a multitude of soldiers, but to depart alone . . . And Aeneas is seene to be accompanied when he fighteth, or doth other ciuill actes; but when he goeth to hell and the Elisian fields, he leaues his followers, accompanied onely with his most faithfull friend Achates, who neuer departed from his

---

[30] *A Booke of Christian Ethics* (1587), sigs. D8ᵛ–Eʳ.
[31] *The Counsellor* (1598), sig. Mʳ.
[32] See the discourse on Allegory prefixed to *Jerusalem Delivered*, trans. Fairfax (1600), sig. A2ᵛ.

side." The modern allegorical epic, then, was one which showed through the plot the active life and through the allegorical meaning the contemplative life. Since they combined in the poem, the Renaissance heroic poem ideally presented a solution to the problem of the relative claims of contemplation and action.

The connection between Spenser and Milton, one which is more likely to be understated than overstated, is partly dependent upon this view of the function of the epic. Milton shows the same concern as that of Spenser, and it will not be very surprising if we find him using the same symbol. "From the time when he wrote *Church Government* until he completed *Paradise Regained*," says Professor Hughes, "Milton must have been concerned over the conflict of the contemplative with the active ideal and its possible solution by some 'heroic' spirit, in art, if not in life." [33] In his juvenile poem on the Passion, Milton described Christ in terms which clearly belong to a picture of Hercules:

> Most perfect Hero, tried in heaviest plight
> Of labours huge and hard, too hard for human wight.[34]

And at the very climax of *Paradise Regained* (Book V, lines 562–568), the overthrow of Satan is compared to the conquering of Antaeus by Hercules. As Mr. Hughes remarks, "Throughout his life Milton instinctively thought of Hercules as symbolically related to Christ." [35]

In such a fashion did the Elizabethan imagination seize upon the concept of the heroic. The Prodican Hercules is only an example, of course, but the figure, with its significance, is central in an understanding of Elizabethan heroic poetry. There is no hero in Spenser's *Faerie Queene* who is not conditioned by this picture of the dilemma of the heroic choice.

More fundamental still, the presence of this commonplace

---

[33] Merritt Y. Hughes, "The Christ of *Paradise Regained* and the Renaissance Heroic Tradition," *SP*, XXV (1938), 265.

[34] Lines 13–14 (*Minor Poems*, ed. Hughes, p. 174).

[35] *Minor Poems*, p. 408.

in Spenser's mind, its powerful effect upon his conception of the hero and the heroic, actually molded his style and accounted for the finest achievements of his poetry as poetry. Professor Bush remarks, in what appears to be a tone of surprise, "It is, by the way, worth noting that Spenser's most uniformly beautiful lines, apart from pageantry, are those which either summon to high endeavor or invite to sensuous ease!" [36] Of course. These beautiful lines are, in effect, the two voices of Virtue and Pleasure exhorting Hercules at the fork in the road. When Spenser's imagination was deep in the heroic, he expressed himself most effectively and most completely in the presentation of these two appeals to the hero, and through him to the reader.

Before we proceed to examine *The Faerie Queene* from this point of view as the chief Elizabethan masterpiece of heroic poetry, it will be well to look at some other examples, at the Elizabethan conception of the ancient epic, as exemplified in Chapman's Homer, and at the English reaction to a modern romantic epic, as indicated by Sir John Harington's translation of Ariosto's *Orlando Furioso*. In this way we will approach *The Faerie Queene* from the right direction, the direction of the tradition of heroic poetry as it appeared to the people for whom Spenser's poem was written.

The modern reader approaches Chapman's Homer with the rapture of Keats's sonnet in his mind, and he is disappointed. Or, he remembers Matthew Arnold on the qualities of Homer and the various ways in which his translators have failed to give the impression which the Greek gives. But the proper way to approach Chapman is rather through a remark of Coleridge's: "It [the *Odyssey*] is as truly an original poem as the *Faery Queene*." [37] Coleridge goes on to say that Chapman feels and writes not as a translator but as a poet, "as Homer might have written had he lived in England in the reign of Queen Elizabeth . . . In the main it is an English

---

[36] *Mythology and the Renaissance Tradition*, pp. 97–98; the exclamation point is his.

[37] *Coleridge's Miscellaneous Criticism*, ed. T. M. Raysor (Cambridge: Harvard University Press, 1936), p. 231.

heroic poem, the tale of which is borrowed from the Greek."

In what sense is it an English heroic poem? First of all, it conforms to the idea of the epic which the English had picked up from the Italian critics of the Renaissance. For Chapman, the works of Homer are educational and moral documents, teaching truth, manners, justice, and piety; they are the highest type of fiction: "Nor is this all-comprising *Poesie,* phantastique, or meere fictiue; but the most material, and doctrinall illations of *Truth;* both for all manly information of Manners in the yong; all prescription of Iustice, and euen Christian pietie, in the most graue and high-gouernd." [38]

There is nothing fundamental to prevent the Elizabethan reader from visualizing Achilles and Ulysses as contemporary Englishmen if he wished to, for the essentials of these heroes were not, in Chapman's opinion, Greek qualities or characteristics peculiar to a more primitive heroic age but the traits which it was desirable to inculcate in young English aristocrats, traits which could even be seen represented in them occasionally by such heroes as Sir Philip Sidney, the Earl of Essex, and Prince Henry. When he is drawing a distinction between the *Iliads* and the *Odysseys,* Chapman shows how he considers the moral qualities to be timeless.[39] Chapman took from Angelus Politianus the doctrine that Homer was a complete cabinet of *exempla,* offering samples of all the types of men with the appropriate moral lesson to be learned from their behavior and what happens to them.[40]

These virtues and vices are of course represented primarily in the characters themselves. Homer is not allegorical in the sense that the events or plot of the poem can convey a moral lesson; the educational and doctrinal benefits of the epic come from a close examination of the characters of the respective heroes. Achilles, for example, is the exemplification of wrath, and Chapman increases the description of his passion at what the hero considers injustice from Agamemnon. The English poet makes him rationalize his anger in the light

[38] Dedication to *Odysseys* (*Poems,* ed. Bartlett, p. 407).
[39] Bartlett ed., p. 406.
[40] *Opera* (Aldine edition, 1498), sig. &ii^r.

of a theory of the proper behavior of a king.[41] And lest he
be a model of the wrong sort, Chapman makes it explicit that
the venting of his wrath is done self-consciously and with an
end in view:

> not for my private bane,
> But since wrackt vertue's generall laws he shameless did infringe;
> For whose sake I will loose the reins, and give mine anger swinge,
> Without my wisdom's least impeach.[42]

But Achilles is not the hero in the *Iliads* who most interests
and attracts the sympathy of Chapman; this place is occupied
by Hector. As Professor Bartlett points out, the reason is that
Chapman is able to see in Hector a man who is eminently
civilized, in comparison to the relatively barbarous Achilles,
and he is a man who, albeit imperfectly, exemplifies the Stoic
ideal.[43] Chapman's additions to his original take the form
of explanation of and emphasis on this aspect of Hector, as
in the lines, when Sarpedon has reproached Hector and the
behavior of the Trojan hero is described,

> This stung great Hector's heart; and yet, as every generous mind
> Should silent bear a just reproof, and show what good they find
> In worthy counsels, by their ends put into present deeds,
> Not stomach nor be vainly sham'd; so Hector's spirit proceeds.[44]

Chapman also interprets the motive of Hector in abandoning
Sarpedon later and pursuing the Greeks instead of rescuing
him: it is an instance of the imperfection of the Trojan hero.
  The most elaborate explanation and unfolding of a character in Chapman's *Iliads* is that of Menelaus. Here Chapman
was no doubt influenced by the common Elizabethan tendency to see in a cuckold something very ridiculous; but he
regards his understanding of Menelaus as a new discovery,

---

[41] See Phyllis B. Bartlett, "The Heroes of Chapman's Homer," *RES*, XVII
(1941), 257–280, where the amplifications made by Chapman are pointed out
and their implications skillfully discussed.

[42] *Iliads* (n.d.), sig. M5^r.

[43] "The Heroes of Chapman's Homer," p. 261.

[44] *Iliads*, V, 487–491, as cited by Bartlett; only the first five words come
from Homer.

not apparent to any earlier critic, and accordingly he lavishes much commentary and explanation upon it. Menelaus is, he feels, an absurd kind of braggart, stupid, humorless, vain, preposterous; yet by the great skill of Homer this is revealed not in any broad satirical way, nor consistently, as in allegory, but naturally, "vsing the hoofe of Pegasus, onely with a touch." [45] This is why the critics have been misled; they see that Homer furnishes Menelaus with some admirable traits, so they are unaware of the absurdities in his character. To Chapman this is all the greater evidence of Homer's skill: "See . . . how ingeniously Homer giueth him still some colour of reason for his senslesnesse, which colour yet, is enough to deceiue our Commentators: they finde not yet the tame figure of our horned." [46] Chapman, like many a later critic of poetry, is overcome with delight at an ingenuity in his author which is in reality only an ingenuity in the critic himself.

In the matter of character consistency Homer was traditionally cited as a corrective to the Stoic position; as Plutarch put it, "The imitation that does not show an utter disregard of truth brings out, along with the actions, indications of both vice and virtue commingled; as is the case with that of Homer, which emphatically says goodbye to that of the Stoics, who will have it that nothing base can attach to virtue, and nothing good to vice, but that the ignorant man is quite wrong in all things, while, on the other hand, the man of culture is right in everything. These are the doctrines that we hear in the schools; but in the actions and in the life of most men, according to Euripides, 'The good and bad cannot be kept apart But there is some commingling.' " [47]

The great value of the *Iliads,* Chapman emphasizes, is moral. Chapman was not much interested in allegory, although he was willing enough to believe, in the traditional way, that the supernatural events in the *Iliads* had probably some allegorical significance. For example, when Sarpedon

45 Commentary on Book II, *Iliads* (n.d.) , sig. D6ᵛ.
46 *Iliads* (n.d.) , sig. R4ʳ; Annotations to Book XIII.
47 *Moralia,* 25 C, trans. Babbitt, I, 133.

is conveyed away in Book XVI by Sleep and Death, Chapman says that poets do not affirm such things personally done, "but to please with the truth of their matchlesse wits, and some worthy doctrine conueyed in it." [48] In the preface to his *Iliads* Chapman promised to write a poem about the "mysteries" to be found in Homer, but apparently he never fulfilled his intention. "Fundamentally," says Miss Bartlett, "he was not interested in the analysis of 'mysteries,' but in the interpretation of Homer's poems as moral documents." [49] By "mysteries" Chapman apparently meant scientific truths, principles of government, and other practical knowledge. In his dedicatory sonnet to the Lord Chancellor, Ellesmere, Chapman urges him to

> heare this Poet sing,
> Most iudging Lord: and see how he reueales
> The mysteries of Rule, and rules to guide
> The life of Man, through all his choicest waies.[50]

Occasionally Chapman will do what we may see other Renaissance critics doing: justify a supernatural occurrence in his original by citing an analogue from sacred scripture. He refutes Scaliger's condemnation of the episode of Achilles' horse uttering words by pointing to Balaam's ass in the Bible,[51] an allusion which Ben Jonson sourly annotated in his own copy of Chapman with the words *profanè, et putidè.*[52]

Homer's chief glory, in Elizabethan eyes, was his "matter and instruction." [53] His lines serve as oracles and mirrors for soldiers, counselors, fathers and children, husbands, wives, lovers, friends, and allies, "all sortes of which concourse and societie in other more happy ages, haue in steed of sonnets & lasciuious ballades, sung his Iliades." [54] Yet, for all this

---

[48] *Iliads* (n.d.), sig. X4ᵛ.
[49] *Poems,* ed. Bartlett, p. 486.
[50] *Ibid.,* p. 396.
[51] *Iliads* (n.d.), sig. E6ᵛ.
[52] See *TLS,* March 3, 1932, p. 155.
[53] "Epistle Dedicatorie" to *Achilles Shield* (1598), sig. A3ʳ.
[54] "To the Reader," *Achilles Shield,* sigs. B2ᵛ–B3ʳ.

didactic value, the artistic eminence of Homer is sufficiently appreciated by the translator.[55]

In spite of the marvelous mirror for all sorts of people contained in the *Iliads,* and despite its dramatic opportunities for opening and exhibiting the characteristics of wrath and of the various other tempers to be observed in rulers, Chapman was really more devoted to the *Odysseys.* This is because, in its hero, the translator was able to see an example of the Stoic virtues, "the Minds inward, constant and vnconquered Empire; vnbroken, vnaltered with any most insolent and tyrannous affliction." Ulysses demonstrated his heroism principally in his capacity to endure, patiently, all that the gods had in store for him. But as Miss Bartlett points out, Chapman added to the Homeric source a Stoic quality: where the Greek original merely records simple fatalism, Chapman embellishes the passage to give Ulysses a chance to preach on the virtue of self-knowledge.[56] Moreover, the habit of classical heroes of breaking into tears at significant moments had been traditionally subject to Stoic objection. Chapman even took steps to reinstate his hero as a good Stoic by giving a rationale for tears as the expression of a sensitive and compassionate awareness of life. Though Homer's hero suffers more than is his just due and complains at the gods for this injustice—a practice very wrong for a Stoic—and though Chapman cannot suppress these complaints, he tries to mitigate them by emphasizing elsewhere the hero's piety and submission to the gods. Ulysses on the whole represents the Stoic hero in action and in precept. He even summarizes the Stoic doctrine:

> But he that fights with heauen, or with the sea,
> To Indiscretion, addes Impietie.[57]

And when he is forced to act himself, after the loss of all his men but one to the enchantments of Circe, he says resolutely,

---

55 "To Prince Henry," dedication to *Iliads,* lines 47–69 (*Poems,* ed. Bartlett, p. 386).

56 "The Heroes of Chapman's Homer," p. 272.

57 *Odysseys,* Book V, *Whole Works* (1614), sig. I.ʳ

I now
Will vndertake th'aduenture; there is cause
In great Necessities vnalterd lawes.[58]

It has often been pointed out that Chapman's Ulysses is a character very much like his Clermont in *The Revenge of Bussy D'Ambois*, as Achilles is like his Byron. Clearly, therefore, the heroes of Homer's epics were to him as understandable and useful educationally as if they had been contemporaries. More so, in fact, because of the *energeia* or clarity of representation which Homer, with Chapman's help, had bestowed upon them.

Poetry and truth are companion qualities, to Chapman. He expresses his conception of their relationship best in a simile:

And, as in a spring,
The plyant water, mou'd with any thing
Let fall into it, puts her motion out
In perfect circles, that moue round about
The gentle fountaine, one another, raising;
So Truth, and Poesie worke.[59]

Homer, as the purveyor of this truth, appeared to Chapman twice, we are told, first to instigate him to translate his works into English and then to teach him the lessons of Peace and the shortcomings of the three types of men, active, contemplative, and intellective, in the world today.[60] But whatever Homer's function personally for Chapman, the Elizabethan felt that his use for the world was still greater:

With eys turnd vpwards, & was outward, blind;
But, inward; past, and future things he sawe;
And was to both, and present times, their lawe.[61]

The way in which the Elizabethan imagination and the prevailing habits of style absorbed all this useful matter and

---

[58] *Odysseys*, Book X, *Whole Works*, sig. O4ᵛ. These two passages, and others, are emphasized by Donald Smalley in "The Ethical Bias of Chapman's 'Homer,'" *SP*, XXXVI (1939), 169–191.

[59] "To Prince Henry," lines 114–123 (*Poems*, ed. Bartlett, p. 387).

[60] *Euthymiae Raptus, or The Teares of Peace*, lines 84–85 (*Poems*, p. 175).

[61] *Euthymiae Raptus*, lines 36–38 (*Poems*, p. 174).

doctrine into themselves illustrates again the acquisitiveness
and positiveness of the Elizabethan mind. Chapman's style
and technique have too often been examined from the point
of view of what would be the ideal translation of Homer
rather than from the point of view of what Homer meant to
the Renaissance. The governing principle for Chapman was
not philological learning, or grammar, or the pedantry of
such scholars as Scaliger. First of all, one must understand
the content. He has no patience with the commentators who
do not see clearly and *a priori* what Homer meant: "But our
divine masters most ingenious imitating the life of things,
(which is the soule of a Poeme) is never respected nor per-
ceived by his Interpreters onely standing pedantically on the
Grammer and words, utterly ignorant of the sence and grace
of him." [62]

That is not to say that Homer was an easy writer; in fact,
according to Chapman, he was quite obscure, at least to previous commentators. This was only natural, for a great writer
was not supposed to be simple: "But that Poesie should be as
peruiall as Oratorie; and plainnes her speciall ornament,
were the plaine way to barbarisme: and to make the Asse
runne proude of his eares; to take away strength from Lyons,
and giue Cammels hornes." [63] Nevertheless, Chapman felt
that much of Homer could be made "pervial" if the translator
knew his business; and he was lacking in neither a sense of
confidence in himself nor a sense of obligation to enlighten
the reader.

His methods have been amply discussed and illustrated by
Miss Bartlett. [64] They include padding of the original, not
only to fill out the verse line of the fourteener which he used
in the *Iliads,* but also for explanation and clarification. Some-

---

[62] Commentary on *Iliads* XVII, *Whole Works,* sig. X4ʳ.

[63] Dedication to *Ovid's Banquet of Sence* (*Poems,* ed. Bartlett, p. 49). Chapman's word "pervial" is one of his favorites; the only quotations of its use
in the *OED* come from him. It is explained in his commentary on Book II
of the *Iliads* when he says, "since a man may peruially (or as he passeth)
discerne all that is to be vnderstood" (*Whole Works,* sig. D5ᵛ).

[64] "Chapman's Revisions in His *Iliads,*" *ELH,* II (1935), 92–119, and
"Stylistic Devices in Chapman's *Iliads,*" *PMLA,* LVII (1942), 661–675.

times this extends so far as to add shades to characterizations, as when, in Miss Bartlett's words, he makes "a knight of Spenserian romance" of Achilles in the scene of his parting from Briseis. These transformations arise often from the problem of dealing with poetical figures. According to Chapman, the translator should not only be observant of the sentences, figures, and forms of speech in his original, but he should also adorn the "true sence and height" of his author with "figures and formes of oration fitted to the originall, in the same tongue to which they are translated." [65]

This decorating the English poet does. He adorns Homer with English colloquialisms, with figures based on physiology and anatomy, with personifications where Homer uses only abstractions, and with epithets varied fancifully and ingeniously rather than repeated traditionally as in Greek.[66] Most important of all, Chapman makes his figures more explicit than those of Homer; he has a tendency to turn his author into a "metaphysical" poet.

In style, therefore, as well as in conception, Chapman's Homer is an English heroic poem. To be sure, Chapman imported some devices from his original, notably the compound epithets, like "great-high-deed-daring men." But on the whole his English is not "translator's English"; it is vigorous, colloquial, sometimes crabbed and harsh, often fanciful and ingenious, a language suited to the poet's conception and purpose.

By his translation of Homer Chapman had offered to the English reader a series of examples of heroic virtue, with indications of their opposites, of their limits, and of their distortions. His Ulysses is a Stoic hero who foreshadows, among others, the Christ of Milton's *Paradise Regained*. His *Iliads* was a mirror of knightly discipline and political and moral regeneration. The *Whole Works* constituted a Bible of that "true learning," that is, moral wisdom and piety, which Chapman felt should guide the revival of the aristo-

---

[65] "To the Reader," *Seaven Bookes of the Iliads* (1598), sig. A6ʳ; discussed by Bartlett in "Chapman's Revisions in His *Iliads*," pp. 110–111.

[66] Bartlett, "Stylistic Devices in Chapman's *Iliads*," pp. 668–671.

cratic class, elevate it above the crass standards of the vulgar
herd, against which he never tired of fulminating, and inaugurate a new era, under Prince Henry perhaps, of nobility
and virtue.

The verse translation of Ariosto's *Orlando Furioso* (1591)
by John Harington is a fair example of what the Elizabethans
considered a modern heroic poem. Legend has it that Harington, the witty godson of Queen Elizabeth, began his project
by translating an indecent and misogynistic selection from
the poem, the tale told by the host to Rodomont at the beginning of Canto XXVIII; Harington is supposed to have circulated this in manuscript about the court, and when it came
to the Queen's hands she imposed upon him the task of translating the whole long poem.[67]

But it is clear that for Harington, as for Spenser and other
Elizabethans, Ariosto's poem was chiefly significant as an
example of heroic poetry, which, as Harington said in his
"Apologie" prefixed to the translation, "with her sweet
statelinesse doth erect the mind & lift it up to the consideration of the highest matters." [68] The translator admits that
lightness and wantonness have crept into poetry in general,
"yet this I will say, that of all kinde of Poesie, the Heroicall
is least infected therewith." [69] When he is forced to confess the
presence of wanton passages, Harington coolly justifies himself, or rather his author: "This lasciuious description of
carnall pleasure needs not offend the chast eares, or thoughts
of any, but rather shame the vnchast that haue themselues
bene at such kinde of bankets." [70] But some lines soon after
are sufficiently monitory to satisfy the sternest moralist:

O poysond hooke, that lurks in sugred bait,
O pleasures vaine that in this world are found,
Which like a subtile theefe do lye in waite,
To swallow man in sinke of sinne profound:

[67] The legend receives support from a modern study of the translation,
Townsend Rich's *Harington and Ariosto* (New Haven, 1940).
[68] Sig. ¶iij^v, ed. 1591.
[69] Sig. ¶v^v.
[70] Note to Canto VII, st. 27, ed. 1591, p. 51.

Princes and peeres, beware of this deceit,
Be not in this sweete gulfe of pleasure dround:
The time will come, and must I tell you all,
When these ioyes shall bitter seeme as gall.[71]

Sometimes his grave justifications have a tone of ironic humor, as when he comments on a *carpe diem* passage: "Namely, I would not haue that xxv. staffe by misapplying it, made worse: being perhaps bad enough at the best." [72]

Harington's chief joke, especially if the legend about the origin of his translation is true, is that he had his engraver alter the illustrative plate for Canto XXVIII, eliminating an architectural framework in the Italian plate of his source in order to make room for pictorial representation of three instances of infidelity narrated in the host's scurrilous story.[73] However, aside from these demonstrations of his wit, Harington's general position is that of the humanistic defenders of the classics. "I must confesse," he says in the notes to Canto XLIII, "these be two knauish tales that be here in this booke, and yet the Bee will pyke out honny out of the worst of them." [74] He is not quite so sanguine about the bee's harvest in the notorious Canto XXVIII, for he says, "Historie nor Allegorie, nor scant anything that is good, can be picked out of this bad booke." [75]

The reason why it is a fruitful heroic poem is that it is grounded upon the two great themes of love and arms, and it brings to bear the greatest variety of applications to these two master subjects. The structure of the poem is determined by the central event of the losing of Orlando's wits through love for Angelica; once his wits are recovered, the successful issue of the war between Charlemagne and the Saracens follows in due course. The meaning of it is given explicitly by Harington:

Of Orlando's restoring to his wit, which is indeed the chiefe Allegorie of all the booke, and where-vpon the booke taketh his name Orlando Furioso. This in briefe is the meaning thereof. Orlando a man of

[71] Canto VII, st. 35, p. 51.　　[72] Notes to Canto XXV, p. 208.
[73] Rich, *Harington and Ariosto*, pp. 56 and 132, reproduces the two plates.
[74] *Orlando Furioso*, p. 373.　　[75] Page 232.

noble byrth, Earle of Aglant, nephew to Charles the great, falls so farre in loue with Angelica, by which (as I haue often noted) is ment pleasure, or honor; that he leeseth his witts and becomes mad: by which may be ment any follie that young men fall into with loue, with prodigallitie, with ambition or vayne studies; (which are at large recited in the 34. booke.) Astolfo with the receit he had of S. Iohn, makes him wise again, that is, by the grace of God & by the Gospell, which teacheth vs how to despise all these worldly things, and either quite leaue them, or turne them to our good and benefite.[76]

The final event of the poem, the defeat of Rodomont by Rogero after his marriage, is explained as follows:

> This is the Allegoricall sence thereof, that Rodomont, which is to be vnderstood the vnbridled heat and courage of youth (for in all Rodomont's actions you shall finde him described, euer most furious, hastie, and impacient) Rodomont I say, is killed and quite vanquished by marriage, and howsoeuer the vnrulinesse of youth is excusable in diuers kinds, yet after that holy state of matrimonie is entred into, all youthfull wildnes of all kinds, must be cast away.[77]

The evident fact that although Orlando is the titular hero of the poem, Rogero is the knight whose exploits receive more attention and whose final success and marriage is the conclusion of the poem, Harington explains by reference to the meaning of the subject: "For these two faults of wantonnesse and wilfulnes, are so coupled commonly with youth, that . . . a man might almost canonize him for a saint, that hath passed the heat of his youth, and not offended in one of these: but many doubtless offend in them both." [78] Orlando's loss of his wits and Rogero's captivity by Alcyna (pleasure) and deliverance from her are the two great examples of this commonplace.

The political wisdom of the poem is shown in the application of examples to the commonplace of arms, and here, says Harington, "mine author hath carried his inuention verie

[76] Notes to Canto xxxix, p. 332.
[77] Notes to Canto xlvi, p. 404.
[78] Page 406, "A briefe Allegorie."

dayntilie, and well worth the marking." [79] The focus is not so much on the two chieftains, Agramant and Charles, as it is upon the various counselors and courtiers who serve them. The consequences of the individual characters of the counselors are seen in the events of the plot. There are so many examples of wise and foolish counselors that the whole becomes a kind of school of politics.

In conclusion, the poem emphasizes the importance of learning, through the horn (betokening eloquence) and the book (representing wisdom) with which the English knight Astolfo accomplishes so many wonders. And this point is of course connected with political wisdom: "In the prayse of learning, and to moue Princes to fauour learning, he shewes how onely the pen of the learned is that, that preserues the good fame of Princes, as for the common foolish pamphlet-writers he condemneth them, likening them to vultures carren crowes and chattering pyes, that are not able to saue their frends names from the lake of obliuion, because their writings are not durable." [80]

All this discussion of the value of heroic poetry needs a perspective different from that to which the modern mind is accustomed. Harington does not approach Ariosto with any pretense of discovering the "intention" of the author, either by external evidence or by examination of structure and artistic methods. He assumes instead that anything profitable which can be gathered from the work is legitimate,[81] though

[79] Page 412.

[80] Page 414.

[81] Apparently the only limitation upon freedom of interpretation on the part of the Elizabethan reader arose when he was tempted to read into a work some libel on a living person. Chapman, for example, does not question the reader's right to read any interpretation he pleases into a poem, short of endangering the author. In his defense of his *Andromeda Liberata* (1614), he asks, "Or doth any rule of reason make it good, that let the writer meane what he list, his writing notwithstanding must be construed *in mentem Legentis?* to the intendment of the Reader? If then, for the mistaking of an enuious or vnskilfull Reader, who commonly bring *praeiudicia pro iudicijs,* I shal be exposed to the hate of the better sort, or taken forciblie into any powrefull displeasure, I shall esteeme it an acte as cruell and tyranous" (*Poems,* ed. Bartlett, p. 330) .

he does include a warning in the notes to Canto 1 against being "so curious to search for an allegorie where none is intended by the Author himselfe." [82] In fact, he lays considerably less stress upon what he calls allegory than upon what he calls the moral. The notes at the end of each book are divided sytematically into "The Morall," "The Storie," "Allegorie," and "Allusion." By "The Morall" Harington means any profitable reflection that may be gathered from the work without interpretation, and of course anything in the poem may be used as an *exemplum* for this purpose. Usually what Harington himself notices is some lesson of practical wisdom or illustration of moral or psychological truth. This is the category in which the reader is given the freest range. The commentator's usual phrase for introducing his discussion of the moral is "we may note" or "we may observe." It is clear that for the purpose of seeing the moral, interpretation or translation from one system to another is not necessary. All the reader need do is to carry with him to the book a normal interest in psychology and morality; if his eyes are open he will find in the plot of the epic plenty of instances or illustrations. When he recognizes them, he is seeing "The Morall."

By "The Storie" Harington means the historical reality or fact upon which the plot is grounded; he calls this alternatively "The Historie." He is glad to find as much as possible of the matter in his poem to be true, or grounded on fact. Sometimes mythological marvels can be adjusted to known historical events, and Harington would willingly accept proof that the three nights in one when Hercules was begotten by Jupiter coincided with the stopping of the sun by Joshua.[83] He is no expert in such matters and defers to "the iudgement of learned Diuines," but his disposition is to believe: "Yet me thinke it is worth the obseruation, how the verie prophane, and vaine writings of old times, do concurre with the sacred scriptures"—not of course for verifying the

[82] Page 7.
[83] Just so, in the *Iliads*, does Chapman justify, against the arguments of Scaliger, the supernatural event of Achilles' horse having the power to speak.

scriptures, which were historically true beyond cavil, but for
the purpose of validating classical mythology.[84]

The "Allegorie," Harington's third class, includes first of
all representational elements which are obvious, like the
colors worn by characters, which Harington says will be immediately recognized as symbolic by English courtiers who
follow the same practice. Allegory also accounts for supernatural elements both of plot and of character. The hippo-
griff represents unbridled desires or passions, and the ring,
as well as the horn and book already mentioned, has allegorical significance. The enchantments which occasionally add
an element of the marvelous to the story are in reality the
illusions produced by love.[85] The story of the lapse of Rogero,
his captivation by Alcyna on her isle, and his final deliverance
and journey to Logostilla, told in Cantos VI and VII, is all
allegory, as Harington says, and its meaning is most transparent: "These two bookes be in a manner a meere allegorie
from the beginning to the ending," [86] and they are "an
Allegorie, so plaine to those that will indeed looke heedfully
into it, as needs no exposition." [87] The general sense—the
seductions of sensuality—is indeed plain, since the story of
Alcyna is a version of the myth of Circe; but the specific
applications which Harington makes are sometimes such that
the only kind of attentive reader who would grasp them is one
accustomed to allegorical narratives. For example, Logestilla
represents not only Virtue but the true Christian religion.[88]

Improbabilities and wonders are justified by their allegorical significance. Thus, when Harington is translating Ariosto's
first stanza of Canto VII he adds an explanatory note in the
margin, identifying the "fond and simple sort" as "those that
cannot vnderstand the allegorie of it." Ariosto himself claims
here only that intelligence is needed:

A uoi so ben, che non parra manzogna,
Che'l lume del discorso hauete chiaro.

[84] Notes to Canto XXXII, p. 266.
[85] Canto VIII, sts. 1–2, p. 57.
[86] Page 55.
[87] Page 47.   [88] Page 47.

But Harington adds both the allegorical warning in the margin and a statement about the moral significance in the text itself:

> For some there are, may fortune in this booke,
> As in a glasse their acts and haps to looke.[89]

On the other hand, Harington is careful to exclude allegory when the story itself is credible enough without it. In the story of Genevra in Canto v, the plot which Shakespeare presumably used for the Hero-Claudio element in *Much Ado About Nothing*, Harington finds a great deal of moral having to do with the proper relationship between husbands and wives, jealousy, equality in marriage, and other matters more remote from the story. But as for allegory, "there is none," he says, "in this booke at all." [90]

By "Allusion" Harington means the use of a visible and recognizable source—another tale or motif which bears the same relation to Ariosto's narrative as the historical facts bear in the "storie" element of the poem. Thus, Alcyna and her effects on her lovers constitute an allusion to Homer's Circe, as well as the allegory already spoken of. The ring which Melissa brings to Astolfo to free him from the bondage to Alcyna, the ring which allegorically means Reason, is also an allusion: "The ring that had the vertue beside dissoluing inchauntments to make one go inuisible, alludeth to Gyges ring, of which it is sayd, that by the helpe thereof he became King of Lydia." [91]

The position of Ariosto's *Orlando Furioso* was established for the Renaissance by comparing the poem with Virgil's *Aeneid*. It was generally accepted that the *Aeneid* was a moral and noble poem, that the reading of it, as Scaliger said, might make a man honest and virtuous. According to Harington, it

---

[89] St. 2, p. 49.
[90] Page 39.
[91] Page 55. I have referred to these interpretations as Harington's for sake of brevity. They of course come in part from the explanations, allegorical and other, which Harington found in the Italian editions of the sixteenth century. For a discussion of these editions and the editorial interpretations inserted into them, see Rich, *Harington and Ariosto*, chap. IV.

is on just this ground of comparison that Ariosto can be most fully justified. "As I sayd before so I say still," he insists, "whatsoeuer is prayseworthy in Virgill is plentifully to be found in Ariosto, and some things that Virgill could not haue, for the ignoraunce of the age he liued in." [92]

The most important advantage the later poet enjoyed was of course his Christianity. Harington points out that the prayer of Charlemagne in Canto xiv and the preparation of Rogero for baptism as a Christian are far more fruitful in "exhortation, doctrine and example" than anything that could be found in the pagan poet. Moreover, Ariosto is superior to all the ancient poets because in his work there are to be found "no Gods, and of them so many fowle deeds, their contentions, their adulteries, their incest, as were both obscenous in recitall & hurtful in example." [93] When the Italian poet imitates a heroic funeral from Virgil, as he does in the forty-third canto, his version is superior because it "is set forth with deuout and Christian termes, and therefore more to be commended." [94]

The heroes of Ariosto's poem are analogous to heroes of the Bible.[95] The valiant heroine, Bradamant, who overcomes even the terrible Rodomont the Turk in battle, is an "allusion," Harington says, to Judith, who slew Holofernes. The most significant supernatural machinery in the poem is Astolfo's journey to paradise, where he sees Saint John and receives from him the knowledge and means to restore Orlando's wits.

In the plot itself Harington finds many instances of divine justice and points out the value of these to the reader: "All which examples (whether true or fained) haue this chiefe scope and end, to make men know there is a diuine power, that will iudge and punish the actions of men, be they neuer so secure or so secret." [96] These instructive events serve not only as a warning but also as a comfort: "In Zerbino's happie deliuerance, from a shamefull death, by Orlando's means, we

[92] "An Apologie of Poetrie," 1591 *Orlando,* sig. ¶6ᵛ.
[93] *Ibid.,* sig. ¶7ᵛ.
[94] Page 373.
[95] Canto xxxiv, st. 63, p. 285.
[96] Notes to Canto xxii, p. 175.

may obserue that which can neuer be too much obserued, namely how diuine prouidence, neuer failes the innocent." [97]

Closely allied to this Christian edification is the utility of Ariosto for the teaching of chivalric virtues. "Noble and princely inclination" or virtuous and gentle discipline are exemplified everywhere. The necessity of this kind of education is felt to be very great because of the decline and perversion of courtly ideals in Elizabethan times. The holding up of the picture of earlier knights (whether true or feigned) served as a criticism of the present time. For example, the point of honor used to be the main incentive of knightly actions, but the modern version of this code is nothing but a vanity.[98] There is the same difference between true honor and false as there is between true religion and heresy or superstition, Harington, goes on. The trouble is that now the social practices of chivalry have survived to our own time, but the ethical or moral content which gave those practices validity has disappeared somewhere on the way. Is it not ridiculous, he asks, to see a man who is a liar, a gourmand, a swearer and gamer, as chaste as the town bull, "and now and then (of the gentlenes of his nature) not scorning a Pandars occupation" standing somewhat nicely upon his point of honor? In the plot, the marriage of Angelica, beloved of Orlando and other champions, to the lowly Medore is to be understood as an allegory of the pursuit of honor. "Angelica is taken for honor, which braue men hunt after, by blood, and battells, and many hardie feats, and misse it: but a good seruant with faith and gratefulnesse to his Lord gets it." [99]

Achievements of valor are of course not to be disdained; they form the chief action of the poem, and they are held up to imitation to the courtiers of our own time. When he pursues pleasure, and specifically love, rather than feats of arms and true honor, Rogero becomes the type of the effeminate courtier.[100]

Equally inimical to the ancient ideals of chivary are the motives of covetousness and ambition. The forty-fourth canto

[97] Notes to Canto XXIII, p. 185.
[98] Page 324.
[99] Page 151.
[100] Canto VII, sts. 46–47.

opens with two stanzas which point out that often nowadays true faith to one's word, concord, and friendship are better kept in houses of mean estate than in prince's or emperor's court. "Ambition is as vnsatiable as anie other humour of man," [101] and Rodomont, as a descendant of Nimrod, represents the vices of the aspiring mind.[102] Covetousness is portrayed as a beast in one of the sculptures in the cave of Merlin.[103] Harington calls this description better than Dante's because it gives the animal more attributes and hence more significations.[104] The reader of Spenser notices here, as elsewhere, that Spenser's allegorical *method* is closer to Ariosto's treatment of works of art than it is to his general treatment of actions.[105]

Besides these qualities of Ariosto—his superiority to the ancients because of his Christianity, his illustration of divine justice and Fortune, and his value as a courtesy-book—his work is significantly modern in that it is not exclusively an epic of a man's world, as the ancient epics were (despite Homer's Penelope and Virgil's Dido and Ovid's Medea), but also includes women. There are several indications in the poem that women are visualized as its readers.[106] The two great heroines of the book, Bradamant and Marfisa, overthrow male knights in combat and are as often the center of action as Orlando or Rogero. Canto XXXVII is designed to vindicate the female sex, both socially and politically, and the law that Marfisa finally imposes gives women the sovereignty over men. The professed purpose of the canto is to make ladies amends for the wrong done them by anti-feminist writers in the past.

On the whole, then, the nature of English appreciation of

---

[101] Notes to Canto XIV, p. 111.

[102] Canto XIV, st. 102.

[103] Canto XXVI, st. 27.

[104] Page 213.

[105] I do not find this observed in S. J. McMurphy, *Spenser's Use of Ariosto for Allegory*, University of Washington Publications in Language and Literature, vol. II (Seattle, 1924); or in the monographs of R. E. Neil Dodge in *PMLA*, XII (1897), 151–204, A. H. Gilbert in *PMLA*, XXXIV (1919), 225–232, and Dodge in *PMLA*, XXXV (1920), 91–92.

[106] Canto XXXVIII, st. 1, and others.

the *Furioso* as heroic poetry is what we should expect from the sixteenth-century understanding of Hercules and from the Elizabethan attitude toward Homer. First and most important is the moral significance, a mirror of those qualities which the young man should aspire to imitate. Then comes the historical reality, then the allegory, and finally the "allusions." Combined, all these served to bring home to men's business and bosoms the convincing picture of heroic qualities which had to be revived if chivalry, morality, and religion were to characterize the men of the modern world. Harington's interests were hardly exceptional; it is clear from his "Apologie" that he thought Sir Philip Sidney would have regarded the poem in much the same light as he did, and Dodge answers the question "How did Spenser interpret Ariosto?" by the confident answer, "Certainly very much like Harington." [107] It is only too evident that a most striking effect in the Italian, the pervasive and marvelous irony, was lost on English readers. This irony, which is largely at the expense of the seriousness of chivalric pretensions, would have been destructive of what the English were most ardently searching for—some lively and convincing literature which would reverse the course of history and infuse the decayed chivalric social forms with a renaissance of the ethical and ideal spirit which was formerly thought to inhabit them.

As recently as a generation ago, Harington thought, the knightly virtues which he found in Ariosto might be discovered in Englishmen. He points out how his own father translated the first stanza of Canto xix and applied it to the Lord Admiral Seymour "very aptly diuerse wayes." [108] Even the combat in tournament to win a lady was not entirely the stuff of romancers in his eyes, for he records his belief (mistaken, as it happens) that Sir Charles Brandon had won Mary, Dowager of France and sister of Henry VIII, by defeating four French knights in a joust.[109]

[107] R. E. Neil Dodge, "Spenser's Imitations from Ariosto," *PMLA*, XII (1897), 168.
[108] Page 151.
[109] Notes to Canto xxxii, p. 266.

Heroic and pastoral always imply each other, for one is in a sense the obverse of the other. The great nexus in which they meet is the question of ambition. Pastoral renounces worldly aspiration because the game is not worth the candle; heroic poetry celebrates the winning of glory by action. One has the value of "content," the other of fame. In style and general strategy also, the two kinds were contrasted. Pastoral, because of its humility and simplicity, was felt to be the lowliest of respectable forms, as Sidney indicates when he supposes that the enemies of poetry might attack pastoral first, "for perchance, where the hedge is lowest they will soonest leape over." [110] Heroic, on the other hand, was the highest kind of poetry, possessing the greatest dignity and of such worth that its very name should daunt all backbiters.[111]

Following the example of Virgil, the poet might logically progress from the writing of pastoral in his youth to the composition of heroic poetry in his maturity. Spenser clearly had this pattern in mind, for in the October eclogue of *The Shepheardes Calender* he has Piers urge Cuddie to

Abondon then the base and viler clowne:
Lyft up thy selfe out of the lowly dust,
And sing of bloody Mars, of wars, of giusts;

and he introduces himself in the opening of *The Faerie Queene* with

Lo! I the man, whose Muse whylome did maske,
As time her taught, in lowly shephards weeds,
Am now enforst, a farre unfitter taske,
For trumpets sterne to chaunge mine oaten reeds,
And sing of knights and ladies gentle deeds.[112]

In fact, the seeds of heroic poetry lie in pastoral, for as Valerius remarked, "There is no life so lowly that the sweetness of glory does not appeal to it." [113]

---

[110] *An Apologie for Poetrie,* ed. Shuckburgh, pp. 28–29.
[111] *Ibid.,* p. 32.
[112] *Faerie Queene,* I, Proem, 1.
[113] Quoted by Boccaccio; see C. G. Osgood, *Boccaccio on Poetry* (Princeton, 1930), p. 121.

The desire for fame, for glory, which motivates heroic action, leads finally to something beyond action, of course—to the desire for immortality, for a heaven which is fundamentally a contemplative, not an active, state. We see it in the tenth canto of Book I of *The Faerie Queene,* when Red Cross is prepared for his final feat as a champion by the sight of the heavenly city and the promise of his own sanctification as Saint George of England. Struck with awe at the prospect of such glory, he asks the aged holy man if he must then abjure his knightly life:

> "But deeds of armes must I at last be faine
> And ladies love to leave, so dearely bought?"

And he receives the answer:

> "What need of armes, where peace doth ay remaine,"
> Said he, "and battailes none are to be fought?
> As for loose loves, they are vaine, and vanish into nought."

He is immediately persuaded:

> "O let me not," quoth he, "then turne againe
> Backe to the world, whose joyes so fruitlesse are,
> But let me heare for aie in peace remaine." [114]

Heroic poetry, then, posits an ideal comparable to that of pastoral, with the difference that the desired state must be earned, must follow the achievement of fame and glory through action. The resolution is therefore on a higher level. The guiding and predominating motive was that of Virtue, pictured symbolically as the lady whose path Hercules chose to follow, as a kind of Venus-Beatrice of a neo-Platonic scheme. Professor Hughes has pointed out how Spenser's Belphoebe represents not only Queen Elizabeth but also this Virgilian, neo-Platonic Venus, and how in the sixteenth century these related or half-identified figures "could be accepted as guides through the mazes of the active life to the perfection of the life contemplative." [115]

---

[114] *Faerie Queene,* I, x, lxii–lxiii.
[115] *Virgil and Spenser,* p. 364.

The essence of heroic poetry, according to the Elizabethan view, is that it is fundamentally moral, both in concept and intention and in its effect upon the reader. "But if any thing be already sayd in the defence of sweete Poetry, all concurreth to the maintaining the Heroicall, which is not onely a kinde, but the best and most accomplished kinde of Poetry. For as the image of each action stirreth and instructeth the mind, so the loftie image of such Worthies most imflameth the mind with desire to be worthy, and informes with counsel how to be worthy." [116] So says Sidney, expressing the common view. And he goes on to cite the example of Aeneas, whose behavior in a great variety of circumstances offers a model to those who would be worthy; and finally, says Sidney, you get not only the hero's actions but his "inward selfe" to emulate. Renaissance commentary on the *Aeneid* had stressed the point; according to Landini, Aeneas was made perfect by the love of God, and he was disciplined for his mystical experience or final contemplative state by the perturbations of the active life. [117]

It is primarily because of his moral understanding of the heroic that Spenser puts his poem in the past. For in the past, he asserts over and over, the virtues which compose and identify the true hero were common:

> Let none then blame me, if in discipline
> Of vertue and of civill uses lore,
> I doe not forme them to the common line
> Of present dayes, which are corrupted sore,
> But to the antique use which was of yore,
> When good was onely for itselfe desyred. [118]

Spenser's romanticism, his love for the past, is misunderstood without a full awareness of his moral concern. Mr. Stoll, for example, equates Spenser's romanticism with that of the nineteenth century: "Chivalry and feudalism are dead and gone, and quite properly Spenser puts a medieval flavor into

[116] Sidney, *Apologie*, ed. Shuckburgh, p. 33.
[117] Hughes, *Virgil and Spenser*, p. 405.
[118] *Faerie Queene*, V, Proem, iii; see also V, I, i, and the Proems to Books IV and VI; also IV, VIII, xxix–xxxii.

his language as he treats of them. Really, he is like Sir Walter Scott in his poems and novels, Coleridge in the *Ancient Mariner,* or the preraphaelite Morris and Rossetti, as he turns from the present to the past. He takes to the poetic beauty of a period now gone by. But though he returns to it, like them he is not of it; there's the blue haze of distance upon it, or the ivy and the mellow patina of time." [119] Surely this is wrong. For whatever picturesque elements Spenser saw in the Middle Ages, his fundamental interest in earlier times was not atmospheric but moral. For him there was no such sharp distinction between heroes of epic and heroes of romance as there is for us. They all served to illuminate the heroic spirit, one which was intent, in Hercules or Arthur, Aeneas or Saint George, to win heavenly peace by earthly struggle.

His model, Ariosto, offered him plenty of encouragement in the moral interpretation of the heroic, and the commentaries of Fornari and others had shown that Astolfo and Ruggiero were comparable with Aeneas in their moral effectiveness. [120] The element of love in the romance was simply a motive for virtue; again and again Spenser emphasizes how the pursuit of virtue and the achievement of heroic deeds are motivated by love. [121] The hero is distinguished from the sluggard partly by the way in which love operates on him:

> The baser wit, whose ydle thoughts alway
> Are wont to cleave unto the lowly clay,
> It stirreth up to sensuall desire,
> And in lewd slouth to wast his carelesse day:
> But in brave sprite it kindles goodly fire,
> That to all high desert and honour doth aspire. [122]

The one criticism of *The Faerie Queene* to which Spenser deigned to reply was that the elaborate celebration of love in his poem was not morally uplifting. It belongs prominently in a heroic poem, he says,

[119] E. E. Stoll, *Poets and Playwrights* (Minneapolis, 1930), p. 172.
[120] See McMurphy, *Spenser's Use of Ariosto for Allegory,* p. 14.
[121] *Faerie Queene,* III, III, i.
[122] III, v, i.

For it of honor and all vertue is
The roote, and brings forth glorious flowres of fame.[123]

He appeals to antiquity, to Socrates specifically, in support of the notion that all brave exploits performed by classical heroes were either ended or begun in love.[124]

From this position, which Spenser merely joined all his contemporaries in holding, that the ancient heroes of epic, romance, and legend are models of the moral virtues, it is not a very great step to the specialization which constituted a plan for Spenser's poem. Since the character of the hero is the most important thing in the poem, because its justification lies in the exhibition of qualities to emulate, and since the epic, ancient or modern, needed explanation and commentary to enforce its meaning on the reader, why not analyze the virtues and present them separately? Make one virtue the subject of each book, with a knight to exemplify it; tie the virtues together by showing these knights aiding each other and by representing one, Prince Arthur, as the exemplar of them all and of the highest virtue, Magnanimity, which is a combination of all of them. But an even more important result of the conventional approach to the ancient hero was that Spenser's imagination was forced to see moral qualities and heroic splendor as one. The most impressive thing about *The Faerie Queene* is not the word painting or the mellifluous music, however much tribute they deserve. It is what Ben Jonson saw in the poem when he said he would have Spenser read for his matter, and what Milton saw in it when he said that Spenser was a better teacher than Scotus or Aquinas. It is the unified vision of the moral virtues as heroic qualities. Illustration could be chosen from many places in the poem, but the one which shows Spenser speaking most clearly, in connection with a character who is one of his greatest successes, may perhaps be offered, even though the virtue represented is the one dearest to an Elizabethan and most unsympathetic to the twentieth century. It is his description of Belphoebe:

[123] IV, Proem, ii.
[124] *Ibid.*

In so great prayse of stedfast chastity
Nathlesse she was so courteous and kynde,
Tempred with grace and goodly modesty,
That seemed those two vertues strove to fynd
The higher place in her heroick mynd:
So striving each did other more augment,
And both encreast the prayse of woman kynde,
And both encreast her beautie excellent;
So all did make in her a perfect complement.[125]

The important thing here is to realize how seriously
Spenser means "her *heroick* mynd"; the competition of these
two qualities, chastity and courtesy, for preëminence increases the strength of each of them, and the gains in "the
prayse of woman kynde" and in her own beauty result from
this competition. This analysis, so curious in its details, so
oddly based on the apparent opposition between the unyield-
ing, firm, hard virtue of chastity and the soft, sympathetic
quality of courtesy, tempered as it is with kindness and grace
and goodly modesty, is designed not as mere description but
as serious support for the conception of these qualities as
heroic.

We have come this far in the discussion of *The Faerie
Queene* without mentioning the letter to Ralegh with which
most such discussions start. The purpose has been to show
that the most important elements in Spenser's conception of
the heroic poem are things which he found it unnecessary to
mention to Sir Walter Ralegh. *The Faerie Queene* would
have been an intensely moral poem if it had had not one
trace of conscious allegory in it. And contemporary readers
would have felt, even without the letter to Ralegh, that the
poem was in the tradition of Homer, Virgil, and all the great
heroic poetry of the past. Nor is there anything particularly
medieval about Spenser's conception of the main purpose and
nature of the heroic poem. Professor Bush remarks that "the
Elizabethan author, as we have frequent occasion to observe,
was, in his treatment of mythology and his general mental
habit, nearer 1400 than 1700. Spenser would have been more

[125] III, v, lv.

at ease with Chaucer than with Dryden." [126] No doubt; so would most of us. Yet Dryden's "Dedication of the *Aeneis*" (1697) opens with a passage which would have seemed to Spenser to fit *The Faerie Queene* with precision: "A heroic poem, truly such, is undoubtedly the greatest work which the soul of man is capable to perform. The design of it is to form the mind to heroic virtue by example; 'tis conveyed in verse, that it may delight while it instructs." [127] There is no danger that the allegory in Spenser will be ignored; the usual approach to the poem is through the letter to Ralegh, and C. S. Lewis has made *The Faerie Queene* the culmination of an extensive and fascinating study of medieval love allegory. But to keep the balance right we should perhaps remember that the Elizabethan reader would need no explanatory letter to guide him in the reading of *The Faerie Queene* as a moral heroic poem, like those of Homer and Virgil and Ariosto.

Those who are fond of emphasizing the medieval elements in Spenser draw a sharp contrast between *The Faerie Queene* and the classical epics. "There is almost no allegory in the classics," they say, "and Spenser abounds in allegory." [128] Beside the literary allegorical tradition studied in C. S. Lewis' book, there was, it must be remembered, a prevailing custom of flattering the Queen by allegorical shows and pageants.[129] And allegory, even in these shows, was not easy to understand. The contemporary account of one of them remarks that allegories "are hard to be vnderstood, without some knowledge of the inuentors." [130] "Sir, knowing how doubtfully all allegories may be construed," begins Spenser, and the modern reader of the notes in the great Hopkins Variorum edition

---

[126] *Mythology and the Renaissance Tradition,* p. 90.

[127] *Essays of John Dryden,* ed. W. P. Ker, 2 vols. (Oxford, 1926), II, 154.

[128] Stoll, *Poets and Playwrights,* p. 172.

[129] See C. R. Baskervill, "The Genesis of Spenser's Queen of Faerie," *MP,* XVIII (1920–21), 49–54; Edwin Greenlaw, *Studies in Spenser's Historical Allegory* (Baltimore, 1932); Ivan Schulze, "Notes on Elizabethan Chivalry and *The Faerie Queene,*" *SP;* XXX (1933), 148–159, and "Elizabethan Chivalry and the Faerie Queene's Annual Feast," *MLN,* L (1935), 158–161; and Ray Heffner, "Spenser's Allegory in Book I of the *Faerie Queene,*" *SP,* XXVII (1930), 142–161.

[130] Baskervill, "The Genesis of Spenser's Queen of Faerie," p. 53.

tends to agree with him. But Spenser is trying to provide that knowledge of the inventor's by which the reader can get the intention of the conceit and from that a grip on the discourse which might otherwise, as he confesses, seem tedious and confused.

The peculiarity of Spenser's plan is the attempt to extend the allegory so far. Allegory itself was usually defined as "continued metaphor," but there is little or no Elizabethan practice which continues allegory beyond relatively short passages.[131] Chapman once speaks of "the allegory driven through the whole Odysseys," but in general he considers that the Homeric heroes are representatives of qualities rather than embodiments of those qualities, and he is especially enthusiastic about Homer's refusal to be more consistent than nature, as indeed the allegorist must always be. Therefore, since the scope of the allegory in *The Faerie Queene* was so large, it needed explanation. But it does not follow that the prime effect to be achieved in the poem came from the allegorical, as distinguished from the moral, nature of the narrative. Spenser thinks of Homer, Virgil, Ariosto, and Tasso, not the *Roman de la Rose* or the *Confessio Amantis*.

Mr. Lewis thinks that the allegory in Spenser is what he calls "radical allegory"—that is, medieval in spirit, "true incarnations of inner experience, like the characters of the *Romance of the Rose*,"[132] not Renaissance allegory, "mere pageant figures put in for decoration," such as you sometimes get in Boccaccio. He is able to support this contention, and to escape such difficulties as the meaning of Arthur's rescue of Red Cross, by reiterating the fact that the poem is unfinished.[133] But a case could be made out for the contention

---

[131] See Joshua McClennen, "On the Meaning and Function of Allegory in the English Renaissance," *University of Michigan Contributions in Modern Philology*, VI (April 1947).

[132] *Allegory of Love*, p. 175. The distinction between medieval and Renaissance allegory is best illustrated by the story Mr. Lewis tells about himself, when reading Chaucer, on p. 174; the statement about Spenser's position relative to this distinction is on p. 298.

[133] See, for his difficulties with Arthur, p. 337, and the summary statement on p. 353, "In the poem as a whole, our understanding is limited by the absence of the allegorical centre, the union of Arthur and Gloriana."

that *The Faerie Queene* is a heroic poem before it is an allegory; such an interpretation would at least fit better with what we have.

The influence of the instructive feats of classical heroes, moralized and explained by Fulgentius, Natalis Comes, and Boccaccio, is pervasive in Spenser's poem. Mr. Lewis, for instance, chooses the episode of Maleger in Book II and the similar episode of Orrilo in Boiardo in which the hero finds a way to overcome an enemy who is not susceptible to the usual dispatching by spear or sword. The knight in the Italian romance finds a solution which Mr. Lewis happily compares to one by Mickey Mouse; the whole episode, he rightly says, is fun. In Spenser, on the contrary, Maleger is described as a kind of ghost, so that the effect, instead of being fun, is rather like a nightmare.[134] But the significant difference here is not merely one of the temperaments of the two poets or their nationality; it is that the Maleger story is Spenser's version of one of Hercules' feats, the conquering of Antaeus, seen by Spenser as symbolic of the natural man's need of grace to overcome human depravity. In the mythological authorities the victory over Antaeus symbolized man's victory over lust, since Antaeus was earth-born and regained his strength from earth.[135] The core of the episode is thus heroic, with an obvious moral significance, like that of Ulysses encountering Circe and the Sirens, which accounts for some other passages in Book II; the allegorical matter consists principally of the furnishing Maleger with two hag attendants named Impatience and Impotence. This, then, can hardly be called "radical" allegory so far as the episode itself is concerned; it looks more like the pageantic allegory which Mr. Lewis calls Renaissance.

The whole problem is really a matter of emphasis rather than a matter of distinction. As Tasso reminds us, heroic poetry is like a living creature, wherein two natures are con-

---

[134] *Allegory of Love,* pp. 307–308.

[135] See the commentary of Upton and Lotspeich in Variorum *Faerie Queene,* Book II, p. 347, and the important article by A. S. P. Woodhouse, "Nature and Grace in *The Faerie Queene,*" *ELH,* XVI (1949), 194–228.

joined. The "imitation" or plot is a pattern of human action; like all heroic story it offers a model. But if the "imitation" is like the body of a man, the allegory is like the mind: it is hidden and inward, not always apparent even from the actions of the person concerned. One does violence to Spenser not to recognize the large elements of story—heroic narrative—of the kind which Sidney would have praised as stirring up the noble spirit to emulation. Then the poem also contains the allegory, which, as Tasso realized, prepares for the contemplative side of life rather than for action.

If we suppose that Spenser understood this, where are we to conclude that he placed the emphasis—on the heroic or on the allegorical? He is apparently aware, in the letter to Ralegh, of Puritan critics, who will prefer "good discipline delivered plainly in way of precepts, or sermoned at large, as they use," rather than in cloudy allegories, but he argues that for the taste of the present day, at any rate, doctrine by ensample is much more profitable and gracious than doctrine by rule.[136] He is also clear that the romance plot he chose was of the kind which "the most part of men delight to read, rather for variety of matter then for profite of the ensample." But in his treatment he has followed, he claims, the great writers of heroic poetry: Homer, Virgil, Ariosto, and Tasso. He would be surprised, I think, at the modern concern with working out his allegory, detail by detail; he would be surprised to find himself grouped with Gower and Thomas Usk and gratified at those other studies which consider him with Virgil, Ariosto, and Milton.

The six books which we have of Spenser's poem are bounded by the virtues of the first and sixth books, Holiness and Courtesy. These two ideals, of Christianity and of Chivalry, encompass the "vertuous and gentle disciple" in which the gentleman or noble person was to be trained. Between

---

[136] Mr. de Sélincourt says Milton "obviously had in mind these words, as well as the poem which prompted them," when writing a passage in *The Reason of Church Government* (which he misquotes). See Ernest de Sélincourt, *Oxford Lectures on Poetry* (Oxford, 1934), p. 109. The passage is in the Columbia Milton, vol. III, pt. 1, p. 238; Milton is talking about *lyric* poetry.

them there are the related virtues of Temperance, Chastity, Friendship, and Justice, which are linked together in Spenser's mind, and his narrative, in a very important way. Friendship and Justice are both modes of concord and order; Temperance and Chastity are similarly related. In fact, through these four books the virtues tend to blend into each other, as in the action the knights come to each other's aid.

The combination of the allegorical devices, from the masques and pageants, and the romance plot, largely from Ariosto, makes an effect in Spenser which is difficult to evaluate. On the one hand it makes for pictorial vividness and decorative beauty; on the other hand it results sometimes in a static impression which is quite inappropriate to heroic poetry. It is, therefore, no wonder that the criticism of Spenser has largely started with the allegory. Professor A. H. Gilbert has tried to oppose this overconcern with the allegory by an emphasis upon the romance in the poem, and especially the influence of Ariosto. "In so far as Spenser is a follower of Ariosto," he says, "romantic action is the life of the poem." [137]

The most striking quality in Spenser is his great seriousness. The Arthurian material, which he says in the letter to Ralegh he used because most men delighted to read it for variety of matter, becomes for him a means of glorifying the Tudor regime and particularly Queen Elizabeth. Of course, this kind of glorification was within the heroic tradition; Virgil had celebrated the *gens Julia* and Ariosto the house of Este: And recent scholarship has undertaken to show that the Arthur legend had its place in a general combination of antiquarianism, national feeling and political intention which was not peculiar to Spenser at all. It is perfectly natural that the knight who represents Holiness should receive his preparation for his final conquest in the form of religious discipline and nurture, in the House of Holinesse in the tenth canto of Book I; but it requires an understanding of the Elizabethan way of looking at things to see why the comparable training of the champion representing Temperance, in Book II, Canto ix, has to be followed by a reading of a

[137] "Belphoebe's Misdeeming of Timias," *PMLA*, LXII (1947), 643.

chronicle of "Briton kings and Elfin emperors." [138] The combination of patriotism, religion, and love cult which was the
Elizabethan feeling about the Queen is infused throughout
Spenser's poem. It is idle to speculate on the sincerity of this
feeling. It makes no difference, because Elizabeth had become
such a complex symbol—of Protestantism, of legitimacy,
of unification of the conflicting sects of Englishmen, of the
legendary past through her Welsh ancestry and the Arthur
tradition, of the stimulus to honor and achievement and the
rewarder of them, of God's grace, and of the resurgent power
and confidence of England, especially after 1588—that a
single attitude toward her, testable by such a criterion as
sincerity, was impossible for any one of her subjects.

The fairy mythology in Spenser's heroic poem is put there
less for romantic reasons, for atmosphere and wonder, than
for serious political and patriotic purposes. The works of
Greenlaw and Professor Millican, and more recently Miss
Rathborne's book, have shown how profoundly the romantic
material in *The Faerie Queene* is rooted in serious political
ideas, antiquarian knowledge, and patriotic zeal. [139] This is
important, for it gives to the poem an epic basis and scope,
it makes of it a national monument. The identification of
this or that character in the historical allegory is of secondary
importance, but the realization of the seriousness and significance of the underlying political concerns is essential to an
adequate reading of the poem.

What are we to say, then, in judgment of it? We must read
it as a heroic poem, with an understanding of its moral and
political implications. It is not a treatise on the virtues, such
as Bryskett gave from Giraldi in *The Discourse of Civil Life*.
It is instead the poet's method of handling the same assign-
ment, namely, to show these virtues in action. The hero will
encounter monsters, spirits, enchantments with which he
must deal; he is himself equipped with supernatural aids.

[138] See the discussion of the structure of Book II by Ernest Strathmann,
Variorum *Faerie Queene*, Book II, pp. 467–471.

[139] Greenlaw, *Studies in Spenser's Historical Allegory;* C. B. Millican, *Spenser and the Table Round* (Cambridge: Harvard University Press, 1932) ; I. E.
Rathborne, *The Meaning of Spenser's Fairyland.*

He must joust with opposing knights and rescue ladies in distress. He must punish evil customs in castles, he must tie up or strip or subdue the practitioners of evil when he encounters them. The events of the poem themselves are romantic, and of course the decoration is romantic. As Professor Osgood has remarked, there are frequent indications that Spenser approves the enjoyment of the element of pure delight in *The Faerie Queene.*

"He [Spenser] would, then, approve our pleasure in the poem's pageantry, the fair processions of men old and young, of frolicking children and of dancing maidens and graces

> with girlands dight,
> As fresh as flowres in medow greene doe grow,
> When morning deaw upon their leaves doth light:
> And in their handes sweet timbrels all upheld on hight.

Grotesque ballets, of satyrs and Sins and sea-monsters; strange mysterious rites; sun-flooded gardens; dark and deep reaches of forest-shade or sea depths, inland rivers, rich old myth and symbolism, grim castles and gorgeous palaces—[140]

—all this romantic world Spenser evokes, but he does not consider it the main element in his poem. Ever and again he pulls the reader's attention out of the romantic dream or out of the purely intellectual analysis of vice and virtue in the allegory to watch heroic action. To see this we must often stand back from the picture and view it from a distance. The details are so lovely, or so curious, that they sometimes absorb our attention at the expense of the larger outline and meaning of the design.

In Book I the allegory is firmly emphasized, and the model for the book is usually said to be the morality play. But Red Cross, for all his defeat by Orgoglio and his seduction by Despair—situations from which he must be saved by Arthur and Una—is nevertheless a hero, carrying out an exploit which is like one of the labors of Hercules. When the narrative becomes too strictly allegorical, we see Spenser interrupt-

[140] "Spenser and the Enchanted Glass," *Johns Hopkins Alumni Magazine,* XIX (1930–31), 9–10.

ing it with heroic action. The house of Lucifera, for example, is the clearest allegory in the book; it is pictorial in its effect, transparent in its meaning, sharply composed. Yet Spenser does not allow the allegorical and pictorial atmosphere to persist too long; he produces the battle with Sansjoy and introduces it with a typical reminder of heroic motive.[141]

In Book II the commentators have generally found that Spenser maintained a firm hold on his allegory; but here also the most definitely allegorical passages are followed by something positively heroic, something which presents an action for imitation. Sir Guyon is a kind of Ulysses; he differs from the hero of the first book in that he demonstrates his heroic qualities largely by resisting temptation. Even allegorical elements are modified with heroic motifs, as when, in the twelfth canto, Guyon and the Palmer steer between the Quicksand of Unthriftyhed and the Whirlpoole of Decay, to gain the beach, and, looking back,

> Suddeine they see from Midst of all the maine
> The surging waters like a mountaine rise,
> And the great sea, puft up with proud disdaine,
> To swell above the measure of his guise,
> As threatning to devoure all that his powre despise.[142]

When Sir Guyon is in the House of Alma, one of the most precise of allegorical details is introduced when he sees a bashful, blushing lady and is surprised at her behavior

> Till Alma him bespake: "Why wonder yee,
> Faire sir, at that which ye so much embrace?
> She is the fountaine of your modestee;
> You shamefast are, but Shamefastnes it selfe is shee." [143]

This is "radical" allegory like that of the *Roman de la Rose;* but the effect is not sustained, for almost immediately Spenser changes the emphasis to the heroic by taking survey of the castle and comparing it with those of Thebes and Troy.[144] In larger sections of the poem, the whole House of Alma with

---

[141] I, v, i.
[142] II, xii, xxi.
[143] II, ix, xliii.
[144] II, ix, xlv.

its allegorical, physiological-psychological matter is followed by the chronicles of Elfin and British history and narratively by the defeat of Maleger in Canto XI, which is, of course, a version of one of the feats of Hercules.

Books III and IV are closer in method to Ariosto than the first two books, and such static descriptive sections as the Garden of Adonis and the Temple of Venus are followed by romantic episodes. But even in Book III there is the same conjunction of allegorical matter and the heroic. The Maske of Cupid, with its parade of characters named Reproch, Repentance, Shame, Strife, Anger, Care, and so on, is followed rapidly by the rescue of Amoret, and it is only a few stanzas after the exit of the parade when

> So mightily she smote him, that to ground
> He fell halfe dead; next stroke him should have slaine,
> Had not the lady, which by him stood bound,
> Dernly unto her called to abstaine
> From doing him to dy.[145]

A comparable sequence in Book V is the episode of Isis Church followed by the fight between Britomart and Radigund in Canto VII. Again, the trial of Duessa, which has, of course, large amounts of moral allegory as well as the obvious political allegory in it, is followed by the heroic episode of the deliverance of Belgae.

One of the links between Books V and VI is that, in spite of the allegory, representing in Artegall Spenser's patron Lord Grey, the virtue of Justice is firmly asserted to belong particularly to antiquity; so, though the present age seem prolific in the other virtue of Courtesy, yet it is a mere appearance in comparison with antiquity. Courtesy, which grows on a lowly stalk, yet branches forth in nobility and results in heroic deeds.[146] Yet the poet confesses that his usual method of finding a pattern of the virtue in antiquity must now be abandoned because he has a finer one in the Queen.[147] Spenser is in some difficulty here, because the virtue of Justice was readily exemplifiable with the heroic performances of a champion like Hercules. As we have noticed before, the

[145] III, XII, xxxiv.   [146] VI, Proem, iv.   [147] Sts. vi–vii.

symbolic unification of Hercules' feats and the achievement of Justice had already been made and was available for Spenser's hand:

> Next Hercules his like ensample shewed,
> Who all the West with equall conquest wonne,
> And monstrous tyrants with his club subdewed;
> The club of Justice dread, with kingly powre endewed.[148]

But Courtesy could hardly be so exemplified. Its doctrine came not from classical legends but from such sources as Castiglione's *Courtier*. Moreover, of all the virtues, Courtesy most definitely owes something to birth; it is the best illustration of the idea Spenser suggests throughout the poem that blood will tell:

> Thereto great helpe Dame Nature selfe doth lend:
> For some so goodly gratious are by kind,
> That every action doth them much commend,
> And in the eyes of men great liking find;
> Which others, that have greater skill in mind,
> Though they enforce themselves, cannot attaine.[149]

Therefore, the events of Book VI are largely pageantic and illustrative. The function of the hero is primarily to punish violations of courtesy and in so doing to exemplify in himself the proper gentleness and humility. The comparison between this book and Book III is interesting. In both cases the principal character is off the stage about half the time. The chief problem is the analysis of the virtue by showing its opposites, its false approximations, its excesses and distortions. But in Spenser's view Chastity is a more heroic virtue than Courtesy; it is more positive and more capable of representation in a heroic manner. He speaks of Britomart's "huge heroicke magnanimity," [150] and her victories stand out in the memory. But the exposition of Courtesy depends upon the contrast between pastoral and court life, or rather, the exercise of Calidore's courtly virtue among the shepherd swains—behavior which is truer and more profound than what commonly goes for courtesy at court. In spite of this, the final

[148] V, I, ii.   [149] VI, II, ii.   [150] III, XI, xix.

episode in the book, the overthrowing of the Blatant Beast, reminds the poet of two feats of Hercules, the slaying of the Hydra and the leading of Cerberus up from Hell.[151]

The great significance of *The Faerie Queene* lies not in its puzzles or their solution; Professor Osgood has well characterized much modern Spenser scholarship and criticism by referring to "feats of highly elaborate and subtle lock-picking." "Now," he continues, "I cannot but suspect that there is no need of such subtlety; that the doors are unfastened, nay, ajar; that, once inside, nothing especially strange, or subtle, or esoteric will be found, unless it be some fanciful and ingenious construction which the student himself, in his zeal, has unwittingly 'planted' there. In short, the secret of the moral allegory, if secret there be, is but the character and quality of Spenser himself, the wars and the loves and aspirations of his own spiritual problem, and of the world in which he moved." [152] To this one would only wish to add that the conscious purpose of the poem was not to reveal the character of the poet but "to fashion a gentleman or noble person in vertuous and gentle discipline," and that this meant, for Spenser and for his age, the projection of moral qualities as heroic ideals.

The reader Spenser had in mind was someone like the courtier in *Mother Hubberds Tale,* whose reading of poetry he describes:

His minde unto the Muses he withdrawes;
Sweete Ladie Muses, ladies of delight,
Delights of life, and ornaments of light:
With whom he close confers, with wise discourse,
Of Natures workes, of heavens continuall course,
Of forreigne lands, of people different,
Of kingdomes change, of divers government,
Of dreadfull battailes of renowned knights;
With which he kindleth his ambitious sprights
To like desire and praise of noble fame,
The onely upshot whereto he doth ayme.[153]

[151] VI, xii, xxxii and xxxv.
[152] "Spenser and the Enchanted Glass," p. 16.
[153] Lines 760–770.

A continuously troublesome question about Spenser's art is one which takes its point of departure from the destruction of the Bower of Bliss in Book II. It is evident that Spenser lavished the utmost of his artistic gifts on the description of sensual delights; in his twelfth canto he turns to Tasso and follows the Italian's descriptions, even translating sometimes with great faithfulness. Yet he changes the emphasis: where Tasso has his Rinaldo merely leave Armida's bower and the enchantress herself destroy it, to take part in the war against her lover but finally to renounce for him her religion and accept him again as her servant, Spenser has Guyon destroy the Bower and bind Acrasia in chains of adamant. For this striking difference, with which few modern readers are in sympathy, Spenser's "Puritanism" is usually blamed. C. M. Bowra, for example, says, "Spenser of course wrote for an England touched by a Puritanism which felt that sexual irregularity was a grave sin and almost past forgiveness . . . The Protestant, with his horror of the flesh, felt that its sins were worse than those of the spirit, which can be corrected by instruction. Tasso, with an insight beyond Spenser, makes Armida's love for Rinaldo, base and selfish though it is at first, become the means for her salvation. He felt that love of this kind had in it something good and noble and that it could, if properly treated, get rid of its corruption and baseness." [154]

Apparently the modern resentment at Spenser would be less if he had not so lovingly described the Bower of Bliss in the first place. Virgil's Aeneas is not portrayed as having enjoyed his stay with Dido; the whole episode is presented tragically. But Spenser was working under the associations which clustered around the figure of Hercules at the fork in the road. The claims of Pleasure were very powerful; to slight them would be to make the dilemma less than heroic. But the decision, in Spenser's mind, in favor of Virtue involved not merely a certain standard of sexual behavior; it involved also a whole concept of moral, social, and political responsibility. Sir Guyon was after all sent on a mission by

[154] *From Virgil to Milton,* pp. 188–189.

Gloriana, the Faerie Queene, who represented not only a moral trait but also his country. Greenlaw's emphasis upon the historical and political idealism of Spenser's poem is very significant here. The political symbol of England was also a symbol of chastity. And it is not in the book devoted to Temperance, or even the book devoted to Chastity, that Spenser places his treatment of the story of Hercules in sexual subjection to Omphale (or Iole, as Spenser has it) ; it is in the book devoted to Justice.[155]

Heroic poetry, we may conclude, was the most comprehensive, the most serious, and the most valuable expression of the Elizabethan mind. It worked out most fully the relationship between classical antiquity and modern life and in doing so made the revival of learning practical and functional. Its mode of expression was particularly satisfying to the Englishman of the sixteenth century because it reconciled imagination and conscience. Socially and morally justified, it offered the greatest stimulus, the greatest possibility of scope and variety, to poets and readers. It promised fame to the doers of glorious deeds and to the writer who celebrated them. At the same time it served immediate moral and social ends.

In contrast with pastoral, which inculcated ideals of contentment, of order and acquiescence, of the good life on a level of simplicity, heroic poetry aroused the ambitions, directed and guided the aspiring mind to worthy purposes.

> Fame is the spur that the clear spirit doth raise
> (That last infirmity of noble mind)
> To scorn delights and live laborious days.

And that last infirmity itself was cured when heroic effort reached its final stage and turned from action to heavenly contemplation.

The Elizabethans searched in their history, even in their topography, for heroic subjects; on the outskirts of our topic lie such poems as Daniel's *Civil Wars*, Drayton's *Barons' Wars*, and Drayton's *Poly-Olbion*, as well as lesser works like Warner's *Albion's England*. There were also naïve attempts to

[155] V, v, xxiv.

utilize Elizabethan explorers and sea dogs as heroic figures. Charles Fitz-Geffrey, for example, calls upon Spenser, "whose hart inharbours Homers soule," and Daniel, and Drayton, to abandon their chosen heroic subjects and celebrate Sir Francis Drake.[156] But for all the glorification of Lord Grey as Artegall, or the various celebrations of Sidney, the Elizabethan poet working on a heroic subject could not make much use of his contemporaries for models. He could not fit the heroic into the "picturesque" version of today, nor could he use the hero as matter for a curious study in "personality." He was concerned first with the meaning of heroic effort, and only after that with the feats themselves. Herculean endeavor seemed to him always to begin with a moral choice; the labors followed and derived their significance from that choice.

[156] *Sir Francis Drake his honorable lifes commendation* (1596), sig. B5^{v}.

INDEX

A